INTRODUCING ANTHROPOLOGY

INTRODUCING ANTHROPOLOGY

An Integrated Approach

Michael Alan Park
Central Connecticut State University

Mayfield Publishing Company
Mountain View, California
London • Toronto

Copyright © 2000 by Mayfield Publishing Company

Library of Congress Cataloging-in-Publication Data

Park, Michael Alan.
    Introducing anthropology: an integrated approach / Michael Alan Park.
        p.   cm.
    Includes bibliographical references and index.
    ISBN: 0-7674-1184-6
        1. Anthropology.   I. Title.
    GN25.P293   1999   051872
    301—dc21   CIP

Manufactured in the United States of America

10   9   8   7   6   5   4   3   2   1

Mayfield Publishing Company
1280 Villa Street
Mountain View, CA 94041

Sponsoring editor, Janet M. Beatty; production editor, Melissa Williams Kreischer; manuscript editor, Dale Anderson; art director, Jeanne M. Schreiber; design manager, Glenda King; text and cover designer, Linda M. Robertson; art editor, Robin Mouat; illustrators, Joan Carol, Alice Thiede, and Parrott Graphics; photo researcher, Brian J. Pecko; manufacturing manager, Randy Hurst. Cover photo, © Jonathan Wright/National Geographic Image Collection. The text was set in 10/12 Sabon by GTS Graphics, Inc., and printed on acid-free 45# Somerset Matte by R. R. Donnelley and Sons Company.

Preface

Modern anthropology has become extraordinarily diverse, with a wide variety of schools of thought and theoretical models within the discipline. Not surprisingly, this breadth in the field has led to a range of approaches to thinking about and teaching those courses traditionally called four-field introductions to anthropology. In short, we anthropologists each have sometimes very different answers to the question: What *is* anthropology?

The ideas about the nature of anthropology that have guided this book's organization, discussions, and selection of topics center on the field's identity as scientific, humanistic, and holistic:

- **Anthropology can be, should be, and is scientific.** That is, it operates by inductively generating testable hypotheses which are then deductively tested in an attempt to derive working theories about the areas of human biology and behavior that are our focuses. This is not to say that applying science to cultural variation or the abstract aspects of cultural systems is easy or particularly straightforward, or that science has even come close to satisfactorily answering all the major questions anthropologists ask about our species. Far from it. I simply believe that—if it is to be truly scholarly—the *process* of anthropologically investigating humankind is a scientific one.

- **Anthropology can be, should be, and is humanistic.** A scientific orientation and focus does not preclude nonscientific investigations and discussions of human behavior, or humanistic applications of anthropology. We are, after all, dealing with human beings who have motivations for their behaviors that fail to respond to fixed laws as do chemicals or subatomic particles. Moreover, because we deal with people, we cannot help but develop a concern for the welfare of our fellow humans. Indeed, this is what leads many to choose anthropology as a career in the first place. It becomes, then, only natural—if not morally incumbent on us—to apply what we have learned about humans and human behavior to give voice to those without one, and to lend our knowledge to the agencies and governments that administer, guide, and, sometimes, compel and manipulate social change.

- **Anthropology can be, should be, and is holistic**—*because its subject is holistic.* Thus, affiliation with one of the traditional subfields of anthropology should be no more than a starting point to the scholarly investigation of the nature of our species. In short, despite the enormous breadth of anthropological subject matter and approaches to studying those subjects, there *really is* a field called anthropology which has a distinctive viewpoint and methodology that make it uniquely valuable.

FEATURES

The assumptions that guided my writing have been concretely applied though the following features:

- To convey the holism of the discipline, the traditional subfields are not used to divide the text into major parts, nor are they titles of chapters. The standard subfields are described and defined in the first chapter, but subsequently, the methods and contributions of each are interwoven throughout the book. In other words, the text is organized around the unique subject matter of anthropology—the human species in its holistic entirety—rather than being organized around the current subfield structure of anthropology itself.

- To convey the multidimensional holism of the field at the introductory level requires choosing a theme that can act as a common thread tying all the parts together. Just saying anthropology is holistic and giving a few specific examples is not enough. There are, of course, any number of themes that would be equally useful as such a pedagogical device. The one I have chosen is that of adaptation, broadly defined. I am not using the term in just its biological, ecological sense, although, of course, this definition does apply to human biological evolution and to the direct responses of cultures to their environments. But even abstract aspects of culture are adaptive responses to *something*. In other words, to paraphrase the title of an old reader, my theme is that "humans make sense." Even if we have a hard time making sense of some of our behaviors, my central integrative assumption is that behaviors have *some* explanation within their cultural contexts.

- I've assumed that student readers have no familiarity with anthropology or, if they do, it is incomplete. I am introducing them to the field from the ground up, starting from scratch, and having in mind courses whose goal is to truly *introduce* rather than supply an encyclopedic survey. For the introductory student, none of the detail about models, paradigms, or current theoretical debates makes a bit of sense unless and until that student has a basic knowledge of the general approach, subject matter, methodology, history, and facts of our field. Then—for students going on—all the nuances of opinion, and the current not-so-subtle differences, can be examined, understood, and appreciated. Discussions, for example, about whether variation in kinship systems is best explained through materialism, structuralism, psychology, sociobiology, Marxism, post-modernism, or any other model are meaningless unless one knows what kinship is all about in the first place. Although I do briefly discuss the area of anthropological theory and note several current debates, a text that focuses on that subject, or that is written from just one perspective would fail to do justice to the field. And it would certainly fail to convey to the introductory student the basic identity of anthropology, the basic facts that anthropology has discerned about the human species, and the richness of our subject matter, our scholarly world view, and our contributions to knowledge and human welfare.

- To get students to feel that I am talking to them personally, I have mixed an appropriate level of informality with the more formal style that must be used to convey the ideas of anthropology and the seriousness with which we approach our subject. I want the students to feel that I am taking a journey through anthropology with them, not that I have just given them a map and guidebook and left them on their own.

- Because a common misconception of our field is that we only study old dried-up fossils and exotic living peoples with their bizarre behaviors, I have tried to emphasize that anthropology studies the world's peoples in all their guises—ordinary and extraordinary, next door and in remote places. I have used as many examples and analogies as possible from North American cultures, groups, and situations. Students should know that anthropology doesn't stop the moment they walk out the classroom door—that they too can do anthropology and that they too are anthropological subjects.

- No one really understands anthropology unless they can and do apply it to thinking about their own lives. To further encourage this, the text includes a Contemporary Issues feature at the end of each chapter that specifically applies the topic of the chapter to some question about the contemporary world, with a focus, where possible, on America and American culture. Questions range from "What Responsibilities Does the Anthropologist Have When Studying Other Cultures?" to "How Can We Account for the Recent Interest in Witchcraft?"

- Stories have worked well for most of human history as a vehicle for transmitting facts and ideas. They are more memorable than lists. I have written this text keeping in mind the narrative approach. There are a few literal stories, such as the one about my fieldwork that begins the book. But narrative in a more general sense refers to a causal sequence of events and I have tried to show how the various topics within anthropology connect with one another in this manner. The student readers should be able to navigate their way through the book and know where they are within the broad and diverse field of anthropology. I have provided signposts in the form of part, chapter, and subheading titles that logically and descriptively divide the subject as I have ordered it. The number of cultures used as examples is limited, so that the same groups may be referred to throughout the book in different contexts.

- A true introduction should be short and to the point. Achieving brevity while trying to introduce such a broad field is a challenge. I have tried to omit no major topic within mainstream anthropology, but, rather, have managed the amount of detail presented. If, for instance, I can convey a sense of a topic through one clear, interesting, memorable example, I think this is more efficient, at this level, than four or five examples. One's own favorite example can always be discussed or more detail added in class.

- Finally, the text is as accessible, attractive, straightforward, and uncluttered as possible. Important terms are boldfaced where they first appear and defined briefly in a running glossary in the margin. A more comprehensive glossary is at the end of the book. A standard bibliography is also included. The text itself is not interrupted with specific references and citations. These are included in a section at the end of each chapter called **Notes, References, and Readings,** along with other references to the topics covered and to some specific studies or facts for those interested in pursuing a subject further. A chapter summary precedes this section. Photographs and line art are in color where possible and captions add information rather than simply label the illustrations.

ANCILLARIES

The **Instructor's Manual** includes a test bank of about 500 multiple choice and short answer/essay questions, as well as chapter outlines and overviews, suggested activities, lists of key words, and sample syllabi.

A **Computerized Test Bank** is available free of charge to qualifying adopters. It is a powerful, easy-to-use test generation system that provides all test items on computer disk for IBM-compatible or Macintosh computers. Instructors can select, add, or edit questions, randomize them, and print tests appropriate to their individual classes.

ACKNOWLEDGMENTS

Once again, the folks at Mayfield have done a remarkable job turning my ideas and words into a finished product. Special thanks go to sponsoring editor Jan Beatty (whose knowledge of both publishing and anthropology makes her a true exemplar of applied holism); production editor Melissa Williams Kreischer (who keeps these projects organized and on schedule despite my best efforts to the contrary); art manager Robin Mouat (who yet again turned my doodles into actual art); copyeditor Dale Anderson (who has, over several books, taught me a great deal about the art of writing); photo researcher Brian Pecko (who managed to locate some strange-sounding photo requests); and designer Linda Robertson and design manager Glenda King (for designing such an attractive book).

Thanks also, as always, to my friend, colleague, and ofttimes co-author Ken Feder for his help with references, photos, archaeological data, and computer advice. Laura Donnelly provided advice for and posed for the sign language photos. For those times when I ventured into the physical sciences, Bob Weinberger checked my facts, but remains innocent of any final transgressions. Over more than a quarter century, my students at Central Connecticut State have been my "guinea pigs" for teaching ideas, and my most candid, most vocal, and most helpful critics.

The following colleagues reviewed the manuscript: Jeff Behm, University of Wisconsin–Oshkosh; Lourdes DeLeone, Central Washington University; Les Field, University of New Mexico; Diane Freedman, Community College of Philadelphia; Barbara Garrity-Blake, East Carolina University; Steve Hackenberger, Central Washington University; Suzanne Kempke, Armstrong Atlantic State University; Cynthia Mahmood, University of Maine; Mark Mooney, University of Pittsburgh; John Nass, California University of Pennsylvania; Patricia Rice, West Virginia University; David Webb, Kutztown University. Their suggestions and advice were invaluable. Any errors, of course, remain my responsibility.

In memory of her companionship many years ago
as I conceived, researched, and wrote
my first book, this one is for:
Joyce
(1982–1996)

And the patches make the goodbye harder still.
—CAT STEVENS

Contents

A Personal Note to My Readers

I've always appreciated knowing something about the authors of the books I read and so I think you should know something about me—especially since you are relying on me to introduce you to anthropology.

I started my college career at Indiana University as a biology major, then switched two or three times to other majors. I took my first anthropology course because it sounded interesting—and because it fulfilled a university general education requirement and met at a convenient time. But soon I was hooked. Once I learned what anthropology was all about, I realized it was the perfect combination of many subjects that had always interested me. I went on to get my undergraduate degree in anthropology and stayed at Indiana for graduate work, specializing in biological anthropology—first human osteology (the study of the skeleton) and forensic anthropology and later redirecting my interests to evolutionary theory and evolutionary processes as they apply to the human species. This, as you'll read about in Chapter 1, was the focus of my field work and research among the Hutterites. I received my doctoral degree in 1979.

In 1973 I started working at Central Connecticut State University where I've been ever since, teaching courses in general anthropology (the topic of this book), human evolution, human biocultural diversity, forensic anthropology, the evolution of human behavior, and the human ecology. I have also taught courses in the biology department and the university's honors program. I consider myself primarily an educator, so it was a natural step from classroom teaching to writing textbooks. This one is my sixth.

In addition to my personal and professional interest in anthropology, I'm also concerned about the quality of science education and about public knowledge and perception of scientific matters. I have written and lectured on such things as teaching about evolution, scientific investigations of palm reading and psychic detectives, and environmental issues.

On the purely personal side, in case you're interested, I live in rural Connecticut with my wife, two Labrador retrievers, and four cats. When I'm not doing anthropology, I enjoy reading (although most of what I read seems to have something to do with science) and travel (although our trips nearly always include museums and archaeological sites). I'm sort of a vegetarian (but eat fish fairly regularly), a loyal Macintosh computer user, and my current favorite TV show is mentioned on page 296. And since you may wonder when you get to Chapter 3, I've never followed up on my tropical fish experiments.

INTRODUCING ANTHROPOLOGY

PART ONE

Background and Context

1

DOING ANTHROPOLOGY

Taking Fingerprints in the High Plains

IN THE FIELD

We had left behind the spacious wheat fields surrounding the small town in western Saskatchewan, Canada, and were now driving a straight, flat, two-lane road through the open, rolling plains. Lyrics of old songs came to mind as I saw mule deer and pronghorn antelope "playing" in the "amber waves of grain." In fact, on that June day in 1973, I was desperately thinking about anything other than where I was going.

I was on my way to an initial contact with my first real anthropological subjects, a colony of people belonging to a 450-year-old religious group called the Hutterian Brethren, or Hutterites. Up to this point, I had not felt much anxiety about the visit. Other anthropologists had given accounts of contacts with Amazon rain forest warriors and highland New Guinea headhunters. My situation was quite safe—I was in an English-speaking country next to my own, preparing to conduct a study of an English-speaking people of European descent who practiced a form of Christianity that emphasized pacifism and tolerance.

At this point, however, such thoughts were of no help. Nor was the fact that I was accompanied by the wife of a local wheat farmer who was well known and liked by this Hutterite community. I had, it seems, that unnamed syndrome that affects many anthropologists under these circumstances.

The road turned from blacktop to gravel, then to dirt, and, in about 10 miles, curved abruptly to the right, ran through an authentic western ghost town, and crested a hill. I saw below me, at the literal end of the road, a neat collection of twenty or so white buildings surrounded by acres of cultivated fields. This was the Hutterite colony, the *Bruderhof,* or "place of the brethren" (Figure 1.1).

As we drove into the colony, I became more anxious. There was not a soul to be seen. My companion explained that it was a religious holiday that day, requiring all but essential work to cease. The colony minister and the colony boss, however, had agreed to see me.

We knocked at the door of one of the small buildings I assumed was a residence. We were greeted formally but warmly by an elderly man dressed in the Hutterite fashion—black trousers and coat over a white shirt—and with a full beard. The room we entered, clearly a living room, was darkened due to the holiday, and that darkness, combined with my nervous excitement, have erased all impressions of the next few minutes from my memory.

Moments later, however, with my bearings straight and introductions made, I found myself explaining the reason for my visit to the

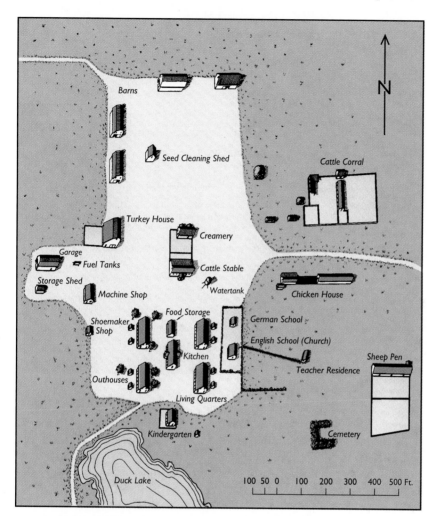

FIGURE 1.1
Diagram of a typical Hutterite colony. The variety of buildings and their functions are indicative of the Hutterites' attempt to keep their colonies self-sufficient and separate from the outside world.

man who had greeted us, a younger man, and a woman. The older man was the colony minister; the other man, who happened to be his son, was the colony boss. The woman, the minister's wife, was also dressed in the conservative style of the Hutterites and related groups. She wore a nearly full-length sleeveless dress—a small floral pattern on a black background—over a white blouse. Her head was covered by a polka-dot kerchief, which they call a shawl (Figure 1.2).

The three listened in silence as I went through my well-rehearsed explanation. My contacts, the wheat farmer and his wife, had previously given them an idea about what I wanted to do, and I had already written them a letter introducing myself. But, I thought, if they didn't like me or my explanation, they could still decline to cooperate. So I started from the beginning, explaining that I wanted to take their fingerprints—which are

FIGURE 1.2
Hutterite women in typical dress.

partially influenced by genes—and collect genealogical data to document genetic changes between populations and across generations.

When I had finished, they asked me a few questions: Was I from the government? (They apparently knew about fingerprints only in the context of law enforcement and personal identification.) Did I know Scripture? (My equivocal answer seemed to create no problem.) What would I use this study for? Was I going to write a book? Did I know Dr. Steinberg, who had been there two years earlier collecting medical data? (I had taken a course from him.)

I expected, when they were done, that they would confer with one another or ask me to come back when they had decided. Instead, the minister, who was clearly in charge, simply said, "Today is a holiday for us. Can you start tomorrow?" And so, for the next month, I took part in my personal version of the anthropological fieldwork experience—taking fingerprints, recording family relationships, observing colony life, and getting to know and become friendly with the Hutterites of this and a related *Bruderhof* in Alberta.

What exactly had brought me 1300 miles from the university where I was doing graduate work to the northern plains, to this isolated community of people whose way of life had changed little over nearly half a millennium and whose lifestyle and philosophy were so different from that of

6

North American culture in general? Essentially, it was the same thing that takes anthropologists to locations from the savannas of East Africa to the outback of Australia to caves in southern France and to street corners in New York City: the desire to learn something about the nature of the human species.

In my case, I was pursuing an interest I had developed early in graduate school. I was curious about certain processes of evolutionary change and how they operated in human populations. To examine them and their roles in our evolution, I needed to find a human group with a few special characteristics. First, the group had to be fairly genetically isolated, which meant most members should find their mates from within the group. The group had to be fairly small as a whole, although it would be helpful if people had large individual families. It would also be helpful if the group had knowledge of their genealogy and if their family relationships reflected genetic as well as cultural categories. (As we will see in Chapter 9, all societies have systems of family relationships but few of these coincide completely with biological relationships.) Finally, it would be ideal if individual units within the group were created through the splitting up of existing units.

The Hutterites fit this description very well. I had learned of them through library research on genetically isolated populations. My opportunity to study them was greatly enhanced by a stroke of luck: A fellow graduate student and friend was the daughter of the wheat farmer and his wife who became my contacts. Let's briefly look at the Hutterites, whom we will use as an example throughout this book.

THE HUTTERITES

The Hutterian Brethren is a Christian religious sect founded in Moravia (part of the present-day Czech Republic) in 1528 by peoples from southern Germany and Austria. They were part of the so-called Anabaptist movement, a religious movement that, among other beliefs, shunned the idea of infant baptism and advocated a free church not under the control of the state. This made Anabaptist groups distinct from and disliked by the Catholic and Protestant mainstreams of their time. Many Anabaptist sects were formed during this period, but only three remain today: the Hutterites; the Mennonites; and a Mennonite branch, the Amish. All now live mainly in North America. (We'll cover more of Hutterite history in Chapter 12.)

One additional aspect of the nonconformity of some of these groups was their belief in communal living and ownership—they were communists in the economic sense of the word. The biblical passage that forms the basis of the Hutterite lifestyle is Acts 2:44, which reads in part: "And all that believed were together, and had all things common."

But the nonconformity of the Anabaptists also led to persecution. Many members of the various sects were imprisoned, and some were tortured and burned at the stake. One of those who was executed was Jacob

Hutter, an early leader of the group that, after his martyrdom, took his name. This persecution resulted in the demise of most Anabaptist groups, but the Hutterites managed, through continual migration and sheer persistence, to survive. Over the next 300 years they lived in Slovakia, Romania, and Russia, coming finally in the 1870s to the United States. Later problems connected with the military draft (the Hutterites, remember, are pacifists) and with taxes led many Hutterites to move again, this time to Canada. Today there are about 35,000 Hutterites in more than 380 colonies. Most are in the Canadian provinces of Manitoba, Saskatchewan, and Alberta; the rest are in Montana, North and South Dakota, Minnesota, and Washington (Figure 1.3).

The sect is now divided into three subsects descended from the three original colonies founded by the Hutterite migrants to North America. They have been genetically isolated from one another since World War I. Members find mates only from within their subsect. The differences among the subsects include degree of cultural conservatism, which is manifested in, for example, clothing styles.

The Hutterites live in *Bruderhofs,* colonies of around 100 people. The lifestyle is communal in every sense of the word: All land, resources, and profits are colony property. An individual's personal belongings are all contained in a hope chest. Decisions concerning the colony are made by elected officials headed by the colony boss. The colony minister, in charge of the group's religious welfare, is also elected. Work is divided along sexual lines and among a number of specialists—chicken men, teachers, cooks, and so on—but the division is not absolute. The community clearly views the completion of required tasks as a community responsibility—when work needs to be done, there is someone to do it.

The Hutterite economy is basically agricultural, and the specific crops and animals raised depend on the geography and economy of the area occupied. Although the Hutterites (like the better-known Amish) have traditionally shunned such worldly items as television, radio, and personal ornamentation, they will readily accept any modern technology or any contact with outsiders that aids them as farmers. As a result of this attitude, and because of the relative wealth of most colonies, you can see people in a *Bruderhof* who look as if they've stepped out of the past, but who use modern tractors, milking machines, fertilizers, antibiotics, telephones, and computers (Figure 1.4).

Children are schooled at the colony by a state or provincial teacher until the legal age at which they can leave. This is called the "English school." The most important schooling, however, given by the colony teacher in the "German school," transmits the ways of Hutterite life and religion, which are one and the same. In addition, practical education is given in the form of an apprenticeship in one of the jobs vital to the colony's existence. This training prepares the child to become a working member of the community when schooling is completed.

The Hutterites are almost completely isolated in genetic terms. Few Hutterites ever permanently leave the group, and converts to their life

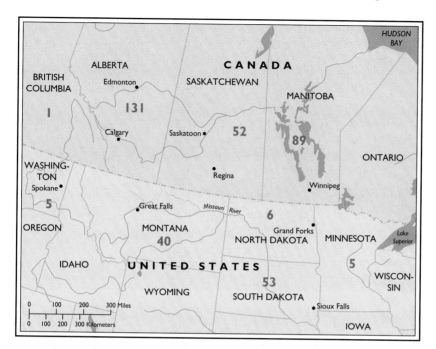

FIGURE 1.3
Map showing the number of Hutterite colonies in each state or province as of 1996.

have numbered only a few dozen since the migration to North America. Moreover, on average about half of all Hutterite marriages take place between members of the same colony. The rest come from another colony of the same subsect.

Hutterites restrict marriage to individuals who are second cousins or more distant. In fact, because individuals within a subsect are all fairly closely related, the most frequent relationship between mates *is* second cousins. The average age at marriage is twenty-four years for men and twenty-two years for women. Only about 2 percent of Hutterite men and 5 percent of women never marry.

An interesting phenomenon with the Hutterites' breeding structure is the frequency with which siblings (brothers and sisters) marry other sets of siblings. In one sample, 20 percent of all marriages were "double sibship" marriages (two brothers marry two sisters or a brother and sister marry a sister and brother). Eight percent were triple or quadruple sibship marriages.

Hutterite families are large, but family lines are relatively few. There are only twenty surnames in the group, and five of these are uncommon. The average family size is around ten children. This is the highest substantiated birthrate recorded for any population. Hutterites maintain a great interest in their genealogies, and they have kept family records with a great deal of accuracy. It is thus easy to trace degrees of biological relationship among individuals even back to the sixteenth century, a fact that has been important for much research on the group, including my own.

FIGURE 1.4
Scenes of colony life. (Top): A kindergarten for young children after they no longer spend all day with their parents and before they begin regular schooling—a Hutterite invention. (Bottom): A young woman packaging eggs in a colony that specializes in this product. Note the modern mechanized equipment.

Completing the match of the Hutterites to my ideal research population is their practice of regularly dividing their colonies, or "branching out" as they call it. When, after fifteen or twenty years, a colony becomes so large (about 130 to 150 people) that social and administrative problems arise and there is increasing duplication of labor specialists, a colony will purchase a new tract of land and divide its population. Usually the minister simply makes two lists, each with about half the colony's families. Family units, of course, are never broken up. The ministers do manipulate the lists to maintain a similarity of age and sex distributions and to ensure that each new colony has the required specialists. At last, lots are drawn to determine which families will remain and which will move to the new land as founders of the new *Bruderhof*.

The two Hutterite colonies I visited in the summer of 1973 were the results of a branching out that had taken place in 1958. Enough time had elapsed for a new generation to be born. Using fingerprint patterns as genetic data, I was able to estimate degrees of genetic relationship within and between the colonies and, most important, to trace changes in genetic makeup from generation to generation. These analyses would help me answer some of the questions I had posed about the evolutionary processes in which I was interested and about the role of these processes in human evolution.

ANTHROPOLOGY

When you think of anthropology—when *I* think of anthropology—the image that first comes to mind is the sort of thing I've just been describing: the fieldwork experience, when the anthropologist visits a land or a people usually very different from his or her own. This is the romantic and exciting part of the discipline, the part that provides the public image and makes for interesting films (dramatic as well as documentary). It is also the part that brings out the humanism of anthropology—the need to understand, to get to know, to communicate with other peoples from *their* perspective.

Fieldwork is certainly one of the things that attracts people to anthropology as a career. And fieldwork *is* important. It is the part of the science of anthropology where basic observations are made, data are collected, and ideas about humans are tested. But does it tell us what anthropology is really about? Does it define the field?

The first problem you may encounter in trying to define anthropology is the great variety of activities that anthropologists engage in. In fact, the field is so broad it is traditionally divided into four subfields (Figure 1.5). I am a **biological anthropologist** (sometimes called **physical anthropologist**). We focus on humans as a biological **species** and study such things as human genetics, human evolution, the fossil record, and the biology of living populations. Some biological anthropologists even study nonhuman species, the other primates (apes and monkeys, for example) to whom we are closely related (Figure 1.6).

Other anthropologists focus on our species' unique ability to create ideas, behaviors, and technologies that we share with one another—**culture**. Such anthropologists are **cultural anthropologists**. They study the nature of culture as a characteristic trait of our species and how and why cultural systems differ among human societies (Figure 1.7). One important characteristic of culture, and one important aspect of any cultural system, is language. **Linguistic anthropologists** study language as a human characteristic and attempt to explain the differences among the 3000 or so existing human languages.

biological anthropologist Specialist in a subfield of anthropology that studies humans as a biological species.

physical anthropologist The traditional name for biological anthropologist.

species A group of organisms that can produce fertile offspring among themselves but not with members of other groups.

culture Ideas and behaviors that are learned and transmitted. Nongenetic means of adaptation.

cultural anthropologist Specialist in a subfield of anthropology that focuses on human cultural behavior and cultural systems and the variation in cultural expression among human groups.

linguistic anthropologist Specialist in a subfield of anthropology that describes the characteristics of human language and studies the relationships between languages and the cultures that speak them.

FIGURE 1.5
The major subfields of anthropology with some of
the topics included in each.
These topics will be de-
scribed later in the book.

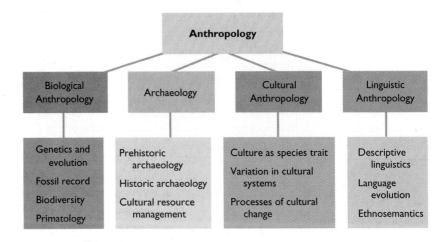

Most cultural systems that have ever existed are no longer in existence. Because for most of human history there were no written languages,
all that these extinct cultures have left behind are their material remains,
often literally their garbage—broken pottery, abandoned dwellings, used
tools, and the like. Reconstructing past cultural systems from such data is
the task of the **archaeologist**—the anthropologist of the cultural past. Archaeology also develops the techniques for locating, recovering, and preserving the often fragile remains of past cultures (Figure 1.8).

Now, how can these sorts of studies all be anthropology? What is the
common theme that ties together such things as the fingerprints of Hutterites, the behavior of chimpanzees, a 3-million-year-old fossil, the culture of a highland New Guinea society, the language of the Eskimo, and
the ancient peoples of southern New England? The answer to that question reveals what anthropology is all about. What all anthropologists are
doing is trying to answer questions about the human species. All anthropologists want to know why humans behave as we do, how we evolved
to look like we do, why we don't all look the same, and why there is such
variation in our cultural behaviors. We may start answering these questions from points as different as ancient fossils and modern Hutterite
farmers, but if our goal is scientific knowledge about the human species,
then we're doing anthropology.

Thus, anthropology, as its name indicates, is the study of humankind. But you might be wondering about many of the other subjects
you're taking classes in. Don't history, political science, sociology, and
even mathematics all study something about humans? What makes anthropology different?

The answer is that anthropology is the **holistic** study of humankind: It
searches for interrelationships among all the parts of its subject. Humans
are a complex species. Like any species, we have an anatomy, a physiology, a set of behaviors, an environment, and an evolutionary history—all

archaeologist Specialist in a
subfield of anthropology that
studies the human cultural
past and the reconstruction
of past cultural systems.

holistic Assuming an interrelationship among the
parts of a subject.

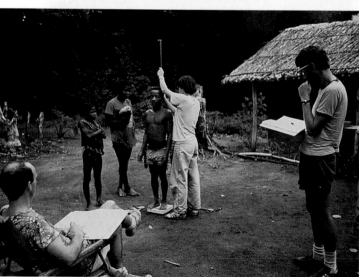

FIGURE 1.6
Biological anthropologists at work. (Clockwise from top left): The author identifies bones from an early New England grave, excavated at the family's request. Primatologist Agustín Fuentes gets close to his subjects, langurs on Bali. Paleoanthropologist Bill Kimbel uses dental tools, a small drill, and a microscope to free fossil fragments from the surrounding stone. Richard Wrangham and Robert Bailey watch Elizabeth Ross measure the stature of an Efe man from Republic of the Congo.

FIGURE 1.7
Cultural anthropologists at work. (Clockwise from top left): Raymond Hames uses a battery-powered computer to collect data about settlement patterns among the Yanomamö of Brazil. Applied anthropologist Miriam Chaiken weighs a child in Kenya as part of her focus on finding ways to improve health and nutrition in rural Third World communities. The late Marjorie Shostak among the San, a foraging people of southern Africa. Sharon Hutchinson among the Nuer, cattle herders of Sudan.

FIGURE 1.8

Archaeologists at work. (Clockwise from top left): Ken Feder shifts soil and examines potential artifacts at an excavation near the Farmington River in Connecticut. Connecticut State archaeologist Nick Bellantoni excavates an early New England grave (see Figure 1.6). Margaret Conkey, a specialist in prehistoric European art, examines an ancient painting at the cave of Le Reseau, France. Terry del Bene studies ancient tool-making techniques by producing replicas.

CONTEMPORARY ISSUES

What Responsibilities Does the Anthropologist Have When Studying Other Cultures?

Living peoples are not chemicals in a test tube or electrons in a particle accelerator. When we visit, observe, and eventually analyze the behaviors of another culture, we have important ethical responsibilities that go beyond those of the chemist or physicist. There are three overlapping and interrelated areas we must be aware of. We have a responsibility to our subjects, a responsibility to the science of anthropology, and a responsibility to ourselves.

Any time scientists observe a subject, they stand a chance of affecting that subject. Even in physics, for example, the act of observing an atomic particle may change the location of that particle and, thus, the observation of it. With people, the changes can be more profound. When anthropologists visit another society, for example, we may introduce its people to new technologies. In sometimes subtle ways, this can bring about changes in their culture. For example, if we give a previously unknown or unavailable tool—say, a metal knife or a cigarette lighter—to some people but not others, it might cause jealousies or even alterations in the power structure. New behaviors that are introduced, if adopted by some of the people being studied, could disrupt the harmony of their cultural system. We may also, of course, introduce them to new diseases, with obvious potential consequences. Some influence from our presence is unavoidable, but we

must be conscious of the possibilities and try, as much as possible, to limit them.

At the same time, we should not withhold knowledge that could be of use to the people we study. When, for example, anthropologists and medical researchers visited the Yąnomamö of the Amazon rain forest, they discovered that previous contact with outsiders had started a measles epidemic. Never having been exposed to measles before, the Yąnomamö had no natural defenses. The scientists brought in a vaccine to try to fight off the disease.

Moreover, we have a responsibility to treat and respect our subjects as equals. This sounds obvious, but some anthropologists have a tendency to think of their subjects, especially if they are from a less technologically complex culture, as childlike and in need of almost paternalistic protection. This is patronizing and insulting. Furthermore, one's study may be far more fruitful if one has gained the respect of the subjects. When I arrived at one of the Hutterite colonies, for example, I found the colony leaders suddenly reluctant to let me conduct my study, despite a previous arrangement. It seems they had been interviewed by a journalist whose subsequent magazine article was inaccurate and somewhat demeaning. My initial inclination was to simply back off and quietly leave. But instead I decided to argue for my position, indicating that I was not a journalist but a scientist and

of which are interrelated. But unlike any other species, we also have culture. We can consciously invent and change our behaviors, and we can think about those behaviors and even about our own consciousness. Thus, all the other academic fields I mentioned, and more, are necessary in order to fully understand every aspect of human biology and culture. However, also necessary is a field that seeks to understand how all those aspects of our species are related—how our biology and our culture interact; how educator and, as such, my job was to present their culture accurately and from their point of view. They said no several times more. I pushed my case. In the end, they agreed, we got along fine, and they provided me with important information.

We also have a responsibility to anthropology itself. As I just noted, we must describe another society from its point of view, without imposing our own cultural values on our description and analysis. We call this cultural relativity. While we may not agree with everything another culture believes and does—and might even be repulsed by it—we are obliged as scientists to assume that the behaviors of others fit somehow into their cultural systems, that is, are acceptable *relative to* their cultural beliefs. We may, for example, find the ritual warfare and killing by the Dani from New Guinea (see Chapter 13) abhorrent by our cultural standards, but we understand that, within *their* cultural system, it makes perfect sense. We can only understand human culture and human cultures if we study them objectively.

Still, we have a responsibility to ourselves, in several ways. First, in the process of practicing cultural relativity, we need not shun or deny our own beliefs and standards. A culture persists because its members adhere to certain standards and, indeed, take them on faith. While one benefit of anthropology is the opportunity to learn about alternative ways of thinking, anthropologists should not simply jettison the beliefs that make them part of their own society. Moreover, by acknowledging reactions to the behaviors of others—even

reactions like repulsion—it is easier to set them aside for the purposes of objective science.

Finally, the concept of cultural relativity has limitations. While certain behaviors may make perfect sense within specific cultural systems and while we must practice cultural relativity in order to understand those systems, the nature of the contemporary world as a global village suggests that there are certain universal standards of behavior. Not everything every society does is morally acceptable, and we have a responsibility to try as best as we can to speak out about such practices in the hopes of changing them. These practices may not be intentional. The subsistence farmers who are burning large areas of the world's rain forests may not have access to the big picture of global ecology and may have perfectly sound personal reasons for their activity. This, however, does not make it acceptable, and we should be trying to provide these farmers with other, less destructive ways of pursuing their livelihoods. In other cases, the acts are intentional. A society, for example, that denies its women equal medical care simply because they are women may be doing so for culturally consistent, long-standing reasons. But such a practice is contrary to ideas of basic human rights that most of the world accepts.

Considerations like these make anthropology a difficult profession, with debatable, and even contentious, issues. But they also make anthropology—the discipline that possesses the broad perspective needed to make these considerations—a very important science.

our past has influenced our present; how one facet of culture, like economics, is related to some other facet, like religion. Trying to understand these relationships is what anthropologists do.

It might be helpful to think of it this way: If you were a zoologist interested in, say, honeybees, you couldn't possibly understand that insect fully unless you understood its anatomy, its physiology, its behavior, its environment, and its evolutionary history. You might specialize in one aspect of its life—say, its complex communication system—but to know just what a honeybee *is*, you must understand the interrelationships among *all* aspects of its life.

Anthropology is much the same—but with the important distinction that what sets humans apart from all other living creatures is our cultural behavior. Culture adds a dimension to our species that is beyond the purely biological. A bee can't change its behavior at will. We can. Thus, culture becomes a central focus within anthropology.

So let's now embark on an anthropological tour of our species, using holism and the focus on culture as our organizing principles. We will view humans from the past and humans of the present; faraway "exotic" cultures as well as those, like the Hutterites, who are right next door. We'll look at mainstream American culture too. We'll examine the environments in which these humans live, and we'll see how changes in those environments have affected our species. We'll even take a look at some other species of living things.

SUMMARY

Anthropology can be defined as the holistic study of the human species. Its central focus is the feature that is unique to humans—our cultural behavior. Culture is the way we as a species deal with our world and with one another. Understanding a species' behavior—even when that behavior is largely cultural—necessarily requires an understanding of all aspects of that species' identity, from its biology to its environment to its evolutionary past to the cultural behaviors that come in many different forms.

NOTES, REFERENCES, AND READINGS

Perhaps the most complete work on the Hutterites is John A. Hostetler's *Hutterite Society*. (All references and reading suggestions are listed, with complete information, in the Bibliography at the back of the book.)

The best description I know of the anthropological fieldwork experience, and one that makes for exciting reading, is *Studying the Yanomamö* by Napoleon A. Chagnon, about his adventures and scientific work with that now-famous South American society. If you like novels, there is a description of an anthropologist doing fieldwork in that form. It's by Elenore Smith Bowen (the pseudonym of anthropologist Laura Bohannon), called *Return to Laughter*. Though fiction, it captures, in an accurate and moving story about West Africa, what fieldwork can be like. A nonfiction account that I enjoyed was Nigel Barley's *The Innocent Anthropologist*, also about West Africa. Finally, I recommend Katherine A. Dettwyler's *Dancing Skeletons: Life and Death in West Africa*. It's not that all anthropological fieldwork takes place on that continent; it's just that some of my favorite fieldwork descriptions do.

2

METHODS OF INQUIRY

Anthropology As Science

From books, movies, and television comes our popular image of the scientist as a walking encyclopedia of facts. Science, indeed, is often understood as the process of fact-collecting. Now, while it's fair to say that scientists certainly need to know a lot of facts, so do a lot of other people. Champions on the TV quiz show *Jeopardy* are not usually professional scientists.

Facts certainly are important to science. They are the raw material of science, the data scientists use. But what scientists really do is *explain* facts, not simply collect them. **Science** is *a method of inquiry, a way of answering questions about the world* that plays by certain rules.

How does science work? Is science the only valid and logical method for trying to explain the world around us? And how is anthropology—the holistic study of human biology and culture—a scientific endeavor?

THE SCIENTIFIC METHOD

The world is full of things that need explaining. We might wonder about the behavior of a bird, the chemical composition of a star in the night sky, the identity of a fossil skeleton, the social interaction of students in a college classroom, or the rituals of a society in the Kalahari Desert of southern Africa. As people, we strive to understand such phenomena, to know why and how these things occur as they do. As scientists we must try to answer these questions according to a special set of rules—the **scientific method.**

The scientific method involves a cycle of steps and, in reality, one may begin anywhere on the cycle (Figure 2.1). The most basic step is asking the questions we wish to answer or describing the observations we wish to explain. We then look for patterns, connections, and associations so we can generate educated guesses as to possible explanations. These educated guesses are called **hypotheses.** In other words, we try to formulate a *general* explanatory principle that will account for the *specific* pieces of real data we have observed and want to explain. This process of reasoning is called **induction.**

Next comes the essence—indeed the defining characteristic—of science. We must attempt to either support or refute our hypothesis by testing it. Tests may take many forms, depending on what we are trying to explain, but basically we reverse the process of induction and go from the general back to the specific by making predictions: *If* our general

science The method of inquiry that requires the generation, testing, and acceptance or rejection of hypotheses.

scientific method The process of conducting scientific inquiry.

hypotheses Educated guesses to explain natural phenomena.

induction Developing a general explanation from specific observations.

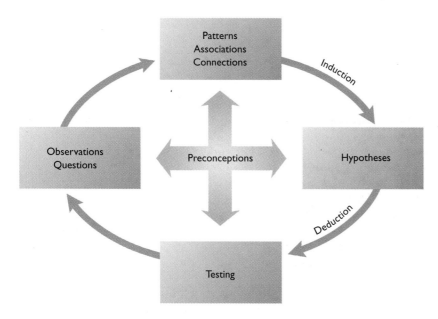

FIGURE 2.1
FIGURE 2.1
Steps in the scientific method. Science is a cycle of asking questions, finding patterns, generating hypotheses, and testing those hypotheses. Even when a hypothesis is well supported enough to be considered a theory, it still must be subjected to scientific inquiry to check its validity and explain its details. Science should always be skeptical, always open to questioning and self-examination. All science is conducted by individuals within the context of a culture and so is affected by preconceptions. It is an important part of the scientific method to try to be aware of these preconceptions.

hypothesis is correct, *then* what other specific things should we observe? This is called **deduction.** For example, we look for:

1. *Repetition:* Does the same phenomenon occur over and over?

2. *Universality:* Does the phenomenon occur under all conditions? If we vary some aspect of the situation, will the phenomenon still occur? How might different situations change the phenomenon?

3. *Explanations for exceptions:* Can we account for cases where the phenomenon doesn't appear to occur?

4. *New data:* Does new information support or contradict our hypothesis?

If we find one piece of evidence that conclusively refutes our hypothesis, we consider it disproved. But if the hypothesis passes every test we come up with, we may elevate our idea to the status of a very good hypothesis, which in science is called a **theory.**

Notice that I didn't say we "proved" the hypothesis. Science is skeptical, always looking for new evidence, always open to and even inviting change. The best we can honestly say about a theory is that *so far* no evidence has been found that *disproves* it.

Of course, some theories are so well supported that we are safe in considering them to be facts and in using them as a basis for further investigation. The theories of gravity, evolution, and relativity are all concepts central to many aspects of our thinking because they are ideas

deduction Suggesting specific data that would be found if a hypothesis were true.

theory A hypothesis that has been well supported by evidence and testing.

supported by every test applied to them and refuted by none. As biologist Stephen Jay Gould says, a theory can be taken as fact when it is "confirmed to such a degree that it would be perverse to withhold provisional assent."

We don't stop when we have developed a theory, however. No theory is complete. The theory of gravity establishes that some force we call gravity exists, but we still don't understand exactly what gravity is and how it works. In other words, we still have questions to answer and observations to explain. Scientists are now testing hypotheses that attempt to explain the origin, nature, and operation of gravity.

Another popular conception of science is that it only studies visible, tangible, present-day things—chemicals, living organisms, planets and stars. But notice that gravity is *not* visible or tangible. We can't see gravity, but we know it exists because all our deductive predictions support its existence. We see gravity work over and over every time we drop an object or jump up in the air and come back down to earth instead of flying off into space. We logically predict that if gravity is the property of objects with mass, the bigger the object the more gravity. We saw this clearly when we watched the astronauts walk around on the moon; they were literally lighter (about one-sixth their earthly weight) because the moon, being smaller than the earth, has less gravity. We also see the increased effects of the gravity of very massive objects (Figure 2.2). We can even explain exceptions *within the context of our general idea.* The reason a helium-filled balloon seems to violate gravity can be explained *by* our theory of gravity: Helium is less dense than the surrounding air and so responds relatively less to the earth's gravity (that is, it is lighter). In other words, the balloon exhibits buoyancy like a boat on water.

Similarly, past events can't be seen or touched. They can't be experimented upon directly or repeated exactly. The evolution of plants and animals is an example. But again, we know that evolution occurred because the idea has passed all our tests. The idea of evolution explains observations of the real world. We have observed everything we predicted we would *if* evolution occurred. (We'll look more closely at how science has derived and supported the theory of evolution in Chapter 3.)

Moreover, we often think of the scientific method as applying only to stereotypical scientific matters like gravity, chemistry, and evolution. In fact, however, we all use the scientific method every day for issues somewhat more down-to-earth than gravity. Remember, science is *a way of thinking.* Consider the steps you take to solve some problem—say, how to most efficiently organize all your activities for the day or how to repair a broken household item. You are probably using a version of the scientific method.

I noted that scientists may begin their investigations at any point on the cycle diagrammed in Figure 2.1. For instance, we might have a flash of inspiration that presents us with some notion of an overarching

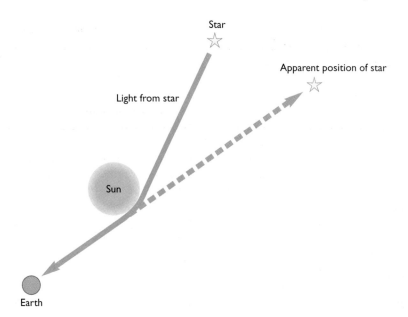

Star

Apparent position of star

Light from star

Sun

Earth

FIGURE 2.2
Light bent by gravity. Einstein predicted that a strong gravitational field could bend light. His prediction was verified when light from stars that should have been blocked by the sun could be seen during a solar eclipse. The effect is greatly exaggerated in this drawing.

concept that might explain many different phenomena. In other words, we might dream up a potential theory. We then, of course, would have to go through all the other steps of making observations, generating individual hypotheses, and testing those hypotheses. As an example, Albert Einstein was working on the nature of light waves when he came up with the idea of the equivalency of matter and energy, his famous formula $E = mc^2$. It was only later that this relationship was experimentally verified and all its implications and applications understood.

Finally, what about the label "Preconceptions" in the middle of Figure 2.1? Don't scientists search for truths—truths that are objective and not influenced by preconceived notions or prejudices? Ideally, yes. But, in fact, scientists are members of their societies and participants in their cultures, and science is always conducted within the context of a particular culture at a particular point in time. Thus, science—as objective as we try to make it—is always constrained by what we already know, by what we still don't know, by the technology available to us to gather and test data, and even by certain influential social or cultural trends.

For example, I recall in elementary school back in the mid-1950s one of my teachers pointing out that the east coast of South America and the west coast of Africa seemed to potentially fit together like a giant jigsaw puzzle (Figure 2.3). Of course, she said, there's no way the continents could move around, so it must just be a coincidence. In fact, she was reflecting our scientific knowledge of the time. There was plenty of geological and fossil evidence that the continents had moved around, but we

FIGURE 2.3
Topographic map of the Atlantic Ocean floor showing the similar outlines of the edges of the Eastern and Western Hemispheres. Also shown is the Mid-Atlantic Ridge—evidence for the plate tectonics that pushed the once-connected continents apart.

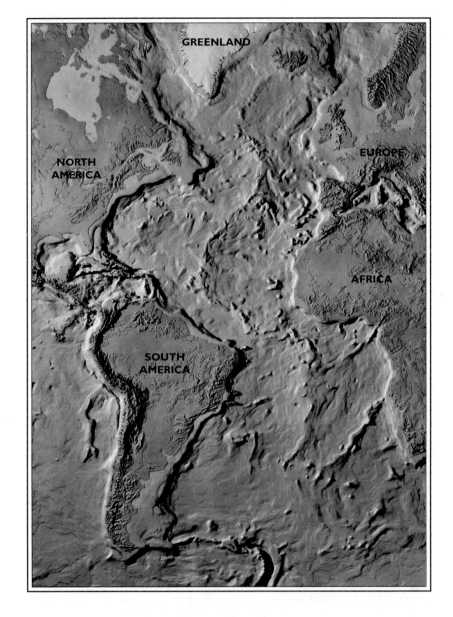

knew of no way then that such movement could possibly occur. Although the idea of continental drift had been proposed in 1912, there was no mechanism to explain it. Beginning in the 1960s, however, new technologies gave us new evidence that provided such a mechanism. We now have a well-verified theory of continental drift by the process of plate tectonics.

An amusing example of an influential social trend comes from a hypothesized explanation for the famous Salem witch trials in Massachusetts in 1692, where a group of young girls accused some adults of witchcraft, with the result that a number of people were executed. One idea was that the people of Salem had consumed bread made from grains tainted with ergot, a fungus that contains alkaloids, some of which are derivatives of lysergic acid, which in turn is used in the synthesis of the hallucinogenic drug LSD. In other words, maybe the young girls that made the witchcraft accusations were inadvertently tripping. (I need not tell you in which recent decade this idea arose. By the way, there is no evidence for this explanation.) These examples show us why scientific skepticism is so important, and why we should always question and re-examine even our most well supported ideas.

So, science answers questions about our lives and about the world in which we live. For an answer to be defined as scientific, it must be testable—and must be tested. Put another way, it must be impossible to find data that would disprove it. For an answer to be accepted, it must pass all those tests and be refuted by none.

As Galileo said—speaking in metaphor—and as Pope John Paul II repeated centuries later—scientific inquiry tells us "how heaven *is*." That is, science tells us what the world is really like and how it really works. In contrast to science are belief systems. They tell us how the world *should* be, or as Galileo put it, "how to *get* to heaven."

BELIEF SYSTEMS

Some questions about the world, even in a technologically complex society like ours, remain beyond the scope of science. Scientific inquiry, as powerful and important as it is, doesn't answer everything. Though we have some well-established theories about how the universe evolved once it began, the origin of the universe remains, for the moment at least, outside the realm of science. For most societies throughout most of human history, many questions could not be addressed scientifically.

Nor does science tell us how to behave. In our society, for example, we treat medical matters scientifically. But science does not, and cannot, inform us how best to apply medical knowledge. Who should practice medicine? How are medical practitioners trained and administered by society? How should they be compensated? What should their relationship be with their patients? Is everyone equally entitled to medical care? Society and the medical profession answer these questions through laws and regulations—formalizations of beliefs. For example, the Hippocratic oath, taken by all doctors, says, in part, "I will not permit considerations of religion, nationality, race, party politics or social standing to intervene between my duty and my patient."

Finally, there are questions that can never be answered by science—matters like the meaning of life, the existence of a higher power, the proper social relationships among people within a society, or the purpose of one's own life.

All these sorts of questions are addressed by **belief systems**—religions, philosophies, ethics, morals, and laws. Belief systems differ from science in that they cannot be tested, cannot be disproved. They are taken on faith, and that, of course, is the source of their power. They provide stable bases for our behavior; for explanations of what is beyond our science; and for the broad, existential questions of life. Belief systems change, but they only change when *we* decide to change them, either as a society or as individuals.

The existence of a supreme being is an example of a value inherent in a belief system. Two of us with opposite views on the subject could debate the issue endlessly, but no scientific test could support or refute either view. If I were to change my mind on the matter, it would be a matter of personal faith, not reason. The supreme being is not to be found in a chemical reaction in a test tube or an observation through a telescope.

Belief systems don't only apply to these big questions. I had a friend in graduate school from a West African society that was **polygynous**—men could have several wives. That is normal for his society, whereas in mine, one wife (at least one at a time) is the norm. We discussed the pros and cons of these two systems at length one day but never, of course, arrived at any "answer." His belief was right for his society as was mine for my society. We each took it on faith that this was so.

Although we often perceive science and belief systems as being eternally and inevitably at odds with one another, nothing could be farther from the truth. Conflicts do arise, as they do among facets of any society. But it should be apparent that, for a society to function, it needs both scientific knowledge and beliefs. Neither, by itself, addresses all the questions.

Understanding the distinctions and the interrelationships between science and belief systems is important for each of us as members of our own culture. It is also important for us as anthropologists because among the things we study are the cultural systems of other people. These systems include scientific knowledge and beliefs but their identity and interaction may well be different from what we are used to in our culture. Furthermore, we need to be aware of the influences of our own cultural background on the science we conduct as we study other societies and their cultures.

To return to Galileo's metaphorical statement, then, while science tells us "how heaven *is*," belief systems tell us "how to *get* to heaven." Or, in the words of biologist John Maynard Smith, science tells us what is "possible," and beliefs tell us what is "desirable." No culture can function without both.

ANTHROPOLOGY AS A SCIENCE

Given the wide range of topics that anthropology studies, and given that much of anthropology studies such abstract areas as human culture and cultural systems, it may be a challenge to understand how anthropology

belief systems Ideas that are taken on faith and cannot be scientifically tested.

polygynous Referring to a society where a man may have multiple wives.

can be defined as a science. Some facets of our field, of course, are clearly scientific. For example, I had some questions I wanted to address about processes of evolution. I generated several hypotheses regarding what I expected to find when I examined these processes among the Hutterites. After collecting relevant data, I tested these hypotheses and drew some tentative conclusions—which, of course, should be further examined in other ways, among other groups of people (anthropology's cross-cultural perspective), and with other types of data.

Also clearly scientific would be our attempts to explain the distribution of human skin color. We observe a connection between skin color and latitude (skin color in **indigenous** peoples is darker closer to the equator) and one hypothesis to explain that connection has been well supported. An explanation for lighter skin in populations farther away from the equator is still under investigation because hypotheses proposed so far have not, at least for the moment, held up to testing (see Chapter 14).

Less clearly scientific at first glance are other areas of anthropology. For example, many of us deal with the past—biological anthropologists with extinct species and premodern forms of humans, and archaeologists with past human societies and cultures. How can we examine something that we can't directly observe and can't replicate? As noted above, we can still collect data concerning such past events. These data come in the form of fossils of extinct species, often found in datable layers of soil; comparative studies of the anatomy and genetics of living species that have descended from previous forms; the material remains of past cultures, sometimes complete and well preserved enough to present us with a picture frozen in time (Figure 2.4); and our knowledge of how living peoples exist and create and use material culture.

We also look for repeated patterns in our evidence from the past. For example, we might note some similarities among the cultures that first began to grow food instead of collecting it. From these similarities, we might generate ideas to explain *why* people made this transition (see Chapter 10).

All these sorts of data, and more, can be used to deductively test the hypotheses we have generated to explain the past. It is really no different from our ability to scientifically examine things we cannot see directly, like gravity or subatomic particles. We know that these exist, and we know a lot about their behavior, because we can observe the results of their existence and behavior.

But what about the study of culture? Culture is not a *thing* like a chemical in a test tube or an electron or even an ancient fossil. Culture is the result of the decisions and actions of people. Are there scientific theories to account for the behavior of groups of people any more than there are scientific theories for, say, our own personal behavior? Some things we do as individuals make perfect, practical sense. Some make sense only to us personally and would not be sensible behaviors for someone else, even someone in a similar situation. Some of our decisions and actions can only be explained by delving deep within our subconscious memories.

indigenous Native; refers to a group of people with a long history in a particular area.

FIGURE 2.4

A moment frozen in time. Skeletons of victims of the eruption of Mt. Vesuvius in A.D. 79 that destroyed the Roman cities of Pompeii and Herculaneum. These people, some of the 150 remains so far discovered in Herculaneum, died embracing one another in their failed attempt to outrun the flow of volcanic ash that entombed their town.

Similarly, some actions of groups of people have obvious explanations. People, for example, have certain direct responses to their natural environments. They eat what human foods their environment provides, and they build their shelters from materials available in designs that make sense for a given set of climatic conditions (Figure 2.5). But many aspects of culture are related to something other than the natural environment. People in Beijing, China, and in Philadelphia in the United States have very different cultures despite being at the same latitude and having similar climates. Languages, beliefs, clothing styles, political systems, family organizations, and so on obviously require far more complex explanations. Sometimes this complexity may lead us to wonder if any scientific explanation is possible at all.

And it may be that a scientific theory for all aspects of human cultural behavior may forever elude us. Some cultural features may be so idiosyncratic to groups of people that no one explanation can account for them. This doesn't, however, mean we should not try. Remember that a first step in the scientific method is to look for patterns, associations, and repetitions. We do find these when we examine cultural systems and we can use them to generate hypotheses about interconnections among aspects of culture. We

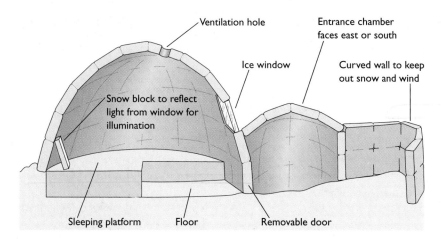

Ventilation hole

Entrance chamber faces east or south

Ice window

Curved wall to keep out snow and wind

Snow block to reflect light from window for illumination

Sleeping platform   Floor   Removable door

FIGURE 2.5
The well-known igloo of the Inuit, made from the only material readily available in the Arctic winter and including many ingenious features that make it remarkably adapted to life in a harsh climate.

can then test these hypotheses by seeing if they hold true for all cultural systems, by seeing if we can describe a cause-and-effect relationship, by finding exceptions to the observed connections and seeing if we can explain them. Maybe such connections exist only under certain circumstances so we have to look for additional relevant variables.

For example, in Chapter 7 we will discuss an observed association between subsistence pattern (how a group of people acquires their food) and number of recognized supernatural beings (gods, spirits, ancestral ghosts, and the like). The connection holds true often enough to allow us to make a generalization and to propose a reason for it. We can test our general hypothesis by seeing if *all* cases show the same association. We can also find exceptions—which there are—and see if we might make sense of them *in terms of our hypothesis.*

Now, we may discover—at least for some aspects of culture—that such hypotheses don't pan out, that no overall idea explains all cases and exceptions. A cultural system, after all, is an incredibly complex web of relationships. And this web is the creation, conscious and unconscious, of real people making decisions, responses, and actions for all the complex reasons people do such things.

But, if we *can* find generalizations—and we can—we have come a long way in understanding our own behavior and the behavior of other societies, and in being able to at least make educated predictions that might help us cope with all the changes and challenges that the modern world imposes on human societies and their ways of life. This is true even if we never achieve any overall theory of culture.

It should be pointed out that, while anthropology is a science, it is also a humanistic endeavor. Indeed, this is what draws many into anthropology as a profession, and in fact, many anthropologists see humanism, rather than the scientific approach, as the major focus of at least cultural anthropology. For in the process of observing, learning about,

CONTEMPORARY ISSUES

Isn't Science Sometimes a Threat to Society?

From Mary Shelley's *Frankenstein* (published in 1818) to modern blockbuster movies like *Jurassic Park* and TV shows like *The X-Files*, science is often portrayed as a potential evil, something that is far too easily abused and that, when abused, wreaks havoc on people and their societies. We often use the phrase "playing God" when referring to scientific endeavors, like genetic engineering, that we perceive as being an affront to human spirit and individuality. Science is blamed for many of today's social and environmental ills—and there *are* plenty of them—from global warming to radioactive contamination to the proliferation of weapons of mass destruction. Science is also thought of and depicted in the media as conspiratorial—covering up certain facts for nefarious reasons and ignoring or denigrating ideas with which the scientists have philosophical or ideological differences.

There are several errors in these views of science. First, although science has put forth and scientists have embraced ideas that have resulted in human suffering, one of the hallmarks of science—as opposed to belief systems—is its ability for self-correction. For example, at the end of the nineteenth century and beginning of the twentieth, the eugenics movement held that many human behaviors were hereditary and that therefore selective breeding could improve the species. This idea was based upon current scientific understanding of the processes of evolution and genetics. Such ideas resulted (even in this country) in the forced sterilization, without the consent or even the knowledge, of many individuals who were deemed less fit because of a characteristic that society felt was undesirable (below average intelligence, for instance, or having borne illegitimate children). This is abhorrent, and was considered so by many people at the time for ethical reasons. Through scientific progress we now know much more about the nature of human heredity and behavior and so such practices, based on then-current science and often applied by well-meaning people, are unlikely in the future. At least science cannot be used to justify them.

Second, the view of science as a potential danger ignores the fact that *anything* may be a danger

and trying to understand culture in general and other cultures in particular, we come to better understand humanity as a whole. We appreciate our species' unique position in the world. We better understand our own society and, perhaps most important, we come to understand other societies, other cultures, and other people. We see that, despite all the striking differences among us—in religion, clothing style, language, and countless other areas—there are lots of similarities in those things that really matter—the needs, desires, potentials, and limitations shared by all people. We may have our different ways of thinking and of doing things—and these certainly can lead to unfortunate and even tragic misunderstandings and conflicts—but the goals of all these behaviors are, in the end, the same for all of us. This, perhaps, is anthropology's most socially important contribution to knowledge.

if used incorrectly or for evil purposes. One has but to examine world history to see that even religious ideals are not always put to positive uses. Indeed, several present bloody hostilities are based on religious conflicts—in some cases involving religions that specifically prohibit the taking of human life.

Third, in focusing on the negative results of science, we all too easily forget or take for granted the positive results. People today who are the most vocal critics of science still promote their ideas over the electronic media, write them down on computers, travel in airplanes, and enjoy all the medical and nutritional benefits of a modern scientific society. The late astronomer Carl Sagan tells of asking a group of people how many of them would not be alive today if it weren't for modern medicine. Most raised their hands. I tried this with a class of undergraduates, average age about twenty, and still about half raised their hands.

Finally, are scientists conspiring to withhold information from us about certain things? Have we really been visited by extraterrestrial aliens? Has Noah's Ark been found? Are there serious holes in the theory of evolution? Do some people really have telekinetic powers? These ideas, after all, are popular and have been around for some time despite sound scientific evidence to the contrary. Why *would* scientists cover up these facts?

I have no doubt that there have been coverups and the withholding of knowledge. But I am also sure that the vast majority of scientific investigators are honest and completely forthcoming with their knowledge. Many of us have, in fact, actively researched some of the ideas that are usually passed off as nonsense to give them a fair scientific hearing and to show, if they have no basis, *why* they have no basis.

We may someday find new evidence that changes our ideas about things like alien visits, psychic powers, and the like; the universe, someone once said, is not only stranger than we imagine, but stranger than we *can* imagine. But, at any given point in time, I think we can rely on the work of scientists in all fields to indicate for us what current evidence points to about the nature of the world. "The truth is out there," it says on *The X-Files*. Some truths, indeed, have yet to be discovered, or maybe even imagined. But the truths, as science understands them at the moment, are "out there" in the sense of being out there for all to see, understand, appreciate, and use.

SUMMARY

Science is the method of inquiry that generates testable hypotheses to explain the real world and then tests those hypotheses with the goal of deriving theories—broad explanatory principles. Belief systems are another method of inquiry. Beliefs are taken on faith. They are not open to testing in a scientific way, although we all regularly test our beliefs on a personal level.

Although we may have the idea that belief and science are eternally at odds with one another—and while conflicts between the two do arise—both methods of inquiry are essential for the smooth operation of any cultural system. Any culture requires both scientific knowledge (what is possible) and belief (what is desirable) in order to function and survive.

Anthropology is a science in that it attempts to explain observed phenomena of human biology and culture, and it does so by generating and testing hypotheses. Although aspects of human cultural behavior may be too complex and idiosyncratic to ever be accounted for by a scientifically generated theory, we still gain immeasurably in just the attempt to apply scientific inquiry to cultures. We achieve a better understanding of ourselves and others, and we become more likely to learn how to cope with the numerous and rapid changes that confront us in the modern world. At the same time, the humanism of anthropology provides us with a better personal and philosophical understanding of our species, its nature, and the wealth of diversity within it.

NOTES, REFERENCES, AND READINGS

One of the best complete discussions of the scientific method I know of is Chapter 2 in Kenneth Feder's *Frauds, Myths, and Mysteries: Science and Pseudoscience in Archaeology,* third edition. This book also, as the title indicates, describes and scientifically examines various claims within archaeology, clearly showing how science works, and how it can be misused and misunderstood. Another good treatment of the scientific method is in Chapter 1 of *The Sciences: An Integrated Approach* by James Trefil and Robert M. Hazen.

The quote from John Maynard Smith is in the November 1984 *Natural History* in an article titled "Science and Myth," which nicely discusses the differences and relationships between science and belief systems. Anthropology as a science is the topic of "Science in Anthropology" by Melvin Ember and Carol Ember in *The Teaching of Anthropology* edited by Conrad Kottak et al. The quote by Stephen Jay Gould is from "Evolution as Fact and Theory" in his book *Hen's Teeth and Horse's Toes,* another good discussion of the nature of the scientific method. Carl Sagan's question about modern medicine, described in the Contemporary Issue, is from his *The Demon-Haunted World.*

3

EVOLUTION

Change in Nature and
the Nature of Change

Each of us lives in a world made up of our society and of that society in interaction with all the societies on earth. We live, in other words, in a social and cultural environment. In addition, even with all our technological achievements, we humans are still part of another world—the natural world. We are, after all, a type of animal. Even though we sometimes forget it, we, like all life on earth, interact continually with the natural environment. We affect it, it affects us, and we are dependent upon it. Moreover, our species has descended from nonhuman ancestors, has changed over time into modern *Homo sapiens,* and is still changing—in other words, we have evolved. And our **evolution** has occurred through the actions of the same natural processes that have affected every other living organism.

THE EVOLUTION OF EVOLUTION

The idea that biological species, including humans, have changed through time and have given rise to other species can be traced all the way back to some of the ancient Greek philosophers. Our present-day understanding of evolution, however, begins in Europe in the late 1700s.

Before that time, the study of biology was limited by two assumptions, derived in part from literal interpretations of the Bible, in part from ancient philosophical ideas, and in part from a simple scarcity of data. Living things were thought to have undergone no change since they were first divinely created. They were thought, in other words, to be "fixed" or "essential" both in terms of their appearance and the number of existing kinds of organisms. Moreover, the variety observed among living things was thought to represent a "great chain of being," a hierarchical organization leading from simplest and least perfect to most complex and most perfect—with human beings, of course, as the last link in that chain.

In addition, the earth was conceived of as very young. This idea was formalized in 1650 by Irish Archbishop James Ussher (1581–1656), who calculated—using passages in the Bible as well as some historical records—that the biblical creation had begun at noon on Sunday, October 23, in the year 4004 B.C. Thus, the earth was less than 6000 years old.

By the latter half of the eighteenth century, however, these ideas began to change. **Fossils** were beginning to be recognized as the remains of creatures that once existed but existed no longer, or at least not in that particular form. Previously, fossils had been interpreted as everything

evolution In biology, the idea that species change through time and that existing species give rise to new species.

fossils Remains of life-forms of the past

inheritance of acquired characteristics The incorrect idea that traits acquired during an organism's lifetime can be passed on to its offspring.

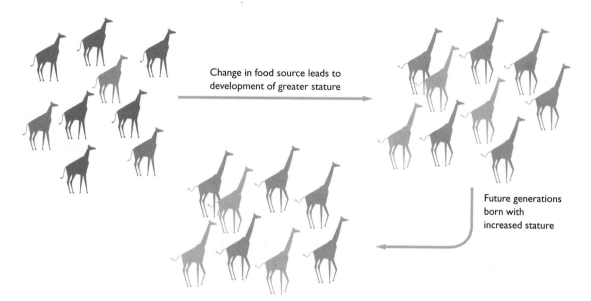

Change in food source leads to development of greater stature

Future generations born with increased stature

FIGURE 3.1
Lamarck's model applied to the evolution of long necks and tall bodies in giraffes. In the past, giraffes were short, but environmental change altered their food source, placing the foliage they ate high up in the trees. Confronted with this problem, each giraffe was able to stretch its neck and legs enough to reach the leaves. This greater height was automatically passed on the giraffes' offspring, who had to make themselves even taller, and so on, giving rise to the 18-foot-tall giraffes of today. (Compare with Darwin's model, Figure 3.4.)

from deformed individuals of existing species to mere "tricks of nature." The nature of the geological record was also becoming clear, and it was seen that the earth itself had undergone enormous change, over what must have been more than 6000 years. By the beginning of the 1800s what was at issue was not so much *whether* change had occurred but *how* it occurred.

Numerous models were proposed to account for the fossils and for the obvious lack of fixity in species that they demonstrated. One of the best known of these was proposed by French biologist Jean Baptiste de Lamarck (1744–1829). Lamarck said that living things are adapted to the environments in which they live. Since the geological record, as well as simple observation, shows that environments continually change, it stands to reason that living things must change their adaptations in order to survive. No problem there.

But Lamarck went on to propose a mechanism to explain how animals and plants change in response to changing environments. His idea, which he refined from earlier, similar proposals, is called the **inheritance of acquired characteristics** (Figure 3.1). Species, said Lamarck, have a "will" that enables them to recognize that some environmental change has taken place and to "carry out" the proper adaptive actions. The organs necessary for these actions are then changed accordingly. Species can even develop new organs if needed. These new or changed traits are then passed on, in their new form, to the organism's offspring. Thus, the "inheritance" of characteristics "acquired" during an individual organism's lifetime. Furthermore, Lamarck proposed that this evolution was "progressive," always working toward producing more-complex and

FIGURE 3.2
Charles Darwin in 1869, by famed photographer Julia Margaret Cameron.

thus more-perfect forms. You can guess what species he thought the most complex and perfect.

For many years, Lamarck's model, or something like it, was accepted by biologists. There was, after all, a certain comfort in his idea. If we have to accept that living things have changed over time, at least they changed in a particular (and human-oriented) direction, and they changed by a process dependent upon something within the organism itself—Lamarck's "will." It was also a process that was unfailing. There was, in other words, no extinction. Creatures represented only by fossils were simply creatures that had undergone so much change that they now looked very different.

But Lamarck's model doesn't work. We know of no way in which traits can arise automatically when they are needed, whether through the organism's own will or some action of the environment. Furthermore, traits that are acquired during an organism's lifetime cannot be passed on to its offspring. To use one of Lamarck's own examples against him, the blacksmith's strong right arm *will not* be inherited by his sons. It should also be clear that species can't just create new organs when they might be useful.

So, although Lamarck's model was popular, many scientists at the same time searched for a better mechanism for evolution. Enter Charles Darwin (Figure 3.2).

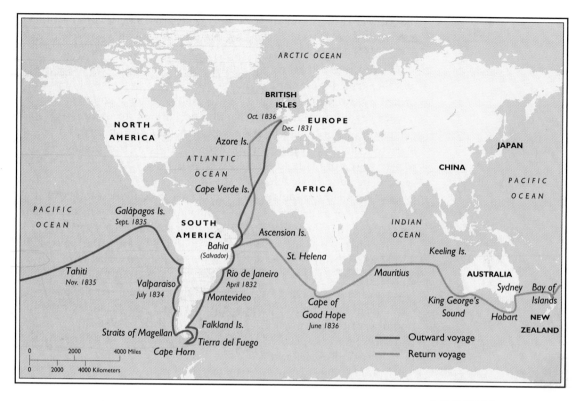

FIGURE 3.3
The route of Darwin's voyage aboard the H.M.S. *Beagle* from 1831 to 1836. This trip provided Darwin with observations and thoughts vital to his formulation of the theory of natural selection. Especially famous and important was his visit to the Galápagos Islands in the eastern Pacific.

Charles Robert Darwin was born into a well-to-do British family on February 12, 1809 (the same day as Abraham Lincoln). As a boy and a young man, Charles seemed to lack a direction in life, at least one that pleased his father. Careers in both medicine and the clergy failed to interest him. Natural history was his passion. It was with some reluctance that, in 1831, Charles's father gave him permission to join H.M.S. *Beagle* for its voyage of discovery around the world. The elder Darwin, unknowingly, changed the history of science.

The story of the voyage of the *Beagle* is itself a fascinating one. For our purposes here, suffice it to say that the voyage provided Darwin with a perspective, rarely available to men of his time, on the nature of living creatures. Darwin was able to observe and collect data, literally from around the world, on geological formations and the fossils they contained, on the geographic distributions of species, on the adaptations of various creatures to their environments, and on how individual populations varied from one another according to environmental differences (Figure 3.3). The data not only indicated to Darwin that organisms changed through time (which was generally accepted by then), but also hinted that species could give rise to other species. Perhaps it hinted as well at the mechanism that brought about these processes. In addition, the works of other thinkers, especially geologists and social philosophers, contributed to Darwin's thinking by introducing new perspectives on natural and social change.

Oddly, rather than writing about the transmutation of species—as it was then called—on his return from the *Beagle* voyage, in 1836, Darwin turned his attention to other scientific subjects. He mentioned what we now call evolution only privately to friends and wrote about it only in his personal notebooks and in two trial essays published in the early 1840s. Darwin's silence can probably be explained by his fear that science and society were not ready to accept his explanation. The process he had discerned, he may have felt, was too dependent on random, fortuitous events. Recall the popularity of Lamarck's idea at the time, which appealed to people because it said that when change was needed, it occurred, and that there was no extinction of species.

But history was not to leave Darwin alone. In 1858 Darwin received a brief paper from a young, lesser-known British naturalist named Alfred Russel Wallace (1823–1913). Wallace, suffering from a malaria-induced fever during a collecting trip in Indonesia, had glimpsed the basics of a mechanism that might explain, better than had Lamarck, the transmutation of species. Later, working it out in more detail, Wallace felt his idea had merit, and he decided to check it out with the most renowned of British naturalists, Darwin.

Upon reading Wallace's paper, Darwin's hand was called. For Wallace had described the same idea, in nearly the same terms as Darwin. Darwin was urged to publish, and the following year, 1859, *On the Origin of Species by Means of Natural Selection or the Preservation of Favoured Races in the Struggle for Life* hit the bookstores and sold out in a single day. Possibly to Darwin's surprise, the time was ripe for his idea of **natural selection,** which was heralded by most of the scientific community (Figure 3.4). "How extremely stupid of me not to have thought of that!" one colleague is reported to have remarked.

Charles Darwin died in 1882, but not before authoring numerous volumes on various scientific topics, including a second major work on evolution, *The Descent of Man* (1871). In this book Darwin did what he dared not in 1859. He applied his ideas explicitly to humans, and by that time they were accepted with little problem.

But Darwin did die without ever finding out the answers to two important questions. First, he did not understand exactly *how* traits in living organisms are passed on. Obviously, the ability of successful parents to give their traits to their offspring was vital to natural selection. There were, at the time, some vague ideas about a blending of substances from father and mother, but no substantial theory.

Second, Darwin did not know where variation came from. Without variation selection cannot operate; there is nothing to select *from*. He recognized that variation was always present in a species, even after years of

natural selection Evolutionary change based on the differential reproductive success of individuals within a species.

genes Technically, those portions of the DNA molecule that code for the production of specific proteins.

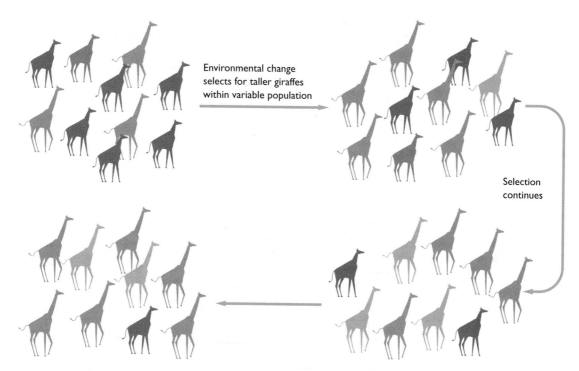

Environmental change selects for taller giraffes within variable population

Selection continues

selection to the same environment—even after years of selective breeding. But as to the origin and maintenance of that variation, Darwin had no answer.

Ironically, the answers to both questions were available during Darwin's lifetime, and they came from the same source. At about the time Darwin was writing *Origin of Species,* an Austrian monk named Gregor Mendel (1822–1884), working in a monastery in what is now the Czech Republic, described the basic laws of inheritance. Experimenting with pea plants, no doubt the culmination of many undocumented years of research, Mendel arrived at a number of important conclusions regarding the passing on of traits.

First, he realized that, rather than being carried in some substance (as was then thought), traits are controlled and passed on by individual particles or factors—we now call them **genes.** Moreover, these factors occur in pairs, both members of a pair not necessarily coding for the same expression of a trait. For example, Mendel's pea plants came in both short and tall varieties. From his breeding experiments he reached the conclusion that there was an individual factor for plant height that came in two versions, one for tall and the other for short plants. An individual might have both factors in its pair, but in this case the factor for tall plants overrode that for short plants. He called it a dominant—and we still do today.

FIGURE 3.4
Darwin's model of natural selection applied to the evolution of long necks and tall bodies in giraffes. An environmental change, perhaps in the location of food sources, made the taller giraffes within a variable species relatively more reproductively successful. These giraffes thus passed on their tallness to a greater number of offspring, making succeeding generations taller on average. (Compare to Lamarck's model, Figure 3.1.)

Mendel's second major conclusion concerned reproduction. A plant, he said, passed on to each of its offspring only one factor from each pair. Thus, every new plant would have a new pair of factors made up of one from each of its parents. In inheritance, factor pairs are broken up and then recombined in the offspring.

Here, then, were the answers to how inheritance takes place *and* to why there is variation within species: Traits are controlled by individual factors, and these factors are shuffled during reproduction to produce new combinations.

In 1900, almost twenty years after Darwin and Mendel died, Mendel's work, which had fallen into obscurity, was rediscovered. In that year three investigators, working independently, came upon the monk's obscure paper and realized what they had found. One of these men was the Dutch botanist Hugo de Vries (1848–1935). De Vries had been trying to explain the rare variations that sometimes appeared in plants and animals—things like a single flower of the wrong color or a plant that was far smaller or larger than other members of its species. Breeders called these oddities "sports." De Vries called them mutations. Now, with his discovery of Mendel's work, de Vries understood that his mutations were the results of sudden changes in Mendel's factors.

With this, the final link in a basic theory of evolution was in place, for mutations explained the source of new variation—where the different versions of factors or genes came from in the first place. Upon this base is built our current understanding of evolution. To be sure, much has been added, many mistakes have been made, and we are still debating the details. But we can use what we've discussed so far to describe the state of evolutionary theory today.

ECOLOGY, ADAPTATION, AND EVOLUTION

Consider two familiar animals (Figure 3.5). Though they look different, they are surprisingly similar in other respects. According to several measures, they are 98.5 percent genetically identical. Thus, many products of their genetic codes are identical—the hemoglobin on the surface of the red blood cells that carries oxygen, for example, and the ABO blood types. They can contract many of the same diseases. As we will see later, they also share striking anatomical and behavioral similarities. It has been concluded, in fact, that a mere 5 million years ago (not long in the grand scheme of things) these two had a common ancestor; that is, they were the same creature. And yet, they cannot interbreed now; that is, they cannot produce offspring. They are, in other words, clearly different species.

What processes bring about new species, and why do species look and behave as they do? There are two parts to the answer to that question.

First, a species (notice that *species* is both singular and plural) looks and behaves the way it does because, as Lamarck observed, it is **adapted**

adapted When an organism has physical traits and behaviors that allow it to survive in a particular environment.

to its environment. In other words, it possesses physical characteristics and patterns of behavior that help it survive in a given set of natural circumstances. It is able to find shelter, acquire food, locate mates, produce offspring, keep from being something else's food, all in step with—and in spite of—the climate, geography, and other inhabitants of the area where it lives.

Second, different species exist because in the continual process of adaptation species can and do give rise to new species. Environments to which species are adapted are always changing. Organisms, for various reasons, are always moving around. Populations of living things sometimes split up, and the resulting subpopulations become adapted to different environments and, under the right circumstances, evolve into different species. Thus, any two species will have a common ancestor somewhere in

41

the past. How far back in time this common ancestor is determines to a great extent how similar any two species are, that is, how closely related they are biologically. This idea—that species can change and give rise to new and different species—has been called **descent with modification.**

Here's an analogy: You are biologically related to all members of your family. But you and your sister are very closely related because you both have two immediate ancestors in common—your parents. You and your first cousin, although related, are more distantly related than are you and your sister because the common ancestors—either your father's parents or your mother's parents—are a generation farther back. Species of living things are related in the same fashion—like a branching tree. In fact, we often depict biological relationships with a tree diagram, just as we speak of and draw family trees (See Figure 3.13).

The complete process that results in the origin of new species is, as you will see, somewhat more complicated than this, but these two concepts—adaptation and descent with modification—are at the heart of the matter. Let's look at each of these important ideas more closely.

Adaptation

When we consider the adaptation of a plant or animal to its environment, we have two basic questions to ask: (1) To *what* is the organism adapted? (2) *How* is it adapted? The science concerned with the first of these questions is the study of **ecology.**

Ecology comes from the Greek *oikos*, meaning "house." It studies the "houses" or habitats of living things. More technically, it is the science concerned with discovering and explaining the network of relationships between organisms and all the various aspects of the environments in which they reside. Now, a moment's reflection should reveal that this could be a fairly complex topic. Imagine all the climatic factors, all the species of plants and animals, all the relationships just in your backyard. Obviously, we need some way of organizing such a study, and the central organizing concept in ecology is the **niche.**

An ecological niche may be defined as all the environmental factors with which a particular species normally comes into contact, and the ways in which that species is adapted to those factors. *Anything* that directly affects the life of the organism in question is included in its niche.

That's complicated enough, but it gets worse. Niches overlap. In other words, even if we are concerned with a particular species, we must learn a great deal about the ecology of the other species that make up its ecological niche. Ecology is a holistic study.

Consider bats. Most bats are active at night and in the air, so they have adaptations that allow them to fly, to navigate, and to find food under the special conditions of winging rapidly through dark skies. Since the food of many bat species—insects—also flies, they have to be able to catch it while they are both on the wing, and to do this bats have developed special

descent with modification An old term for what we now call biological evolution.

ecology The science that studies the network of relationships within environmental systems.

niche The environment of an organism and its adaptive response to that environment.

FIGURE 3.6
Bat catching insect.

anatomical and sensory structures (Figure 3.6). But adaptation is not a one-way street. To appreciate and understand fully the bats' adaptation, we have to realize that the insects it eats are adapted to the presence of the bats in their niches. Some insects that are hunted by bats have an adaptation that allows them to pick up the bats' navigation and food-finding signals (called echolocation) and so be better able to avoid becoming a meal. The full story of the bats' adaptation must include a study of the adaptations of the insects on which they feed.

Two more concepts result from this idea of complex systems of overlapping niches. They come from the fact that if you keep describing overlapping niches, you'll end up with an ecological description of the entire planet. One concept is the idea of the habitat. A habitat is not really strictly defined. It depends on the type of organism you are interested in and the number of environmental factors that directly affect it. If your species is a small insect, its habitat would be the local area in which it lives. The habitat of the St. Lucia parrot is the rain forest of that small Caribbean island, for the bird lives nowhere else. The blue whale's habitat is the world's oceans. In short, the set of niches that directly overlap with the niche of the species you are studying makes up the relevant habitat. Finally, a set of interacting habitats make up an **ecosystem**.

These ideas relate to humans in two ways. First, we are a biological species that evolved from other biological species. We thus have to understand ecological relationships in order to understand our basic nature. Second, this natural model can also be applied to the cultural environment of our species. We can each be thought of as living in a particular cultural niche, which is affected by other cultural niches, which collectively make

ecosystem A specific set of environmental relationships. The unit of study within ecology.

FIGURE 3.7
A cheetah hunting.

up the human cultural environment. We are also adapted to these cultural niches and this general cultural ecosystem.

Now, the second question: *How* are organisms adapted to their environments? Each living species has its own unique set of adaptations to its own unique environmental niche, and these can be described. But is there any general concept we can use to study adaptation, any one thing we can focus on?

We tend, both literally in laboratories and figuratively in adaptation studies, to "take organisms apart," to look at and explain their individual traits. For example, one of my favorite animals is the cheetah, an African cat (Figure 3.7). The cheetah is covered with fur that is yellow with dark spots. Its body is smaller and sleeker than other African cats, with a unique skeletal and muscle structure. Its spine is extremely flexible. If we were to look at its physiology, we would note certain distinct features about the way the cheetah uses energy. In the end, we could list dozens of characteristics that make the cheetah different from other species.

But does this list of features fully describe the cheetah's adaptation? Of course not. The cheetah doesn't survive by having anatomical and physiological traits. It survives by using them—by doing something, by behaving. And this is true of any organism, even the simplest single-celled animals, even plants. They all function, behave, do something—and this is how they interact with their environments: through the ways they get food, elude predators, find shelter, reproduce, and so on. Anatomy and physiology make behaviors possible. A certain muscle structure, a certain digestive system, a particular nervous system—we can think of these as having evolved along with behaviors to facilitate those behaviors. Thus, behavior is the key to understanding adaptation. Behaviors, like physical features, are the results of natural processes.

But how can this idea be applied to humans? After all, we are not programmed to behave in all the ways we do. In fact, we are unique in that we can think up our behaviors and change them at will if they are not giving us the desired results. We have, in other words, culture.

Think of it this way: Our cultural behaviors and the strictly biological ones of other organisms *serve the same function.* They help us adapt and survive in a given environment. Considered that way, the focus on behavior makes sense whether the environment and adaptations to it are natural or are created by the organism. Moreover, our behavior—our culture—is not entirely separate from our biology. We are, in a sense, biologically programmed to have culture in the first place through the structure and functions of our brains. And, as I'll describe later, there may even be some more direct connections between our biological heritage and some of the general themes of our behavior. So, as long as we keep in mind that there are differences between our cultural adaptations and the instinctive ones of most other animals, a focus on behavior is quite appropriate for the anthropologist studying the adaptations of the human species.

Descent with Modification

If environments always stayed the same, organisms would not have to change their adaptive characteristics and behaviors. All living things today would be essentially like the very first living things. This, of course, is not the case. Ecological conditions are in a constant state of flux. The geological record shows this over long periods of time. We can see smaller changes such as streams changing their courses, hills eroding, old farmland turning to woods, or any of the numerous human actions that alter our environment. In addition, organisms don't stay put. Plant seeds get blown by wind or carried by birds to new locations. Animals wander, or for some reason get pushed into new environments.

In some cases the changed or new environment is too different from the old one, and organisms won't survive. But there is always a chance that they will be able to adapt to the new conditions. So, when environments change, or when populations within species move into new environments, species may change. When a species is split up, with some populations isolated from the parent population and able to thrive under new ecological circumstances, new species may come about. Species change over time; this is modification. Populations within species may change enough to give rise to new species; this is descent.

There are two aspects to this idea that must be considered: (1) the *evidence* for change through time, and (2) the *processes* that bring this change about. If you think about it, descent with modification is a bold idea. It says that living creatures are not stable, unchanging entities. Such a broad, important idea requires a good deal of supporting scientific evidence. That evidence exists in ample quantities.

I've already noted one basic piece of evidence. This is the fact that species are not separate and equally distinct but are, like members of a family, similar to and different from one another in varying degrees. Specie, then, appear like members of a family line that have descended from earlier members. And there's more.

For one thing, despite the great diversity among the earth's living things, there exists a certain unity of life. All living creatures on the planet are composed of cells, all of which have a similar basic structure and are made up of **proteins,** which themselves are made up of **amino acids.** All living forms make their proteins from combinations of the same 20 amino acids. Furthermore, all organisms use the same code for building their proteins from amino acids. This is the genetic code, which uses **deoxyribonucleic acid (DNA)** and ribonucleic acid (**RNA**). Finally, living things do not exist independently of one another. In addition to being biologically related, they are all functionally related. They exist within a complex web of ecological interrelationships, each species dependent on the existence of many other species.

Of course, it's conceivable that all species could have arisen (or have been created) at the same time, already exhibiting these similarities and connections. The type of evidence I've given so far that evolution took place is, as they'd say in a courtroom drama, circumstantial. What we need is not only supporting evidence for what *could* have happened, but evidence for what *did* happen. And we have this too. It's the evidence from the geological and fossil records—the story of the earth's history and life, often literally written in stone. The story these records tell is clearly one of descent with modification.

If you've ever visited the Grand Canyon or any similar geological formation, or if you just take a good look at the walls of rock along a road that cuts through a hill instead of going over it, you will notice that the sides of the canyon or the wall of the roadcut are layered, like a gigantic layer cake. Closer inspection reveals that the layers are not all the same. They are of different thicknesses and are made up of different kinds of rock (Figure 3.8). It should be obvious from this structural relationship of the **strata** ("layers") that they were not laid down all at the same time, but were deposited in sequence, from bottom to top, as different geological events gave rise to different sorts of rock. The record of **stratigraphy,** then, is a record of change through time. When you consider that in some areas there are hundreds of strata, it becomes obvious that we are dealing with immense amounts of time.

Now, if we find fossils in certain strata, we can assume relative dates for them. That is, even if we don't know exactly how old a certain fossil

proteins are made up from combination of 20 amino acids

proteins Molecules that make cells and carry out cellular functions.

amino acids The chief components of proteins.

deoxyribonucleic acid (DNA) The molecule that carries the genetic code.

ribonucleic acid (RNA) The molecule that, in two forms, translates and transcribes the genetic code into proteins.

strata Layers; here, the layers of rock and soil under the surface of the earth.

stratigraphy The study of the earth's strata.

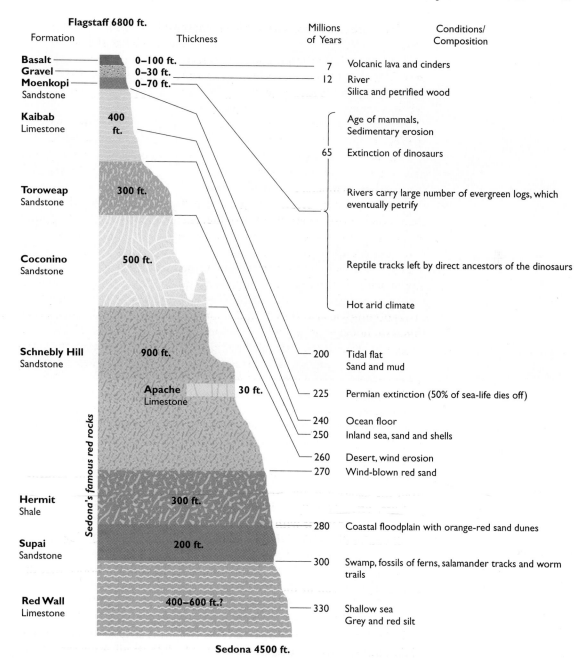

Flagstaff 6800 ft.

Formation	Thickness	Millions of Years	Conditions/Composition
Basalt	0–100 ft.	7	Volcanic lava and cinders
Gravel	0–30 ft.	12	River
Moenkopi Sandstone	0–70 ft.		Silica and petrified wood
Kaibab Limestone	400 ft.		Age of mammals, Sedimentary erosion
		65	Extinction of dinosaurs
Toroweap Sandstone	300 ft.		Rivers carry large number of evergreen logs, which eventually petrify
Coconino Sandstone	500 ft.		Reptile tracks left by direct ancestors of the dinosaurs
			Hot arid climate
Schnebly Hill Sandstone	900 ft.	200	Tidal flat Sand and mud
Apache Limestone	30 ft.	225	Permian extinction (50% of sea-life dies off)
		240	Ocean floor
		250	Inland sea, sand and shells
		260	Desert, wind erosion
		270	Wind-blown red sand
Hermit Shale	300 ft.		
		280	Coastal floodplain with orange-red sand dunes
Supai Sandstone	200 ft.		
		300	Swamp, fossils of ferns, salamander tracks and worm trails
Red Wall Limestone	400–600 ft.?	330	Shallow sea Grey and red silt

Sedona's famous red rocks

Sedona 4500 ft.

FIGURE 3.8
Geological cross section of the area around Sedona and Flagstaff, Arizona, showing the variation in composition and thickness of the strata and some of the events represented in those strata.

is, we can tell if it is older or younger than some other fossil by noting the number of strata separating the fossils.

Fossils, in their stratigraphic relationships, show us biological change through time in a number of ways. For one thing, the fossil remains of a particular group of organisms show change. As we'll discuss in Chapter 5,

FIGURE 3.9
Fossil of feathered dinosaur.

there is a nice sequence of fossils showing change within the human fossil record. We have similarly good records of change for the horse and elephant families. At a broader level, we can even see the evolution of one major type of organism from another. It was suggested over a hundred years ago that birds evolved from dinosaurs. We now have fossils that give evidence of forms transitional between these groups (Figure 3.9). Similarly, we have transitional fossils showing the evolution of mammals from early reptiles, and even of humans from apelike ancestors.

The fossil record of the earth's life also shows an increase in the range of diversity through time. The earliest fossils are all of fairly simple, single-celled organisms, and these remained the *only* kind of organism for over half the history of life. Then, about 1.7 billion years ago, multicellular creatures arose. As evolution accelerated, we begin to see fossils of early plants, animals with hard shells, animals with skeletons, flowering plants, flying insects—all the amazing array of life we now observe around us.

Related to the increase in diversity is an increase in complexity. This does not mean all types of organisms are always evolving to become more complex. Some organisms stay simple. In fact, most species on earth today are bacteria, among the simplest of creatures. Other species may become simpler through time by evolving a smaller size or losing some anatomical structure they once had. But, as time goes by, one finds *more kinds* of more-complex living things. This is what you would expect if types of creatures arose from earlier types. Just as technological innovations become more complex not all at once but by building on the base laid down by previous inventions, so too living things can increase in complexity only by adding new structures or functions on already existing ones.

So every individual piece of evidence in the geological and fossil records supports the idea that changes in the earth itself and in its inhabitants have taken place over great spans of time and that living things, including us, are related to one another as in an enormous and complex family tree. Within science these ideas are not really an issue today, nor have they been for some time. But precisely how all this happens—the processes by which descent with modification, or evolution, takes place —is still an important area of research and was the real scientific issue in Charles Darwin's day. And the centerpiece of these processes is Darwin's great contribution, natural selection.

NATURAL SELECTION

Natural selection is not always easy to understand right off. I had a hard time with it as an undergraduate, and when I began teaching I noticed the same problem among my students. I finally figured out why this was so. As contradictory as this may sound, natural selection is initially hard to understand because it's so straightforward. Because of this, we have a tendency to try to make it more complex, to read things into it that just aren't there.

The funny thing is, many of us practice a form of selection when dealing with pets, plants, or livestock. In high school I kept and bred tropical fish. One of my favorites was a live-bearing fish called a swordtail (Figure 3.10). Once I tried to breed a bright red strain of the fish, which didn't exist at the time. I have forgotten the exact details so I hope experts will forgive me any inaccuracies.

I started with a pair of the reddest fish I could find and mated them (which just involved putting them in a tank together). From the first generation of this mating—a dozen or so babies that quickly grew up—I chose the reddest and put them in a separate tank to breed. Then, from the second generation I again selected only the very reddest to breed the third generation, and so on. In this way, I hoped to get redder and redder fish until I had a pure strain of bright red ones. In case you're wondering, I ran out of room for aquariums before I found out whether my goal was even possible.

Now, notice that I was making two assumptions. First, I assumed that reddish swordtails were likely to produce reddish offspring—in other words, that children tend to resemble their parents. But second, I

FIGURE 3.10
Swordtails.

knew that not all the offspring of reddish parents would be equally red. In every generation I had to eliminate from breeding the offspring that were not the reddest (don't worry, I just moved them), and some of these were not even as red as their parents. In other words, any group of organisms shows variation in certain characteristics, within each generation and from generation to generation. Look around the classroom and even at the members of your own family for examples of this principle.

In general terms, I had set up a mini-habitat in which the most important adaptive characteristic was reddish body color. I then selected from the natural variation of the group the individuals in each generation that possessed an acceptable expression of that trait. These were the ones I allowed to reproduce, and they tended to pass on their body color to their offspring. Thus, fish with the favorable expression of the trait would increase in frequency (become a larger percentage of the whole population) and those with an unfavorable expression would decrease in frequency. If I hadn't run out of room, and—this is important—if the potential *natural* variation of the swordtails included a bright red color, I might have been able to alter the nature of my swordtail population from an original group whose average color was just reddish to one whose average color was bright red. Of course, I would still have to continue weeding out from succeeding generations any individuals that were not acceptably red.

If that makes sense, you need only take one more step to have a basic understanding of natural selection. But it is an important step, and it's the one that causes the most difficulty in understanding this process. The example I just gave is of **artificial selection.** A conscious agent—me—was making choices and taking direct action to implement them. Such an agent doesn't exist in nature, and trying to insert one into the process of natural selection is what gives people problems. Nothing directs the process in nature; it just happens.

[handwritten margin note: With our human eyes we don't see that God directs all the things that happens in the nature process!]

So, aside from the conscious agent, simply translate all the parts of my fish example to a natural situation. The artificial environment of my aquariums becomes the natural environment of a particular ecosystem. The reddish color I selected for becomes *all* the adaptive traits that allow a species to survive in its niche. Selection is no longer a matter of being moved to a different aquarium if a fish is the wrong color. Now it is based on variation in the expressions of all the adaptive characteristics and the degree to which the variation affects survival—and thus the ability to pass on those adaptive characteristics to the next generation.

Wild swordtails from Central America, for example, live in an ecological niche that requires the expression of adaptive traits within a limited range of variation. These traits would include things like body color; swimming ability; normal vision, smell, and other senses; and instinctive behaviors. Selection starts right away. Each female swordtail gives birth to many more young than can eventually survive, and she helps cut down the number herself by eating any newborn she can catch. Thus, swimming speed, protective coloration (wild swordtails are a dull green), and perhaps some sort of fleeing instinct are immediately important. As life goes on, the ability to find food, to keep from becoming food, to ward off disease, to find a mate and reproduce—all these and more "select" the swordtails better able to thrive—we can call them the better "fit." These individuals are generally the most successful at producing offspring and thus passing on the characteristics that made them fit. Favorable expressions tend to increase in frequency, unfavorable ones to decrease. That's the essence of natural selection.

The primary result of natural selection is to maintain a species' adaptation to its niche, an effect referred to as **stabilizing selection.** It occurs because those individuals who possess poorly adapted traits are less reproductively successful than those with well-adapted traits. Well-adapted traits remain the norm; poorly adapted traits are rare.

But, somewhere, sometime, into the life of every species some environmental change occurs. When that change occurs, different expressions of certain traits may be more adaptive than had been the case. Previously adaptive traits may now be poorly adapted. Once-important traits may now be neutral. If sufficient variation exists, natural selection may take a new direction. A species may undergo change through time.

artificial selection Selection for reproductive success in plants and animals that is directed by humans. Also called selective breeding.

stabilizing selection Natural selection that maintains a species' adaptation to a particular set of environmental circumstances.

This is called **directional selection**. I was attempting a form of directional selection in my swordtails, toward a red fish. If I had succeeded, I would then have needed to practice stabilizing selection to maintain the red strain.

It may seem that selection would be able to work any time it's needed—that it can adapt and readapt, over and over again, any species to any environmental change that species may encounter. That's not the case, however. Remember that there is no directing force at work in natural selection. The characteristics of a species do not vary according to what environmental changes may happen in the future. Variation is the result of chance alterations in a species' genetic code and of the trait expressions that have been selected for so far. Selection can only operate with variations that are *already present.* It can't make new traits because they are needed or may be needed in the future. I could not *make* red fish by producing the right genetic combination. All I could do was hope I had redder and redder fish from which to select my breeding pairs.

Eventually, then, in the life of all species, some environmental change occurs with which the species can't cope. None of the existing variation in adaptive traits gives any individuals enough of an edge to produce sufficient offspring. When that occurs, the species becomes extinct. This is the norm, not the exception. Estimates indicate that over 95 percent of all species that have ever lived are now extinct. Selection has its limitations. But it is the central process behind all adaptive evolution and thus is the factor that brought about the diversity of life we see today and in the fossil record.

THE OTHER PROCESSES OF EVOLUTION

One wonders what Charles Darwin would think if he could be here today and listen to an explanation of modern evolutionary theory. I think he would be pleasantly surprised to find that his idea of natural selection is still at the center of the concept. But he would also probably be amazed at all the new things that have been added. Remember, Darwin didn't know about genetics. I also like to think he would have no trouble grasping all the new ideas. Evolution is a complex topic, but if you take things step by step, it all falls into place with beautiful logic (Figure 3.11).

We've already described the nature of the relationship between a species and its environment: A species is adapted to the environmental habitat in which it lives. This relationship, however, is not static. Environments are constantly changing—as the stratigraphic record, as well as our own observations, clearly shows. Species, if they are to continue to exist, have to undergo change in their adaptations to keep pace. This is accomplished, when it *is* accomplished, by natural selection, the process of evolution that acts to maintain the adaptive balance between a species and its environmental circumstances.

directional selection
Natural selection for new adaptations in response to changing environmental conditions.

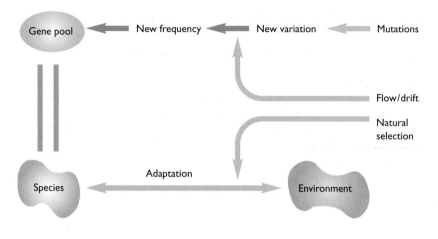

FIGURE 3.11
The processes of evolution. A species is in an adaptive relationship with its environment. This relationship is maintained by natural selection. Environments, however, are constantly changing, so the adaptive characteristics of species change through time. In addition, the gene pool of a species is always changing, altering the traits upon which selection acts. Mutation provides new genetic variation by producing new genes or otherwise altering the genetic code. Flow and drift mix the genetic variation within a species, continually supplying new combinations of genetic variables.

But the species itself is changing as well, because the genes making up the species' **gene pool** are changing. There are other processes of evolution that bring about genetic change by affecting the gene pool of a species, which in turn affects the traits of the species upon which natural selection operates. The first of these is **mutation.** A mutation is any spontaneous error in the genetic code and can take place at the level of an individual gene or may involve an entire **chromosome.**

These errors are brought about in a number of ways. Cosmic radiation, X rays, gamma rays from radioactive substances, and certain chemicals are all known **mutagens.** But most mutations take place during the two normal but very complex processes when the genes copy themselves during cell division and when the genetic code is read and translated into proteins—the family of chemicals that make up cells and carry out cellular functions. Such mutations happen all the time. In fact, some took place in some of your cells as you read this sentence.

But not to worry—too much. Nature takes care of many mutations by immediately correcting them. Others are dealt with when the cell that contains them dies. Many mutations are neutral, making no functional difference in the cell. Many others, however—because, by definition, a mutation is abnormal—are deleterious. Some produce a slightly abnormal cell which will then reproduce other slightly abnormal cells. Such cells accumulate, which may in part explain why our tissues break down and begin to malfunction as we age. Others can bring about illnesses in the organism. Many human ailments—from cancers to sickle cell anemia to schizophrenia to Down syndrome—have been linked to genetic mutations.

There is, however, another side to the story, for all these deleterious effects are the price living things pay for evolution. Without mutations there would be no new versions of genes and therefore no variation. If the first life-forms on earth over 3 billion years ago had always reproduced

gene pool All the alleles in a population.

mutation Any spontaneous change in the genetic code.

chromosome Strands of DNA in the nucleus of a cell.

mutagens Environmental factors that cause genetic mutations.

themselves absolutely without error, nothing would have changed, and the first type of living thing would still be the *only* type of living thing. Thus, mutations are the raw material of evolution, adding new genetic variation to a species' gene pool and giving natural selection new choices to select from.

After new variation has been added to the species' gene pool, it then gets distributed within the species. There are two more processes of evolution that affect this distribution of genes. Think of this analogy: If I have a gallon can of white paint and add a small amount of red paint to it, the red paint will remain in one spot. If I give the paint a couple of stirs, the red will be distributed in a long streak through the white. If I stir the paint well, I will end up with a can of evenly colored light pink paint. How, and how much, the new color is distributed within the existing color affects the color produced by the mixing of paints.

The same thing is true with new genetic variation: How new variation is distributed within the species will affect what natural selection has to work with at any point in time and in any given individual populations within the species.

One process affecting the distribution of variation is called **gene flow.** It operates among populations within a species. (Remember, genes cannot be exchanged *between* different species.) As interbreeding takes place among populations, genes are exchanged. This may result when populations move to new areas, or when small groups move from one population to another, or when mating takes place between members of neighboring groups. The result is new genetic combinations, new variations, and, thus, new raw materials for natural selection to work with.

A human example comes from the Hutterites, the group you read about in Chapter 1. On average, half of all Hutterite marriages take place between colonies, and they involve the bride moving to the colony of her husband. The woman thus brings her genes into the population and contributes them to subsequent generations. In one colony I visited, 70 percent of the female parents came from other colonies, and marriages involving these women produced nearly 60 percent of the children of the next generation. In the other colony, 75 percent of the female parents "flowed" in, and their marriages produced 47 percent of the next generation. Changes from one generation to the next in a Hutterite colony are greatly affected by this continual flowing and mixing of genes among individual populations.

The second process that distributes genetic variation is **genetic drift.** Actually, there are two processes that are usually included under this label. The first is **fission** and its result, the **founder effect.** Sometimes populations split up (fission) and found new populations. When this happens, the two or more new populations are not genetically representative of the old, original population, nor are they genetically the same as each other. In other words, fissioning creates new sets of genetic combinations.

gene flow The exchange of genes among populations through interbreeding.

genetic drift Genetic change based on random changes within a species' gene pool; includes fission and the founder effect, and gamete sampling.

fission Here, the splitting up of a population to form new populations.

founder effect Genetic differences between populations produced by the fact that genetically different individuals established (founded) the populations.

Try an experiment. Take 100 coins and arrange them so you have 50 heads and 50 tails. Mix them up and then, without looking (that is, at random), select 10 coins. They will probably *not* be 5 heads and 5 tails, 50 percent each as in the original group. (The odds of this happening are about 25 percent.) Your sample of 10 is not representative of the whole population of coins.

The same is true of genes in biological populations. Again, the Hutterites provide an example. Recall that Hutterite colonies split or "branch out" with regularity. I found in my study that branching out can produce marked genetic differences between the original whole population, the half that stays in the original location, and the half that founds a new colony.

Fission and gene flow are particularly important for our species as a whole. For most of our history we have been divided into many small populations defined by such things as kinship, religion, and politics. But these populations have always mixed genes, and they have split up to found new populations that have then mixed *their* genes. In the past few centuries, of course, gene flow has increased enormously as our species' mobility and motivations for moving around have increased. Our history of gene flow and fissioning, then, have resulted in constant rearranging of genetic combinations and constantly changing distributions of genes throughout the species.

The second form of genetic drift is **gamete sampling.** Just as genes are not sampled representatively when a population splits, they are not sampled representatively when two individuals produce offspring. An organism passes on only one of each of its pairs of genes at a time, with chance dictating which one will be involved in the fertilization that produces a new individual. Suppose each of two pea plants, for example, possesses one gene variety for tallness and one for shortness. (Both plants would, as you recall, be tall.) They would not necessarily, in their reproductive lifetimes, pass on an equal number of short and tall genes. It's a matter of chance. It's possible that they could pass on only their tallness genes, and so their offspring would have 100 percent tallness genes even though the parents had 50 percent of each.

On the level of a whole population, then, where each mating may alter the relative number of gene varieties between parents and offspring, the overall effect could be great. This process has the greatest effect in small populations because any chance change in gene variety numbers would have the greatest impact. In a large population, a change in one direction might well be balanced by a change in the opposite direction.

Thus (see again Figure 3.11), all these processes of evolution are continually in operation—providing new genetic variation, affecting the distribution of that variation throughout a species, and, through natural selection, maintaining, if possible, a species' adaptive relationship with its environment.

gamete sampling The genetic change caused when genes are passed to new generations in frequencies unlike those of the parental generation.

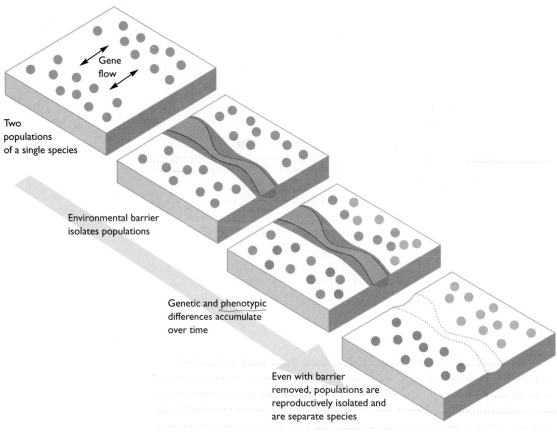

Gene flow

Two populations of a single species

Environmental barrier isolates populations

Genetic and phenotypic differences accumulate over time

Even with barrier removed, populations are reproductively isolated and are separate species

FIGURE 3.12
A simple example of speciation through environmental isolation.

THE ORIGIN OF SPECIES

So far in this chapter we've mostly talked about the modification part of descent with modification—that is, how evolution takes place within a species. How does the descent part work—that is, how do new species evolve? That was the real topic of Darwin's *The Origin of Species*—the "mystery of mysteries" as he called it.

The evolution of new species—**speciation**—is based, as is the modification of species, on environment and adaptation. To take the simplest case (Figure 3.12), say a species inhabits a wide geographic range with populations at opposite ends of the range having slightly different adaptive responses to their environments. Now, say some environmental change—a river changing its course, the destruction of some important resource, or the advance of a glacier—splits the species, isolating one portion from the other. Over time, each population will continue to adapt to its environment, but without being able to exchange genes with the other

speciation The evolution of new species.

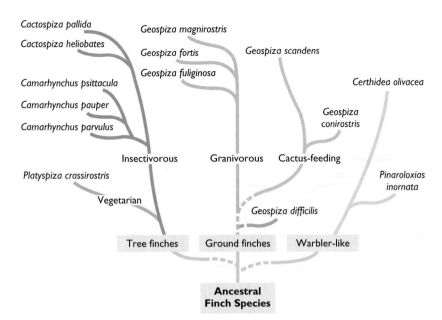

FIGURE 3.13
A family tree for the fourteen species of birds collectively known as Darwin's finches, named for the naturalist who described seeing them in the Galápagos on his famous voyage. Notice that they have all evolved from a common ancestor (a species from South America), and that the species are grouped by general type of adaptation (tree, ground, and warbler-like) and then by shared feeding habits (vegetarian, insectivorous, and so on). (We will take up the process of naming species and building such trees in the next chapter.)

population. There is, in other words, no gene flow. Each population will accumulate different genetic and physical traits. Quite possibly one or more of these traits will, by chance, affect the ability of members of the two populations to reproduce with one another. If, at some point in the future, the barrier were removed so that the two populations *could* mix, they would not be able to interbreed. They would be separate species.

Speciation may be accelerated when a group within a species shares a mutation with extensive physical effects. Such mutations are called **macromutations**. Most macromutations are, as you would expect, deleterious. But, by chance, some might be neutral or even beneficial. Those macromutations would be retained by natural selection, and they might serve to very rapidly make a small population within a species isolated from the rest of the species. Speciation can be given a "head start" by macromutation.

The evolution of new species from existing ones has given rise to all the diversity we see in our planet's living forms, now and in the fossil record. Since we assume that life started just once, we may picture the history of life on earth as a giant, complex family tree, with each branch representing a species, and clusters of branches representing groups of related species with shared characteristics (Figure 3.13). In actuality, a depiction of all species, even for a portion of life's family tree, would more closely resemble a dense bush, with countless twigs each standing for one of nature's adaptive experiments—an individual species.

macromutations Mutations with extensive and important phenotypic results.

SUMMARY

The history of evolutionary theory is the story of the application of the scientific method to the questions of the origin and nature of living organisms, as scientists learned to gradually give up their presuppositions and look to nature herself for the answers. Adhering faithfully to the spirit of the scientific method, Charles Darwin was able to synthesize his observations and thoughts with those of many others to formulate a theory that laid the groundwork for our modern understanding of biological evolution.

The evolution of organisms is based on the concepts of ecology and the adaptation of species to their habitats. Since environments are always changing, it stands to reason that changes in species' adaptations can account for evolutionary change. The basic process that brings this about is natural selection, which maintains a species' adaptive relationship with its environment and, if there is sufficient variation, alters a species' adaptations in response to changed environmental circumstances.

Change also occurs within a species gene pool. Mutations supply new genetic variation. Gene flow and genetic drift affect the distribution of genetic variation within a species. Thus, not only do environments change through time, so do species themselves—all this constantly providing natural selection with new and variable sets of relationships between species and environments.

When a portion of a species is isolated from the rest of the species, the stage is set for speciation, the evolution of a new species. If the isolated portion accumulates enough genetic and therefore physical differences through time, it becomes reproductively isolated from the original species; that is, it may no longer be able to produce offspring with members of the original group. A new species has evolved.

The diversity of life on earth—the result of countless speciation events—can be depicted as a huge, incredibly complex bush. A single stem represents the single origin of life, but it then begins branching, producing millions upon millions of twigs, each standing for a new species, a new natural experiment in adaptation.

NOTES, REFERENCES, AND READINGS

The history of evolution is nicely covered in C. Leon Harris's *Evolution: Genesis and Revelations*, which contains numerous selections from original works, and in John C. Greene's *The Death of Adam*. The impact of Darwin's work on modern knowledge in general is the theme of Philip Appleman's *Darwin: A Norton Critical Edition*. A good biography of Darwin is John Bowlby's *Charles Darwin: A New Life*.

For examples of animal and plant adaptations to various environments, try three books by zoologist and filmmaker Sir David Attenborough: *Life on Earth*, *The Living Planet*, and *The Trials of Life*. These each accompany a video series.

CONTEMPORARY ISSUES

Is Evolution a Fact, a Theory, or Just a Hypothesis?

It may at first be surprising that the answer to this commonly asked question is *all of the above*. Evolution, as a broad topic, incorporates theory, fact, *and* hypothesis. This is because the scientific method is not a nice, neat, linear series of steps from first specific observation to final all-encompassing theory. Rather, science works in a cycle (see Figure 2.1), and the inductive and deductive reasoning of science are applied constantly to the different aspects of the same general subject. Data and hypotheses are always being re-examined, and each theory itself becomes a new observation to be questioned, tested, explained, and possibly changed.

A theory is a well-supported idea that explains a set of observed phenomena. Evolution is a theory in that all our observations of life on earth—fossils, the geological formations in which they are found, and the biology of living creatures—make sense and find explanation within the concept of evolution, the idea that living things change through time and that organisms are related as in a huge branching bush with existing species giving rise to new species.

Moreover, there is so much evidence in support of evolution that this tried and tested theory may reasonably be considered a fact. Of course, new data could conceivably change that, but with an idea as well supported as evolution, it is highly unlikely. A good analogy is the accepted fact that the earth revolves around the sun and not, as people thought for so long, the other way around. But how do we *know* the earth revolves around the sun? It certainly appears, upon daily observation, to do just the opposite. We accept the heliocentric (sun-centered) theory because there is so much data in its support. It makes so much sense and explains so many other phenomena that we consider it a

fact and take it for granted, never giving it much thought on a regular basis. I would be very surprised to read in tomorrow's newspaper that some new evidence refuted the idea. Similarly, that evolution occurred and accounts for the nature of life on earth is, for all intents and purposes, a fact.

But that fact poses more questions. A big one (the one that confronted Darwin) is how evolution takes place. The fact of evolution now becomes a new observation that requires explanation through the generation of new hypotheses and the subsequent testing and re-testing of those hypotheses. Darwin proposed a mechanism he called natural selection and then, over many years, examined this hypothesis against real-world data. The mechanism of natural selection is now so well supported that we call it, too, a fact.

But an overall explanation for how evolution works—a theory (or set of theories) to explain the observed fact of evolution—is far from complete. We know that mechanisms in addition to natural selection contribute to evolution. The relative importance of all these mechanisms is still being debated. The broad picture of evolution—the "shape" of the family bush of living things—is a matter of much discussion. The specific genetic processes behind all evolutionary change are really only beginning to be glimpsed as new technologies are letting us look closer and closer at the very code of life. In other words, we are still examining hypotheses to account for *how* evolution takes place.

Evolution—like any broad scientific idea—involves a complex and interacting web of facts, hypotheses, and theories. It is the never-ending nature of scientific inquiry that can make science so frustrating, but that also makes it so exciting.

There are many good general books on evolution. I especially recommend Edward O. Wilson's *The Diversity of Life,* and, for a more technical treatment, Mark Ridley's *Evolution,* second edition.

For a very readable narrative of the whole panorama of the evolution of life, try *Life: A Natural History of the First Four Billion Years of Life on Earth* by Richard Fortey. Another, somewhat more technical treatment is *The Book of Life: An Illustrated History of the Evolution of Life on Earth* edited by Stephen Jay Gould.

Another example of natural selection, this one in a human population, can be found in Jared Diamond's article "Curse and Blessing of the Ghetto" in the March 1991 *Discover.*

PART TWO

The Identity and Nature of Our Species

4

OUR PLACE IN NATURE

Humans as Primates

Entomologists study insects. Ichthyologists study fishes. Herpetologists study reptiles. Anthropologists study humans. Although we approach our study of humans in the same general way these other scientists study their organisms, anthropologists are limited by their focus on just a single species, at least just a single living species, *Homo sapiens*. To be sure, humans are a complex enough species to warrant a whole discipline. But to do the job right, we anthropologists need some perspective. We need to see where humans fit in the overall biological scheme of things. We need to be able to compare and contrast humans with other organisms. We need to answer the question of just what the human animal is.

Because all organisms are related on that giant family bush of evolution, there are many groups to which we could compare humans. In the following pages, I will do this briefly. But to narrow it down to the level that will really indicate humans' identity, we should see what group of organisms makes up the local cluster of twigs on that bush. These are the organisms to which humans are most closely related. As you already realize, this group is the primates—the approximately 200 living species that includes monkeys, apes, humans, and some other animals you may be less familiar with.

How best to organize this comparison? There are many ways to categorize the features that identify a species, but four seem most relevant and useful to our focus on adaptation:

1. *Place in nature*—where a species fits into the kingdoms of living things and how it is related to other organisms.

2. *Anatomy and physiology*—what an organism looks like and how its body functions.

3. *Reproduction*—the process whereby a species perpetuates itself (which, as you recall, is what distinguishes and separates one species from another).

4. *Learning how to survive*—the organism's behavior; its adaptations to its habitat.

Using these categories, we may consider humans as members of the primates. We can then identify our species as the bipedal primate, the sexual primate, and the cultural primate. Let's take these ideas one at a time. As you will see, however, they are intertwined in a holistic way into a single evolutionary story.

TABLE 4.1 Taxonomy of Five Familiar Species

	Human	Chimpanzee	Bonobo	Gorilla	Wolf
Kingdom	Animalia	Animalia	Animalia	Animalia	Animalia
Phylum	Chordata	Chordata	Chordata	Chordata	Chordata
Class	Mammalia	Mammalia	Mammalia	Mammalia	Mammalia
Order	Primates	Primates	Primates	Primates	Carnivora
Family	Hominidae	Pongidae	Pongidae	Pongidae	Canidae
Genus	Homo	Pan	Pan	Gorilla	Canis
Species	sapiens	troglodytes	paniscus	gorilla	lupus

NAMING THE ANIMALS

Recognition of some relationship among living things is not new. It is probably as old as human intellect itself. But formalizing this recognition was not always seen as important, even to the emerging science of biology at the beginning of the eighteenth century. After all, the plants and animals were then thought to be the unchanging products of divine creation, and an understanding of the evolutionary implications of biological relationships was many years in the future.

One eighteenth-century biologist, however, thought that a formalized view of the relationships was important, even if he thought species were specially created and forever fixed. This was the Swedish botanist Carl von Linné (1707–1778), known to us by his Latinized name, Carolus Linnaeus. Linnaeus sought to devise a system of names that would reflect the various relationships among all the plants and animals on earth. He felt, of course, that he was proposing a way to describe what God had in mind when He created living things. (Linnaeus was never known for his modesty!) But the system he came up with is still used today, and it carried more meaning than Linnaeus ever dreamed.

What Linnaeus did was create a system of categories of increasing specificity. The largest category contains within it many smaller categories, and so on, down to the most specific, which contains one item—the species. Such a classification system is known as a **taxonomy**, and Linnaeus proposed his taxonomy for living organisms in his *Systema Naturae*, published in final form in 1758.

Our present taxonomic system, based on Linnaeus's original scheme, uses seven basic categories: kingdom, phylum (plural, *phyla*), class, order, family, genus (plural, *genera*), and species. Each organism to be classified is given a name indicating its place within each of these categories and, thus, its relationship to other organisms. Table 4.1 shows the taxonomy of five familiar species.

taxonomy A classification based on similarities and differences.

Obviously, these are all mammals and that is reflected by their all being grouped within the same class, Mammalia. It follows, then, that they all share membership in the two larger categories, phylum and kingdom. Below the level of class, the five clearly fall into two groups. Four are primates, and one, the wolf, is a carnivore. So the four primates are more closely related to one another than any is to the wolf. Now, within the primates, the chimp, bonobo (sometimes called the pygmy chimpanzee), and the gorilla are all more closely related to one another than any is to humans. The three apes are in family Pongidae, and the human is in family Hominidae. Among the apes, the most closely related are the chimp and bonobo, which differ only at the most specific level—they are different species within the same genus. So, even without knowing just what all those strange looking words mean (we'll get to that in a bit), you can easily see the relationships that the taxonomy is reflecting.

It should be noted briefly that an organism can be referred to by just its genus and species names, for this combination is shared by no other living thing. The species name alone won't do, however, since these are generally descriptive and can be used for more than one organism. For example, the chimpanzee shares its species name, *troglodytes,* with the winter wren, a small North American bird (the name conveying the erroneous assumption that these species were cave dwellers). To clearly refer to chimpanzees, then, you must say *Pan troglodytes.* Genus names begin with a capital letter; species names with a small letter. And since these are foreign names (usually either Latin or Greek), they should be italicized.

Now, as far as Linnaeus knew, he was describing a static, divinely created system of living things. Today, however, we know how the relationships among organisms have come about—through the processes of evolution. And Linnaeus's taxonomy also reflects evolutionary relationships. Why? Simply because the degree of similarity or difference between two organisms is a direct result of the amount of time they have been evolutionarily separate. It is evolution in different directions—along different branches—that makes organisms different. So a taxonomy, although it can't give us specific dates for branchings, can tell us something about the *relative* times of important evolutionary events.

Figure 4.1 is an evolutionary bush based on the information contained in the taxonomy of the five species. Clearly, the first evolutionary episode here was the split between the wolf group, order Carnivora, and the primate group, order Primates. The next split is between the apes, family Pongidae, and the humans, family Hominidae (collectively referred to as **hominids**). The gorillas, genus *Gorilla,* branch off next, and the last split to have taken place was that between the chimp and bonobo, different species within genus *Pan.*

This bush is, of course, an approximation based upon our assessment of the obvious similarities and differences among living species. With new information about actual dates of divergence, the shape of the bush could

hominids Modern human beings and our ancestors, defined as the primates who walk erect.

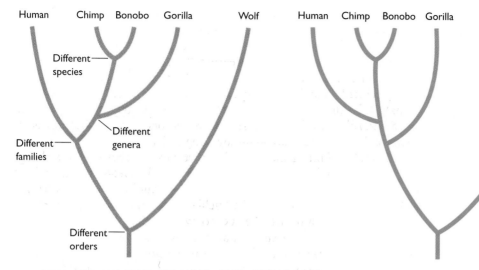

FIGURE 4.1
Evolutionary tree for the five species in Table 4.1.
We infer the evolutionary relationships from the
taxonomic classifications.

traditional

FIGURE 4.2
A cladistic tree for the five species in Table 4.1 based
on latest data for actual order of branching. Accepting
this tree would require reclassifying either humans or
chimps, bonobos, and gorillas because humans branched
off *after* gorillas. Compare carefully to Figure 4.1.

cladist.

change. Moreover, with our modern ability to delve into the very genes of living species, we have seen that sometimes we've been fooled by outward appearances, and so we have to change the order of branching on our evolutionary bush diagrams.

For example, genetic data and evidence from **paleontology** indicate that chimps and bonobos are actually more closely related to humans than those two apes are to gorillas—outward physical features notwithstanding. In addition, the branching between humans and the chimp-bonobo line took place a mere 5 million years ago while that between carnivores and primates can be traced back to *at least* 65 million years ago. So, in fact, the bush for these species should look more like Figure 4.2, which would require a reclassification of some of these species—humans would be lumped into the same family with the chimp and bonobo, or those two species would have to be considered hominids.

The difference between the two diagrams, the traditional (Figure 4.1) and the **cladistic** (Figure 4.2), represents an ongoing debate within modern taxonomy over which view best represents the reality of nature. That debate is beyond the scope of this book. Suffice it to say that scientists tend to pick and choose the taxonomic names that fit the way we each see the data for particular groups of organisms. I prefer, for example, keeping chimps, bonobos, and gorillas together in one family and humans in another because *no matter how they got to their present state*, they still

fossil — ископаемое

paleontology The study of past life forms using fossil remains and geological context.

cladistic A classification system based on order of evolutionary branching rather than on present similarities and differences.

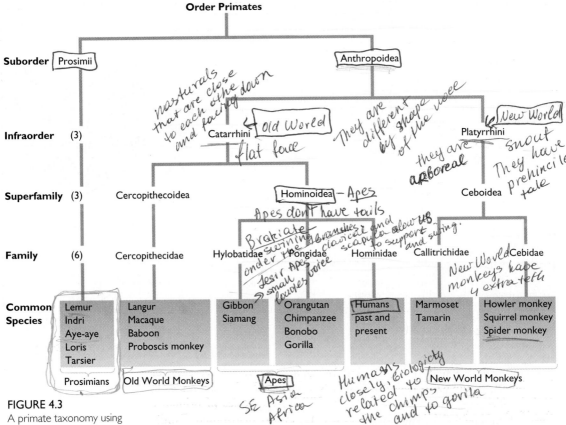

Order Primates

Suborder	Prosimii	Anthropoidea
Infraorder (3)		Catarrhini [Old World] ... Platyrrhini [New World]
Superfamily (3)	Cercopithecoidea	Hominoidea – Apes ... Ceboidea
Family (6)	Cercopithecidae	Hylobatidae Pongidae Hominidae Callitrichidae Cebidae

Handwritten annotations:
- nosturals that are close to each other and facing down
- Old World — Flat face
- They are different by shape of the nose
- New World — snout They have prehincile tale
- they are arboreal
- Apes don't have tails
- Brakiate — order the branches and swining
- lesir Apes → small lower voice
- clavical and scapula to alow US to support and swing.
- New World monkeys have 4 extra teeth
- SE Asia Africa
- Humans closely, biologicty related to the chimps and to gorila

Common Species

Lemur Indri Aye-aye Loris Tarsier	Langur Macaque Baboon Proboscis monkey	Gibbon Siamang	Orangutan Chimpanzee Bonobo Gorilla	Humans past and present	Marmoset Tamarin	Howler monkey Squirrel monkey Spider monkey
Prosimians	Old World Monkeys	Apes				New World Monkeys

FIGURE 4.3
A primate taxonomy using traditional categories. The numbers in parentheses refer to groups in that category where particular names are not given for sake of space.

fall into two easily recognizable, logical, and adaptively distinct groups —apes and us.

Now, let's look at a family bush for the primates (Figure 4.3). Notice that we've had to add categories—in this case, suborder, infraorder, and superfamily. We do this to better capture the various actual relationships among organisms. (As an extreme example, look at a taxonomy for insects—it's even more complex.)

Members of the primate order come in two basic types, the two suborders. The second suborder has a major division along geographic lines: Some of these primates inhabit the New World (Central and South America) and the rest live in the Old World (Europe, Africa, and Asia). Humans are Old World primates because that is where our ancestors first evolved and where our evolutionary line has lived for over 99 percent of our history (Figure 4.4). Such a major geographical separation is of obvious evolutionary importance, and thus taxonomic categories must reflect it. Finally, there are groups of families that arrange themselves into larger categories called superfamilies based on some shared adaptive characteristics.

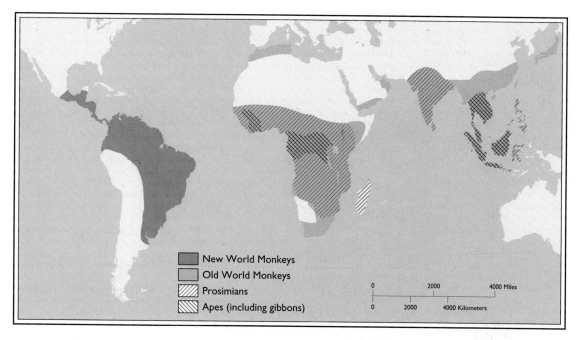

New World Monkeys
Old World Monkeys
Prosimians
Apes (including gibbons)

0   2000   4000 Miles
0   2000   4000 Kilometers

FIGURE 4.4
Distribution of the living nonhuman primates.

The bush in Figure 4.3 doesn't include genus and species names for the sake of simplicity. It lists some common names of a few examples in each family. There are, as noted, about 200 living species of primates, classified into about 60 genera. These are not evenly distributed. Family Cercopithecidae has about 15 genera, while Hominidae has only 1 living genus (there are 1 or 2 fossil ones) and only 1 living species—us, of course.

Now that you understand the mechanics of the taxonomy, let's move to the primates and the definitions of some of those taxonomic categories.

INTO THE TREES

The organization of the anthropoid *Quadurmana* [four-footed apes] justifies the naturalist in placing them at the head of brute creation, and placing them in a position in which they, of all the animal series, shall be nearest to man.

That statement appeared in the December 1847 issue of the *Boston Journal of Natural History* in an article containing the first scientific description of a gorilla. What is interesting is that even twelve years before Darwin's *Origin of Species,* scientists recognized the similarity between humans and the apes and monkeys. In fact, that recognition had been formalized by Linnaeus a hundred years before when he placed both humans and the known monkeys and apes in the same order, Primates.

So just what is a primate? Why are humans included in this group? How are humans similar to the other primates? In what ways are we different?

Primates are members of the kingdom called Animalia. We have sense organs and nervous systems, ingest our food, and are capable of intentional movement. We are not members of any of three other kingdoms of organisms whose cells have nuclei: complex single-celled organisms (amoebas and the like), fungi (mushrooms, molds, mildews), or plants (roses, ferns, broccoli, pine trees). There are also two kingdoms of single-celled organisms that lack nuclei: bacteria and the most primitive of earth's life, archaea.

Within kingdom Animalia are about thirty phyla, which include groups such as sponges, jellyfish, starfish, several types of worms, mollusks, and arthopods (insects, spiders, and crustaceans). Primates are members of phylum Chordata because we have a bony spine, the evolutionary descendant of a notochord, a long cartilaginous rod running down the back to support the body and protect the spinal chord. Chordates with a bony spine are grouped into a subphylum, Vertebrata. All the species in Table 4.1 are vertebrates.

There are seven classes of vertebrates: jawless fishes (an ancient group represented by only a few existing species), cartilaginous fishes (sharks and rays), bony fishes, amphibians, reptiles, birds, and mammals. Primates are mammals because they have hair, can maintain a constant body temperature (commonly called being "warm-blooded"), give birth to live young and nourish their young with milk from mammary glands (the characteristic that Linnaeus used to name the group), and have relatively large, complex brains.

Notice that the items on this list are not exclusive to mammals. Birds are also warm-blooded as are, believe it or not, great white sharks. This trait has also been attributed to some dinosaurs. Some sharks, some bony fishes (like my swordtails), and some snakes give birth to live young. At the same time, some mammals lack an important mammalian trait. The duckbill platypus and the spiny anteater, both from Australia, are mammals even though they lay eggs. But otherwise, these two are perfectly good mammals, while snakes, dinosaurs, and birds are not. Only mammals possess the whole list of traits (or, in the case of those Australian species, all but one).

Class Mammalia contains about nineteen existing orders. The best known are the flying bats (that make up nearly one-quarter of all mammalian species); the fully aquatic whales and dolphins; the partially aquatic seals, sea lions, and walruses; two orders of hoofed mammals; rabbits and hares; rodents; meat eaters; insect eaters; the pouched marsu-

[handwritten margin notes:]

Animalia kingdom:
★ sense organs
★ nervous system
★ ingest our food
★ capable of intentional movement

Seven classes of vertebrates:
★ jawless fishes
★ cartilaginous fishes
★ bony fishes
★ amphibians
★ reptiles
★ birds
★ mammals

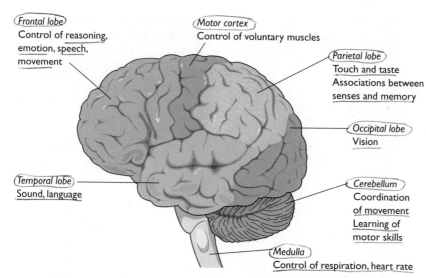

Frontal lobe
Control of reasoning, emotion, speech, movement

Motor cortex
Control of voluntary muscles

Parietal lobe
Touch and taste
Associations between senses and memory

Occipital lobe
Vision

Temporal lobe
Sound, language

Cerebellum
Coordination of movement
Learning of motor skills

Medulla
Control of respiration, heart rate

FIGURE 4.5
The human brain with major parts and their functions. The lobes and the motor cortex are all part of the neocortex.

pials; and a group of large-brained, tree dwellers with three-dimensional vision and dexterous hands. These are the primates.

The Primate Traits — характерные черты ~~характе~~

With 200 species of living primates, we are confronted with a great deal of variation in anatomical, physiological, and behavioral features. We can, however, make some generalizations and point out some of the range of variation. We'll use the following categories:

1. **The Brain.** The two words that describe the primate brain are *large* and *complex*. Large is used in a relative sense. A sperm whale, for example, with its 20-pound brain, has a brain ten times the size of the average human's. A sperm whale's body, however, is over *five hundred* times the size of ours. Humans have bigger brains than a whale relative to the size of our bodies. In fact, larger relative brain size is true of the primates in general. (Figure 4.5).

In addition, the primate brain is complex, especially in the neocortex, the part of the brain where memory, abstract thought, problem solving, and attentiveness take place. In short, primates are intelligent, which may be defined as the relative ability to acquire, store, retrieve, and process information

2. **Vision.** Vision is the predominant sense for the primates. Most primates in the anthropoid suborder see in color. The prosimians, members of the other suborder, generally do not see colors; most of them are

FIGURE 4.6
The southern lesser bush-baby or galago, a prosimian primate from Africa. Note the large eyes, large, mobile ears, and moist, naked nose—all adaptations to a nocturnal way of life.

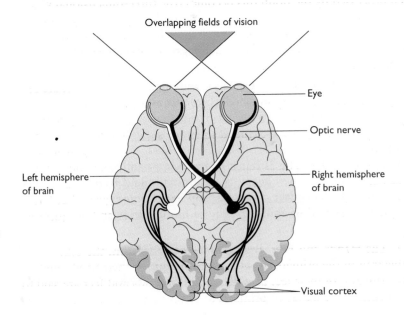

Overlapping fields of vision

Eye

Optic nerve

Left hemisphere of brain

Right hemisphere of brain

Visual cortex

FIGURE 4.7
Stereoscopic vision. The fields of vision overlap and the optic nerve from each eye travels to both hemispheres of the brain. The result is true depth perception.

FIGURE 4.8
The generalized primate dentition, here in a De Brazza's monkey from Africa. The different tooth forms allow the processing of a variety of foods. As in humans, all the Old World monkeys and apes have, in each quadrant of the mouth, two incisors, one canine, two premolars, and three molars. The New World monkeys and prosimians have three premolars in each quadrant.

nocturnal (Figure 4.6). All primates, however, have **stereoscopic** vision, that is, they have true depth perception, made possible because the eyes face forward and see the same scene from a slightly different angle. When processed by the brain this becomes true three-dimensional vision (Figure 4.7). The delicate nerves and muscles of the primate eyes are enclosed and protected within bony sockets. The area of the brain that processes vision, in the occipital lobe, is greatly expanded in primates over other mammals.

3. **The Face** The faces of primates, as viewed from the side, are relatively flat. Most lack the long, protruding snout of a horse or even a cat or dog. A related feature is that primates have a relatively reduced sense of smell. Primates have traded smell for sight. There is some variation here: The nocturnal prosimians have a better sense of smell than the **diurnal** primates. This is reflected by their moist, naked outer nose, as dogs and cats have (see Figure 4.6). Primates tend to have a smaller number of teeth than other mammals, and have a more generalized dentition, that is, geared toward a variety of food sources and not just one type of food (Figure 4.8).

4. **The Hands and Feet.** Besides stereoscopic vision, the other most notable trait of the primates is the grasping ability of their hands, and, in many primates, of their feet as well. Grasping hands and feet are said to be **prehensile**. The hands of primates also have **opposability**, that is, the

nocturnal Active at night.

stereoscopic Three-dimensional vision; depth perception.

diurnal Active during the day.

prehensile Having the ability to grasp.

opposability The ability to touch the thumb to the tips of the other fingers.

FIGURE 4.9
The slender loris from India and Sri Lanka, another nocturnal prosimian. The primate prehensile hands and feet are clearly visible. Note also the grooming claw on the toe in the upper part of the picture, a prosimian trait.

thumb can touch, or "oppose," the other fingers (Figure 4.9). There is variation in the dexterity of the hands, but these traits still apply in general to our order. Primates also have nails instead of claws on the tips of their fingers and toes, although some prosimians have retained a grooming claw on a couple of fingers or toes, which is used for cleaning or to help acquire food (see Figure 4.9).

Some species of New World monkeys have a fifth grasping organ, a prehensile tail. Monkeys hanging by their tails have become a stereotyped image of this group of primates, but this is not a general primate trait (Figure 4.10).

5. The Limbs. The arms and legs of primates are characterized by great flexibility. The arms, especially, attached at the sides of the shoulders, are capable of all manner of twisting and turning. The acrobatics of a **brachiating** gibbon (Figure 4.11) or the grace and power of a gymnast on the rings or uneven parallel bars clearly demonstrates this. For primates that clamber about in the trees using both hands and grasping feet, the legs as well are strong and flexible. To help support the stresses placed

brachiating Moving using arm-over-arm swinging.

FIGURE 4.10
A tufted or brown capuchin monkey from South America, breaking open dead twigs in search of insects. He is gaining extra support from his prehensile tail which has a hairless patch of skin on the inside surface to enhance friction.

FIGURE 4.11
White-handed gibbon from Southeast Asia suspended by one arm. Notice the long, hooklike fingers and that it is also grasping with its feet.

FIGURE 4.12
A bonobo standing bipedally. He is collecting and carrying stalks of sugar cane in his hands, now freed from locomotor activities.

quadrupedal Walking on all fours.

bipedal Walking on two legs.

on the arms and shoulders, primates have a well-developed clavicle, or collarbone, that acts as a brace between the shoulder girdle and center of the body. (Feel your own as a perfect example.)

Most primates are **quadrupedal**, that is, their locomtion uses all four limbs, either on the ground or in the trees. Many primates can also stand or even walk on two legs for brief periods, meaning they are **bipedal** (Figure 4.12).

FIGURE 4.13
A gorilla female and young. The primates have an extended period of dependency and thus parents (usually the mother) take an active and long-term role in the care and nurturing of their offspring.

6. Reproduction. Most primate species give birth to one offspring at a time, though some, such as some of the South American monkeys and some of the Madagascar lemurs, normally produce twins and triplets. As is typical of mammals, primate parents (only the mother in most species) take an active role in protecting, nurturing, and socializing their young (Figure 4.13). Because of their large, complex brains and because of the importance of learning, primates take a long time to mature. How long depends upon the size of the species. During this time, the young primates are dependent on adults. The primates, relative to size, have the longest period of **dependency** of any mammal.

7. Behavior Patterns. Primates are social animals. Most primate species live in groups. So do many organisms, but primates are different because they recognize individuals. A primate group is made up of the collective relationships among all individuals who are members. As physical evidence of this, it may be noted that primates are among the most colorful of mammals, and most of the color patterns are on their faces. One primate species even purposely enhances the colors on its face (see Figure 6.8). So the attention of one primate to another is drawn to the face, to the primate's identity as an individual.

In some primates, each individual may have a rather specific status within the group. Some have more social power and influence than

dependency Here, the period after birth during which offspring require the care of adults to survive.

FIGURE 4.14
Chimps grooming, an activity that rids them of dirt and parasites and, more important, helps maintain group unity and harmony.

others. They are said to be dominant, and a structure based on the relative power and influence of a group's individuals is called a **dominance hierarchy.**

Primates maintain their social groups through communication. Primates have large repertoires of vocalizations, facial expressions, and body gestures. Touch is also an important form of communication and often takes the form of **grooming,** an activity that serves the practical purpose of removing dirt and parasites but also acts as a source of reassurance to maintain group harmony and unity (Figure 4.14).

Given this general set of characteristics, and keeping with our theme of adaptation, what can we say about the adaptation of the primate order? The basic primate environment is **arboreal**—primates live in the trees. To be sure, several species—gorillas and baboons—spend more time on the ground, and we humans are thoroughly terrestrial. But most primates spend most of their time in the trees, and the primate traits we just described all evolved in response to an arboreal environment. (There are other responses to this environment, of course, such as that seen in squirrels, who lack color vision, prehensile hands and feet, and particularly large brains, but who do just fine with their arboreal adaptations.) Even the partially and completely terrestrial primates possess features that are variations on this arboreal theme. Thus,

A primate is a mammal adapted to an arboreal environment through well-developed vision, manual dexterity, and large complex brains that rely on learned behavior. The latter is aided by the birth of few offspring and the direct and extensive care of those offspring during a long period of dependency while they are socialized into groups based on differential relationships among individuals.

dominance hierarchy Individual differences in power, influence, and access to resources and mating.

grooming Cleaning the fur of another animal, which promotes social cohesion.

arboreal Adapted to life in the trees.

The Human Primate

Since our species is the focus of this book, what can we say about the human primate? Each species of primate has its own version of the basic primate adaptive theme. What is ours? Let's use the seven categories we used above.

1. **The Brain.** The human brain is the largest primate brain, both absolutely and relatively. Brains are measured in cubic centimeters (cc) or milliliters (ml). The brain of an average gorilla, the largest living primate, is about 500 ml (about the size of one-and-a-half cans of soda). The average human brain is 1450 ml. In fact, humans have brains three times the size one would predict for a primate of our body weight. Thus, based on our definition of intelligence, we are clearly the most intelligent of the primates.

2. **Vision.** Human eyes are typical for diurnal primates. The world we see is the same as that viewed by monkeys and apes.

3. **The Face.** The human face is among the flattest of primate faces and human teeth among the most generalized for processing a variety of foods. Our sense of smell is probably about the same as that of the anthropoid primates.

4. **Hands and Feet.** The human hand has the longest thumb and thus the most opposability and most precise grip. Our manual dexterity, also involving enlarged areas of the brain, is the greatest of any primate. Our feet, of course, have no prehensile ability whatever because we use them for walking on the ground.

5. **The Limbs.** Human arms are the most flexible among the primates, being entirely freed from locomotor activities and therefore available for a multitude of other purposes. Our legs are less flexible but are longer and stronger than our arms. All this is because humans are habitually bipedal, the only primate with this locomotor behavior. In fact, this was the first human characteristic to evolve.

6. **Reproduction.** Humans normally give birth to a single offspring (twins occur in about 1 of every 250 births). Of all the primates, we take the longest time to mature and so have the longest period of dependency. Chimps, for example, reach sexual maturity in nine years and physical maturity in twelve. For humans, the averages are thirteen and twenty-one. We are born far more helpless than most other primates. In addition, there are important differences in our sexual behaviors, which we will take up in Chapter 6.

7. **Behavior Patterns.** Like most Old World primates, humans live in societies that are based on the collective conscious responses of a group of individuals. The difference is that our groups are structured and maintained by cultural values—ideas, rules, and behavioral norms that we

FIGURE 4.15
Renaissance engraving by Albrecht Dürer of the expulsion of Adam and Eve from the Garden of Eden shows our species' general physical features, the differences between the sexes, and the importance of symbolic meaning.

have created and shared through a complex communication system, the topic of Chapter 11 (Figure 4.15).

In the next chapter we will take a look at how our rather odd terrestrial, bipedal, big-brained version of the primate adaptive theme evolved.

SUMMARY

Using the taxonomic system created by Linnaeus in the eighteenth century for classifying living organisms, we may see humans as animals, vertebrates, mammals, and, most important, as primates. Primates may be generally defined as large-brained, tree-dwelling mammals with

CONTEMPORARY ISSUES

Should Nonhuman Primates Have Rights?

This is part of a larger question that has become one of today's most contentious issues: Do animals share with us any of our basic rights and do they, consequently, deserve considerations equal to those accorded humans? Opinions on this issue vary enormously. Some animal rights advocates endorse the view that we should not consider animals as property and so should treat them as independent, autonomous individuals and not in any way exploit them. At the other extreme is a letter that appeared in my local newspaper in which the writer seriously claimed that animals lack souls and brains and that God put animals on earth, among other reasons, to entertain people at circuses and provide fur coats for women so men's spirits would be uplifted seeing them.

Ideas on the subject vary even more when put into actual practice. Many supporters of some form of animal rights adamantly refuse to eat mammals or birds but continue to eat seafood— apparently drawing some sort of ethical line between warm-blooded and cold-blooded creatures. Many who are sickened at the sight of a fur coat still wear leather shoes. Hunters easily justify killing wild creatures for sport while, at the same time, treating their hunting dogs as members of the family. Veterinary researchers, interested in promoting the health of animals, will subject other animals to experimentation and practice surgery. Clearly, this is a complicated issue involving many aspects of a thinking person's moral, emotional, and material life.

The question is perhaps most profound and intense with regard to our closest relatives, the nonhuman primates, especially the apes. These species have always struck us as being very much like our own, probably because, as we've learned in recent years, some apes share nearly 99 percent of our genes. The African apes and we share a recent common ancestor. Only 5 million years ago, we and they were the same creature.

Some have claimed that this genetic closeness itself makes obvious the need to extend basic human rights to apes. But this brings up the problem of where to draw the line. *Is* there a line? Chimps and humans are 98.5 percent similar. The orangutan shares about 96 percent of our genes. Is that enough dissimilarity to warrant doing things to orangs we would not do to a human? What about monkeys, who are even less genetically similar, or prosimians, or nonprimates?

The detailed genetic data are, in fact, not relevant to this issue, but there are *relevant* similarities as well as differences that can be considered. For example, vegetarians are often sarcastically asked how they can kill and eat plants. There is a serious answer: Because plants lack nervous systems and sense organs, they don't feel pain or emotion. This is a natural, documented, and relevant difference. The intellectual differences between us and the apes are certainly relevant in some regards. No one would seriously suggest giving bonobos the right to vote.

And there are relevant similarities too. The reason apes are used as human surrogates in medical experiments—their extreme similarity to us—is the very reason we might consider not so using them. Experimenting on an ape is the same as experimenting on a human in terms of the physical and emotional stress and pain the subject may feel. What we know factually about the anatomy, physiology, and behavior of apes supports such a view.

Many people (me included) constantly struggle with the emotional, philosophical, and practical questions involved in this issue. Even those who agree that some human rights should be extended to apes must still cope with such moral matters as balancing our needs against theirs in such areas as medical research. But—especially after considering the question from the point of view of our closest biological relatives—the one thing one cannot do with this issue is ignore it.

three-dimensional vision and grasping hands that produce few offspring at a time but take extended and direct care of those offspring, preparing them to live in groups.

Like each of the existing 200 primate species, the human primate exhibits its own unique version of the primate theme. Humans have extremely large brains with the ability to create cultures with complex symbolic communication systems, are completely terrestrial, and, unlike all other primates, are habitually bipedal. We also display some differences in our sexual behaviors that are connected to these other characteristics.

NOTES, REFERENCES, AND READINGS

A nice brief introduction to the cladistic system of taxonomy is in the June 1995 issue of *Natural History* in an article by Eugene S. Gaffney et al. called "Why Cladistics?" It expands on the dinosaur-bird example. The use of cladistics with the primates is explored in Stephen Jay Gould's "The Telltale Wishbone" in his *The Panda's Thumb*.

An excellent technical book on the primates is John Napier and P. H. Napier, *The Natural History of the Primates*. Noel Rowe's *The Pictorial Guide to the Living Primates* is a beautifully illustrated, up-to-date, and informative reference to all living primate species. A collection of articles covering primate taxonomy, evolution, behavior, and conservation is Phyllis Dolhinow and Agustín Fuentes's *The Nonhuman Primates*.

A comprehensive and readable book comparing humans with other primates is Richard Passingham's *The Human Primate*.

For more on the behavior of our closest primate relatives see Jane Goodall's *Through a Window: My Thirty Years with the Chimpanzees of Gombe*, Dian Fossey's *Gorillas in the Mist*, Biruté Galdikas's *Reflections of Eden: My Years with the Orangutans of Borneo*, and Frans de Waal's *Bonobo: The Forgotten Ape* with Frans Lanting's wonderful photos.

Some good references regarding the Contemporary Issues feature on animal rights are *Created from Animals* by James Rachels; *Animal Rights and Human Morality* by Bernard Rollin; *Animal Experimentation: The Moral Issues* edited by Robert Baird and Stuart Rosenbaum; and, for a focus on the apes, *The Great Ape Project* edited by Paola Cavalieri and Peter Singer.

5

ANATOMY AND PHYSIOLOGY

The Bipedal Primate

Pangea

More than 200 million
years ago

Laurasia

Gondwana

180 million years ago

65 million years ago

Present

FIGURE 5.1
The relative position of the continents over the past 200 million years. Continental drift occurs as the motion of the molten rock in the interior of the earth causes the individual plates that make up the earth's crust to change shape and location. This in turn causes the continents—those parts of the crust that protrude above sea level—to shift.

The characteristic that strikes us today as the most important feature distinguishing humans from our closest primate relatives is our big brains—three times the size, on average, as those of a chimp or gorilla. It is a satisfying idea that brain power is what makes us different. So satisfying, indeed, that a famous anthropological fraud was committed using the expectation that this difference surely must be the *first* difference to have arisen when our line split from that of the apes. In England in 1912, someone buried a modern human cranium along with the jaw of an orangutan. It was then "discovered" and, named *Eoanthropus* (the "dawn man"), was claimed to be the missing link between humans and apes. Scientists expected that the first human would be an ape with a big brain, and that's what was offered. It was not until forty years later that this famous fossil, known more commonly as Piltdown Man, was proved fraudulent. And, by that time, we knew that the first human was quite different—not an ape with a big brain, but an ape that stood upright. Bipedalism in our line evolved millions of years before any increase in brain size. In an evolutionary sense, *it* is our most distinguishing feature. How, when, and why did it evolve? And what evolutionary trends followed?

OUT OF THE TREES

Before discussing how our variation of the primate theme evolved, we need to give a brief account of the evolution of the primates in general. Fossils representing the precursors of the primates may go back before the extinction of the dinosaurs 65 million years ago (mya). There are some primatelike teeth and bones found in Montana and Wyoming dated from 60 to 65 mya, but the first undisputed primates appear about 55 mya. Their fossils are found in North America, Europe, Asia, and Africa, which, at the time, were in different positions than they are today (Figure 5.1).

These early primates, despite the modern primate arboreal theme, may not themselves have been arboreal. Rather, the primate hallmarks of prehensile hands and feet and stereoscopic vision may have evolved to aid in leaping to move through dense undergrowth and to promote fruit eating and the sight-oriented hunting of insects. As the primates continued to evolve, these basic traits proved a useful adaptive response to a more generalized life in the trees (and even, of course, set the stage for one group of terrestrial, bipedal primates).

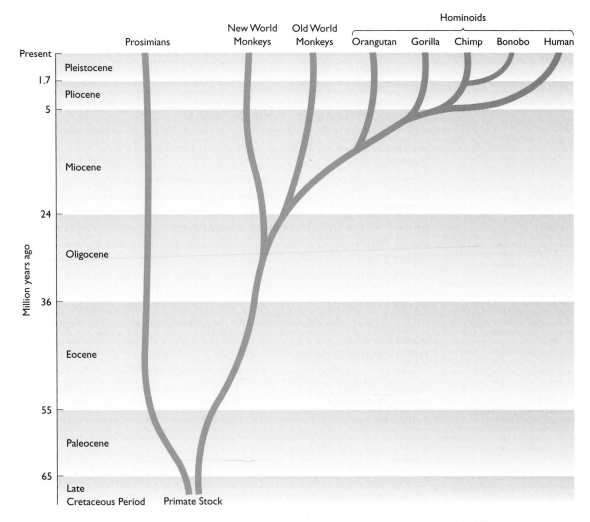

FIGURE 5.2
A generalized evolutionary tree for the primates with major geological epochs and dates. There are at present several models for the specific evolutionary relationships among living primate groups and fossil forms.

The earliest primates appear to come in two groups, one giving rise to the modern prosimians and the other to the anthropoid primates (Figure 5.2). By 40 mya early monkeys appear in the Old World. They expanded and began to outcompete the prosimians, pushing them into marginal areas. Most prosimians now live—as endangered species—on the island of Madagascar, which they probably reached by rafting or possibly over a land bridge.

Later the Eastern and Western Hemispheres (the New World and Old World) became completely separate, dividing the early primates into two geographical groups. Although this topic is still being researched, the early New World primates were apparently replaced by more advanced monkeylike primates that rafted from Africa to the Americas when the two continents were closer together than today, floating on logs and branches or "island hopping" over a chain of volcanic islands. (As incredible as this may seem, it does happen. Recently, a group of fifteen iguanas rafted 200 miles from the Caribbean island of Guadeloupe to Anguilla, where that species was not found but has since established a small reproducing population.) All the modern New World monkeys, then, trace their ancestry to the Old World.

Apes appear in the fossil record about 23 mya. At first, they were monkeylike but with a few anatomical details that foreshadow later, more typical apes. With the evolution of larger bodies and larger brains, they became a successful group of primates. Between 23 and 5 mya there were an estimated thirty or more types of apes throughout Europe, Africa, and Asia. Some of these species were the ancestors of modern groups. An ape from India and Pakistan, dated at 12 to 15 mya, is so similar to modern orangutans, the big red apes from Southeast Asia, that it must be ancestral to them.

We are most interested in the early African apes, however, because it is from one of them that the hominids evolved. Unfortunately, the fossil record of the African apes is scanty from about 10 mya on. When we pick it up again, around 4 mya, what we see is clearly hominid. The early hominids can be exemplified by one of the most famous hominid fossils, popularly known as Lucy, found in Ethiopia and dated to 3.2 mya (Figure 5.3).

Lucy (so called because her discoverers were playing the Beatles's "Lucy in the Sky with Diamonds" the night they examined her skeleton) is remarkable because, as old as her fossilized bones are, she is 40 percent complete, with all parts of the body, except the cranium, well represented. Lucy was, indeed, a female who stood about 3 feet 8 inches and weighed around 65 pounds. She and other members of her species (about 300 specimens have been found so far, representing a number of individuals of both sexes) had the brain size of a chimpanzee and in many respects resembled chimps. Their faces jutted forward, a condition called **prognathism**, and their canine teeth were pointy like an ape's. There is, in some individuals, the hint of a crest running along the top of the skull from front to back for the attachment of a major chewing muscle. Gorillas have such crests. The arms are proportionately longer than in modern humans, and the legs relatively shorter. The bones of the arms and shoulders show evidence of heavy musculature. The hands and feet are long and show curvature of the finger and toe bones.

In nearly every respect, Lucy and her kin looked like apes—except that they walked bipedally. The bones of the pelvis and legs clearly show this, as does the large hole in the base of the skull from which the spinal cord emerges and around which the top of the spine attaches. This hole is underneath the skull, rather than in back, and indicates a creature that faced forward while its spine dropped straight down. Lucy was a bipedal ape, and, therefore by definition, a member of family Hominidae, the only primate family that is habitually bipedal.

prognathism The jutting forward of the lower face and jaw area.

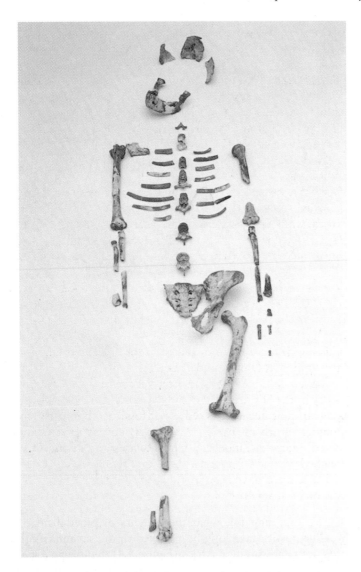

FIGURE 5.3
The-3.2 million-year-old skeleton of "Lucy" (technically *Australopithecus afarensis*), the most complete early hominid fossil found to date. Her pelvis and leg bones are those of a biped but otherwise she was quite apelike.

1974

So bipedalism was the first hominid feature to evolve—millions of years before our big brains and flat faces. A major question, then, becomes why did bipedalism first evolve? What environmental circumstances would have selected for that form of locomotion while leaving the other apelike traits pretty much intact?

Many answers to this question are being hypothesized, and those hypotheses are being scientifically tested. Each new fossil or new date or new interpretation of ancient environments changes the outlook slightly. There is, at present, no definitive answer. But I can relate the scenario that seems to me the best supported at the moment. It is at least a reasonable one and shows how the evidence is brought to bear on the question.

FIGURE 5.4
The climatic zones of Africa today, except for the large deserts of the north and south, were similar when hominid evolution began 5 mya.

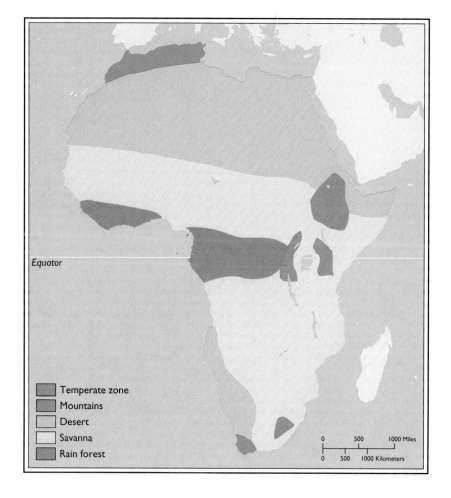

Equator

Temperate zone
Mountains
Desert
Savanna
Rain forest

0   500   1000 Miles
0   500   1000 Kilometers

We may first ask what the benefits of bipedalism could be. Early hominid fossils have long been linked to the **savannas**—the open plains of eastern and southern Africa (Figure 5.4) that began expanding because of climatic changes about 5 mya. In that environment, it is hypothesized, bipedalism could serve four functions. First, and probably most important, it frees the forelimbs to carry things. With food appropriate to an ape less concentrated on the plains, and with dangerous animals around more than willing to make a meal out of a small primate, the ability to search for food while possibly carrying one's offspring and to carry the food back to a safe location would certainly be a benefit. Second, by elevating the head, bipedalism provides better views of food and danger. Third, the vertical orientation helps cool the body by presenting a smaller target to the intense equatorial rays of the sun and by placing more of the body above the ground to catch cooling air currents. Fourth, bipedalism,

savannas The open grasslands of the tropics.

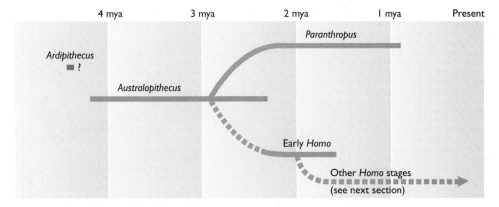

FIGURE 5.5

A generalized evolutionary tree for the early hominids. There are at least a half-dozen specific models that differ in terms of number of species for each genus and precise evolutionary relationships. Most of them, however, are versions of this basic model. The tree will be completed in Figure 5.11.

while using a great deal of energy for running, is very efficient for walking. Long periods of steady walking in search of food require less energy if done in an upright, bipedal position.

Walking bipedally, in other words, makes a lot of sense in the environment of the African savannas. Two problems have arisen with this nice connection, however. First, if you look back to Figure 4.12, you see that bonobos are at least occasionally bipedal and they live in very dense forests. Recall, too, that the bonobo is one of our two closest relatives, separated from us modern hominids by a mere 5 million years and a mere 1.6 percent of our genes.

Second, recent analyses have shown that some of the earliest hominid fossils are from creatures who resided not on the open plains but in forests. And other research has indicated that there was no abrupt change in ancient East Africa from forest to savanna, but, rather, a mixture (a mosaic, as some call it) of forest and plains. Moreover, climatic changes were taking place, beginning 5 mya, in an increasing range of variation, from cool to hot and moist to dry. This led to great fluctuations in water and vegetation.

It has been suggested, then, that the evolution of bipedalism—with the retention of long, strong arms and powerful shoulders—was an adaptation to living in an environment of *both* arboreal and terrestrial settings, giving our earliest ancestors great adaptive flexibility. As we will see, when the open plains later became the hominids' main habitat, arboreal adaptations disappeared (we're really very poor tree climbers), and bipedalism became our adaptive focus.

Once we find the first evidence of habitual bipedalism—human pelvic and leg bones—a little over 4 mya, the hominid fossil record becomes more complete and more complex. Although there is much information, there is really no agreement on how it all goes together. Especially at issue is the question of just how many species of early hominids there were (Figure 5.5). Some paleoanthropologists (called

FIGURE 5.6
Map of early fossil hominid sites.

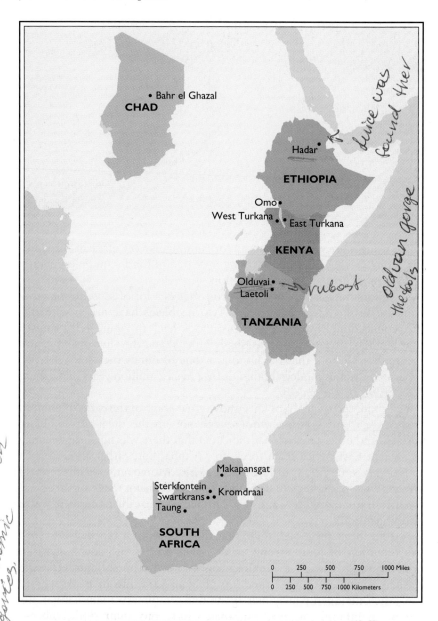

"lumpers") group fossils together into a small number of species, focusing on the degree of physical variation found within modern species. Others (called "splitters") emphasize the differences among fossil specimens and interpret those as indicating different taxonomic categories. It is beyond the scope of this book to cover all the details of the debate—at least six different, and reasonable, lines of descent have been proposed—but I can give you a general idea of what we think happened (see Figure 5.5).

FIGURE 5.7
A reconstruction, part of a display at the American Museum of Natural Hstory in New York, of a pair of australopithecines. These are based on analyses of the remains of members of Lucy's species (see Figure 5.3). Note the retention of apelike physical features combined with complete bipedalism.

The hominid fossil record begins with an enigmatic set of specimens from Ethiopia (Figure 5.6) dated at 4.4 mya. At present placed in a separate genus, *Ardipithecus* ("ground ape"), these fossils have been described as belonging to a forest-dwelling, very apelike biped. As of this writing, however, we still await publication of a full description.

We know more when we pick up the fossil record at 4.2 mya. The earliest well-established hominid fossils are placed in genus *Australopithecus* ("southern ape") and are often divided into as many as three species. The famous Lucy belongs to this group. Their fossils have been found in Ethiopia, Kenya, Tanzania, Chad, and South Africa and are dated at 4.2 to 2.3 mya. The australopithecines, as they are generally called, might well be described as bipedal apes. Their bones show full upright walking, but their faces are apelike, their brain sizes those of chimpanzees (around 450 ml), their bodies average about 105 pounds, and their arms are long and heavily muscled (Figure 5.7). They were probably well adapted to both arboreal as well as terrestrial environments, and microscopic analysis of their teeth indicates a mixed vegetable diet of fruits and leaves.

FIGURE 5.8
An example of a robust early hominid, often included in genus *Paranthropus*. Note the large crest on top of the skull for the attachment of chewing muscles, as well as the large cheekbones, and the broad, dished-out face —all evidence of a diet of tough, gritty vegetable matter. This specimen, from Kenya, shows the most extreme expression of these robust traits.

Around 3 million years ago there is evidence of a drying trend in Africa that caused further decline of the forests and expansion of the savannas. The fossil record appears to show two responses to this environmental change. One comes in the form of the so-called robust early hominids, placed by many scientists in their own genus, *Paranthropus* ("nearly human"). As many as three species have been recognized. Their fossils have been found in Ethiopia, Kenya, Tanzania, and South Africa and are dated at 2.8 to 1 mya. The word *robust* applies not to body size or shape. In these features and their brain size they resemble *Australopithecus*. What is robust are all the features involved in chewing (Figure 5.8). They have crests along the top of the skull for the attachment of important chewing muscles, broad, dished-out faces, large cheekbones, huge lower jaws, and large back teeth. These all point to a diet of large amounts of vegetable matter with an emphasis on hard, tough, gritty items like seeds, nuts, hard fruits, roots, and tubers—the kinds of foods more likely to be found in open areas. Microscopic analysis of tooth wear confirms this. Although *Paranthropus* appears to have been a good

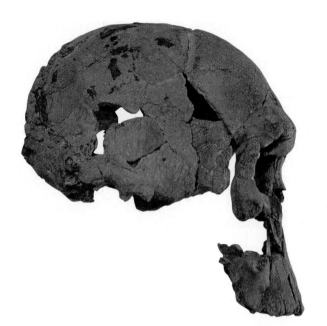

FIGURE 5.9
An example of early *Homo* from Kenya. Note, relative to the other early hominids, the flatter face, less sloping forehead, more rounded braincase, and generally smoother contours. The brain of this individual is estimated at about 775 ml, notably larger than in *Australopithecus* or *Paranthropus*.

climber, their main adaptation seems to have been to the open plains, achieved by the evolution of chewing areas adapted to the kinds of plant foods found there.

But there was a second evolutionary response among the hominids to the expansion of the savannas. This was the beginning of the genus *Homo*, to which we modern humans belong. Early members of this genus, making up one or two species, are found in Ethiopia, Kenya, Tanzania, and possibly South Africa, and are dated at 2.3 to 1.6 mya. They retain the body size and possibly the long, powerful arms of *Australopithecus* and *Paranthropus*, but their crania show important differences. Their faces are much flatter, their foreheads less sloping, and their brains much bigger. From an average brain size of about 480 ml for all the other early hominids, early *Homo* jumps to an average of 680 ml, with a maximum of 800 (Figure 5.9). (For comparison, the modern human range is 1000 to 2000 ml.) It is this evidence for the beginning of a trend to increased brain size that prompts us to classify these fossils in our genus.

What were they doing with those big brains? We can speculate that they were better able to perform intellectual tasks—learning about their environment, altering their behaviors to fit specific circumstances and address specific problems, manipulating social situations, forming more conscious and intimate relationships with other members of their group. Unfortunately, these behaviors do not leave direct remains. We do, however, have concrete evidence of the brain power of early *Homo* in the form of the tools they made.

FIGURE 5.10

A sample of Oldowan tools. The stone at upper left was used unmodified. The two at lower right are flake tools. The rest are core tools from which flakes have been taken off to create sharp edges. A major use of such tools may have been the quick dismembering of animal carcasses.

It is likely that the other early hominid species also made tools. After all, chimpanzees use simple tools, such as rocks to crack open hard-shelled nuts. They even make tools, like their famous termite fishing sticks (see Chapter 7). Such materials, however, would not leave evidence of their use as tools.

But early *Homo* made tools from stone (Figure 5.10), as far back as 2.6 mya. Stone tools last, for millions of years, and provide evidence that they *were* tools (see Chapter 10). More important, there is nothing in an unmodified stone to suggest that sharp edges or points can be found within it. It takes a leap of the imagination to understand this and to picture the process needed to produce those edges or points—hitting the stone with another, harder stone at just the right angle and force. This also takes a great deal of manual dexterity. (These tools look simple to us but are not easy to make, as I can attest.) Moreover, it seems as if the earliest stone toolmakers not only used the core stone once the flakes had been removed, but also used the flakes themselves as tools for finer work.

What sort of work were these tools used for? Many of their probable uses have left no concrete evidence—things such as sharpening branches for crude spears or sticks for digging up roots, or cutting up plant material for food or other purposes. But one use *has* left evidence, and it may provide the key to explain why *Homo* survived while the other genera of early hominids became extinct. Stone tools appear to have allowed early *Homo* to better exploit a source of food that was no doubt exploited before but would have been a difficult and dangerous enterprise—the scavenging of meat and bones from the carcasses of dead animals.

There is new evidence—from chemical analyses of australopithecine teeth—that these hominids ate animals that ate grasses. These, however, were probably mostly small creatures, maybe even grass-eating insects (grasshoppers are a baboon favorite). But scavenging the carcass of large savanna ungulates (antelopes and their kin) would have been difficult. These animals may have been killed by dangerous predators such as lions, leopards, and cheetahs and would have been scavenged by dangerous meat eaters such as hyenas, jackals, and wild dogs. Use of this source of food was probably rare among early hominids—until they had a means to quickly cut up a carcass so they could then carry the parts to a safer location for further processing and eating.

There is evidence that this was a major use of stone tools by early *Homo*. Animal bones found at early *Homo* sites in Tanzania were mostly lower leg bones of antelopes. These bones carry little meat and, along with the skull, are about the only parts left after a large carnivore has finished eating. Such bones, however, are rich in marrow, so a major nutritional activity may have been to cut these parts away from the remainder of the carcass, take them to a safe location, cut off what little meat remained, and then break the bones open for the nutritious marrow inside. Microscopic analysis of some of the animal bones found in association with early *Homo* reveal cut marks from stone tools. Sometimes, these cut marks overlie carnivore tooth marks, showing that the carnivores had killed and scavenged the animal first.

So it is a reasonable, but still speculative, scenario that early *Homo*, in the face of expanding savannas and shrinking forests, used their bigger brains and the stone tools they made possible to exploit a new and reliable source of food. Whereas plant foods on the plains may have varied more with changing climatic conditions, there were nearly always vast herds of grass eaters around, many of whom would die natural deaths or be killed by predators. Stone tools made the acquisition of this food source quicker, safer, and more efficient.

We picture, then, early *Homo* living in small cooperative groups, maybe family groups, foraging on the savannas for plant foods and always on the lookout for a large dead animal, maybe watching for a group of scavengers gathered on the ground or a flock of vultures circling overhead. Their big brains allowed them to better understand their environment and to manipulate it, making imaginative and technologically advanced tools from stone, which helped provide them with an important new source of food. The adaptive themes of bipedalism, large brains, complex social organization, and tool technology were established in this primate evolutionary line, and set the stage for the rest of hominid evolution.

AROUND THE WORLD

Evidently, the adaptations of early *Homo* proved so successful that hominid evolution seems to accelerate about 2 mya. Within about 800,000 years of the first evidence of stone tools in Africa, fossils of *Homo* are found as far away as Georgia (in the former Soviet Union), China, and Java.

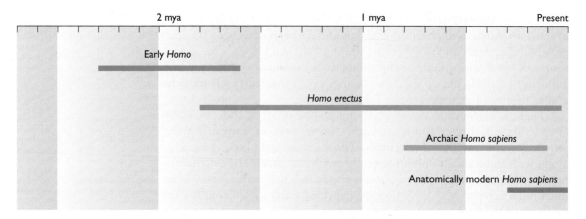

FIGURE 5.11

The stages in the evolution of genus *Homo.* There are major disagreements as to how many species are represented and how they are related to one another. The branching pattern, in other words, is a matter of intense debate.

But if there is little agreement among anthropologists about the taxonomy and relationships during the first 2.5 million years of hominid evolution, there is even less agreement regarding the latest 2 million years —the evolution of genus *Homo*. Extreme lumpers suggest a single species of *Homo* during this time. Extreme splitters see as many as six species. The debate over these models can become rather heated, because what is at issue is the very identity of our species, *Homo sapiens*. Under the extreme lumping model, all the fossil hominids I'm about to describe belong to our species. *Homo sapiens* is seen as a 2-million-year-old species that displays a great deal of variation through time but has always maintained enough gene flow to remain a single species. According to the extreme splitting model, *Homo sapiens* is only the latest of many products of speciation in the hominid fossil record, with all previous species now extinct. Thus, we are a young species—around 200,000 years old.

The details of this debate are complex and change a bit with every new fossil find and each new analysis. I have yet to make up my mind on the issue. But in many ways the outcome of the debate will not change the basic story of our genus's adaptive evolution, which is our focus here. For this section, then, I will discuss the groups of fossils of our genus as three "stages." Whether they are separate species or a single species, there *are* physical characteristics that can distinguish them for purposes of understanding their features, geographical distribution, and behaviors. Figure 5.11 shows a generalized chart of hominid evolution.

The *Homo erectus* Stage

Beginning about 1.8 mya, we find fossils representing what looks like a fairly sudden jump in our evolution. Body size is now within the modern human range and is essentially modern in shape (Figure 5.12). From the neck up, however, the bones reveal the retention of primitive features (Figure 5.13), with one notable exception. Brain size has now evolved to

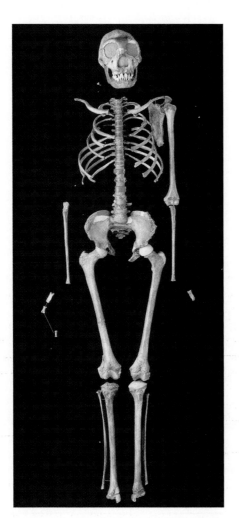

FIGURE 5.12

The "Turkana Boy" fossils from Kenya, dated at 1.6 mya. It is estimated that he was twelve years old when he died. He was about 5 feet 6 inches and, had he lived to adulthood, might have been a 6-footer and weighed around 150 pounds. Although his skull retains some primitive features, from the neck down he was essentially modern.

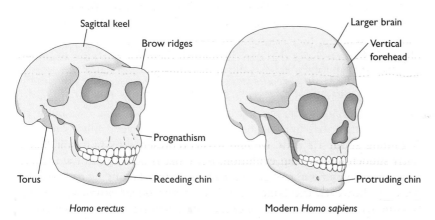

Homo erectus

Modern *Homo sapiens*

FIGURE 5.13

Cranial features of *Homo erectus* compared with those of modern *Homo sapiens*. A sagittal keel refers to a sloping of the sides of the skull toward the top. A torus is a bony ridge at the back of the skull to which heavy neck muscles are attached.

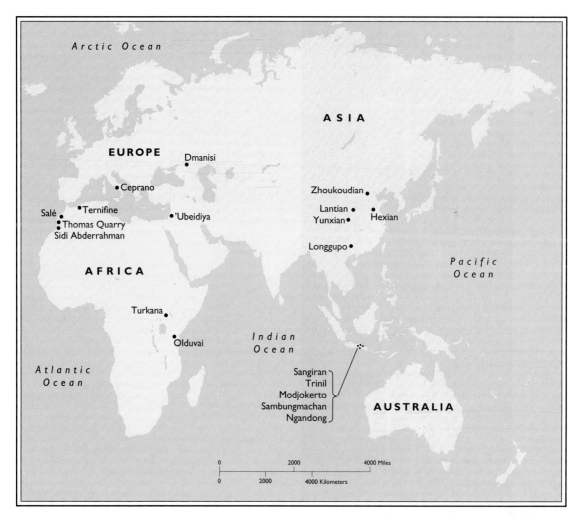

FIGURE 5.14
Map of *Homo erectus* sites.

an average of 980 ml with a maximum of 1250 ml—overlapping the modern human range of 1000 to 2000 ml.

This is the *Homo erectus* stage, so named because, when the first of these fossils were found in Java around the turn of the twentieth century, they were thought to be the first humans to walk upright. (We know today, of course, that upright locomotion was achieved millions of years before this.) These fossils have long been considered by most anthropologists to be a separate species, although some split them into two species and others lump them into *Homo sapiens*. Fossils belonging to the *Homo erectus* stage are dated from 1.8 mya to perhaps as recently as 100,000 years ago, and are found at sites all over the Old World (Figure 5.14).

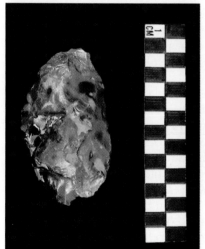

FIGURE 5.15
Bifacially flaked hand axes became one of history's most popular tools and were found in a variety of sizes showing varying degrees of quality.

The key feature of this stage is the expansion of the hominids throughout the Eastern Hemisphere. Success on the savannas of Africa, where the earliest of the *Homo erectus* fossils were found, provided the motivation and the means to expand. This success was made possible by the larger brains and by a product of those brains, more-advanced stone tools. *Homo erectus*, rather than flaking just the part of the stone that would become the business end, now flaked the entire stone, thus controlling the shape of the whole tool. The primary tool associated with this stage is the **hand axe** (Figure 5.15). It is symmetrical, edged, pointed, and **bifacial** (flaked on both sides)—the all-purpose tool of its time.

hand axe A bifacial, all-purpose stone tool, shaped somewhat like an axe head.

bifacial A stone tool that has been worked on both sides.

In addition to hand axes, however, *Homo erectus* also made tools with straight, sharp edges called cleavers. Moreover, making a hand axe or cleaver produces many flakes, and these were also used, sometimes further modified themselves to achieve a particular shape, perhaps for a particular task.

At any rate, expanding on the successful adaptations of early *Homo*, the members of the *Homo erectus* stage may well have rapidly increased their population size, a factor that puts pressure on resources as well as social harmony. Groups on the African plains may well have split up and moved away from familiar areas in search of less competition over food, water, and shelter.

In search of these resources, then, *H. erectus* wandered the Old World, arriving in the Far East in what appears to be only a few hundred thousand years. This may seem highly improbable, but some simple calculations (thanks to science writer James Shreeve) support it. Java is 10,000 to 15,000 miles from Africa, depending upon the route, and Java was connected to mainland Asia at the time because of lower sea levels. If *H. erectus* walked just 1 mile a year, it would only have taken them about 15,000 years to reach Java. Of course, they had to walk that mile every year *in the right direction,* but, remember, we're talking about *hundreds* of thousands of years. It becomes, I think, a plausible, and yet still remarkable, achievement.

But what makes it even more remarkable is the fact that as *Homo erectus* was expanding their range, they were coming into contact with the changeable environments of the Ice Ages, technically called the **Pleistocene.** This was the period, from about 1.6 mya to around 10,000 years ago, when lowering of earth's average temperature caused great sheets of ice, **glaciers,** to advance from the polar regions and out of higher elevations. There may have been as many as eighteen glacial advances during this time, interspersed by warmer periods when the glaciers retreated. We are not yet sure of the reasons for these fluctuations. Suffice it to say, however, that they caused a great degree of climatic and environmental change (Figure 5.16). Another result was the lowering of sea levels as much of the earth's water was tied up in the great ice sheets, which exposed areas of land formerly under water and allowed humans to migrate to previously inaccessible places. For much of the history of our genus, these changes had to be confronted and adapted to.

The other important first normally associated with *Homo erectus* is the first evidence of the purposeful use of fire. Good evidence of this goes back to around 500,000 years ago in China, although there is less well accepted evidence from as far back as 1.3 mya in Africa. Fire, of course, provides heat and can also be used for cooking and protection from animals. Its most important use, however, science writer John Pfeiffer suggested, is as a source of light. As such, fire extended the hours of activity into the night and provided a social focus for group interaction. This is

Pleistocene The geological time period, from 1.6 million to 10,000 years ago, characterized by a series of glacial advances and retreats.

glaciers Massive sheets of ice that expand and move.

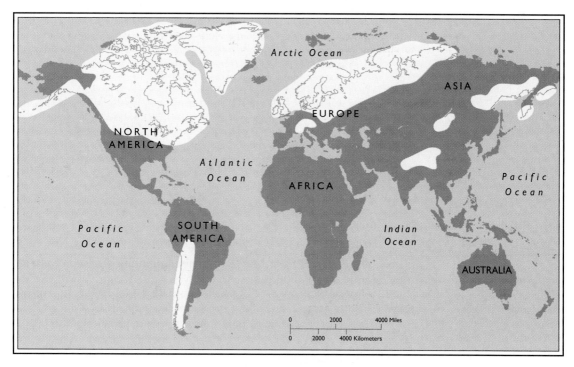

FIGURE 5.16
Maximum extent of the ice sheets during the Pleistocene.

when people experimented, created, talked (in whatever manner they were capable at the time), and socialized. Fire may also have given people a psychological advantage, a sense of mastery over a force of nature and a source of energy.

What else do we know about this stage of our evolution? Apparently, *Homo erectus* was still basically a scavenger, rather than a big-game hunter. Detailed analyses of associated animal bones strongly suggest this.

We also know, from reconstructions based on their fossilized bones, that *H. erectus* probably had a vocal tract more like that of modern humans than like that of apes or the earlier hominids. Thus they *could* have produced all the sounds we can, and so they *could* have had a complex linguistic system such as ours (which we will describe in Chapter 11). There are also features of their brains (seen in casts made from the insides of their skulls) that hint at language ability. Whether or not they *did* have a complex, symbolic language like ours cannot be determined, however. But I think that, given their ability to make fairly complex tools, to control fire, and to survive in different and changing environments, they certainly had complex things to talk *about*. It is not out of the question that they had a communication system that was itself complex.

Fossils with the traits that identify the *Homo erectus* stage—essentially modern bodies with primitive cranial features and a brain size

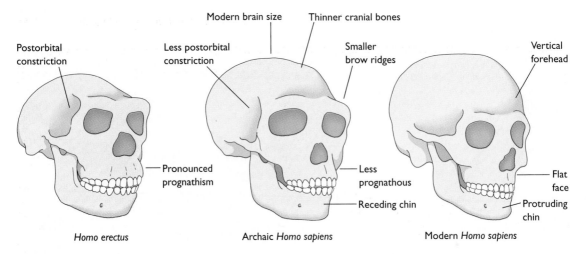

Postorbital constriction

Modern brain size

Thinner cranial bones

Less postorbital constriction

Smaller brow ridges

Vertical forehead

Pronounced prognathism

Less prognathous

Receding chin

Flat face

Protruding chin

Homo erectus

Archaic Homo sapiens

Modern Homo sapiens

FIGURE 5.17
Cranial features of *Homo erectus*, archaic *Homo sapiens*, and anatomically modern *Homo sapiens*. Postorbital constriction refers to a narrowing of the skull behind the eyes, as viewed from above.

Early Homo
Homo erectus
Homo sapiens

average just a bit below the modern human minimum—have been dated to as recently as 100,000 years ago (or even more recently) in Java. The stage—whether a separate species or not—was long-lived. But meanwhile, back in Africa and southern Europe, a new development had taken place, possibly as long ago as 780,000 years. This begins the next stage of our story.

The Archaic *Homo sapiens* Stage

Traditionally, when the brain size average of fossils reaches that of modern humans, those fossils are given our taxonomic name, *Homo sapiens*. That brain size, and some other detailed features associated with modern humans, appears to have been achieved by some fossils from Spain dated at 780,000 years ago and from Tanzania and Ethiopia at 700,000 and 600,000 years ago respectively.

These fossils, however, hardly appear completely modern. Their crania retain so-called primitive characteristics, although with some changes over those of *Homo erectus* (Figure 5.17). Hence, they are often referred to as archaic *Homo sapiens*, including them in our species but indicating that they are not fully modern in their physical features.

Fossils included in this stage have been found all over the Old World and date from nearly 800,000 years ago to perhaps 36,000 years ago (Figure 5.18). Although the oldest examples come from Spain, those are from just a single site. There are several very old sites of archaics from Africa and so the traditional model has this new big-brained hominid evolving on that continent, most likely from a population of the *Homo erectus* stage. As I noted, the exact categories and, thus, the evolutionary relationships of these forms remain an area of intense controversy.

An early achievement of this stage of our evolution, dated to around 200,000 years ago and appearing first in Africa, was a new toolmaking

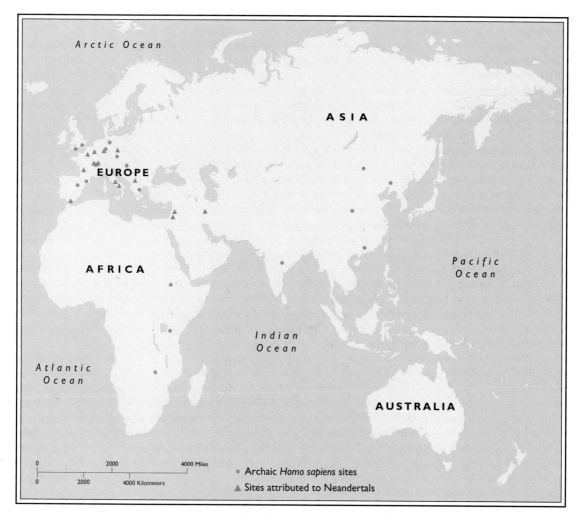

Archaic *Homo sapiens* sites

▲ Sites attributed to Neandertals

technique. It's called the Levallois or prepared-core technique (see Chapter 10) and essentially allows for the production of a number of predictably shaped flakes off of a single core—history's first example of mass production.

Of the earliest three-quarters of this stage we know relatively little, but the last quarter includes one of the most famous human fossil groups, the Neandertals. Sometimes considered a separate species, we will here include them in archaic *Homo sapiens* because of their modern-sized brains and retention of primitive cranial features. They do, however, show a distinctive expression of those cranial traits, as well as some differences in the postcranial (from the neck down) skeleton (Figure 5.19).

FIGURE 5.18

Map of archaic *Homo sapiens* sites. The sites attributed to Neandertals are indicated by a triangle. For clarity, the names of the sites have been omitted. The stress here is on the geographic range of this stage in the evolution of our genus.

FIGURE 5.19

Two Neandertal skulls from French sites showing extreme expressions of archaic *Homo sapiens* features. Note the large brow ridges, sloping forehead, prognathism, receding chin, bulging rear of skull, and overall rugged appearance. Many European Neandertals had brain sizes larger than the modern human average, although this should not be taken to indicate greater intelligence. Within the modern human range of 1000 ml to 2000 ml, there is no evidence of a relation between size and intellect. The Neandertals' large crania match their large, rugged bodies.

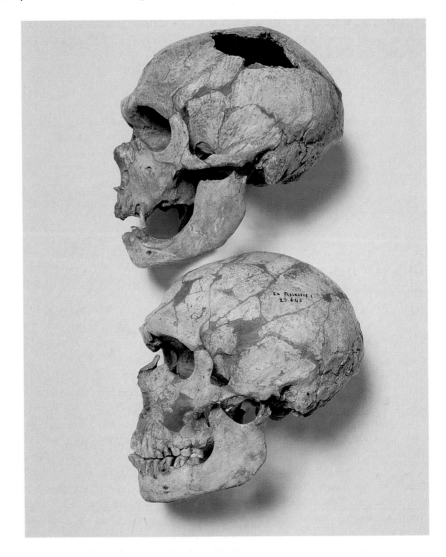

First discovered in 1856 (three years before Darwin wrote *Origin of Species*) and named after the Neander Valley in Germany, this group of archaics dates from 225,000 years ago to 36,000 years ago and their fossils have been identified from Europe and Southwest Asia (see Figure 5.18). Their brain sizes ranged from 1300 to 1740 ml, giving them a larger average than modern humans, but their foreheads were still sloping, the backs of their skulls broad, their brow ridges large, their faces jutting forward, and their chins receding.

From the neck down, there are also striking features. The bones of the Neandertals, even the finger bones, were more robust with heavier muscle markings than modern humans or, for that matter, than other archaics. They were stocky, muscular, powerful people, and these traits are even seen in Neandertal children, so they are assumed to be the result of inheritance, not simply a hard-working lifestyle.

Some of the explanation for their stockiness, as well as their short stature of 5 feet 6 inches for males, may be as an adaptation to the cold conditions of Pleistocene Europe during the glacial advances. Shorter, heavier bodies conserve heat. It has also been suggested that certain unique features in the nasal cavity as well as large sinus cavities might have helped warm and moisten the cold, dry air of Ice Age Europe.

Neandertals are also noted for elaborating on the Levallois stone tools by very precisely sharpening and shaping the flakes taken off the core. Such flakes are called Mousterian (and we will describe them further in Chapter 10). The Neandertals may also have been the first to attach or **haft** a stone point to a wooden shaft to make a spear for hunting larger, dangerous game. They probably also did a lot of scavenging.

Once considered as a dimwitted poor cousin of modern humans, Neandertals are now recognized to display some very modern human traits in their social behavior. At least thirty-six Neandertal sites show evidence of intentional burial of the dead, and in some graves were remains of offerings such as stone tools, animal bones, and possibly, flowers. Moreover, the Neandertals cared for their elderly and infirm. For example, a man from the site of Shanidar, in Iraq, lived for some time with serious injuries that probably resulted in blindness and the loss of one arm. He could only have done this with the aid of his comrades.

Again, it should be pointed out that there is, at present, a heated controversy over the number of species of *Homo* and their evolutionary relationships, and the Neandertals seem to be at the center of that debate. Some authorities adamantly feel they are a separate species that made no contribution to the modern gene pool. The Neandertal set of physical features died out when this species was replaced by more modern humans. On the opposite side are those that consider the Neandertals a variety of *Homo sapiens*, concentrated in time and geographic space. In this model, the Neandertals interbred with more modern types and the genes for typical Neandertal traits were "swamped" by those for more modern traits. Whatever turns out to be the case—and this will require more data and more sophisticated techniques for analyzing fossils— the Neandertals were certainly a long-lived group who were successful in adapting to some harsh and demanding climatic conditions, and who were clearly intelligent and sentient beings.

The Anatomically Modern *Homo sapiens* Stage

Beginning perhaps as early as 300,000 years ago, fossils with near-modern or modern features appear, earliest in Africa and later in other parts of the Old World. We call these fossils anatomically modern be-

haft To attach a handle or shaft.

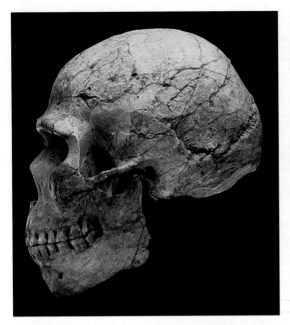 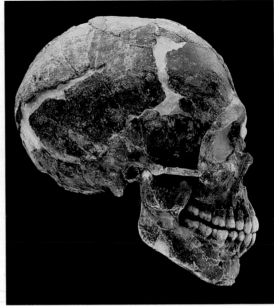

FIGURE 5.20

Two examples of early anatomically modern *Homo sapiens*, both from Israel and dated to around 100,000 years ago. Note the more vertical forehead, more rounded braincase, flatter face, and protruding chin. (See also Figure 5.17.) Although the left skull retains fairly prominent brow ridges, its other features are modern. Indeed, brow ridges are still found in some living populations such as Native Australians.

cause they lack some features characteristic of earlier hominids and possess features common to humans today. Gone is the prognathous profile; the face is essentially flat and there are no heavy brow ridges. The skull is globular rather than elongated, and the forehead more nearly vertical. The face is smaller and narrower, and there is a protruding chin (Figure 5.20). The postcranial skeleton is less robust.

Fossil data, as well as some fairly new techniques of genetic analysis, appear to indicate that modern-looking humans first arose in Africa, probably evolving from a population of archaics, and then spread around the world. Whether they replaced the archaic populations they encountered (because they were a different and more successful species) or interbred with them (because they were members of the same species, only different looking) is a matter of debate.

What we do know is that with modern-looking anatomy came further advances in technology and the expressions of modern behavior patterns. Stone tools now show a great deal of craftsmanship; indeed, some are so thin and delicate that they must not have been made for a utilitarian purpose. There is clear evidence of big-game hunting. And art makes an appearance in the form of carvings (Figure 5.21) and, about 30,000 years ago, paintings in caves that rival any art produced today (Figure 5.22).

At least 50,000 years ago, people moved onto present-day New Guinea and Australia, using land connections with mainland Asia exposed when sea levels dropped during glacial periods. Twenty thousand years ago, and possibly much earlier, humans moved into North America,

FIGURE 5.21
Carved artifacts, including a shaft straightener with carved animals (top), a harpoon carved from antler (left), and an example of the famous Venus figurines (lower right) that may have served as fertility symbols.

FIGURE 5.22
One of many beautiful paintings from the cave of Lascaux in southern France, this depicts an aurochs (an ancient ox) and several horses. There is an antlered animal, probably a deer, in the lower right. Notice that the left front leg of the red horse is separated from the body, adding a three-dimensional appearance. This photograph is really from Lascaux II, a replica near the actual cave, created because of damage to the original from bacteria and carbon dioxide given off by too many visitors. The walls of the replica cave are reproduced to a tolerance of 5 mm, and many of the pigments in the paintings are the same as used by the original artists perhaps 17,000 years ago.

CONTEMPORARY ISSUES

Have We Found the "Missing Link"?

A headline in the December 19, 1912, issue of *The New York Times* proclaimed: "Paleolithic Skull Is a Missing Link." The skull referred to was the now-infamous Piltdown Man, discovered in England, named *Eoanthropus* (the "dawn man"), and forty years later proven to be a fraud. At the time of its discovery, however, it was considered a missing link because it possessed traits that were a perfect mix between those of human and ape. Its cranium was the shape and size of a modern human's and its lower jaw decidedly apelike. (In fact, it *was* the cranium of a modern human and the jaw of a modern orangutan—both modified by the still-unidentified perpetrator to appear ancient.)

For much of the history of evolutionary thought, evolution was conceived of as a ladder or chain progressing from primitive to modern, with living forms representing links on that chain. Even when it was generally acknowledged that humans had descended from apes, this evolution was thought of as unilinear, a single line of progress from ape to man. Modern apes were seen as the remnants of primitive forms that had never evolved further. Thus, as we go back into the fossil record, we should eventually find something that is intermediate—a mix of the traits of *modern* humans and *modern* apes. In our hubris, we were sure it was our big brains that separated us from the apes and that had evolved first, so the combination fabricated to concoct the Piltdown skull fit the bill perfectly.

Indeed, even when evolution was recognized as being a branching tree rather than a ladder or chain, the idea of fossil forms that were intermediates between modern species still held. Famed anatomist Sir Arthur Keith wrote in 1927 that "To unravel man's pedigree, we have to thread our way, not along the links of a chain,

but through the meshes of a complicated network." Then, on the next page, he accepted the Piltdown find as authentic.

We recognize today that living species are not leftover primitive links on an evolutionary chain, but are, themselves, contemporary products of evolution. A missing link in the traditional sense—an intermediate between modern humans and modern apes—simply does not exist. What does exist is a *common ancestor* of humans and our closest relatives, the chimpanzees and bonobos, and we have reason to think that the common ancestor resembled a bonobo or chimp more than a modern human. This is because evolution happens to have taken place at a more rapid pace in hominids than in the apes. But the apes are still modern species.

So what we can look for is that common ancestor. It is a link not in the sense of the part of a chain, but in the sense of being at that point where our two evolutionary lines converge. At the moment, that form is still missing. But as we find older and older fossils, we are closing in on our common ancestor.

What will it look like? It should have characteristics that are shared by both humans and apes, but it will look, on the whole, like neither modern form. Genetic evidence, as well as the fact that we have the very apelike *Ardipithecus* from 4.4 million years ago, suggests that our common ancestor might be somewhere around 5 million years old (see Figure 5.5). In fact, it has been suggested that *Ardipithecus* might *be* the common ancestor, but we still await a detailed report on that form.

In the meantime, if you want to get a glimpse of the missing link in this modern sense, it's probably something between a bonobo (see Figure 4.12) and *Australopithecus* (see Figure 5.7). At the moment, that's the best we can do.

coming across a land bridge between Siberia and Alaska. They soon moved throughout the continent and into South America. Modern *Homo sapiens* had populated every landmass on the planet except Antarctica.

Cultural change then accelerated rapidly, with specific cultural systems geared to the specific ecologies of the areas inhabited. In a few thousand years—a short time when compared to the millions we have been dealing with so far—we find the first traces of farming, metallurgy, cities, and writing. History begins.

But before we can discuss the nature of the cultural systems of modern humans, we still need to look at two more identifying traits of our species and see how they evolved and how they affect the nature of our species.

SUMMARY

The primates are one of the earliest of the mammal groups to evolve after the mass extinction that took place 65 million years ago. They appear to have arisen first in what are now North America and Europe, but the success of their adaptations allowed them to radiate over the Old World and back into the New World after the hemispheres separated. About 23 million years ago, primitive apes first appear, and from one group of African apes our family, Hominidae, branched off around 5 million years ago.

The habitual bipedalism that marks our family seems to have evolved in response to the need of our earliest ancestors to survive in both forest and open plains environments after a climate change that dried the continent, expanding the savannas. These earliest ancestors were essentially small, bipedal apes.

About 3 million years ago, a further drying trend led to two new hominid adaptive responses. One gave rise to another small, bipedal apelike form, but with massive chewing bones and muscles adapted to the tough, gritty vegetation of the plains. The other response was the evolution of larger brains. This hominid, the first member of genus *Homo,* survived by inventing stone tools, which, among other things, allowed them to scavenge the meat of the vast herds of grass eaters.

From this adaptive base, the evolution of our genus accelerated. The *Homo erectus* stage, with its basically modern bodies and even larger brains, migrated all over the Old World, encountering the climatic changes of the Pleistocene, improving stone tool manufacture, and, at least in some areas, taming fire. Modern-sized brains were reached over one-half million years ago, although crania retained some primitive features. These archaic *Homo sapiens,* first seen in Africa and southern Europe, also spread all over the Old World, and exhibit such typically human behaviors as burial of the dead and care of the elderly and infirm. The Neandertals are one of the best-known forms of this stage.

The anatomically modern *Homo sapiens* stage, first appearing in Africa around 300,000 years ago, brings with it further advances in tool-making, the clear practice of big-game hunting, and the first expressions of artistic endeavors. Members of this stage entered Australia and nearby islands and reached the New World. Farming, cities, writing, and all the cultural features we associate with modern humanity follow.

NOTES, REFERENCES, AND READINGS

A detailed account of the Piltdown fraud story that opens this chapter can be found in Kenneth Feder's *Frauds, Myths, and Mysteries.*

Expanded discussions of the story of human evolution are in my *Biological Anthropology* and Kenneth Feder's and my *Human Antiquity.* For even greater detail, I recommend *Lucy: The Beginnings of Humankind* by Donald Johanson and Maitland Edey, and its sequel, *Lucy's Child: The Discovery of a Human Ancestor* by Johanson and James Shreeve. The first of these focuses on the discovery of the famous Lucy and gives a good idea of the work of paleoanthropologists. A different perspective on much of the same material is in Richard Leakey and Roger Lewin's *Origins Reconsidered: In Search of What Makes Us Human.* A beautifully illustrated treatment of the subject, based on an exhibit at the American Museum of Natural History in New York, is Ian Tattersall's *The Human Odyssey: Four Million Years of Evolution.*

A *National Geographic* series, "The Dawn of Humans," appears in the following issues: September 1995; January and March 1996; and February, May, July, and September 1997. The photographs and graphics are, as usual for that magazine, superb.

For more on the debate about the evolution of genus *Homo,* I shamelessly recommend Chapters 11 and 12 of my *Biological Anthropology,* or, for the two treatments by the proponents of the extreme views on the subject, *Race and Human Evolution* by Milford Wolpoff and Rachel Caspari and *African Exodus* by Christopher Stringer and Robin McKie.

James Shreeve's calculations about the migration of *Homo erectus* from Africa to Java are in his article "*Erectus* Rising" in the September 1994 *Discover.*

John Pfeiffer's idea on the importance of fire can be found in *The Emergence of Humankind.*

6

REPRODUCTION
The Sexual Primate

The part of the brain that governs the reproductive function, is the cerebellum or little brain. It is located in the lower back part of the head. The cerebellum also constitutes the organ of amativeness, which, according to the teachings of phrenology, gives loves for the opposite sex. Other things being equal, the strength of the cerebellum is proportionate to its size. . . . You will never find the most popular and successful men and women with a small and weak cerebellum, nor a weak, narrow, retreating chin, because they do not have enough love for the opposite sex to form an incentive to be gallant, polite, attentive, winning, etc.

The above was written in 1895 by V. P. English, M.D., in his book *The Doctor's Plain Talk to Young Men*. The book seems quite humorous to us today, for it is filled with all manner of outdated information and nineteenth-century attitudes toward sex. For example, we know now that the cerebellum (see Figure 4.5), the part of the brain concerned with the learning of motor skills and the coordination of movement, has virtually nothing to do with reproduction. We also know that phrenology —the **pseudoscience** of determining personality and mental traits from the shape of one's head—doesn't work. And we realize that, contrary to what Dr. English implies, human ideas about attractiveness, love, manners, and so on are not species characteristics controlled by the brain but cultural norms, which vary from society to society.

Although we may find his book hopelessly naive, and in some places quite funny, the book demonstrates an important idea: Despite what Dr. English is trying to say, our romantic and sexual behavior is not entirely programmed in our brains. Quite the contrary. We can *think* about sex. Instead of automatically responding to external stimuli, as do most other organisms, we decide when, where, with whom, and how to have sex. We decide, as members of a particular culture, and as individuals, what is sexually attractive and stimulating. And what is attractive and stimulating is all tied up with personality traits, emotional responses, and learned attitudes. To put it bluntly, we know who we are having sex with, and we care. And the ability to think about sex not only makes us different from other organisms, but it may also be the result of important changes that took place at the very beginning of our evolution, when habitual bipedalism was also evolving.

So, as naive as this may sound, we must ask just what sex is, how our sexual behavior is different from that of other animals, and what this has to do with our evolution and behavior.

pseudoscience Scientifically testable ideas that are taken on faith, even if tested and shown to be false.

SEX AND GENETICS

Because we are a sexually reproducing species, as are most species with which we deal directly and are familiar, we tend to think of sexual reproduction as the norm. But in one important sense it's not. Life began on earth about 3.6 billion years ago. For the next 2.6 billion years, so far as we know, the vast majority of organisms were simple single-celled organisms that reproduced **asexually** ("without sex") by dividing or budding.

The first evidence for sexual reproduction dates to about 1 billion years ago, so sex is a fairly recent invention in the history of life. Once it appears, however, the evolution of increasingly complex organisms accelerates. Why? Because asexually reproducing species essentially make carbon copies of themselves. Except for mutations, there is no source of genetic variation, and many if not most mutations are deleterious. Without variation, however, evolution can operate only at a very slow pace.

With sexual reproduction, portions of two sets of genes are being combined to make a new individual, and that new individual is genetically unique. Genes from two sources are now shuffled together during reproduction, giving evolutionary processes an ample supply of variation. This is why, as soon as sex appears, new forms adapted to new niches evolve at a more rapid rate than previously. Most of the evolutionary lineages on earth today arose during the last 30 percent of life's history. (Keep in mind for perspective, however, that most *individual organisms* on earth today are bacteria and bacteria-like creatures—simple, single-celled, and asexual.)

To appreciate fully how sexual reproduction contributes to genetic variation, we must return to Mendel and his genetics. We will use, however, modern knowledge and terminology.

The varieties of each of Mendel's particles (what we call genes) are known as **alleles.** They arise originally through the mutation of one form of a gene into another. Every individual has a pair of each gene, and the alleles don't necessarily have to be the same. In many cases, furthermore, one allele is **dominant** over the other, called the **recessive.** The dominant is expressed in the **phenotype** but the recessive is not, meaning that an organism may possess some hidden variation in its genes. (It is important to remember that dominant and recessive have nothing to do with the adaptive fitness of the allele. Many beneficial alleles are recessives; many deleterious ones are dominants. Most alleles of most genes are in a **codominant** relationship; that is, both are expressed in the phenotype.)

As an example, let's look at a trait in humans that works just like those of Mendel's famous pea plants. It's called the taster trait and refers to humans' genetic ability, or lack of ability, to taste a chemical called phenylthiocarbamide (PTC), one of a family of chemicals found in many plants. The trait is controlled by a single gene, the T gene, which has two alleles: *T,* the dominant, codes for the ability to taste PTC. The recessive, *t,*

asexually Reproducing without sex, by fissioning or budding.

alleles Variants of a gene that code for different expressions of a trait.

dominant The allele that is expressed in a pair of unlike alleles.

recessive An allele that is only expressed if present in a like pair.

phenotype The chemical or physical results of the genetic code.

codominant When both alleles of a pair are expressed in the phenotype.

FIGURE 6.1
Punnett Square illustrating the possible genotypic combinations when two heterozygotes for the taster trait reproduce. Note that, because of the hidden recessive, two tasters have a one-quarter chance of producing a nontaster offspring.

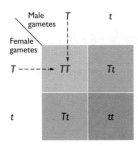

codes for lack of the ability. (PTC tastes bitter. If you find brussels sprouts bitter tasting, you are probably a taster.) Since everyone has a pair of these alleles, there are three possible genetic combinations, or **genotypes:** *TT, tt,* or *Tt*. The phenotypic expressions of the first two are obvious. The phenotype of the third is taster, because the *T* allele is dominant and overrides the expression of the recessive. (That's why it is indicated with a capital letter.) To complete the terminology, genotypes where both alleles are the same are called **homozygous.** If the genotype has two different alleles, it's called **heterozygous.**

What does this have to do with sexual reproduction? In asexually reproducing species both alleles of a parent's pair are passed on to the offspring, making the offspring as similar to the parent as a set of identical twins are similar to one another. Unless mutations take place, there is no chance for genetic variation. But if two parents combine portions of their genes in the production of offspring, there is plenty of opportunity for variety.

Of course, if both parents passed on both alleles, the resulting offspring would have twice the proper number of genes. What takes care of this problem is that in the production of the sex cells or **gametes** (for example, sperm and egg in animals), the gene pairs separate so that each gamete has only one of each pair. Then, when fertilization takes place, the new individual will again have a pair of each gene, one member of each pair from each parent. Using a diagrammatic device called a Punnett Square, we can see how this works for the taster trait when two heterozygotes produce offspring (Figure 6.1).

The gene pairs separate in gamete production but are recombined at fertilization. Thus, brand-new combinations are produced. There is even a one-in-four chance of producing a nontaster child from two taster parents. Now, multiply this simple, one-gene, dominant-recessive example by the 100,000 or so genes a human has, and you can appreciate the enormous potential for genetic variation that results from sexual reproduction. Moreover, most phenotypic traits are influenced by more than one gene, many genes have more than two potential alleles, and most alleles are codominant to some extent. All this adds to the potential variation. That's why sexual reproduction is important in the story of evolution.

SEX AND HUMAN EVOLUTION

genotypes The alleles possessed by an organism.

homozygous Having two of the same allele.

heterozygous Having two different alleles in a gene pair.

gametes The cells of reproduction, which contain only half the chromosomes of a normal cell.

To understand why humans can be called the sexual primates, we need to understand how mammals in general reproduce. In most mammals, sexual activity takes place only when it can do what it's supposed to do—make baby mammals. This is because sex is geared to the reproductive cycle of the female. The eggs of female mammals mature and can be fertilized at certain intervals. These may be regularly spaced throughout the

FIGURE 6.2
A baboon in estrus. The skin around her genital area is swollen, a clear visual sign that she is fertile and sexually receptive. In baboons and other primates, this area may also be brightly colored.

year, or they may be seasonal to ensure the birth of young during times of abundant resources.

Egg maturation, called **ovulation**, has two results sexually. It makes the female sexually receptive to males, and it initiates the sending of signals that act to stimulate the males. During this period, the female is said to be in **estrus** (popularly, in heat). This is when sex takes place, as a result of an instinctive set of stimuli and responses. At other times, when there is no egg to be fertilized, mammals have much better things to do.

This holds true for most primates. Female primates ovulate, and are in estrus, at certain intervals, specific to the particular species. During estrus, the females give off automatic signals that cause sexual stimulation among males. These signals are usually both **olfactory** (based on smell) as in most mammals, and visual, involving the swelling and coloration of the skin in the genital area. Those primates you see in zoos with what look like large, painful growths on their rear ends are females in estrus (Figure 6.2). It is during estrus that mating takes place. Mating may involve a number of males, as in chimpanzees, or just one dominant male who has exclusive mating rights to a particular female, as in some baboons.

The link between sexual activity and ovulation is an adaptive mechanism to give a species the greatest possible chance to produce offspring without wasting a lot of time and energy on sex when it will do no biological good. When primates, for example, are not involved in sexual activity during a female's estrus period, they have more than enough to do just trying to stay alive.

ovulation The period when an egg cell matures and is capable of being fertilized.

estrus In nonhuman primates, the period of female fertility or the signals indicating this condition.

olfactory Referring to the sense of smell.

You can see right away the key feature in which we humans differ: We have lost the signals of estrus. To be sure, female humans ovulate at regular intervals—about once every twenty-eight days, producing an egg that can be fertilized over a period of three to five days. But there is no outward sign of this. No signals tell a male that a female has produced an egg ready for fertilization. Some women can tell when they have ovulated, and there are hormonal changes and a rise in body temperature, but men can't tell. In other words, rather than having an estrus cycle with its automatic signals, we humans have what has been called "concealed ovulation."

Now, one would at first assume this to be a pretty inefficient way of perpetuating our species since it means we don't know when the best time is to have sex. But what our species has evolved to take care of this is, in a sense, continual estrus. We have replaced unconscious, innate sexual signals with sexual consciousness. Sexuality has become part of our conscious thought, taking place in our neocortexes (see Figure 4.5) and thus tied up with all the other reactions and attitudes and emotions we have toward other members of our species and toward ourselves.

We thus express ourselves sexually as individual personalities and as members of particular cultural systems. We respond sexually to individual personalities and according to cultural norms that set standards of behavior and attractiveness. We find a person sexually stimulating not because of a set of automatic signals but because of that person's appearance, personal traits, intelligence, socioeconomic status—all the factors by which we judge and respond to individual people as members of our society.

As further evidence for the psychological and social context of human sexuality, note that we create and recognize symbols for sex. Clothing styles are more than utilitarian; they also become expressions of our sexuality. In this society, the automobile has taken on sexual connotations. Athletic talent is often linked with sexual prowess. A single evening's television viewing or a look at a popular magazine will show that many products are advertised with sex. Although the product itself may have nothing to do with sexuality, the ads subtly imply that the use of the product will enhance one's sexual attractiveness (Figure 6.3).

Now, as with other traits we've discussed, there is no *absolute* difference between our expression of sexuality and that of all other animals. Some other species show a degree of sexual consciousness and a similarity in expression to that of humans. Not surprisingly, we find this in our closest relatives, the chimpanzees and, especially, the bonobos.

Chimps have been seen to engage in sex at times other than a female's estrus, and they use sexual postures as signs of dominance and submission. Some aspect of sex is conscious for them and is separate from purely reproductive functions. But the sexual behavior of the bonobos is strikingly humanlike—or, perhaps, to phrase it with more evolutionary accuracy, our sexual behavior is bonobo-like.

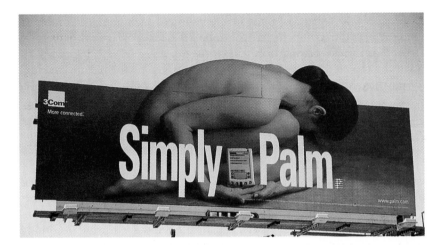

FIGURE 6.3
An advertisement for Palm Pilot, clearly using sex to attract attention to an item not related to sexual matters.

For the bonobo, sex is not only reproductive but also plays a role in interpersonal relationships and group cohesion. Especially when feeding, bonobos constantly posture sexually toward one another, rubbing rumps or "presenting" themselves as if initiating sexual activity. When sex does follow it is often face-to-face, unlike the position of other primates and like that of humans. The genitalia of female bonobos, in fact, seems oriented toward this position for optimal stimulation (Figure 6.4). Sexual activity is not limited to opposite-sex partners. Females commonly rub genitalia with other females, and males will mount each other and even engage in oral sex. Moreover, the signs of receptivity, the estrus swelling and coloration, are present for about 75 percent of the female's cycle (as opposed to 50 percent for the chimpanzee), and there is at least circumstantial evidence that female bonobos experience orgasms.

Sexual activity in bonobos has become separate from purely reproductive activity and is responded to on a conscious level. The motivation for sex seems as much psychological and social as it is reproductive. Primatologist Frans de Waal lists several functions of sexual behavior: the promotion of sharing food and other things of interest (play items, for example), the negotiation of favors, the resolution of social tensions, and reconciliation after aggressive episodes. The nearly constant awareness of sexuality among bonobos also leads to female bonding and mixed (male-female) social units.

Now, can bonobo sexual behavior shed any light on the evolution in humans of continual receptivity and conscious sexuality? There are a half-dozen hypotheses as to why we evolved our type of sexual expression, but I believe what they all amount to is the addition of males to the raising of offspring within the context of a relatively peaceful, cooperative group setting, an usual situation for primates. As de Waal puts it: "Surrounded by predators and enemies, and living a marginal existence,

FIGURE 6.4
Bonobos often engage in sex in a face-to-face position.

in which every source of subsistence counted, male support probably made a huge difference. It made it possible for protohominid females to raise more offspring than the apes from whom they had descended. It might be the chief reason why we, and not they, populated the world."

Sexual interest added to the conscious aspects of social interaction would have strengthened the psychological, personal commitments of males and females to one another in an area directly related to reproductive success. It may have been harder to successfully perpetuate the species in the harsh world of the African plains, and so natural selection —expanding on a theme perhaps already found in our ape ancestors— extended sexual receptivity by concealing ovulation and linking sexual behaviors directly with the conscious parts of the brain.

Thus, at some point in the early stages of hominid evolution, bipedalism helped make physically easier the location and acquisition of food in open areas, and the human sexual pattern—in some respects, an elaboration of that seen in bonobos—helped provide additional motivation for the cooperation needed to share resources, strengthen the group, and successfully raise future generations. As we'll discuss below, this theme eventually established the basis of human social organization—a set of relationships centered around the family unit of parents and their offspring, a unit recognized within all known human cultural systems.

VIVE LA DIFFÉRENCE

All sexually reproducing species display differences between the two sexes, if for no other reason than that the sexes need different anatomical features for their respective reproductive functions. But in some species, unless you look really closely at those anatomies, it's hard to tell male from female. A familiar bird, the robin, is an example. Other species, however, show clear distinctions between the sexes in traits not directly related to reproduction. Such species are said to display **sexual dimorphism**. Another familiar bird, the cardinal, is an example here; males and females are easily distinguishable. The same is true with humans (Figure 6.5). And the nature of our dimorphism is most interesting.

The differences between human males and females begin at the genetic level. Two of the human chromosomes are called the sex chromosomes because they include genes that code for our sexual characteristics (Figure 6.6). The X chromosome is the female chromosome. It is a large chromosome and carries genes for nonsexually related traits as well. The male chromosome, the Y chromosome, is the smallest of the chromosomes and appears to carry only genes related to male sexual characteristics. Each female has a pair of each chromosome, including a pair of X chromosomes, for a total of 23 pairs. Each male has 22 pairs of the other chromosomes, but instead of a twenty-third pair, possesses an X

sexual dimorphism Physical differences between the sexes of a species not related to reproductive features.

FIGURE 6.5
Two sexually dimorphic species, the northern cardinal and *Homo sapiens*. Males and females are clearly distinguishable using only external phenotypic features.

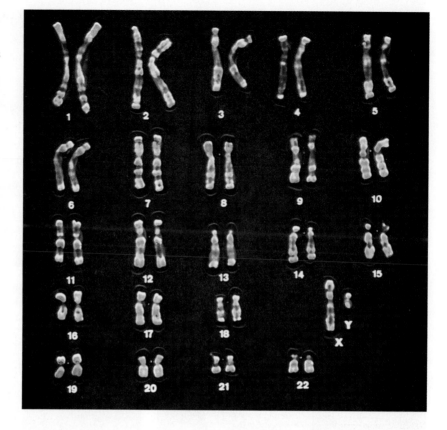

chromosome inherited from his mother and a Y chromosome inherited from his father.

What are the physical and physiological results of the genes on these chromosomes? Can we make any adaptive sense of them?

Human males are, on average, generally larger and more heavily muscled than females (see Figure 6.5). In this humans are like the apes and some of the monkeys. Ape males are much larger than females, as are baboon males. This dimorphic feature is most pronounced in the more terrestrial primates, those that spend a lot of time on the ground. Dangers from predators seem to have led to selection for larger size in males as a means of helping to protect the group. In some of the savanna baboons, males are twice the size of females. We hominids became established on the savannas of Africa, and our sexual size differences may well represent the same original function. We can, in fact, see this basic dimorphic difference in early hominids as well. For both the early hominids and modern humans, males' bones are generally larger and show heavier muscle markings. There are other skeletal differences too, especially in the pelvis.

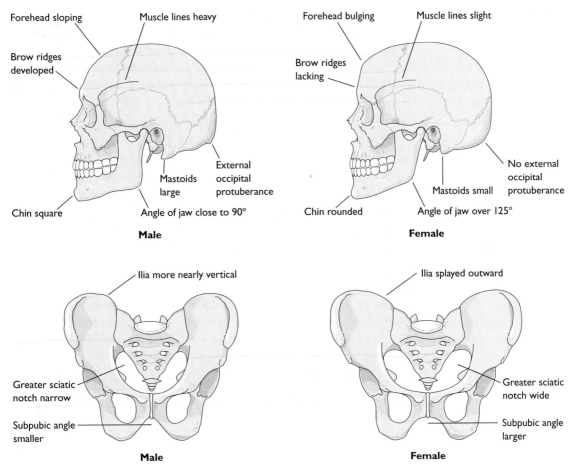

Forehead sloping — Muscle lines heavy

Brow ridges developed

External occipital protuberance

Mastoids large

Chin square — Angle of jaw close to 90°

Male

Forehead bulging — Muscle lines slight

Brow ridges lacking

No external occipital protuberance

Mastoids small

Chin rounded — Angle of jaw over 125°

Female

Ilia more nearly vertical

Greater sciatic notch narrow

Subpubic angle smaller

Male

Ilia splayed outward

Greater sciatic notch wide

Subpubic angle larger

Female

FIGURE 6.7
Sex differences in the skull and pelvis of humans.

Nearly everything about the female pelvis is wider, an obvious adaptation to carrying and giving birth to children (Figure 6.7).

Males have relatively larger hearts and lungs, a faster recovery time from muscle fatigue, higher blood pressure, and greater oxygen-carrying capacity. But males are more susceptible than females to disease and death at all stages of life. During the first year of life, one-third more males die, mostly from infectious disease. Males also are more likely to have speech disorders, vision and hearing problems, ulcers, and skin disorders.

Females have a greater proportion of body fat than do males. They mature faster at almost all stages of life, most notably exhibiting earlier puberty and an earlier growth spurt at adolescence. They are less likely than males to be thrown off normal growth by disease and other factors, and they recover from such problems more quickly than males. Although females appear to have a greater tendency than males to become obese, males suffer more from the effects of too much weight—strokes, for example. Females seem to be more sensitive to touch and pain and, perhaps, to higher sound frequencies, and they are said to be better at locating the sources of sound. Smell sensitivity is about the same in both sexes, but females seem better at identifying smells.

These dimorphic features are not completely understood, and there is a great deal of overlap in the range of variation of these traits—for example, some females are more heavily muscled than some males. But the above tendencies suggest an adaptive explanation. Many of the characteristics of the human male are aimed at sustained, stressful physical action at the expense, however, of overall health and longevity. Females' overall better health, earlier maturity, and greater sensitivity to stimulation of the senses might be geared toward their reproductive and child-rearing roles. Again, perhaps some basic themes of terrestrial primate sexual dimorphisms were retained, and some others selected for among our early ancestors as their small, cooperative bands confronted the challenges of life in the changing environments of Africa.

Are there any sexually dimorphic traits, or, for that matter, traits shared by the sexes, that might be linked to, and therefore be evidence for, our sexual behavior as described above? One obvious difference between us and all the other primates is our relative hairlessness. We are, as biologist Desmond Morris describes us, the "naked ape." The loss of hair may well have been an adaptation to allow more efficient sweating and cooling of the body as we were doing all that bipedal walking (and sometimes running) around the savannas. But we have retained hair in a few places, and there are sexual differences in the pattern of that retained hair.

Males have more facial and body hair than females. Notice the location of this hair—the front of the body (male chest hair) and on the face. Humans are not merely males or females but *individuals* who are male or female. As primates, we recognize one another as individuals. Primate color patterns focus attention on the face, on the individual (Figure 6.8). As humans, with even more conscious, more specific, more variable relationships with one another, and with our sexual consciousness, it seems reasonable that the dimorphic feature of facial hair, or lack of it, would have evolved to clearly draw attention to us as individual males or females and to announce our identities as one or the other. Similarly with chest hair—another area of color patterning in some primates (although not the apes).

Along the same lines of logic, it has also been suggested that human lips, which are everted (pulled outward) with translucent skin showing the color of the muscle underneath, may also be signals, a splash of color drawing attention to the face. It is not irrelevant, in addition, that the lips are rich in nerve endings involved in sexual arousal. Nearly all cultures practice kissing, and women in many cultures enhance the color difference of their lips.

gibbon.

mandrill

bald uakari

human

FIGURE 6.8
Some colorful primate faces, including that of one primate that purposely enhances the color. Colorful faces are evidence of the importance of individual recognition within primate societies. Clockwise from upper left: Chinese white-handed gibbon, mandrill, human, bald uakari.

public

But what about the places where both sexes have retained body hair —in the axillary (underarm) and pubic regions? Both these regions have specialized sweat glands called **apocrine glands** that develop from the hair follicles and, after puberty, discharge a secretion into the hair canal that decomposes to generate a musky odor. In many mammals these secretions are important **pheromones** used to transmit information about, among other things, courtship and mating status. It has been speculated that they serve, or may have served, similar functions in humans. After all, humans in many societies use odors as sexual attractants—although in many places artificial perfumes are applied after washing off the odor nature may have given us.

endowed

Finally, suggesting that size does matter, humans are endowed with the largest primate breasts and penises. In neither case does the size appear to be related to the function of those features. Biologist Jared Diamond proposes that the increased amount of fat and connective tissue surrounding the mammary glands in humans functions as another sexual signal. Breasts are in the front of the body, they are related to reproduction and nurturing of offspring, and they are rich in nerve endings connected to sensations of sexual pleasure.

Similarly, the relatively large size of the penis in human males is a sexual display, although Diamond suggests that, rather than being a display for females, it is a "threat or status display" for other males. He notes, as evidence, the penis gourds worn in many societies in the highlands of New Guinea (see Figure 14.1)—the ultimate in sexually expressive fashion.

To be sure, all these traits and our attitudes about them can be manipulated by culture. Different cultural systems have different standards of beauty, including which parts of the body should be covered and which can be exposed. Breasts, for example, are exposed in some cultures, covered in some, and covered but then enhanced with specialized clothing in yet others. But breasts are hardly ever meaningless characteristics.

Facial hair in males is the norm in some cultures, such as several Islamic societies or the Hutterites, where beards are a sign of marriage. In other societies, beards have certain negative associations and the majority of men shave. In the 1960s, for example, many of us college students grew beards—some pretty scruffy looking—as a sign of our nonconformity. Again, however, facial hair is seldom without some meaning.

So there is strong evidence that our basic sexual behavior is something that was selected for and established early on in our evolution. This behavior has been translated from purely biological to cultural as our species evolved that aspect of its identity (the topic of the next chapter), so that now there are all sorts of variations with regard to normal sexual behavior. But they all seem to be variations on the same basic theme.

What may we say in general, then, about this transition from biological themes to cultural interpretations with regard to sex?

apocrine glands Specialized sweat glands that secrete a substance that gives off an odor thought to be related to sexual stimulation.

pheromones A chemical substance secreted by an animal that conveys information and stimulates behavior responses.

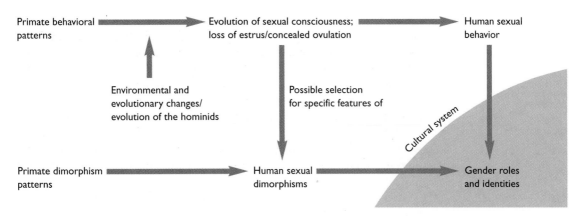

FIGURE 6.9
The evolved sexual identities and roles common to all members of the human species are translated by individual cultural systems into gender identities and roles.

SEX AND GENDER

Although there is some individual and regional variation in the degree and nature of our sexually dimorphic traits, in general we rarely have any difficulty telling the sex of any other human being. Male and female are two biological categories that are objectively real and common to all human groups. As these two categories are incorporated into various cultural systems, however, differences arise. The identity, place, and role of males and females under different cultural systems vary depending upon the nature of those systems—their economics, politics, family organizations, and abstract beliefs. Thus, *males* and *females* of the human biological species become the *men* and *women* of a particular society practicing a particular culture. We refer to the cultural interpretation of biological sex categories as **gender** (Figure 6.9).

From studies by cultural anthropologists we acquire data about the incredible range of variation in gender identity and gender roles among the world's cultures. The variable factors include such things as the roles of each gender in economic activities, differences in political and other decision-making power and influence, and expected norms of behavior.

For example, in the United States only a century ago, men were seen as the gender that properly had political, economic, and social power and that, therefore, should be educated. Women were far less likely to receive a college education, seldom held any sort of management position (if they did any work outside the home at all), and, until 1920, were not even allowed to vote. Women were sometimes thought of as the weaker sex. Obviously, things are different now, at least to a degree. As our culture has changed over the past hundred years, our gender roles and identities have changed to fit our evolving cultural system.

Among the Hutterites, as another example, women are generally believed to be inferior to men and do not formally participate in colony decisions. They cannot even vote for the head cook, who is a woman. There

inferior

gender The cultural categories and characteristics of men and women.

is also a strict division of labor; that is, there are men's jobs and women's jobs. However, as I pointed out in Chapter 1, if work needs to be done, a man may perform a woman's task, and vice versa. In one colony I visited, the official chicken man—literally a man's job—was a woman. Moreover, women can and do voice opinions and have, I was told, a good deal of unofficial influence, through their husbands, in colony business. Roles and identities differ from culture to culture.

We refer to culturally defined categories as **folk taxonomies,** or cultural classifications. A society of people orders its world in ways that reflect objective reality as its people see and understand that reality, and that also meet its particular cultural needs and fit the totality of its cultural system.

To take an example from a different area, our society has a scientific viewpoint about the causes of disease. In our culture we treat diseases as the results of natural processes, and so one way we classify them is by the nature of their cause. Diseases are genetic, bacterial, viral, parasitic, environmental (due to drugs, radiation, pollutants), nutritional, congenital (where the development of the embryo is disrupted), emotional, and so on.

The Fore, a farming people of Papua New Guinea (whom we will discuss in more detail in Chapter 13), also classify disease by cause, but the causes are very different. The Fore believe that all disease is the result of the malicious intent of either sorcerers or spirits. Life-threatening diseases are thought to be caused by sorcery—malevolent action of one person against another. This reflects the political and economic tensions, rivalries, and jealousies that have become prevalent parts of Fore lives. Less severe diseases are caused by nature spirits inhabiting important places, or by the ghosts of the recently deceased. These diseases are punishments for violating important norms with regard to nature or the dead. Minor illnesses are attributed to a person's having violated some social rule among the living. The Fore folk taxonomy for disease, though it differs a great deal from our own, makes perfect sense within the context of the Fore cultural system.

Similarly, folk taxonomies for gender differ to a great degree among the cultures of the world, even though they are all dealing basically with two sexes and two gender categories. We need to note, however, that biological sex is not always unambiguous. There are people born with underdeveloped sexual characteristics or with characteristics (including genitalia) of both sexes. In addition, there are those who are ambivalent toward their own sexual identity. As a result, some cultures recognize more than two genders.

A striking example is the *hijras* of India. The word means "not men," and, indeed, *hijras* are men who have been voluntarily surgically emasculated. They are recognized as a third sex and make up a third gender, and they have very specific identities and roles within the culture of Hindu India. Although often mocked and ridiculed because of

folk taxonomies Cultural categories for important items and ideas.

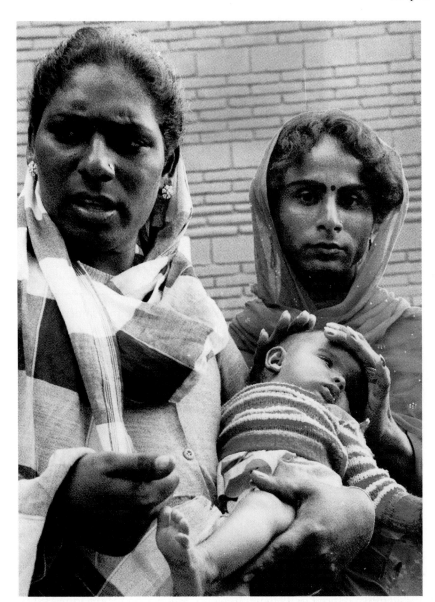

FIGURE 6.10
Hijras, emasculated men who dress and behave like women, make up a third gender category in India. These *hijras* are blessing a child, one important ritual function they perform.

their exaggerated feminine expressions and gestures, they are also in demand as performers at important rituals such as marriages and births (Figure 6.10).

A less extreme example comes from a number of Native American cultures where some men dressed as women and assumed the occupations and behaviors of women. Such men have been referred to by the term *berdache* (a French term with derogatory implications but still in common use). In some cases, they engaged in sexual relations with other men, and certain rituals could be performed only by them. In the cultures in which they were found, *berdaches* were not considered abnormal, but were thought of as another gender.

It appears, then, that some societies acknowledge that certain of their members are, or think of themselves as, ambiguous with regard to the two standard sex categories. These societies evolved third or even fourth gender classifications to accommodate them and these classifications came to have defined places, identities, and roles within those societies' cultures. Sex is biological. Gender is a folk taxonomy—a cultural interpretation of the biological reality.

Finally, has our evolved sexual behavior, and its cultural interpretations, had effects on other aspects of our cultural systems?

SEX AND CULTURAL INSTITUTIONS

Among the most interesting of cultural phenomena, and sometimes the most puzzling, are cultural universals—behavior patterns found in all societies. Because we humans have the ability to invent our behaviors and change them at will, and because most behaviors show a good deal of variation from culture to culture, it may seem strange that a few items are found everywhere. These demand explanation, and there are two that may well be explained by our identity as the sexual primate.

The first is **marriage.** Marriage is a set of cultural rules that bring together male and female to create the **nuclear family** and to define their behavior toward each other, their offspring, and their society. All cultures we know of now or have knowledge of from the past have some form of marriage. Of course, there is a great deal of variation in such things as the number of marriage partners one may have, whom one may marry, how property is owned, and so on. (We'll cover some of these in Chapter 9.) But every society, from every level of complexity and part of the world, recognizes a need to culturally define and acknowledge a male-female unit (Figure 6.11).

At first, that may seem only natural. But that's because it *is* universal. It's what we're used to. Is there, however, any reason for the universality of this institution, especially today when, for many societies, the nuclear family is no longer the center of the social and economic organization? When, in our own culture for example, nearly half of all families are single-parent families, some of which have always had only one parent, often indicating that someone other than a parent is taking a major role in the care and raising of the offspring? A union of male and female is certainly needed to conceive a child, but after that, anybody can raise and

marriage A set of cultural rules for bringing men and women together to create a family unit and for defining their behavior toward one another, their children, and society.

nuclear family The family unit made up of parents and their children.

FIGURE 6.11
A marriage in China. Although the specifics vary greatly, every culture recognizes marriage and celebrates the beginning of such male-female unions with a ceremony.

nurture the child to become a functioning member of the group. Except for rare, individual cases, however, all cultures only accept some version of a marriage unit for this function.

Can the universality of marriage be explained by saying that it is such a good idea that every culture invented it or chose it from among all the possible alternatives? It doesn't seem likely, especially when there *are* other, perfectly viable alternatives. Rather, it seems more likely that it can be explained in much the same way we accounted for sexual dimorphisms—that they had a biological origin and were then translated into a variety of cultural interpretations.

If some sort of male-female bond was crucial to the success of our early ancestors, as I have proposed, and if the social, psychological, sexual, and emotional aspects of this bond became something that was normal and vital for our survival for millions of years, the universality of marriage may be as much a part of our biological heritage as our bipedalism and our sexual dimorphism. In a manner of speaking, we're stuck with being bipedal and sexually dimorphic and so any cultural variations regarding these features must necessarily take them into account. As a simple example, clothing—no matter what sort—has to be made for bipeds, and clothing that is tailored to any extent must vary somewhat depending on which sex it is for.

Similarly, we had little choice but to base our reproductive units, and, indeed, the basic units of our societies, on the unit formed by the cooperative bond and commitment between males and females that evolved biologically in our ancestors. We have created all sorts of variations in the specific ways we have done this, but they are always variations on this theme. Even single-parent families in our society are really not something entirely new but are just a variation, a miniature nuclear family.

The second cultural universal is the incest taboo. A taboo (from a Polynesian word) is a negative rule; it tells you *not* to do something. The Jewish and Islamic prohibition against eating pork, for example (which we'll discuss in Chapter 13), is a taboo. The incest taboo is a rule that says one cannot marry persons to whom one is too closely related. Just who these people are varies enormously from culture to culture, in many cases (as we'll see in Chapter 9) not even corresponding to biological relationships. But every society does include under the incest taboo the prohibition against marriage between siblings and between parents and offspring. This part is the cultural universal.

There are, as usual, a few limited exceptions. Among certain royal family lines, most notably the ancient Incas, Egyptians, and Hawaiians, the preferred marriage partner was someone in the family, often a sibling or parent or offspring. This rule was an attempt to maintain the purity of the royal lines, which were considered divine. But everyone else in these societies lived by the common incest prohibition.

Why is this a universal? One obvious result of close inbreeding is the potential for the production of defective offspring. This occurs because each of us carries several deleterious, even lethal recessive alleles that are not expressed because they are hidden by normal dominants. (Recall here the definition of these terms with regard to genes.) Such deleterious alleles are rare, *because* they are deleterious. When expressed, they are selected against by natural selection. It's unlikely that any two random people carry the same rare deleterious alleles. But who

incest taboo A cultural rule that prohibits marriage with persons defined as being too closely related.

else in the world is most likely to share your particular hidden alleles? Your parents, siblings, and offspring, of course. So a child produced by you and one of these people would stand a very good chance of being homozygous for one of these alleles, thereby expressing the defective traits involved.

[handwritten margin note: homozygous genotypes that have same allele.]

Now, that's a good reason to institute a parent-offspring and brother-sister incest taboo, and that's the stated reason for such prohibitions in many cultures. But not every society knows about this genetic rationale. Not every society has seen such results happen often enough to make the generalization. Many societies lack the scientific knowledge to do so. (Our society has understood this concept for only about a century.) It seems unlikely, then, that the incest taboo originated as a cultural invention to prevent genetic defects.

Another possible function of the incest taboo would be to prevent sexual conflicts within the nuclear family. Having siblings, parents, and offspring competing with one another over sexual access to family members would be disruptive emotionally and economically. Having to seek sexual and marriage partners outside the basic unit would limit this conflict potential. But again, could every single society we know have invented the taboo for this reason? After all, as cultural beings we can come up with all sorts of rules of behavior. To be a bit facetious, what's the matter with one that says, "You can marry your sister, but just don't fight with your brothers about it"? But, except for those few royal lines, no one does.

To be sure, the taboo can and does serve these functions for a society. Moreover, many societies require marriage outside a specific group, using marriage to create social, economic, or military alliances with other groups. However, the present cultural functions of the incest taboo may not explain its origin. (Recall that the arboreal focus of the primate's prehensile hands and feet and stereoscopic vision may have originated as adaptations to something different—catching bugs in dense undergrowth.) As anthropologist Jane Lancaster puts it, people's *motivations* for a behavior may be different from the *original adaptive significance* of that behavior.

It seems that many nonhumans have a biological "incest taboo" that must necessarily be somehow built into their genes. Many of the nonhuman primates, as well as some other social creatures such as wolves, lions, some birds, and even rats, seem to have a mechanism that prevents mating between siblings or between mother and son. (The identity of the father is often unknown in many species, so father-daughter matings stand a chance of taking place.) The adaptive significance of such inborn behaviors is probably the two factors described above: preventing both the expression of deleterious genetic combinations and the disruption of the main economic and social unit. The behaviors were naturally selected for. The same may have been true for

FIGURE 6.12
Children in an Israeli kibbutz. Marriages between people who have grown up together in the same age group on the same kibbutz are extremely rare, although no cultural regulations prohibit them.

our ancestors. As with marriage, then, the explanation for the universality of the incest taboo may lie in a biological norm becoming translated into a set of cultural rules.

So is there any evidence that the incest taboo may, underneath its cultural expression, have a biological basis? Some compelling evidence comes from studies conducted among Israeli kibbutzim—communal agricultural settlements (Figure 6.12). In these communities, children of similar age are raised together in day-care centers while their parents are working. Until about 12 years of age, both sexes play, eat, sleep, bathe, and use the bathroom together. They grow up, in other words, as familiar with one another as real siblings, even though they come from different families. Israeli anthropologist Joseph Shepher found that there have been virtually no marriages between members of one of these age groups. The actual figure is only 6 marriages within age groups out of nearly 3000 kibbutz marriages. This is despite the fact that such marriages are not at all prohibited and in some cases are even encouraged. It seems as if the social situation in the kibbutzim has, in the words of an old TV ad, "fooled Mother Nature." The close proximity and familiarity of age-group kids is apparently siblinglike enough to activate some biological mechanism that turns off sexual attraction between real siblings and between parents and offspring.

We can and do make up cultural incest rules that cover many different groups of people, and this variation, as we'll discuss in Chapter 9, has cultural explanations. But the fact that there are incest rules at all, and that the brother-sister and parent-offspring taboo is universal seems to be explained by delving into our biological past. And, as in the case of the kibbutzim, sometimes even culture can't overcome the remnants of the original behavior.

From our remote beginnings, then, through some of our more obvious anatomical and physiological features, to some cultural institutions so basic we take them for granted, we are indeed the sexual primate.

SUMMARY

Sexual reproduction in general is important in evolution as a supplier of genetic variation, giving natural selection more on which to act. This principle can be seen by examining the basic laws of genetics discovered by Mendel.

Sexual behavior in humans differs from that of most other mammals, including most other primates, in that we have concealed ovulation and sexual consciousness. Sexual attraction, norms, and attitudes are tied up with cultural concepts of personality and standards of beauty as well as individual psychologies.

This difference may have evolved early in hominid history as a mechanism to increase and strengthen the direct involvement of males in the care and raising of offspring, in other words, to add males to the standard primate family unit of females and young. Sexual interest would add to the motivations for forming a personal, emotional, and economic bond between parents. Connected to this was the evolution of bipedalism, which helped facilitate mobility and the acquisition and sharing of resources that were part of this bond. We may glimpse the antecedents of our sexual behavior by looking at our close relatives, the bonobos.

Humans are a sexually dimorphic species and many of our dimorphic features may be understood in the context of the different roles that would have been played by males and females among the early hominids. Other features make sense as clear, visible signs of one's identity as an individual male or female. Still other traits, shared by both sexes, can be seen as evidence for the importance of personal sexual attraction having replaced the automatic, innate signals of most primates.

Sex refers to the biological characteristics of and differences between males and females. These differences are interpreted by cultural systems into the identities and roles of men and women. We refer to these categories as gender. Gender categories differ widely from culture to culture and from time to time.

The universality of two cultural phenomena—marriage and the parent-offspring and brother-sister incest taboo—may be explained as cultural manifestations of biologically based themes related to the

CONTEMPORARY ISSUE

What Causes Differences in Sexual Orientation?

In the fall of 1998, a young Wyoming college student was beaten and left hanging on a fence in the cold to die. At least part of the reason for the assault was because the young man was gay. Clearly, a difference in sexual orientation still troubles many people, even to the point of violence, and even that majority who don't feel violent toward homosexuals still tend to infer additional attributes about a person based on that sexual orientation. We have our stereotypes of gay men and lesbian women.

Science also has shown an interest in this topic. Over the years, a fair number of explanations for homosexuality have been proposed, including such things as hormonal imbalances, early childhood imprinting, and early sexual abuse. More recently, with new technologies that allow us to peer into our genetic code and generate electronic images of brain activity, genetic differences and differences in brain anatomy have also been offered as connections, if not causes.

While any or all of these factors could be related to aspects of one's sexuality and sexual behavior, it makes sense that no single factor can account for all cases of a preference for members of one's own sex. Sexual preference is a far more complex phenomenon than that.

Consider exactly what is being categorized by the terms homosexual and heterosexual. Despite all the connotations of those terms, all they really refer to is the sex of one's partner in a given instance. Either one is having sex with a member of the opposite sex or with a member of one's own sex. Because the vast majority of people are unambiguously biological males or females, there are really no other choices but those two. So the physical, tangible situation generates the dichotomy we make. In anthropological terms, we have created a fairly obvious folk taxonomy with regard to the sex of one's sexual partners.

But does it follow that the sex of a person's sex partner predicts other things about that person? Does it follow that other factors of one's personality and life also fall into two nice, neat, discrete categories? Consider this: If you know that someone is categorized as heterosexual, can you make *any* other inferences about that person other than the sex of his or her sex partners? Hardly. Persons who classify themselves as heterosexual vary widely in every other factor of their

cooperative bond that was the adaptive focus of the evolution of our sexual behavior.

NOTES, REFERENCES, AND READINGS

There are many good introductory genetics texts in which you can find more details about this topic. Most books on evolution and biological anthropology also include a basic chapter. If you'd like to read Mendel's own words (English translation), a long excerpt can be found in C. Leon Harris's *Evolution: Genesis and Revelations*.

lives, *including* their attitudes and behaviors regarding sex. Two heterosexuals will probably find different features attractive in members of the opposite sex, will prefer different sexual activities, and will have different philosophies and moral outlooks regarding sex. Why should the situation be any different for those categorized as homosexual?

Indeed, one finds the same degree of variation in all these factors among homosexuals as among heterosexuals. And this is because attitudes toward sex partners are expressed as a continuum, not as two all-encompassing taxonomic categories. At one end of the continuum are those for whom the only norm regarding sexual activity involves members of the opposite sex. At the other end are those whose focus is exclusively on members of the same sex. In between is everyone else, with enormously varying attitudes about the emotional, physical, and moral considerations involved in the sex of one's partner as well as about all the other complex components of human sexuality. (Think about the complex and varying factors that must motivate the men who become *hijras*.) That our categories are artificial and limited is evidenced by the fact that, for people in the middle range of that continuum with regard to the preferred sex of their partners, we have created yet another category—bisexual. All the wide range of variation in human sexual attitudes and ideas is forced into three categories because the physical expression of those attitudes and ideas must necessarily be limited by our two biological sexes.

Why does this range of variation in attitudes and ideas exist? To ask a related question in evolutionary terms, why do some people prefer sexual activity that cannot conceivably lead to conception and thus to the perpetuation of the species? The answer is simply that, as we detailed in the chapter, during the evolution of our species the components of sex have been extended from the deeper, purely instinctive parts of our brains into the conscious parts. All the components of our sexuality and sexual behavior are now tied up with all the other aspects of our personalities. Since, obviously, our personalities differ in as many ways as there are people on earth, it stands to reason that our sexual personalities will differ to a comparable degree. Thus, it also stands to reason that there is no *one* factor that gives rise to our sexual attitudes, including our choice (or choices) of sexual partners. There is, therefore, no single cause for homosexuality. Indeed, given our nature as the sexual primate, a wide range of variation in what gives people sexual pleasure is to be expected.

More information on the bonobos is in Frans de Waal's delightful *Bonobo: The Forgotten Ape*, which includes Frans Lanting's wonderful photographs. The quote I used is from pages 105–106.

A more detailed discussion of the various hypotheses proposed to account for the evolution of our sexual behavior can be found in Jared Diamond's *The Third Chimpanzee*. He also discusses the adaptive significance of the relatively large sizes of human breasts and penises.

More details on our various sexual dimorphisms are in *Sex Differences* edited by Michael S. Teitelbaum and in several chapters of *Female of the Species* by M. K. Martin and B. Voorhies. The latter also covers variation in sex and gender categories and the various roles of men and women in different societies. This book is out of print but is well worth looking up in the library.

Jane Lancaster's distinction between motivation and adaptive origin can be found in her *Primate Behavior and the Emergence of Human Culture*. Her book focuses on the rationale for studying the beginnings of our behaviors by observing those of our closest relatives.

Joseph Shepher's study of the kibbutzim is included in his *Incest: A Biosocial View*.

7

LEARNING HOW TO SURVIVE
The Cultural Primate

[handwritten margin notes: "culture is behaving in such a way that people don't think you're creaty. Culture – gives an ability to live without chaos. set of rules and regulations, on how they will interact" ; "enculturation – to grow up in section culture."]

Among the most amazing builders in the world are weaver ants from the Old World tropics. Colonies of these ants construct nests in trees in the form of tents made from the tree's leaves. To do this, teams of ants form living staples suspended between the leaves and pulling the leaves together. Then other ants gently carry larvae along the seam, stimulating them to excrete silk which "sews" the leaves together (Figure 7.1).

A few years ago I decided to build a wall and hang a door in order to create a new room for my study. Having virtually no knowledge of such matters, my first step was to purchase a book about home improvements and digest all the necessary information about partition building, lumber, drywall, and tools. Then I drew up my plans and materials list. Still unsure of myself, I consulted with a colleague who is experienced in carpentry and who came over to look at my proposed construction site. Based on his knowledge, he suggested a few amendments to my plans to take into account my particular situation. Off I went to buy my materials and some shiny new power tools and a few days (and half a container of plastic wood filler) later, I had my new room, complete with a door that actually swings open and closed.

Both these examples are amazing feats of engineering—well, at least the ants' is—but they are fundamentally different. My project was cultural. The ants' was not. I had to do all sorts of thinking and analyzing to build my wall. The ants did not think at all about their nest. Indeed, ants don't really have much to think *with*.

This distinction should be obvious, and it's fairly easy to decide, in general, whether a behavior is cultural or not. I've been discussing culture all along so far, and you've probably had no problem understanding what I've meant. We all know what culture is.

Or do we? Can you define culture? Can you create a sentence or two that clearly tells why my wall was cultural but the ants' nest was not? If you can't, don't worry. You're in good company. For the entire history of anthropology, a continual project has been to try to come up with just such a definition. One reason for the difficulty is simply that the phenomenon of culture is so complex. The second reason is that, until recently, we were trying desperately to define culture in a way that made it our species' unique possession. As you can probably guess, it's not.

A concise definition is difficult, if not impossible, but we can list and discuss the characteristics of culture to show, point by point, how cultural behaviors differ from noncultural ones, and to examine in what ways nonhumans exhibit cultural behaviors.

FIGURE 7.1

Weaver ants build nests by pulling edges of leaves together. While some of the ants hold the leaves in this position, others gently carry larvae along the "seam," stimulating them to excrete silk, which "sews" the leaves together.

THE CONCEPT OF CULTURE

Perhaps the easiest characteristic of a cultural behavior to see, and the clearest distinction between the two building behaviors described, is that culture is *learned.* The ants clearly didn't learn how to build nests, even as complex as that behavior might be. Rather, the behavior is built into their genes and is expressed by a complex series of stimuli that elicit a complex set of responses. My accomplishment, on the other hand, was only possible through learning, and the skills and information I learned were in turn learned by those who instructed me, who learned it from someone else, and so on.

Learning used to be considered the only distinguishing feature between cultural and noncultural behaviors, but a moment's reflection will tell you that learning is not enough. Other creatures learn. My dogs, for example, have learned many things, including, of course, the taboo against eliminating in the house, but these things would not really be considered cultural. Why not? What other differences are there?

A second characteristic of culture is that it involves *concepts, generalizations, abstractions, and ideas.* The ants are locked into the specifics of their nest-building behavior. It must work the same all the time. If some important variable is different, the ants cannot make specific adjustments. They don't, in other words, know what they're doing. Their behavior is not part of some larger concept.

My wall building, however, certainly involved concepts. No external stimuli elicited a wall-building response in me. Rather, I decided, consciously, to do the project for my own set of reasons. My book didn't relate to my wall in particular but gave general ideas about partition building that I adapted to my specific situation. As I ran into unexpected problems (and there were lots), I was able to use my knowledge of the general principles to solve them. I now should be able to apply what I've learned to other, similar tasks.

And think about having to learn every specific behavior for every situation you encounter in the course of a day. Life as we know it would be impossible. Rather, because we have learned generalizations, or have generated our own generalizations from specific data, we adapt those generalizations to each new situation—more often than not successfully.

But even concepts and generalizations don't absolutely define human cultural behavior. My dogs have some concept of the elimination taboo. I don't have to take them into every house and building we may visit and teach them all over again. Rather, I'm confident that they have generalized from their training in my house. They have some concept that says something like "Don't go to the bathroom in people's buildings." But that still doesn't make their behavior cultural.

There is another dimension to learning that is important. Learning in most organisms is passive. They learn from imitation or from trial and error. For many birds, for example, singing just the right song is impossible unless they've heard another bird sing it. Singing itself is genetic, but the song must be learned. The wild turkeys in my backyard have learned through trial and error that showing up in the afternoon yields no extra food because I put out corn for them only in the morning. They now show up every morning within minutes of my scattering the corn, and I seldom see them any other time of day.

But learning can also be active, when information is *shared* among organisms, is *transmitted* from one organism to another *extragenetically*, that is, without any direct genetic influence, as in the birdsong example. The ants' basic information about nest-building is solely genetic. The information I acquired about wall building was shared extragenetically.

Now, if I adopted a new puppy and put her in the house with my present dogs, and if I had no input into the situation and allowed the dog to leave and enter the house at will, would she learn the elimination taboo? I doubt it. Each dog can learn it independently, but one can't share the information, and certainly not the generalization, with other dogs. ("Hey listen, never, ever go to the bathroom in peoples' houses, OK?") Dogs can and do learn by imitation and, probably, after a while, the new dog would start to behave accordingly. But she would have learned on her own, passively. It is not culture.

The fourth characteristic of culture is the presence of *artifacts*. An **artifact** is defined as any object made intentionally. It is, in other words, not natural but, in the common phrase, "man made." This book is an artifact. To be sure, the ants made their nest, but that nest is natural. The program for it is genetic and so, in a sense, it is like their hormones and

artifact Any object consciously manufactured. Usually refers to human-made objects, but now includes those made by other primates.

bodies—natural and not the result of learned, shared concepts and generalizations.

Although the usual definition of artifact limits it to concrete items —tools, houses, books, pottery—I'd like to expand it a bit here to include cultural institutions and organizational systems—things like religions, governments, educational establishments. These too are "man made." Artifacts—both concrete ones and abstract organizing principles—facilitate the realization of cultural ideas, and human culture is dependent upon them. Without artifacts, there is no way I could have built my wall—which, of course, is an artifact itself.

So, cultural behavior has these four characteristics:

1. It must be learned.
2. It must involve concepts, generalizations, abstractions, and ideas.
3. It must be shared through extragenetic transmission.
4. It must be realized through the use of artifacts, both concrete and abstract.

At this point a major question naturally arises. If my dog exhibits behaviors that have two of the four characteristics of culture (numbers 1 and 2 above), is it not possible that some nonhuman organisms actually do possess behaviors that could be considered cultural? The answer is yes, and it's no surprise that they are the apes.

As we saw with genetic differences, and in features such as bipedalism and the consciousness of our sexual behavior, we differ from our close primate relatives not in kind but in degree. The same holds true for the mental abilities that make culture possible. And there are some clear examples of cultural behavior, or nearly cultural behavior, among the nonhuman primates.

Perhaps the most famous example was first witnessed by primatologist Jane Goodall in 1960. Goodall has spent nearly forty years studying a large population of chimpanzees in the Gombe Stream Reserve in Tanzania. The chimps there have developed a taste for termites. Except for a short period when African termites sprout wings and fly around forming new colonies, they spend all their time inside tunnels within the large dirt mounds they construct. Most animals that eat termites must wait for such an event to capture them. The chimps, however, have developed a solution to the problem. Some of them, mostly females, will break a twig off a bush and strip off the leaves, or pull a long, stiff blade of grass from the ground and tear off any excess length. They will then insert their termite fishing stick into the opening of a tunnel in a termite mound, wiggle it around to cause the soldier termites to attack it, and carefully draw it out and have themselves a termite snack (Figure 7.2). A clever idea, and it fits our criteria for cultural behavior.

First of all, it is learned and not programmed in the chimps' genes. It is far too complex a behavior for that, and not all chimps perform it, as

FIGURE 7.2

Chimps using tools they have made to extract termites from their mound.

one would expect with a genetically based behavior. It is also shared extragenetically as chimp offspring learn the behavior by closely studying their mothers doing it. It also clearly involves an artifact. A raw material is purposely modified to perform a specific task.

Most important, fishing for termites uses concepts and generalizations. To accomplish the behavior a chimp must (1) understand a behavior of termites that it can only see the results of (that is, the soldier termites attached to the stick or grass by their long, sharp mandibles), (2) understand how to exploit the insects' behavior to get the termites out, and (3) visualize a tool for that purpose within a plant and conceive of and perform the steps needed to modify the plant to produce the tool. Moreover, chimps don't need the stimulus of a termite mound (where the insects have been out of sight anyway) to elicit the chain of behaviors. They have been seen to make their tool and *then* go looking for a mound. Different chimps even have different styles of the tool. It is clear that they have a concept in mind. When the young chimps learn from their mother's actions, they could not perform such a complex set of behaviors unless they conceptually understood what she was doing. It is more than just imitation.

FIGURE 7.3
A macaque washing its food, a behavior that has been termed protocultural because it does not involve a modified artifact. The monkeys are, however, using the water as a tool.

prey — godura.

Chimps use and make other tools as well, and tools are found in all natural populations of chimps that have been extensively studied. Moreover, regional and group differences are observed in type, style, and use of tools—clear evidence for a cultural, rather than a biological, behavior. In addition, chimpanzees hunt, often with other primate species as the main prey. Again, regional and group variations are seen in preferred prey species, favorite parts to be eaten, and whether hunting is solitary or cooperative.

Another primate example shows that possession of culture is a matter of degree. On the island of Koshima in Japan is a colony of Japanese macaques (an Old World monkey) that has been extensively studied for fifty years. The scientists conducting the study put piles of sweet potatoes on the beach to get the monkeys to come into the open and spend time there picking the sand off their food. The monkeys disliked dirty food. In 1953 a young female they had named Imo began taking her sweet potatoes to a freshwater pool to wash off the sand (Figure 7.3). Soon, other members of the group had picked up the idea. Some even washed theirs in the sea, possibly because they liked the salty taste.

Having been thwarted, the scientists then threw grains of wheat onto the sand, hoping it would take the monkeys longer to get the sand off so they could have more time to observe them. But Imo simply picked up a handful of wheat and sand, took it to a freshwater pool, and dumped it all in the water. The sand sank but the wheat floated, and this she scooped out and ate. This behavior too, spread through the group.

Now, there is obviously one criterion missing here: there are no artifacts. The monkeys are just manipulating unmodified natural objects. But it is learned, it is shared extragenetically, and it does involve a concept. And they are using a natural object, the water, for a specific, conscious purpose. Some have termed the water in this case an **ecofact**—a tool that has not been modified. (Another example of an ecofact would be the rocks that some chimps use to crack open hard-shelled nuts, sometimes first placing the nut on another, flat rock.) The washing behavior of these monkeys might be called **protocultural.** It is important to remember, at the same time, that these behaviors of the Japanese macaques resulted from some degree of human influence.

A final example deals not with natural behaviors but with behavioral potentials seen under artificial conditions. For some time, researchers had been trying to see if apes could learn to talk. All attempts failed because apes don't have the vocal apparatus needed to make human sounds (see Figure 11.4). But a lot of humans can't speak either. Many of them use a substitute for spoken language such as American Sign Language for the Hearing Impaired (Ameslan). Perhaps, it was reasoned, this would work with apes. At present, there are a fair number of chimps, gorillas, and bonobos that have become amazingly proficient at Ameslan or other substitute forms, and with these they can communicate using the features of a human language (see Figure 11.7).

I'll detail this phenomenon in Chapter 11. For now, however, suffice it to say that these achievements indicate that, although the apes don't use a language in the wild, they obviously have the mental capabilities that enable them to learn the rudiments of the one cultural trait we always thought was ours alone.

If, then, other creatures have behaviors that we are obliged to consider cultural, how are we different? Very simply, in these nonhumans, behaviors that fulfill the criteria for culture are rare and individual. They don't make up the majority of the animals' behavioral repertoire. For us, however, culture is absolutely vital. We are dependent upon it for our survival. All our behaviors, even though some may have their origins in our biological past, are learned culturally and performed culturally, for cultural reasons, within a system of cultural behaviors. Other species may *have* cultural behaviors, but our species *is* cultural. The difference may be one of degree, but the degree is a large one.

Of course, the ability to have culture in the first place is dependent upon a biological phenomenon—the structure and function of our brains. Just what is it about our brains, and to a lesser extent about the brains of apes, that makes the cultural ability possible? How did this evolve?

ecofact A natural object used as a tool but not modified.

protocultural A behavior having most but not all of the characteristics of a cultural behavior.

BRAINS AND CULTURE

The topic of brain structure and function is, obviously, complex and not yet completely understood, especially with regard to the origin and nature of conscious thought. It is important, however, to try to understand something about the brain in general to get a glimpse into how it makes our cultural behavior possible.

A useful way of picturing the brain, and one that has an evolutionary theme, is a model devised by Paul MacLean of the National Institute of Mental Health. He calls his model the triune (three-part) brain, and it refers to three evolutionary stages seen in the mammalian cerebrum (see Figure 4.5). Understand that these are not three absolutely distinct, clear-cut sections of the brain. Rather, they refer to areas that are associated with different functions but that are certainly interrelated in complex physical and functional ways. Think of this as a way of describing how the brain operates rather than specifically how it is structured.

The first, deepest, and oldest part is the **R-complex** (for reptilian). It is shared by all vertebrates and deals with such basic self-preservation functions as aggressiveness, territoriality, mating, and social hierarchy. Above this is the old mammalian brain, the **limbic system.** This appears to be the area that controls strong emotions like fear, rage, altruism (self-sacrifice), and care and concern for the young. Also part of the limbic system are areas dealing with basic sexual functioning and with the sense of smell. The association of these two should sound familiar. Some aspect of memory seems also to be housed in the limbic area. Surrounding these two parts is the new mammalian brain or **neocortex. This is where we think.** Various parts of the neocortex are concerned with perception and deliberation, spatial reasoning, vision and hearing, and the exchange of information between the brain and body.

So we humans have inherited the basic survival behavior of reptiles, the emotional responses of mammals, and the thought processes that became more elaborate during mammalian evolution. And all these operate together, influencing one another in a complex feedback system. Take for example, the aggressive action of a soldier at war or a police officer in the line of duty. Their actions are not simply automatic stimulus-response functions but involve logical deliberations and emotional reactions. At the same time, their taking aggressive action in the first place may have nothing directly to do with their own survival, but, rather, is related to abstract concepts of law, patriotism, group identity, or ideology. In other words, when all these evolved areas of the brain work together this way, we have the basis for the complex abilities of consciousness, reasoning, and, eventually, culture.

Moreover, within the neocortex—and again, this is metaphor, not a realistic description of brain anatomy and physiology—all the information acquired by the senses is stored and accessed through a highly cross-referenced retrieval system. There is a debate as to whether memories are stored in multiple places, or whether there are multiple pathways to each

R-complex A primitive portion of the brain involved in self-preservation behaviors such as mating, aggressiveness, and territoriality.

limbic system A portion of the brain involved in emotions such as fear, rage, and care of the young.

neocortex A portion of the brain involved in conscious thought, spatial reasoning, and sensory perception.

memory. At any rate, our brains can store massive amounts of information and we are not stuck with just memories of whole events but of the individual pieces of those events. Nor are those pieces dissociated. We can associate our mental pieces of information with related pieces, or even with unrelated pieces if we wish. When we retrieve information, we can use only those pieces of information that we deem relevant, and we can put pieces from various events together in all sorts of combinations to create solutions to problems, scientific hypotheses, philosophical ideas, generalizations, and so on.

Put another way, what we can do is experience events in our nervous systems. That is, our mental experiences are not limited to what our senses are sensing at the moment but to what they have sensed in the past, what they may sense in the future, and even to what they would sense in hypothetical situations. Only humans can make up stories. Only humans have philosophies. Only humans are good liars.

Keep this model in mind as we move on in subsequent chapters to talk about human culture and cultural adaptations. Note how these would be impossible without brains that work in some manner such as described.

In addition, keeping all the above in mind also helps us understand how some animals can exhibit a degree of cultural ability. Apes, for example, have relatively large neocortexes. Their brains have the same basic structure and function as ours, only less complex. After all, we both evolved from a common ancestor in the relatively recent past. The conscious thought, complex social behavior, and tool use of our closest relatives is really no surprise. In fact, since a neocortex is possessed by all mammals, it's reasonable to attribute some thinking ability to them all. It's clear to any pet owner that dogs and cats can reason. Whales and dolphins are also known to be highly intelligent. We humans are different in degree, not kind.

This difference in degree—and it is a rather large difference—can be accounted for evolutionarily. In conjunction with the trends toward bipedalism, conscious sexuality, and cooperative, committed family and social groups, there was also selection at some stage of our evolution for individuals who had larger neocortexes and who could reason at a more complex level. This would have enhanced the conscious controls over social and psychological relationships, and over the problems posed by the environment. We see the results of this evolution in the gradual but steady improvement in tool technology, and in the successful expansion of the hominids into new geographic locations and diverse environments.

This, then, is the story of *culture* as a species characteristic shared by us all. But there's another level, the level of *cultures*—the specific systems that characterize the societies within our species. How do we study, describe, and explain all the world's cultural systems? Why do we find such an enormous amount of variation from one culture to the next?

A MODEL FOR THE STUDY OF CULTURAL SYSTEMS

If we think of culture as an adaptive mechanism, it's easy to understand some of the cultural variation we observe around the world. Important aspects of people's cultures are geared to the conditions of their habitats. The Netsilik people of the Canadian Arctic have all sorts of cultural ideas and technologies for hunting seals but not for hunting kangaroos. For Native Australians it's just the opposite. Living in New England, I own all manner of clothing and heating devices to keep me warm during the winter. Native Americans in the tropical rain forests of Brazil, however, are concerned very little about warmth.

But what about peoples who live in almost the same environment but whose cultures still differ? As I noted in Chapter 2, Philadelphia in the United States and Beijing in China, being at the same latitude, have very similar climates, but the cultures of those two cities differ in everything from language to economics to clothing styles to eating habits. The climate of highland New Guinea is fairly homogeneous, yet that area is the home to hundreds of similar yet distinct cultures. How can we explain these differences in terms of the adaptive theme we've been following?

Culture has two identities. It is our major adaptive mechanism for coping with our basic biological needs. But at the same time, it is such an important, pervasive part of our lives that it has actually *become* our environment. Look around you: Everything you come in contact with, everything you're concerned about, all the solutions to your concerns—they are all cultural. And in that light we can see that most cultural adaptations (once we've taken care of basic biological needs) are adaptations to culture itself. Most changes in a cultural system are responses to other changes in that cultural system. So we must look within cultural systems and view them as their own integrated environments in order to understand just how they work and why we see such a great degree of variation from society to society.

There are as many specific ways of going about this as there are anthropologists, and there are, as we'll discuss in Chapter 15, several major schools of thought about the nature of culture and how to study it. The following discussion represents my way of looking at these issues; I have no doubt other anthropologists would suggest at least minor changes. But I think it reasonably captures the basic approach of anthropology and so is a useful model for examining cultures and explaining cultural variation (Figure 7.4).

We begin, naturally, with the biological characteristics of humans. We should never lose sight of the fact that, despite the power of culture, we are still limited by our biological structure, function, and needs. However, because part of our biology includes a brain capable of culture, there is a variety of specific ways we can go about fulfilling our basic needs. There are many possible behavioral patterns and our task as

FIGURE 7.4
A model for the study of cultural systems as described in the text.

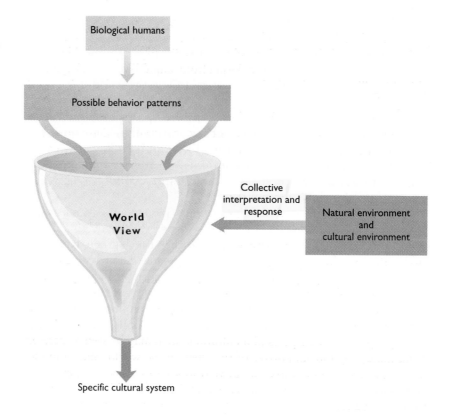

anthropologists is to figure out why, from all the possible patterns, each society exhibits and practices its unique combination, its specific cultural system.

I like to visualize all the potential possibilities going into a metaphorical filter, like the filter in a drip coffeemaker. All the unwanted behaviors are filtered out. Those that are wanted, that work for the society in question, pass through and are combined and integrated to form the cultural system. The problem now becomes, what to label the filter? To what single thing may we link all the aspects of a cultural system, as well as the combination that becomes the system itself?

I think the best label is **world view.** World view is, as someone once put it, "a set of assumptions about the way things are." What sorts of "things"? Well, as vague as this sounds, just about anything. The nature of the world and its living creatures; the place of humans in the natural world; the proper relationships between humans and nonhumans, between individuals and groups of people; the explanations for why all these are as they are—these and many more items are the "things" with which the world view of a culture concerns itself.

But why do I prefer the label "world view" and not "environment" or "conscious choice"? Simply because those other alternatives, while

world view The collective interpretation of and response to the natural and cultural environments in which a group of people live. Their assumptions about those environments and values derived from those assumptions.

partially accurate, are incomplete explanations. As noted, not every aspect of a cultural system can be explained as a direct adaptation to the environment. And claiming that culture was directly determined by environment is too mechanistic. It makes culture sound like an entity, a tangible thing like some chemical in a test tube. It leaves real people out of the equation.

On the other hand, to claim that all aspects of a cultural system are the results of conscious, rational choice is to say that there are no generalizations we can make about human culture, no trends or tendencies that make some sense out of cultural history. That point of view would mean that every cultural system is idiosyncratic, making sense only in terms of the minds of the people who created it.

World view, as the term implies, must be a view of the world that a group of people knows. It includes their natural world and their cultural world, that is, their cultural system at a point in time as well as the history of that culture, how it got to be the way it is. These two factors, of course, interact as people move around, encounter other peoples, and develop new and different ways to cope with their environments.

World view, then, can best be thought of as the collective interpretation of and response to the worlds (natural and cultural) in which a society of people live. All aspects of a cultural system may be seen as derived from, linked to, and supportive of this view of the world. Such a model takes into account both direct adaptive responses that make logical sense as well as the idiosyncratic responses of real people, which may or may not make logical sense to others but which are perfectly reasonable and consistent to the people in question.

Obviously, some examples are in order at this point, but not without two words of caution. First, these examples are simplifications. I will be trying to narrow things down as much as possible in order to show what we mean by world view and how it serves as a label for our imaginary filter. In real life, much more would be involved. A cultural system is a complex, integrated whole. All aspects of a cultural system interact with all other aspects and with all the facets of a society's natural and cultural worlds. You will see this clearly as we examine specific aspects of cultural systems in the following chapters and some of the questions you may have about these examples will be addressed later.

Second, we must appreciate the difficulty of trying to understand and describe another culture's world view. Remember, world view is not a thing. It is an abstraction, a term we have put on the totality of the collective interpretations and responses of a society of people. One cannot ask members of another culture what their world view is. It is not something people articulate because it is really in the background. (In a bit, we'll see how this is so by trying to describe an American world view.)

We can, however, open a window onto another group's world view by looking at their religious beliefs. Religion is not the same as world view. Religion is one aspect of a cultural system. But one function of religion (about which more in Chapter 12) in all societies is to allow people to codify their world view—to talk about, share, and pass on those assumptions about the way things are. Most, if not all, religions include a creation story (how the world and its people began); the history of a people; stories that indicate a people's relationship to the supernatural, to each other, and to the other species on earth and to the earth itself; and basic rules of behavior.

So with these cautions in mind, let's compare two rather distinct world views—that of Arctic peoples with those of certain societies from Southwest Asia (also called the Near East or Middle East) around 10,000 years ago.

The environment of peoples of the American Arctic (whom we may collectively refer to as Eskimo, although there is some disagreement over that usage) live in one of the harshest environments of any human group. It's not that the Eskimo are poorly adapted. On the contrary, even before acquiring modern technological items, they were known for their ingenuity and inventiveness at using natural resources cleverly and efficiently to satisfy their needs (see Figure 2.5). They saw themselves not as separate from the land and its life, but at one with it. As writer Barry Lopez puts it, their relationships with animals, even those they hunt, are "local and personal" and those animals are "part of one's community." Their lives are, he says, "resilient, practical, and enthusiastic."

But this intimacy with nature comes at a price. The Arctic is never an easy place to live, and the Eskimo saw that world as one over which their control was limited, tenuous, and unstable. They live, says Lopez, with "a fear tied to their knowledge that sudden, cataclysmic events are as much a part of life, of really living, as are the moments when one pauses to look at something beautiful."

How is this view reflected in Eskimo religion? In other words, how did the Eskimo codify this world view? There are many different Arctic peoples, both in North America and Asia, and so there are many specific individual cultural systems. We may look at a few aspects of one and, because there are certain similarities among peoples of this region, it can represent some generalizations about them all.

The Netsilik people live in the Hudson Bay region of Canada (Figure 7.5). Their name means "people of the seal" because seal hunting in the winter is a major focus of their lives, although they also hunt caribou and fish for salmon in the spring, summer, and fall. The Netsilik express their view of the world by believing that the natural world, the supernatural world, and the world of human moral order are one integrated whole. But the natural world is under the control of the spirit world and important natural phenomena—as well as all humans and animals—have spirits or souls. There are other spirits with various degrees of control over the world as well. We say technically that the Netsilik, like many hunting peoples, are **polytheistic**—they recognize multiple supernatural beings.

codify To arrange systematically. To put into words.

polytheistic Refers to a religious system that recognizes multiple supernatural beings.

FIGURE 7.5
A Netsilik hunting for seals. Since the seals are below the ice, the hunter must harpoon them sight unseen. He has placed a bit of swan's down in what he hopes is a seal's breathing hole, which had been located by his dogs. When the seal uses the hole the disturbed air will move the swan's down and the hunter will throw his harpoon down the hole. If he strikes the seal he must then enlarge the hole to pull it out.

The control of these souls over the physical world helps explain why things are as they are, especially why things can go wrong. Souls are seen as, at best, unreliable and are generally considered evil or capable of becoming evil. Souls that have been wronged can cause misfortunes and thus there are many rules about how they should be treated. A newly killed seal, for instance, must be placed on fresh snow rather than the dirty floor of the igloo. The hunters beg the forgiveness of the spirit. Water is poured in the dead seal's mouth because its soul is still thirsty. Caribou souls are especially sensitive and no work on caribou hides can be done in sight of living caribou. If they see and are offended, their souls will not allow them to be caught. By adhering to these taboos the Netsilik gained at least some sense of influence over their difficult lives. Thus, not only the technology of the Netsilik but more abstract aspects of their culture can be linked to their interpretation of and response to the real world in which they live.

Contrast this with a second example. In Southwest Asia prior to about 10,000 years ago, people also lived as hunters of wild animals and gatherers of wild plants. The lives of these peoples were not, perhaps, as hard life as those of the Eskimo, but they were still dependent upon naturally occurring resources in an environment where humans were pretty much at the mercy of nature. Religions in the area were probably also polytheistic, with various supernatural entities controlling important natural phenomena.

But about 10,000 years ago, a major cultural event began to take place in the area—the invention of farming (which we'll detail in Chapter 10). People with this cultural ability had direct control over the most important natural resource, food (Figure 7.6). Think of how that cultural change would eventually alter the world a people lived in and change their feelings about that world and their place in it. As the long history of farming influenced the physical and cultural worlds of this area, we see a change in world view reflected in three important religious traditions that originated in Southwest Asia—Judaism, Christianity, and Islam.

All three of these religions are **monotheistic,** that is, they recognize one supreme supernatural being. That one being, whom we can refer to as God in all three cases, brought about and has control over all natural phenomena, including human affairs. But things are not entirely out of human hands. First, humans are said to have been created in God's image, so humans have a closer connection to the supernatural than do any other living things. In the Judeo-Christian tradition, for example, humans are given dominance over the other creatures of the earth (Genesis 1:28); it is the first human, Adam, who names the animals (Gen. 2:19–20); and humans are enjoined to multiply and subdue the earth (Gen. 1:28, 8:17).

Second, humans are not so much at the whimsical mercy of the supernatural as they are in Eskimo tradition. In the Judeo-Christian-Islamic tradition, humans may petition God through prayer and action. They can ask God for favors and, if God is pleased and willing, stand a chance of having those requests granted. Humans have some sense of personal control in their dealings with the supernatural, even with an all-powerful being.

This is a clear reflection and articulation of a world view in which people are coming to see themselves as having a real ability to know and understand the world around them and to use that knowledge to exercise real control over their world for their own benefit. As humans now have some dominion over the natural world, so God has dominion over humans. As people begin to view the world as clearly divided into the human and the natural, so too is there a division between humans and a single, omnipotent supernatural entity. Gone are the multitude of spirits and souls, fairly equally powerful and able to control aspects of the real world at will and under only minimal influence from people.

Thus, world view is, I think, a useful focus around which we may describe the other aspects of a society's natural and cultural worlds. Doing so allows us to take into account both the practical and the more abstract connections within the integrated whole we call a cultural system.

As an exercise, try putting into words some important facets of a modern American world view. Remember that world view is not the

monothesitic Refers to a religious system that recognized a single supernatural being.

FIGURE 7.6
A farmer in Egypt uses techniques that are essentially unchanged from thousands of years ago to grow crops that were among the first domesticated plants.

same as religion; it's far more abstract. When I ask my classes to consider this question, a common contribution is that we value individualism. Think about our folk heroes, past, present, real, and fictional—Daniel Boone, Davy Crockett, Paul Bunyon, Harriet Tubman, John Glenn, Muhammad Ali, to name a few, are all embodiments, in their own ways, of the rugged individual we so admire.

Others have said that we Americans expect, value, and embrace change. Our clothing styles, automobile designs, and musical trends change annually. We place term limits on those who run our government. We focus intently on some news event and then quickly move on. (As I'm writing this, the scandal surrounding President Clinton, now a year old, is fast becoming "old news" and the public in general is eager to be done with it.) As Bob Dylan once put it in a song, "OK, I've had enough! What *else* can you show me?"

Still another aspect of the American world view might be the way we value size. We like things big. We've always seen the country as big. The early history of the United States is full of stories of the explorers and pioneers (more rugged individuals) setting off into the unknown expanses of a huge continent. There's always been room to grow. We've built, at one time or another, the tallest building, the biggest sports stadium, even the largest shopping mall. We even admire physical size in people. Studies have indicated that taller men are more likely to be hired for some jobs than shorter men, even if height is irrelevant to the work. Try it. I'm sure you can come up with other expressions of our world view.

For the sake of introducing the concept and my model, the above examples leave out a lot. To even begin to fully analyze a cultural system one would have to include data about every aspect of that system and every aspect of the natural and cultural environment to which it is a response. We will do a more complete (though not entirely complete) job with some other examples in Chapter 13. For the moment, however, to show that this model can apply to all sorts of human matters, I give you the following parable.

AN ANTHROPOLOGICAL ANALYSIS OF THE NECKTIE

In class several years ago, after I had presented the model you've just read about, one perceptive student raised her hand and asked, a bit sheepishly but with a touch of a challenge in her voice, "What about your tie? It doesn't have a practical purpose for survival. Can you explain *that* with your coffee filter?"

"Well," I faltered, "sometimes certain cultural practices are so obscure and indirectly related to whole systems that it's nearly impossible to explain them in this perspective. Oh look, time to go!"

Overnight, though, I gave it some thought and in the next class I proudly presented my analysis. The origin of this specific item—a colored piece of cloth tied around the neck of males—is obscure. It seems to have come by its modern form during the reign of Louis XIV of France when, called a *cravat* (from the French word for Croatian), it was worn as part of the uniform of Croatian soldiers as a sign of rank. The French, always on the cutting edge of fashion, liked the idea and adopted it as a normal item of clothing.

But what does the tie *mean* to us? Although not as common as it once was (my father would even wear one shopping or attending sports events), the tie is still a symbol of status. It is worn in certain situations where one is expected to display one's social status, socioeconomic position, and attitude about the situation. For example, certain jobs require a necktie. A man nearly always wears one to job interviews, even if the job itself doesn't require one. We wear ties to court, regardless of whether we're defendant or plaintiff. We wear them to weddings, funerals, bar mitzvahs, and christenings to show that we acknowledge the importance of the event. When worn in a seemingly inappropriate situation—say, at an archaeological excavation—a tie is a clear sign of one's high socioeconomic status. I have been treated very differently by clerks in the same store depending upon whether I'm wearing a suit and tie or jeans and sweatshirt. This useless and often uncomfortable item lacks any practical purpose but is obviously full of meaning.

This relates to our general discussion when you realize that not all cultures recognize the concept of differential status and wealth that something like a tie symbolizes. Among hunters and gatherers—peoples like the Eskimo who rely solely on naturally occurring resources—it would prove at least inefficient, if not possibly detrimental, if some people had more wealth than others. Rather, in such societies (which we will discuss in detail in Chapter 8) wealth is distributed equally among members, and there are no recognized differences in social status. To be sure, some people are better hunters than others, or are more adept at decision making, but these differences are not institutionalized or formalized. They can't afford to have anything but a group of people working together as harmoniously as possible for the common good. As a result, there are no symbols of status or wealth differences, such as different clothing for those of higher position.

In societies that farm, however, we find a new phenomenon: surplus resources. At least when things are going well, a family can produce more than they need to feed themselves. The excess can be traded to someone else for some other resource that that person has a surplus of. Or it can be traded for a service that person may perform, which might include leadership activities. With all that wealth changing hands, and all those resource surpluses, and all the specializations in labor, it is inevitable that some people are going to have more than others—both more wealth and more status, with the two generally going hand in hand. Status differences arise and symbols of those differences develop, including, of course, items of personal adornment.

Western civilization can trace much of its cultural heritage back to farming societies of Southwest Asia and early Europe. Our cultural tradition has long had the concept of status differences built into it. So, the necktie has a history of its own, but its use as a symbol denoting differential wealth and power can be linked to world view.

Now that we understand the nature of the upright, sexual, cultural primate, we can proceed to look at the individual categories of our species' adaptations. The categories we'll work with could be used for any organism. They are essentially a list of the major behaviors needed for survival. Where we differ from other species is in the fact that our adaptive behaviors are cultural and must be analyzed and understood within the complex and integrated set of relationships we have outlined in this chapter.

SUMMARY

A cultural behavior is a concept or idea that is shared among members of a population, transmitted extragenetically through learning, and made possible through artifacts. Culture is the major adaptive mechanism of our species, which we absolutely depend upon for our survival. The rudiments of culture can be observed in some other organisms, especially the nonhuman primates. Indeed, chimpanzees who manufacture tools are clearly engaged in cultural behaviors, though these behaviors are not vital to the perpetuation of their species.

CONTEMPORARY ISSUES

Can Anthropologists Study Their Own Cultures?

Anthropologists can and do study the cultures in which they grew up, but doing so involves a somewhat different approach from that used to study a culture foreign to us. When we study another people, our goal is to understand their world view so we can then understand how all the features of their culture interrelate to each other and to the world that the people observe, live in, and interpret. When we seek to anthropologically understand our own culture, we need, in a sense, to begin by stepping away from our world view.

By definition, one's world view is not something one is aware of on a daily basis. World view is an abstraction—the name anthropologists give to the complex web of interpretations and responses of a society to its natural and cultural environments. Everything we do as members of our culture is linked, as we described in the chapter, to our world view. Even trying to describe components of one's world view can be difficult, because we don't think in those terms. My motivations for my daily behaviors are fairly

basic. Many things I do, I simply do because I've always done them or they're expected of me or they fit the immediate situation. Rarely do I acknowledge that I do things because they relate to my society's world view. So a first step in making your own culture your anthropological subject is to try to view it from the outside, as an objective observer.

How does one accomplish this? One way is simply to start thinking about your society's behaviors and ideas in the same anthropological terms you would apply to a foreign society. In 1956, Horace Miner wrote a piece in *American Anthropologist* called "Body Ritual among the Nacirema" which described and analyzed the meaning of various behaviors related to the human body performed by an exotic culture. It included passages like the following:

> The daily body ritual performed by everyone includes a mouth-rite. Despite the fact that these people are so punctilious about care of

The human brain—the organ that enables us to have culture—may be pictured as having different functional levels, the results of different stages of our evolutionary history. All these levels operate together to produce our basic behavioral repertoire. The thinking part of our brain, our cerebral cortex, is a complex, highly cross-referenced system that allows us to store data from our memories and experiences and to manipulate those memories to produce the ideas that make culture possible.

Culture is a species characteristic, but individual cultural systems differ greatly. To explain, understand, and analyze a given cultural system requires that we see each system as an integrated set of ideas and behaviors, all of which are related directly or indirectly to the abstract assumptions we call world view. World view in turn may be defined as the collective interpretations of and responses to the natural and cultural environments in which a group of people lives.

the mouth, this rite involves a practice which strikes the uninitiated stranger as revolting. It was reported to me that the ritual consists of inserting a small bundle of hog hairs into the mouth, along with certain magical powders, and then moving the bundle in a highly formalized series of gestures.

Miner is obviously describing Americans (look at the word Nacirema closely) brushing their teeth. (Toothbrushes used to be made with hogs' hair bristles, and tooth powders rather than pastes were common in 1956.) The article may seem like a cute trick, but reading it provides for many people (including me as a young anthropology student) a first realization that our culture is as much a subject for anthropology as any other.

Another way to begin understanding one's own culture in anthropological terms is to focus on a specific subculture. Each such subculture has its own unique set of beliefs and behaviors —indeed its own unique world view—but is still a variation on the world view, beliefs, and behaviors of the larger culture of which it is a part. A geographically large, populous, multicultural, pluralistic, and free society like ours in North America contains many groups worthy of study as subcultures. For example, there are anthropological descriptions and analyses of religious isolates like the Hutterites and Amish, urban street gangs, inner-city ethnic communities, baseball, business corporations, the health food movement, hospital operating rooms, cocktail waitresses, retirement communities, the public school classroom, courtrooms, prisons, tattooing and body piercing, motorcycle societies—I could go on and on. Understanding one or more of these subcultures or practices in the end sheds light on the larger society that gave rise to them and in which they exist.

Knowledge of one's own culture is important simply because all anthropological knowledge helps us understand our species and its behaviors. Such knowledge is also especially valuable on a personal level. There is certainly a satisfaction about seeing one's own culture from a new perspective and understanding something about the origins and meanings of its components. And, for those who wish to contribute to their culture and effect change within it, an anthropological understanding and context is, I think, vital.

NOTES, REFERENCES, AND READINGS

The emergence of culture from the basic primate behavioral repertoire is the topic of Jane Lancaster's *Primate Behavior and the Emergence of Human Culture.* The question of the presence of culture among the non-human primates is addressed in W. C. McGrew's "Culture in Nonhuman Primates?" in the 1998 *Annual Review of Anthropology.* In the process of addressing this question it also nicely deals with the characteristics that define a cultural behavior. More on the behavior of chimpanzees is in Jane Goodall's *Through a Window.*

The late Carl Sagan won a Pulitzer prize for his *Dragons of Eden: Speculations of the Evolution of Human Intelligence.* It includes more detail on the structure and function of the human brain and McLean's triune brain model. Much of the book is now outdated and large portions are, as the subtitle admits, highly speculative, but it still holds up as a thought-provoking way of thinking about the nature and evolution of the human mind. Another, and more recent, approach to the relationship between the mind and its products is Steven Mithen's *The Prehistory of the Mind: The Cognitive Origins of Art, Religion, and Science.* I also recommend *How Brains Think* by William H. Calvin.

Material on the Netsilik can be found in Asen Balikci's *The Netsilik Eskimo.* On the Arctic and Arctic peoples in general, see Barry Lopez's *Arctic Dreams.* The quotes I used are from pages 180 and 181 of that book.

PART THREE

Adapting to Our Worlds

8 *Food: Getting It, Growing It, Eating It, and Passing It Around*
The importance of food throughout human history. Descriptions of societies that collect their food and of those that produce it through farming or herding. Some basic categories of economics, the distribution of goods and services.

9 *Nature of the Group: Arranging Our Families and Organizing Our People*
Social organization among the nonhuman primates. Variation among human societies in the organization of nuclear and extended families and in family lines. The importance of what we call family members. Types of political organization.

10 *Material Culture: The Things We Make and the Things We Leave Behind*
Archaeology, the science of recovering, identifying, dating, and interpreting the cultural past. Three prehistoric highpoints that archaeology has illuminated.

11 *Communication: Sharing What We Need to Know*
The characteristics of language, the human communication system. The evolution of human language and the attempts to teach it to apes. The relationships between languages and the cultures that use them.

12 *Maintenance of Order: Making the World View Real*
Defining religion and the variable characteristics of religious systems. The relationships between religion and culture, using Christianity as an example. Laws, nonreligious systems of social maintenance.

13 *The Evolution of Our Behavior: Pigs, Wars, Killer Proteins, and Sorcerers*
Analyzing whole cultural systems. Some general schools of thought compared and combined, using the biblical dietary laws as an example. Two cultural systems described and analyzed. A discussion of the interaction of biology and culture.

8

FOOD

Getting It, Growing It, Eating It, and Passing It Around

In Part Two we discussed food in two important contexts. First, the quest for food in the shrinking forests and expanding savannas of Africa is thought to have played a major role in the explanation for human beginnings, linked with the evolution of bipedalism, social consciousness, and, later, our big brains with their cultural faculties. Second, in a cultural context, when I told my necktie story I analyzed differences in social status in terms of differences in food-getting techniques. The Eskimos relied on naturally occurring resources, while the Southwest Asian groups grew some of their own food. These differences gave rise to and helped explain the status differences—or lack of them—in these cultures.

All this is not really surprising, of course. Food is obviously important. No organism can survive without nutrients to build its structure and run its functions. If there's not enough food, a living thing doesn't have to worry about finding shelter or reproducing. This is as true for humans as for any creature. In many ways, food has been a moving force behind human evolution and culture history. Indeed, when anthropologists categorize the rich array of human cultures into a reasonable number of meaningful types, we often do it on the basis of food-getting techniques, or **subsistence patterns.** How a society gets its food has important ramifications for all other aspects of its cultural system. What food is available and how we get it clearly has a lot to do with our world view, which in turn affects our culture.

FOOD AND HUMAN EVOLUTION

Once the quest for food under new environmental circumstances established our bipedal version of the primate order, further environmental changes and adaptations to food sources influenced what appears to be the next major event in hominid evolution. About 3 million years ago, two new branches diverged from the apparent original hominid line, genus *Australopithecus*. These original hominids had a mixed diet of vegetables from the forest and open ground. One new branch, genus *Paranthropus,* seems to have begun to specialize in the vegetable foods of the open plains. The other branch, genus *Homo,* facilitated by their larger brains and ability to make stone tools, made the important addition of large quantities of scavenged meat to the diet. This provided the early members of our genus with some dietary flexibility that allowed them to continue evolving when further environmental changes brought about the extinction of the other two hominid genera.

subsistence pattern How a society acquires its food resources.

This adaptive success was put to the test around 2 million years ago when humans began to spread throughout Africa and into other Old World continents. As they migrated they encountered new and changing environments—including the advances and retreats of the Pleistocene glaciers—and, thus, new and changing sources of food. In northerly and glacial areas, edible plants were scarce, and so hunting took on an increasingly important role, as we see from the specialized hunting tools associated with anatomically modern *Homo sapiens*. Note too, that much early cave art had game animals and hunting as a theme (see Figure 5.22 and Chapter 10).

It should be mentioned that, as important as hunting may have been in our evolution, that importance can be overemphasized. Anthropologists used to think humans *began* as hunters on the savannas—the old "Man the Hunter" scenario. One also can get the idea that among peoples with a **hunter-gatherer** subsistence, the hunting part is by far the most important. Neither idea is accurate. We have already described evidence indicating that meat eating was based on scavenging for much of our evolution. Scavenging was replaced by hunting only later. And as far as recent cultures are concerned, except for Arctic groups, gathering of plant foods is usually the more important activity in terms of the relative amount of nutrition it supplies. In indigenous southern African hunter-gatherer groups, for example, around 75 percent of the food eaten is plant material gathered by the women.

Anthropologists, I hate to admit, were guilty of a bit of sexism for a time. The field, long dominated by men, perhaps found some satisfaction in the idea that our first ancestors invaded the savannas with their weapons and started killing things. It was not a very pleasant idea that we waited for lions and other predators to finish their meals and then picked up the leftovers. Similarly, the idea that gathering roots, nuts, leaves, and tubers was nutritionally more important than "bringing home the bacon" was brushed aside. More objective observations and analyses have shown us otherwise.

But there is a second reason for this misinterpretation. Hunter-gatherer groups themselves tend to emphasize the hunting part of their subsistence, despite its statistically limited role in their nutrition. This is because hunting is the more tenuous of the two activities, the more dangerous, the one less likely to yield results on a regular basis, and the one that causes the most anxiety. There are few rituals related to success in gathering but many that seek to ensure success in hunting. People seldom tell exciting stories about collecting roots, but they enjoy a good antelope hunting tale (Figure 8.1). Hunting is more exciting. So we must be careful not to let our own cultural biases—or those of the people we're studying—affect our attempts to objectively describe and interpret facts. At the same time, of course, a people's view of their own world and behaviors *is* part of those facts that we anthropologists study.

hunter-gatherer A society that relies on naturally occurring sources of food.

FIGURE 8.1
Two San boys, from Namibia, play a story-telling game. Stories, accompanied by gestures and body language, are often used by the San to tell about hunting adventures, with the storyteller performing creative and humorous mimicry of the animals involved.

There is another possible food-related facet of our evolution. Recall the gradual smoothing out of the facial features and decrease in the size of the teeth that took place in hominid evolution, including the relatively recent change from the rugged features of archaic *Homo sapiens* to the more graceful ones of modern humans. One explanation for this change is that our teeth and jaws became less important as tools because of advances in stone tool technology, the habit of cooking meat and other foods, and, with the final recession of the glaciers, a shift from an emphasis on big-game hunting to a more mixed diet. It has also been suggested that the invention of eating utensils may have brought about a decreased robusticity in the chewing areas of our crania.

Food has, of course, continued to play an important role in historic events, as countless examples show. The potato, for instance, domesticated in South America and imported to Europe, was suggested as a good, easily grown crop to stave off famine. It later became such an important part of Irish agriculture that when a blight caused the potato crop to fail in 1845 and 1846 the results were the death by starvation and disease of about a million Irish and the emigration of about a million more to the United States.

Food has often been used as a tool to manipulate people and events. During war, the two items that opposing forces try hardest to keep from their enemy are ammunition and food. Many a battle has been won or lost as a result of the availability of food supplies. "An army marches on its stomach," Napoleon is reputed to have said. Similarly, a people can best be subjugated by withholding food, as during sieges or blockades.

Food can even supersede arms in importance. Despite the military tension and cultural differences between the United States and the former Soviet Union, there was a great deal of trade between the two countries. Especially important were shipments of wheat that the United States and Canada sold to the U.S.S.R., because Soviet agriculture, unlike other aspects of its technology, was not nearly as productive as that of the West. The Soviets relied on this trade to maintain adequate food supplies.

One reason for the problems of Soviet agriculture is interesting and relevant to several themes in this book. In the 1930s, a Russian agronomist (a specialist in agricultural science) named Trofim D. Lysenko proposed a theory for cultivating plants that was based not on Darwinian evolution and Mendelian genetics, but on Lamarckian ideas about the inheritance of acquired characteristics. Lysenko thought he could impart the characteristics of winter wheat to spring wheat by refrigerating spring wheat seeds—thus, in his words, "training" them. Lysenko promoted his idea not scientifically but politically and ideologically, claiming it fit Marxist-Leninist social theory better than did Darwin's and Mendel's theories. It was officially accepted as Soviet scientific doctrine in 1948. Needless to say, it didn't work too well, but it wasn't until 1965 that mainstream science with regard to plant breeding was reinstated in the U.S.S.R. By that time, Soviet agriculture was far behind the West's.

It should be clear that the acquisition of food is a central concern to our species (as any) and to the individual populations within our species. We can thus use subsistence patterns as meaningful categories to organize our examination of cultural variation, and we may make some generalizations about other aspects of cultural systems within each category (Table 8.1). We may divide subsistence patterns into two main types: food collecting and food producing. Within the latter, there are several more specific types.

These are not mutually exclusive categories. Most societies practice more than one subsistence technique. For example, although I speak of the United States as a food-producing society, we still get some of our food through collecting. Most of the fish one orders in a restaurant, for instance, has technically been collected and not produced. But most societies have one subsistence pattern that supplies the majority of their diet. It is this pattern that becomes the integral part of the society's cultural system and that is related to other features of that system. Table 8.1 reflects, as noted, *generalizations* that provide us with a starting point for organizing our examination of human societies. I will point out some other exceptions as we go along.

TABLE 8.1 Subsistence Patterns and Associated Traits This table represents generalizations about each subsistence pattern. Exceptions exist, some of which are noted in the text. The terms are defined in the text and glossaries. Kinship and politics are covered in Chapter 9. Religion is the topic of Chapter 12.

Pattern	General	Social Stratification	Labor Specialization	Resource Distribution	Kinship	Religion	Politics
Foraging	Natural resources Hunting and gathering Small population Nomadic	Egalitarian	By sex	General reciprocity	Bilateral Monogamy	Polytheistic (not hierarchical) Animistic	Band
Horticulture	Farming with human labor and simple tools Larger, more sedentary	Rank	Part time	Balanced reciprocity Redistribution	Unilineal Polygyny	Polytheistic (hierarchical)	Tribal
Agriculture	Farming with animal (or mechanical) labor Large, sedentary	Class/caste	Full time	Balanced reciprocity Market system	Unilineal/bilateral Polygyny/ Monogamy	Polytheistic (hierarchical) Monotheistic	Chiefdom/state
Pastoralism	Focus on herding Nomadic Highly variable	Egalitarian/rank	By sex	Redistribution Balanced reciprocity	Patrilineal Polygyny	Ancestors	Tribal

FOOD-COLLECTING SOCIETIES

When I began full-time teaching in 1973 and was preparing notes for my first classes, I recall, I read somewhere that there were only 30,000 people in the world who still lived as hunter-gatherers, also known as **foraging societies**—approximately the number of full-time students at the university I attended. I would imagine that at present there are none left. That is, there are no groups who rely strictly on collecting naturally occurring resources. The modern industrial world has encroached everywhere, bringing its technology, medicine, and education, as well as its problems and abuses. Populations that acquire some food by hunting and gathering still exist, but they also use foods that they or some other people have grown.

Although access to food, health facilities, and technological innovations can be a positive development, it also has its negative side. There are numerous cases of small groups of foraging peoples who have been moved off their land to make room for farms or roads or logging. Many were relocated to refugee camps or reservations where their culture, not to mention their dignity, was obliterated. In the worst cases, some groups have simply been killed.

So it is probably impossible today to observe a true foraging culture. Fortunately, however, there are still people in these populations who remember the way it used to be. Also, some foraging cultures remained relatively untouched until recently, so we have firsthand anthropological descriptions of them, as well as photographs and films. We can, then, get a glimpse into this way of life.

Why is it so important to learn about foragers? Aside from ethical considerations (which we'll take up in Chapter 15), it is important because the foraging way of life is, in one respect, *the* human subsistence pattern. Even if we take a conservative view and say that human refers to anatomically modern *Homo sapiens* and is thus at most 300,000 years old, humans were foragers for 96 percent of our tenure on earth. We have been food producers for only the last 12,000 years. Thus, all of our basic physical characteristics, cultural abilities, and cultural practices arose within the context of foraging. To adopt a common phrase, we might see foraging as "the human condition," at least in an evolutionary sense.

Among the groups from whom we have gathered knowledge about this way of life are the Arctic peoples from Greenland to Alaska and into Siberia; peoples (often collectively referred to as Pygmies) from the Central African rain forests; the Bushmen of the Kalahari Desert of Angola, Namibia, and Botswana; Native Australians; peoples from the Andaman Islands in the Bay of Bengal; and some Native Americans such as the Shoshone and Cheyenne from North America and several cultures from Tierra del Fuego at the tip of South America (Figure 8.2).

We have already mentioned two characteristics of foraging groups: Such societies tend to lack formalized status and wealth differences and they are generally polytheistic.

foraging society Another name for hunting-and-gathering society.

FIGURE 8.2
A Yahgan hunter from Tierra del Fuego, photographed around 1890. Darwin encountered these people on his famous voyage.

The first trait—the lack of **social stratification** (from "strata" for layers)—is called **egalitarianism**. Although, obviously, some individuals have skills and talents not shared by others, and some have more influence on decision making in certain areas, in foraging societies there are no *recognized, formalized* status differences, and there are most assuredly no differences in access to resources. As explained in the previous chapter, such a society simply cannot afford to have it otherwise. The social order, not to mention the physical welfare of the people, would suffer.

Hunter-gatherer groups tend to be polytheistic, recognizing many supernatural beings with equal or close to equal power and influence over the material world. This is a direct reflection of the world views common to such groups—world views that see the environment as predictable yet unstable, with humans pretty much at its mercy.

Foraging cultures as a whole are fairly small, with individual units averaging about fifty persons—although there is great variation in this from society to society and within a society in different locations and during different seasons. It's usually difficult to support large numbers of people using only what nature provides. But it's not that such people are—as we tend to visualize them—always on the brink of starvation. Indeed, they can be very successful (after all, we lived like this for most of

social stratification The presence of acknowledged differences in social status, political influence, and wealth among the people within a society.

egalitarianism The practice of not recognizing, and even eliminating, differences in social status and wealth.

our species' history) and in fact they often require methods of limiting their birthrates. These may involve prolonged nursing (because lactation interrupts ovulation), a **postpartum sex taboo,** or, more drastically, methods of abortion or even **infanticide.**

The individual units of a foraging society, called **bands,** are usually made up of several related nuclear families probably with some grandparents, siblings, or cousins. Family relationships are, thus, the basis for social organization. Food, for example, is distributed along lines of kinship. Foraging bands tend to be flexible in their membership. In times of scarce resources, the band may contain only a handful of nuclear families. When times are better, several of these small bands may join together to pool their resources and talents. When important resources, or even a single important resource, are found in great abundance, a foraging society's population may number in the thousands, with individual units of hundreds of people. This was the case for the Kwakiutl of Vancouver Island, British Columbia, Canada (about whom more shortly). Among other bountiful resources were the great yearly salmon runs that provided them with huge supplies of meat.

With rare exceptions like the Kwakiutl, foragers are **nomadic.** Rather than stay put, they move around, following the animals and plants they rely on. The degree of movement depends upon the degree of seasonal climatic fluctuation and the response of the resources to it. The Mbuti of the tropical forests of the Republic of the Congo don't have to move around much. There is relatively little seasonal change and there are many species that can be exploited year-round. The Netsilik of the Arctic, on the other hand, travel great distances as they seasonally hunt for seal, caribou, and salmon.

To maintain their egalitarian social organization, foraging societies distribute important resources equally among their members. Distribution is usually along kinship lines and the rules for who gives what to whom can be complex. In the end, however, each family receives an equal share. Every resource is not distributed, however. Plant foods are typically used only by the immediate families of the women who gathered them. Plants are often a more dependable source of food, so they may be used in this way without adversely affecting the welfare of the whole group.

As the above indicates, foraging societies typically display a **division of labor** in which men hunt and women gather. This is practical since hunting is generally the more dangerous and stressful activity and can take hunters away from a home base for extended periods. Since the women carry, give birth to, and care for the society's offspring, it makes sense not to place them and their children at risk or under extreme stress. Beyond this there is no **labor specialization.** Not everyone does everything, but there are no full-time leaders, weapons makers, or food preparers. Within the gender roles noted above, each person does whatever he or she is capable of. The society wouldn't work otherwise.

postpartum sex taboo The practice of prohibiting sex for a certain period of time after a woman gives birth for purposes of limiting the birth rate.

infanticide The killing of infants.

bands Small autonomous groups, usually associated with foraging societies.

nomadic Referring to societies that move from place to place in search of resources or in response to seasonal fluctuations.

division of labor When certain individuals within a society perform certain jobs. Usually refers to the different jobs of men and women.

labor specialization When certain jobs are performed by particular individuals.

FIGURE 8.3
Map of the San area of southern Africa, with the Ju/'hoansi, one of the best-studied groups, indicated. (Data from Lee 1993).

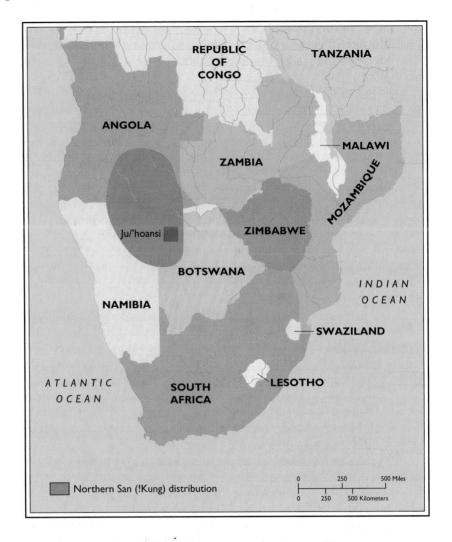

Northern San (!Kung) distribution

Finally, in foraging societies there is no ownership of resources or land. A band may forage in a particular area, but it is not considered their territory. Groups must be able to move around in search of resources. Keeping an outsider off your "property" may someday backfire when your resources fail. There is thus sharing between bands as well as within bands.

All the above are generalizations. Because even recent foragers live, or have lived, in such a diverse array of environments, it is hard to pick one group as a typical example. But one society stands out as giving us a glimpse into this lifestyle. It has been extensively studied, the people were strictly foragers in the fairly recent past, and they are African, so—although they are fully modern human beings—many of their environmental situations and food resources are similar to those of many humans throughout much of our evolutionary history. These are the so-called "Bushmen" of Angola, Namibia, and Botswana (Figure 8.3).

FIGURE 8.4
A San woman and her daughter showing typical physical features. The mother is instructing the girl in the preparation of mongongo nuts, an important food source.

The term "Bushmen" was applied to these people by the Dutch settlers of South Africa and carries racist connotations. The name San is often applied to this group as a whole, referring to a language family noted for its use of click sounds. Perhaps the best-known population within the San has traditionally been called !Kung, also a language family reference. The ! denotes a click sound, one of four in their language. Among these peoples, the most extensively studied are a group from Namibia and Botswana who call themselves the Ju/'hoansi (meaning "genuine people"). The / is another click sound but an acceptable pronunciation would be zhut-wasi. For our purposes here (in part because it's less awkward for English speakers), I'll use San and let the following description, taken largely from studies of the Ju/'hoansi, serve as a generalization for the whole group. I'll also describe them using what we call the "ethnographic present," speaking in the present tense about their lives as foragers, even though, as we'll discuss later, their lives today are actually much different.

There are about 80,000 San in the Kalahari Desert. The Kalahari is not, by the way, technically a desert because for several months of the year it has a good deal of rain. There is archaeological and biological evidence that the San and related peoples have lived in this area for about 11,000 years and that they were once more widely spread over the continent.

The San have a characteristic set of physical features (Figure 8.4). They are short people, the men averaging around 5 feet and the women a little under. Their skin is a reddish brown and their facial features are youthful looking, even those of the elderly. Their hair has been referred to as "peppercorn" because it grows in tightly curled tufts. The eyes of many of the San have the shape, sometimes called "almond shaped," that we associate with people from East Asia.

The San live in small bands that average ten to thirty people. Their camps, made up of grass huts, are temporary because the San are regularly on the move in search of food and, especially, water. The inhabitants of a camp are usually related—a "chain of sibs and spouses," as anthropologist Richard Lee puts it. Membership in a band, however, changes with the seasons and for reasons such as internal conflicts, commonly solved by one family's moving away. A camp, as Lee says, is made up of a group of families that "work well together" (Figure 8.5).

Most of the San's food comes from some 100 species of plants recognized as edible and gathered by the women. One of the most popular foods is the mongongo nut, a good source of protein and other nutrients. Game, hunted by the men, are usually ungulates (hoofed animals), which they bring down with poison-tipped arrows.

While we tend to think of such a way of life as harsh and unstable, the reality is usually quite different. Certainly nature can seem whimsical, and unforeseen environmental changes can mean the difference between life and death. But when things are going as planned, a foraging group actually spends less time than one would imagine in basic subsistence. The San, for example, can acquire the necessary calories by working 20 hours per adult per week. Not bad when compared to the 35- to 40-hour work week many of us consider normal.

The San are egalitarian. There are, for example, no formal leaders. There are individuals who are more important in terms of such things as settling conflicts or making decisions about where to hunt, gather, or move. But these individuals lead by influence and suggestion rather than by power and command. The San don't consider themselves led by anyone. One San, in response to a request to identify his group's leader, is reputed to have responded that they were *all* leaders. As a logical part of this, neither sex is seen as superior to the other.

Though plant foods are, because of their relative abundance, generally kept by the gatherer's family, great pains are taken to be sure that meat is evenly shared. Although the hunter whose arrow killed the animal is said to "own" the meat, this merely means that he is responsible for beginning the distribution, which is done according to kinship lines. The concept of sharing of meat and even of the arrows used to acquire meat is of central importance to the San's social structure.

The idea of equality with regard to meat is so important that the San have a way to ensure that a hunter who has supplied the camp with a fine, meaty animal will not feel in any way superior or even praiseworthy. The people of the camp, rather than showing their joy at the successful hunt, make negative and derisive comments about the quality of the ani-

FIGURE 8.5
A San campsite among mongongo nut trees with huts used as windscreens and for storage. The people spend most of their time outside.

mal killed. Richard Lee calls this "insulting the meat." Some men are bound to be better, more successful hunters than others, and this social leveling device covers up a natural inequality.

As is the general case for foraging peoples, the majority of San men, about 93 percent in one sample, have just one wife. They practice **monogamy**. But a small number, around 5 percent from the same sample, have two or three wives. They practice **polygyny**. All the men involved in polygynous marriages are healers, men possessed of special powers that allow them to cure illness (Figure 8.6). This is one of the few symbols of differential status seen among the San. Women, by the way, may also be healers, but these women do not seem to have any special privileges.

San religion is polytheistic. There are two very important, powerful gods who are largely responsible for the creation of the world and for keeping it running. There are also lots of individual spirits, as well as the ghosts of deceased people, who tend to be malevolent. There is also the healing power, said to be a substance possessed by the healers that they can call up through a dance. It causes them to go into a trance during which they are able to cure illnesses and speak with the ghosts of the dead.

The last trait of foragers I noted was their lack of a concept of land and resource ownership. This is true for the San. It's not that each band of San roam wherever they want. Each band has an area in which it normally hunts and gathers, and this area is acknowledged by other bands. If, however, the home range of one band runs out of a resource—say, if their water hole dries up or becomes contaminated—that group may use

malevolent
злобный, недоброжелательный
roam
странствуют

monogamy The marriage unit made up of only one husband and one wife.

polygyny Where the marriage unit includes multiple wives.

FIGURE 8.6
A San healer (left) in a trance tries to discover the cause of the other man's illness.

the water hole normally used by another band. They simply ask permission to do so. Permission is always granted—after all, the tables may be turned next time. So it's not technically a territory, but more a matter of courtesy, functioning to promote an egalitarianism among bands as well as within them.

As you can imagine, there is a good deal of variation from one foraging population to the next, depending upon the specific nature of the environment in which they live and their specific cultural history. But all exhibit more or less the basic traits listed. The study and understanding of any of these groups gives us a picture of how we existed for most of our evolutionary history, keeping in mind that this picture is limited because all the foragers we have been able to study are fully modern. Still, we can say that everything our species is today stems from the foraging lifestyle.

So it was for all our ancestors until about 12,000 years ago. Then began, in a few populations, what has been termed a "revolution." Not one of riots and warfare, but a peaceful one, a change from within a group's own cultural system. This change altered everything that came after. The revolution was that some people began to produce, rather than collect, their food.

FOOD-PRODUCING SOCIETIES

The change to food producing, of course, was not abrupt. Major changes in any aspect of culture seldom come about instantly. No one simply picked up some seeds, planted them, and invented farming one day. The shift to food producing came about gradually. We are left, however, with the impression that it was rapid because our evidence is in the form of remains from the past, and such remains rarely show all the steps involved in a change.

Evidence for the transition to food producing comes in two types. First, there are artifacts related to the use of domestic plants, things like stones used to grind grain, pottery used to store it (sometimes still containing some ancient grains), or instruments used to harvest plants. I will go into more detail about the archaeological aspects of this in Chapter 10. The second type of evidence comes from our knowledge of the biological differences between wild and domestic plants and animals. By comparing, say, wild ungulates with domestic cattle or wild grasses with familiar wheats, oats, and maize (what Americans call "corn"), we can observe certain distinctions in such things as bone structure of animals and seed characteristics of plants. Looking into the past, we search for the earliest evidence of organisms possessing these features (Figure 8.7).

Transition to Food Production

Common sense and what we understand about the lives of foragers tells us that this cultural transition must have begun in some populations long before we actually find hard evidence for it. Foragers are intimately familiar with the living things in their environments. They must understand the behavior of animals and the life cycle of plants in order to survive. People had probably understood for thousands of years that plants grow from seeds and that some animals can be manipulated. Modern Lapps from Arctic Scandinavia and Russia, for example, control wild herds of reindeer but have not actually domesticated them in the sense of

FIGURE 8.7

A series of maize cobs from Tehuacán, Mexico. The cob on the left is dated at 5000 years ago and is barely an inch long with only eight rows of six to nine kernels each. The one on the right is a modern variety with hundreds of kernels.

conducting selective breeding for desired characteristics (Figure 8.8). Their control is based on an understanding of the behavior of those creatures—an understanding that all foragers possess about the animals they hunt or trap. Human ancestors may well have acted in a similar way with another animal or have experimented with planting seeds or tending an area where an important plant grew.

The real question in evolutionary perspective is not so much how they switched to producing food, but *why.* If you were to present the idea of full-scale farming or herding to a real group of foragers, they might find the idea rather strange, if not actually humorous. "Why," they might ask, "should we go to all that trouble when the animals and plants we eat are right out there?" This is a good question, because remember, when things are going normally, foraging populations tend not to spend nearly as much time as we once imagined in their basic subsistence activities.

We are, in fact, still trying to account for the changeover to food producing in those areas where it first occurred. One proposed explanation deals with the retreat of the Pleistocene ice sheets and the attendant climatic alterations that occurred around 12,000 years ago. Large areas of land underwent substantial ecological change. Where once people living in cold areas near the glaciers subsisted primarily from big-game hunting, now they had access to the greater variety of foods characteristic of habitats not in the grip of the ice. We know from archaeological evidence that people in such areas developed ways of exploiting all the new food

FIGURE 8.8
Lapp with reindeer. The Lapps traditionally followed the reindeer herds on their migrations. Sometimes the people captured a male and castrated him to make him more docile, then led him where they wanted to go so that the rest of the herd would follow.

docile – покрушивое

sources at their disposal. We call this **intensive foraging.** It may have been in such newly rich environments that people became extremely knowledgeable about the biology of plants and animals and began to use that knowledge for domesticating them.

But wouldn't such a climatic change, with an increase in possible food sources, just make hunting and gathering easier and more reliable? Food producing would seem even less desirable in such an environment. Anyway, glacial retreats were nothing new. They had occurred between glacial advances many times before. What was different 12,000 years ago?

One difference was population. As people improved their abilities to find food and deal with environmental pressures, populations increased. Estimates vary, but around 12,000 years ago there may have been something like 10 million people in the world, mostly in the Old World. That seems small by our standards, when there are about 6 *billion* of us. But twelve millennia ago, considering that people were relying pretty much on naturally occurring resources, a large and increasing population could put a good deal of pressure on some resources in a particular environment. Perhaps such population pressure caused some groups to try to use their knowledge of plants and animals in an attempt to gain more control over food resources.

intensive foraging Hunting and gathering in an environment that provides a very wide range of food resources.

There is a problem with this model as well, at least on the surface. The early centers of farming, such as the Fertile Crescent of Southwest Asia, Southeast Asia, and Central America, were fairly rich in wild plants and animals. Perhaps, as archaeologist Kent Flannery has suggested, farming began at the edges of these rich areas. Groups pushed out of the optimal areas by a rapidly expanding population found themselves in locations that were marginal with regard to wild food sources. One answer to this problem for such groups was to apply their knowledge of wild species to gain control over them and thus enhance their productivity and reliability.

Whatever the specific reasons for the transition to food production—and they probably differ somewhat in each area where it occurred independently—the new idea spread rapidly and brought with it other ecological and cultural changes that altered forever the nature of our relationship with the environment and with one another.

Horticulture

There are, within the food-producing category, three basic subsistence patterns: **horticulture, agriculture,** and **pastoralism.** Horticulture refers to societies that focus on farming and use only human labor and simple tools such as a digging stick or a hoe (Figure 8.9). It does not, in other words, include animal or mechanical labor or more complex technologies such as plows and fertilizers. As we did for foragers, we may describe some of the characteristics we can expect to find among horticultural groups.

Examples of horticultural societies are many of the indigenous groups of the Amazon rain forests, the forests of Central Africa and Southeast Asia, and the highlands of New Guinea.

Horticulturalists tend to live in larger groups than foragers. The greater control over at least some of their food sources and the surplus that results allows them to support a greater number of individuals. Their populations are also more **sedentary,** that is, they can stay in one area for longer periods of time since the people can grow food where they *are* rather than having to go where the food is. Population size tends to be more stable than in foraging groups because there is less seasonal fluctuation in resource availability. Though populations are larger than among foragers, groups are still organized around kinship. They are made up of several nuclear families, most of whom are probably related. A striking feature of many horticultural groups is that their nuclear families are polygynous—men have several wives. (Marriage patterns and other aspects of kinship will be covered in Chapter 9.)

Horticultural groups maintain an essentially egalitarian outlook but because there is now the possibility of surpluses and because there are more people and thus more need for formal organization, we see in these groups the beginnings of leaders and labor specialists, though these are often part-time. For example, a man is not, say, always a leader in battle,

horticulture Farming using human labor and simple tools.

agriculture Farming using animal or mechanical labor and complex technologies.

pastoralism The subsistence pattern characterized by an emphasis on herding animals.

sedentary A human settlement pattern in which people largely stay in one place year-round, although some members of the population may still be mobile in the search for food and raw materials.

FIGURE 8.9
A woman from the Mount Hagen region of Papua, New Guinea uses a digging stick to plant seeds.

or always a healer. Most of the time he is a farmer and hunter like everyone else. He takes on his specialized role when needed.

We also see in horticultural societies the beginning of the concept of ownership, on both the family and population levels. Land on which plants are cultivated may be the property of a family, as are the plants themselves. A herd of animals, for example the pigs ubiquitous to horticultural groups in highland New Guinea, are likewise owned. Despite this, though, members of horticultural societies still work for a common good, and the products of their labors, although family owned, are nonetheless shared within the group. The techniques for sharing them, as we will see, are more complex than among foragers.

Horticultural societies also recognize the concept of territory. With growing control over food resources, there is less need to share resources on an intergroup basis—say, between villages within a society—and more need to protect one's own resources. Indeed, there is an idea that the advent of farming was also the advent of war (defined as conflict between populations or between groups within a population). Put bluntly, when one society or unit within a society had something another did not, the have-nots tried to take it away and the haves tried to keep it (Figure 8.10).

Indeed, there is an association between warfare and horticulture. Many horticultural societies live in rain forests, and such areas—although they have more species of living organisms than any other land ecosystems on earth—have certain important limitations. There are so many species that no individual species are found in abundance. With reference

FIGURE 8.10
A group of Yąnomamö in the Amazon rain forest prepares for a raid against an enemy village, the purposes of which are the acquisition of land for farming and hunting and, perhaps, wives (see Chapter 13).

to human food sources, there are few large animals in the rain forests. Finally, rain forest soil is not particularly fertile. The rain leaches out nutrients fairly quickly, and the abundance of living creatures means that nutrients get recycled quickly and don't have a chance to build up, as they do in temperate climates where there is an annual leaf fall and where biological processes slow down in winter. As a result, societies in rain forests, especially those that farm and so build up their populations and remain somewhat sedentary, can overexploit natural resources, forcing them to shift areas of cultivation as natural nutrients are depleted. This can lead to tensions over land and food, which in turn can lead to war.

Finally, horticulturalists, like foragers, tend to be polytheistic. But unlike the case with foragers, the supernatural beings tend to be arranged in a hierarchy. Some, in other words, are more powerful and important than others. This seems to reflect the people's growing control over nature. They may not see themselves as having mastered nature (as do, for example, modern industrial societies), so natural phenomena are still explained as under the influence of supernatural beings, whom humans must be aware of and propitiate. The most important supernatural beings, however, are often those with direct connections to humans—humanlike deities that gave rise to and control the lives of people, or, perhaps, the spirits or ghosts of the dead.

Agriculture

Agricultural societies are so defined because they use animal (or, in recent history, mechanical) labor and more-complex tools like the plow. Agriculture is found in areas that require more-complex technologies in order to grow plants in large, concentrated plots. Remember, any farming in-

FIGURE 8.11
A farmer with his oxen plowing a field in Egypt. The remains of the Colossi of Memnon are in the background. The great civilization of ancient Egypt was made possible by the use of agriculture.

volves growing plants under conditions in which they don't normally grow in the wild (Figure 8.11). Thus, some farmers need plows to break up compacted, rocky soil and draft animals to pull those plows. Irrigation systems and fertilizers (often the manure of the draft animals) are also often needed to manipulate wild species.

Due to even greater control over plant food sources, groups with this subsistence pattern can support greater numbers of people than can horticulturalists. Agricultural populations, quite expectedly, are more stable and sedentary, tied to the land they have cultivated and on which they depend.

With surpluses virtually ensured, there can be full-time labor specialists—not everyone has to devote all their time to getting food. If I'm good at growing wheat, I can concentrate on that and trade my surplus produce (what's left after I've supplied my family's needs) to, say, the family that makes plows in exchange for one of the tools. There are also those whose full-time specialty is carrying out religious rituals, healing, or providing military or political leadership. With more than enough food to go around, such specialization is possible. With the great numbers of people involved and the growing complexity of social and economic interactions, such specialization is necessary.

And with surplus and labor specialization, some people inevitably accumulate more resources than others. Wealth and power are usually found in the same hands. Thus, we see a formal social stratification. Obviously, a central concept in such situations is ownership of one's wealth.

Religion in agricultural societies may still be polytheistic, as with the complex pantheon of ancient Egypt, but if so the deities are hierarchical,

FIGURE 8.12

Amun-Re, king of the gods (left), and Horus, lord of heaven, who shared divinity with the pharoah. Among the many other gods of ancient Egypt were Thoth, god of the moon, time, and healing; Anubis, embalming; Min, fertility; Seth, violence; Nut, the sky; Geb, the earth; Shu, the air; Ptah, the creator of all things; Hapi, the Nile; and Bes, the household.

some having greater importance than others, and there are usually direct human connections to the most powerful (Figure 8.12). As social situations become increasingly complex, and with a greater sense of control over food resources, the tendency was toward monotheism, a belief in one all-powerful god and, thus, a reflection of the power of humans over nature. This is what we see in Judaism, Christianity, and Islam, all of which arose in agricultural societies in Southwest Asia.

In agricultural societies that evolved to be very complex and very populous, we see one of the important results of the so-called farming revolution. At some point of complexity, there is a need for a centrally located government and a center for economic transactions. In other words, cities developed. The term **civilization**, although often used as a value judgment, literally means "city making," and refers to urbanized societies and their characteristic features (Figure 8.13).

For example, with all the information about trade transactions, ownership, and social and economic positions that such a society needs to keep track of, forms of recordkeeping arose, evolving eventually into writing. It is no surprise that some of the earliest examples of writing are

civilization Cultures with an agricultural surplus, social stratification, labor specialization, a formal government, rule by power, monumental construction projects, and a system of recordkeeping.

FIGURE 8.13
A New World city, the spectacular ruins of the Inca fortress city now called Machu Picchu (the original name is unknown) 8000 feet up in the Peruvian Andes. This site was only discovered in 1911.

associated with cities in Southwest Asia, where farming may have first developed (Figure 8.14).

There would also have been a need for public works, such as roads from outlying farming areas into the urban center. Monumental structures are also found early on. Temples, statuary, pyramids, and the like all represent the centralization of political and religious power, and they would not be possible without the release of large numbers of laborers from basic subsistence activities. Defensive facilities—walls, moats, and fortresses—and standing armies are also associated with urban centers.

Finally, the need to improve the tools on which the success of such systems is based gives rise to another major cultural innovation associated with civilization. This is metallurgy, the extraction and working of natural metals. Cities, centralized governments, writing, monumental

183

FIGURE 8.14
A clay tablet from Mesopotamia dated at about 5000 years ago. The text, written in what is called cuneiform (Latin for "wedge-shaped" referring to the shape of the impressions), records the sale of a slave.

and public works, a military, and metallurgy all follow from an economy based on intensive agriculture.

Now, keeping in mind our themes of adaptation and evolution, some questions arise: Why are some people horticulturalists and some agriculturalists? Is agriculture better? Is it a more advanced form and thus a logical evolutionary outcome? Do all people who practice horticulture eventually become agriculturalists as soon as they acquire the skills?

The general answer is that a group of people uses the subsistence pattern that works for them under existing environmental conditions—keeping in mind from Figure 7.4 that the "environment" to which a society responds includes both natural and cultural factors.

Most horticultural societies live in the tropical forests, areas with sufficient rainfall, abundant useful plant species, and year-round sun and warmth. People who cultivate in such areas don't require more complex technology. On the other hand, one tends to find agriculture in areas where natural conditions must be manipulated to grow plants. These are places where the ground must be turned and broken to prepare it for planting, where rainfall is not always enough to nourish plants that are not in their natural growing conditions, and where the soil's nutrients may have to be augmented. A society, in other words, does what it must to survive. Doing more would be a waste of energy.

To be sure, when you acquire the skills and technologies necessary to grow plants in the latter situation, you can feed large numbers of people and produce large surpluses. In that sense, agriculture is "better." But there is no inexorable trend toward it. In some areas, like the tropical forests, agricultural techniques would not increase production anyway.

There are negative aspects to agriculture as well, for with such a specific set of circumstances necessary for successful subsistence, more can go wrong. If, for example, something happens to draft animals, if there is not even enough rain to channel through irrigation ditches, if a disease or insect infestation kills off the few species of plants grown—such events can have devastating effects on a society's ability to feed itself. Because societies that practice intensive agriculture have often altered their natural environment, eliminating some native plant and animal species, there may be few alternative sources of food available.

Other problems arise as well. Overall nutrition may be adversely affected because of the smaller variety of foods eaten. Far more energy is expended in agricultural societies than in foraging societies for the same nutritional results. It is necessary to store food, and stored food is prone to attract vermin that may carry diseases. Crowded populations make epidemics possible and pose problems of sanitation and waste removal. Deep socioeconomic differences may lead to class conflicts.

When everything is working well, agriculture can lead to larger populations and give people longer, more stable lives. But it is also prone to disruption much more easily than subsistence by foraging. So there is no overall better or worse way of obtaining one's food. There is just what works for a particular group in a particular environment at a particular point in its history.

Many anthropologists list **industrialism** as a subsistence pattern. This is generally defined as a system based on mechanical rather than biological power. There are obvious social and economic ramifications of such a system. Populations are very large; there is extreme labor specialization; the emphasis is on the individual, rather than the family, as the unit of labor; governmental systems become very complex; and secular laws take over for religious beliefs as reflections of world view and behavioral norms.

Industrial societies are different enough from the other types we've examined that they might be considered a separate and unique subsistence pattern. But, for a general overview, I tend to stick with the food theme and categorize societies like ours in North America as agricultural. Despite our industrial base, and despite the fact that under 3 percent of the United States population live on farms, our subsistence is still based on agriculture. Our society still exhibits the general set of characteristics discussed for agriculturalists. Industrialism is just a *very complex* form of that subsistence pattern.

industrialism Sometimes recognized as a subsistence pattern characterized by a focus on mechanical sources of energy and food production by a small percentage of the population.

FIGURE 8.15
The Masai of East Africa build *kraals* of thornbush to protect their cattle, goats (lower center), and homes from lions and leopards at night. The word *kraal* is possibly a borrowing from the Portuguese and Spanish and thus related to the English *corral*.

Pastoralism

Pastoralism is subsistence based on the herding of animals. Certainly, nearly all farmers have some domestic animals for food or labor or both, and pastoralists may well do some hunting, gathering, or even farming. But pastoralists are those whose herds are the basis for their subsistence and whose world view and cultural system is built around this pattern. Examples are the cattle herders of the dry savannas of East Africa (Figure 8.15) and the Indian subcontinent, sheep and goat herders from Southwest Asia, and yak herders on the Tibetan Plateau.

Most pastoralists are nomadic—the people go where there is food for their animals. They are egalitarian with regard to use of pastureland within their group but territorial with regard to other populations. Within pastoral societies there is socioeconomic stratification based largely on the number of animals owned. Leadership is present but is rather vague with regard to how it is achieved and who has it. It is not formalized and so is probably similar to the situation of informal influence found among foragers.

Labor is divided by sex, with the men being largely responsible for the care of the animal herds and the women handling household tasks and childrearing. In some pastoral societies, however, women have a say in whether, to whom, and for how much to sell animals. Beyond this, there is no labor specialization.

Pastoralists' religions tend to involve ancestor worship. Their supernatural world is populated by the spirits of the dead. This hints at an emphasis on human control and on a general cultural conservatism. One pleases the spirits of the dead by doing things in a traditional way, the way *they* would have.

Pastoralists are found in areas unsuitable for other subsistence activities, areas where it would be hard to grow anything and where the wild plants are primarily grasses, which don't provide humans with much nutrition but are fine for ungulates that can digest cellulose. The animals turn the plant nutrients into milk products, blood, and, less often, meat for human consumption.

Now, once a group of people has collected or produced the food they need, once they have the tools to get and process that food and to take care of other technological concerns, and once they can provide all the services necessary to maintain their social structure—how do all these resources get to the people who need them? How do they make sure that the resources are distributed? Does everyone share equally? Is there any correlation between distribution of goods and services and type of subsistence pattern?

SOME BASIC ECONOMICS

How do *you* go about getting the goods and services you need? Because you provide society with certain goods you help manufacture or services you perform, you receive **money, a symbolic representation of some value equivalent**. This you exchange with other individuals for the goods and services they produce. The quality and quantity of the goods and services you can purchase depends on the amount of money you can spend, which in turn depends on how much society values your services or the goods you help produce. This is all familiar and seems perfectly logical; but is there any other way?

Let's assume you live in a family with two working parents and two siblings. Within your family, goods and services are distributed in a different fashion. Your parents bring home money they earn, which is used to purchase food and pay for housing. Each also performs certain jobs around the household. They certainly don't expect each other, you, or your sibs to repay them in kind or equivalence. No one is keeping a ledger of all the transactions to make sure things balance out. Everyone contributes and receives in return only whatever contributions other family members are capable of providing (depending on their age, health, and occupational status) as well as the physical and emotional security that family membership provides.

money Symbolic representation of wealth. Used for exchange in place of the exchange of actual products or services.

This kind of giving and taking of goods and services without expectation of immediate and equivalent return is called **general reciprocity**. It's what happens within your family—and it's what happens within foraging societies. Such societies are, in fact, made up of individual units that are often themselves small family groups. Moreover, since the only efficient way to run a population with a foraging subsistence is to practice egalitarianism, general reciprocity is the only method of distribution that makes sense for these groups. Any recognition of what we might call "an imbalance of trade" would break up the equality of wealth and status that is so vital for foraging peoples.

A group may also practice **balanced reciprocity, the exchange of goods and services with the clear expectation of the relatively immediate return of something of agreed-on equivalent value**. In the earlier example, when I traded some of my surplus wheat for a plow someone else made, that was balanced reciprocity. This kind of system tends to be found in horticultural and agricultural societies with their larger communities, surpluses, labor specialists, and greater need to exchange goods and services in order to survive.

An example of balanced reciprocity exists within North American industrial society: gift giving at birthdays and other important holidays. Despite the ethic we profess that "giving is better than receiving" and "it's the thought that counts," we in fact go through all sorts of mental trauma worrying about how much to spend on so-and-so's gift so it won't be any more or less expensive than the one we last received or next expect to receive from that person. It's neither explicit nor a formal part of our economy, but it's balanced reciprocity just the same.

This also shows that a society may practice several of the resource distribution types we're discussing, depending on the people involved. The Mbuti, for example, foraging peoples of Central Africa, practice general reciprocity among themselves, but they also carry on trade with outside farmers conducted by balanced reciprocity.

When a society gets so large and the economic transactions within it so complex that the trading of actual items and services becomes difficult, symbolic representations of the value of resources may be used. These can be traded in place of actual products so long as the system is part of the culture as a whole and there is some mechanism for determining and maintaining the value equivalents. This symbolic representation, of course, is money, and a system that uses money is called a **market system**. A market system is, in a sense, balanced reciprocity with symbols and is found in intensive agricultural and industrial societies.

Between systems that maintain overall egalitarianism and those that recognize and support socioeconomic stratification is a system of distribution that attempts to level out inherent inequalities. When the goods and services within a population are not distributed on an equal basis, this mechanism tries to counteract that. It's called **redistribution**. Surpluses are collected under the direction of some governing body, perhaps

---

general reciprocity Giving with no expectation of equivalent return.

balanced reciprocity Giving with expectation of equivalent return.

market system Where money is used for exchange in place of the actual exchange of goods and services.

redistribution Where surplus goods are collected centrally and then given out to those persons in need of them.

FIGURE 8.16

In this artist's rendering, guests arrive in their huge, elaborately decorated canoes for a *potlatch,* a feast of extravagant giving that seems to have served as a redistribution system.

an individual, and then redistributed according to the needs of the recipients. Such a system is common among horticulturalists. The larger number of people in some of these societies and the existence of surpluses ensures that wealth will not be evenly distributed. At the same time, some horticultural societies are still small enough and closely related enough to want to maintain an egalitarian outlook. A system of redistribution addresses this need, using some social mechanism—a feast perhaps—to gather and dole out surplus wealth. (We'll look at an example from highland New Guinea in Chapter 13.)

Perhaps the most famous example of a large-scale redistribution system comes not from a horticultural society but from a foraging one. (This is also a good example of an exception to the general correlations we've been discussing.) The Kwakiutl of British Columbia, mentioned earlier, were unusual for foragers in that they had a large overall population with large, fairly sedentary communities. This is because of the abundance of natural resources, especially the annual salmon runs (where, in essence, the food came to *them*). The Kwakiutl would hold periodic feasts called *potlatches,* the immediate point of which was for the host to try to give away, or even destroy, more food and other goods than any of his rivals (Figure 8.16). If the host was getting behind, he might even burn down his own house as the ultimate display of his wealth. Early anthropologists

CONTEMPORARY ISSUES

Is There a World Population Crisis That Is Putting Pressure on Food and Other Resources?

A major influence on Darwin's thinking was the English economist Thomas Malthus (1766–1834). In *An Essay on the Principle of Population* (1789), he wrote "Population, when unchecked, increases in a geometrical ratio. Subsistence increases only in an arithmetical ratio. . . . I can see no way by which man can escape from the weight of this law which pervades all animate nature." Malthus predicted famine and war if humans continued the population increase that even he in his day perceived. He should only have known.

Since Malthus's time, the human population has increased nearly sixfold and, given the war, famine, and environmental degradation we see around us, we have every reason to believe that Malthus was right and that, with our current 1.5 percent per year population increase, we will eventually run out of something—most likely food, but possibly also water, land, clean air, or patience with one

another—and our species and its world will be in for some very bad times indeed. The human species has even been likened to a cancer that grows uncontrolled, spreads, and eventually destroys its environment.

So, in theory, it looks as if the answer to the question in the title of this feature is yes (see also Chapter 16). But we don't always really see this problem firsthand, and so we don't always acknowledge it or respond to it in practical ways.

In fact, it is tempting to those of us in the developed West to place the blame for rampant growth on the developing countries of Latin America, Africa, and Asia, where some fertility rates (the number of children a typical woman has during her lifetime) have been as high as eight. Indeed, nearly every night on the TV news, or in ads for charitable organizations, we are shown starving people in those countries. We tend to

were puzzled by this seemingly wasteful behavior. Upon closer examination, however, it makes sense.

The Kwakiutl, because of their large populations and abundant resources, moved away from the strict egalitarianism of foragers. Still, they were a single, integrated society and were thus concerned about inequalities among their people. In this, they resemble horticulturalists. Specifically, annual fluctuations in the salmon migrations and in the availability of wild plant foods led to some Kwakiutl villages having more food than others. The potlatch, it turns out, was a redistribution system. During the giving away of surpluses by the haves, the have-nots tended to receive in the long run, making up for their deficiencies.

Moreover, the potlatch system was tied up with status seeking (which was the immediate motivation for it), so there was continual pressure to produce as much as possible so one could give away more at the next potlatch. The result benefited the entire population.

You might, of course, be wondering why the Kwakiutl went to such see no evidence of a population problem here in North America (the infertility business is booming here now) and comfortably see the Malthusian predictions as only affecting *other* countries. *We* have enough food. If only *they* would change, the problem could be solved.

But in fact, many people *are* changing. In some undeveloped and developing nations, frequent birth has been traditionally promoted in order to make up for high infant mortality and high mortality rates in general. But many developing countries are experiencing a fairly rapid decline in birthrates, not as a result of their becoming more like the West but from having better education about and access to contraceptive technology. People in many of those countries realized the problems inherent in overpopulation but lacked the means to address them. In Thailand, to give just one example, fertility dropped by 50 percent from 1975 to 1987.

It is rather arrogant to think that *we* are not part of the problem. We do live, as the cliché says, in a global village. All parts of the world are now interrelated in every way imaginable. Global ecological effects are well known. Politics and economics are no different. *Every* new human, no matter where they live, will help use up the world's food, water, and energy resources, and will contribute to the buildup of waste products. *Every* new human adds to the population density of the world and encourages the further spread of people with its resultant alteration of environments.

Aspects of the population problem are still, to be sure, being debated. There are arguments as to how many people the planet could ideally support, as well as arguments as to how best to (or if it is even possible to) bring about those ideal conditions. It has been argued, for example, that there *is* enough food but that, for various reasons, it does not get equitably distributed. But, that there *is* a population problem, and thus a resource problem, is undeniable. And to think that it is not *everyone's* concern is complacent at best.

extremes, even if the explanation makes economic sense in the end. Why not just decide that everyone will contribute some of their surplus, which will then be collected by a leader of some sort who then determines who needs it and passes it out? The potlatch is a good example of the complexity of any cultural system. Although the potlatch can be interpreted economically, and although it became a vital part of Kwakiutl culture because it worked economically, the origin of the practice is submerged within the whole of the Kwakiutl world view, which, you recall, involves not only their present but their past history as well. It is probably impossible to reconstruct the origin of the idea, which may have begun for different reasons than those that now motivate it.

A second example of a redistribution system comes from within a market economy, and also provides a glimpse into the complexities of cultural systems. In North America we live in a stratified society but we consider some inequities to be unacceptable. Part of our tax money is used to provide goods and services to those who cannot otherwise afford them. On the whole it works well, but this redistribution system itself involves inequities, and these inequities demonstrate the power of a whole cultural system and the world view that generates it.

As a stratified society, we recognize differences in status and wealth and acknowledge them within the system. One way in which our system supports such strata is through our complex laws of ownership, protecting what we consider the rights of individuals to possess property and wealth and to keep it. So pervasive is this concept that it is difficult to define what constitutes "surplus" to a particular person. Thus, figuring out just what part of a person's wealth goes into taxes, especially income tax, is incredibly complex. In fact, it turns out that owning things is given so much credit in this society that the ownership of something can actually allow you to contribute less of your income to the redistribution pool. Our intent may be in keeping with certain ethical precepts, but this particular mechanism has inconsistencies with regard to our whole cultural system.

Finally, we may define some more terms for ideas we've been discussing. These refer to the degree to which a society is stratified. Egalitarianism—the absence of formalized differences in status and wealth—has been covered at length. Again, it is common to foraging societies. Horticultural societies are often considered **rank** societies. This means that they try to eliminate differences in wealth but do so with a redistribution system that necessarily must recognize differences in status, although temporary ones. That is, persons in charge of redistributing the surplus are those who, at the moment, have the most of it, and thus are recognized as having a differential status. From the western Pacific comes the name we use for such temporarily powerful people—"big men." One attempts to become a big man by accumulating wealth, but that status essentially gives one the opportunity and obligation to give away some of that wealth to those who need it.

North American society is an example of a **class** system. It recognizes and builds into the system formal differences in both status and wealth. A class system, however, is open. That is, an individual has the opportunity to acquire more wealth and status and move to a higher stratum. Or, of course, one can also lose both and move to a lower stratum.

Another system freezes strata. In these societies, you are born into a socioeconomic layer and stay there. Access to resources, occupational opportunities, and potential marriage partners are all decided by birth as well. This is a **caste** system. The best-known example is perhaps that of India.

Food acquisition and distribution may now provide us with a basis for discussing all other areas of cultural variation. Let's begin with the following consideration: If you were a San hunter who had brought back to camp a nice fat antelope you had killed, you would distribute the meat according to kinship. That is, you would give some meat to certain of

rank Refers to a society that strives for equal distribution of goods and services but that achieves this through the use of recognized status differences.

class A system of socioeconomic stratification where the strata are open and a person may move to a different stratum.

caste A system of socioeconomic stratification where strata are closed and a person's membership is determined at birth.

your relatives, who would give some to certain of their relatives, and so on until everyone had their share. Sounds easy enough. Everyone knows who's related to whom and how. Kinship is basic biology. Or is it? In the next chapter, I'll show you how, in some societies, your uncle is the same as your father, and your cousin is the same as your brother.

SUMMARY

Perhaps the most important relationships between a species and its environment focus on the processes of food acquisition. For humans, the ways in which societies acquire their food—their subsistence patterns— are so central that we may use them to categorize types of cultures. Thus, we speak of a society as food collecting or food producing. A synonym for the former is foraging. Within the latter are the subcategories of horticulture, agriculture, pastoralism, and industrialism.

Many, if not most, of the other basic features of a cultural system can be seen as more or less related to subsistence pattern. Generalizations are possible with regard to things like mobility, population size, basic economics, social stratification, labor specialization, kinship, and religion.

NOTES, REFERENCES, AND READINGS

Information on the San can be found in Richard Lee's *The Dobe Ju/'hoansi.* It includes his famous and delightful article, "Eating Christmas in the Kalahari," about the practice of "insulting the meat." Also included is an annotated list of films about the San. One of the most famous of these is "The Hunters" by John Marshall, an excellent look at San life, but one which also overemphasizes hunting and gives the impression that foraging life is unstable and the people often on the verge of starvation.

For more on Lysenko see "A Hearing for Vavilov" by Stephen Jay Gould in *Hen's Teeth and Horse's Toes.*

Hypotheses on the origins of farming are discussed at length in Ken Feder's and my *Human Antiquity,* and the archaeological evidence in Feder's *The Past in Perspective.*

A good look at a horticultural society, and one characterized by warfare, is Napoleon Chagnon's *Yąnomamö,* fourth edition.

The Kwakiutl potlatch is described and interpreted by Marvin Harris in his famous and provocative book *Cows, Pigs, Wars and Witches: The Riddles of Culture.* A more traditional interpretation is Ruth Benedict's in *Patterns of Culture.*

Two good articles on the population crisis are "Ten Myths of Population" by Joel Cohen in the April 1996 issue of *Discover,* and "The Fertility Decline in Developing Countries" by Bryant Robey et al. in the December 1993 *Scientific American.*

9

NATURE OF THE GROUP

Arranging Our Families and Organizing Our People

One of the biggest problems facing the anthropologist is the question of **ethnocentrism**. People are all ethnocentric, which means we feel our particular cultural system is the "correct" one and that our way of doing things is the "right" way. And indeed it is. If every person on earth didn't live within some sort of cultural system, human life as we know it would not exist. Without some set of agreed-on ideas and practices, our social fabric would come unraveled. You *should* think your culture is the right one for you.

The problem arises when one makes value judgments about a different culture based on one's own cultural ideas or, worse, when one people force their culture on another. As we discussed earlier, a major task for anthropologists is to try not to analyze the cultures we study from our own cultural perspectives.

We have to practice, in other words, cultural relativity. We have to try to get inside the heads of other people, to see things from their perspective. We have already talked about the idea of world view and about different sorts of economic systems. You should now understand something about the world of egalitarian societies, for instance, even though you are part of a class society.

In this chapter we'll look at one of the facets of culture I've always thought was among the most difficult in this regard. It deals with our family relationships, something basic to our lives both as individuals and as a species. For most societies, family relationship, or **kinship,** is the basis for social organization in general. As you might expect by now, not every society looks at kinship the way we in most of North America do. But if you can understand kinship systems that differ from your own, you'll have come a long way toward understanding and being able to apply cultural relativity.

PRIMATE SOCIETIES

ethnocentrism Making value judgments about another culture from the perspective of one's own cultural system.

kinship Your membership in a family and your relationship to other members of that family. May refer to biological ties or to cultural ties modeled on biological ones.

As noted in Chapter 4, primates are social creatures who recognize and respond to one another as individuals. Primate societies are made up of the collective relationships among individuals, and an individual may hold a particular status relative to others in the group. The degree of individual recognition and the general details of primate social organization differ widely from species to species, of course, but a common occurrence, at least among the anthropoid primates (see Figure 4.4), is that of a strong bond among individuals who are closely biologically related—that is, among members of some family unit.

FIGURE 9.1
A family of olive baboons in Kenya—a group of related females and their young—focuses on the oldest female, right. Such family units form the core of baboon troops.

For example, in some baboons the social center of the troop, and the subgroup that ties generations together, is made of related females. These females form alliances with one another that help ensure their own reproductive and childrearing success, as well as the passing on of their genes via the reproductive success of their close relatives who share many of those genes (Figure 9.1).

In chimpanzees perhaps the strongest social bond is that between mother and infant. This is not unusual for mammals, but in these apes, with their large, complex brains and the amount they need to learn to become functioning adults, the mother-infant bond is particularly long lived and important. The nature of that interaction can have a lasting effect on the rest of a chimp's life. Poor treatment by the mother, for example, often makes a chimp a poor mother herself when she bears young. Chimps, in other words, *raise* their young, and the family bonds that result may last a lifetime.

Members of this chimp family unit may, throughout their lives, protect and care for each other, especially during illness and injury. Offspring often remain close to their mother for many years, helping her in her old age. Older daughters help their mothers with her younger babies. Males have been known to help brothers in their competition for dominance.

Interestingly, this sense of caring can extend outside the actual family unit. Offspring are important to the group as a whole, and adults will come to the aid or protection of a youngster threatened with harm, possibly risking their own welfare, even if the youngster is not necessarily theirs. Once, according to famed chimp researcher Jane Goodall, an adolescent male adopted an unrelated youngster who had been orphaned. In a sense, then, chimps have extended the concept of family beyond just easily recognized biological relationships.

In bonobos there is even a stronger and longer-lasting mother-son bond. Sons may stay with and travel with their mothers well into their adulthood. There is also a strong bond between brothers.

There are also many bonds, both temporary and long-lasting, among unrelated nonhuman primate individuals. Bonds among adult females are a focus of bonobo society, and those females are not necessarily related to one another. In chimps, bonds among unrelated males are important. But in all cases there is some recognition of and importance given to relationships between individuals that *are* related. In other words, kinship in many primates—although not formalized as among humans—is more than just the temporary bond between mother and dependent young. It is an integral part of the larger social order.

In the human primate, the social system in most cultures is based on family. One's place in society is influenced, if not determined, by one's membership in a family and one's specific relationships to other members of that family. And the basic biological relationships of family are interpreted and translated by culture into an almost bewildering array of kinship systems.

KINSHIP

For most of human evolutionary history, and for recent foraging groups, society literally was family. Social units were made up of small groups of nuclear families that were no doubt related—several biological brothers and their wives and children, for example, with perhaps some grandparents. Social interaction was thus based on family relationships, and these would have been rather obvious and easily kept track of. After all, there were not a lot of individuals involved and the intimacy with which such groups lived meant that biological events—births, deaths, even sexual relations—were known about and observed.

As food production made possible larger populations, social interactions got more complex. Now there were more people to deal with, more goods and services being produced and passed around, more than just a few biological families present. There were groups other than close relatives to interact with. There was a need for some sort of leader or overseer to handle interactions within the group and between one group and others. A new social organization was required—one based not on natural groupings but on cultural ones, ones that could be geared to the specific needs and desires of the population and cultural system concerned.

But must a social system be created from scratch? Just sit down, dissolve all existing social relations, and make up new ones? Hardly. For there already *is* a model for organizing a society: the kinship relations around which less complex societies were arranged. What apparently happened was that food-producing societies, needing new and varied schemes of organization, created cultural variations on biological kinship themes. What family you belonged to, your place in that family, and where your family line fit relative to other family lines still determined your place in society. But the system, even though it looked like and used the terminology of biological kinship, was a cultural one. It may have ignored some biological relationships. It may have created categories that cross-cut actual biological groups, or may have lumped, under one name, people of quite distinct biological identities. The model is from biology, but the specific features are cultural.

The base of any kinship system remains the nuclear family. Anthropologists have devised diagrams to represent this unit and its extensions (Figure 9.2). In these diagrams, triangles represent males, females are circles, an equal sign means marriage. A vertical line is descent, the offspring from a marriage. A horizontal line means sibship, brothers and sisters. From this base we may begin to examine the wealth of variations on the kinship theme.

The number of spouses one may have varies from culture to culture and is the criterion for the two basic types of nuclear family. Most people in the world today live in societies where marriage involves just one of each spouse, the practice called monogamy (*mono*, one; *gamy*, marriage), a term introduced in Chapter 8. But in some societies a person may have more than one spouse. The general term for this is **polygamy** (*poly*, more than one). Obviously, there are two versions of this. If a man has several wives it is polygyny (from the Greek *gyne*, woman), also introduced in Chapter 8. If a woman has several husbands, it's **polyandry** (from the Greek *andros*, man).

Now, those of us from monogamous societies no doubt think of that system as the normal and correct one, and for us it is. But the statistics show something else. In a survey of 565 world societies, only about 25 percent were strictly monogamous, that is, never allowing multiple marriages. You can literally count the number of polyandrous societies on the fingers of one hand—only 4, or less than 1 percent, in this same survey. Polygynous societies are the statistical norm, accounting for over 70 percent of societies in the survey. What explains this statistic?

In Chapter 8, we noted a correlation between marriage pattern and subsistence pattern—monogamy tended to be practiced in foraging, complex agricultural, and industrial societies. Polygyny is associated with horticultural and nonindustrial agricultural societies (see Table 8.1). I believe a basic answer lies in these relationships. In horticultural and

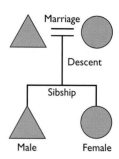

FIGURE 9.2
A basic nuclear family with one husband, one wife, and two children; a boy and a girl.

polygamy Any marriage system that allows multiple spouses.

polyandry A marriage system with multiple husbands.

FIGURE 9.3
Johnny Bungawuy, a native of Arnhem Land in northern Australia, with seven of his eleven wives and some of his children who accompanied him on a successful hunt for a pelican. This is an example of a foraging society that practices polygyny, a not uncommon situation in northern Australia, which has abundant food resources.

nonindustrial agricultural societies, the nuclear family is the basic economic unit. Whether the family is relatively self-sufficient, as in horticulturalists, or involved in a more complex trade network, as in agricultural groups, the family is the unit of production. Thus, the more adult members in the family, the more workers there are. When one wife is limited in her work by pregnancy or caring for a young child, having multiple wives means that there are still other adult women to contribute their labor. Moreover, with a husband and several wives, the reproductive potential of the family is enhanced (Figure 9.3).

Now, an obvious objection arises here: Aren't such families making things harder on themselves, economically, by having the additional children that multiple wives would produce? If there were fewer mouths to feed, two adult workers in the family would probably suffice. Remember, however, that the fairly low rates of infant mortality (death within the first year of life) that we take for granted are a recent phenomenon that occurred first in industrialized societies with adequate nutrition and medical care. For most people during most of human history, infant mortality was much higher. So, to have enough children who will grow up to perpetuate the family, and the society, each household must increase its *potential* reproduction, because parents are aware that a fair number of the children born will not survive to adulthood. Thus, the large number of human societies that are horticultural or nonindustrial agricultural societies accounts for the statistical popularity of polygyny.

Why, however, does not the same hold true for industrial and foraging societies? In industrial societies, production becomes more dependent on nonhuman energy. Fewer people can produce more food than in the

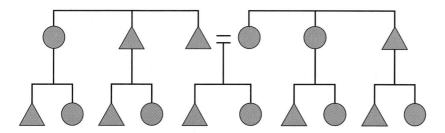

FIGURE 9.4
Horizontal extension of the nuclear family. The married couple in the center has two children, one of each sex. Each parent has two siblings, one of each sex, each of whom also has two children, one of each sex. For simplicity's sake, the spouses of the parents' brothers and sisters—and their relations—have been left out.

other types of subsistence. (Recall that less than 3 percent of the United States population live on farms. The food we eat is produced by a tiny proportion of the people.) In a sense, the individual, rather than the nuclear family, is now the basic economic unit. Moreover, with better nutrition and medical care, more children live to reach adulthood. Very large families would, in most cases, put a strain on a family's economics.

In foraging societies, the whole society is the basic economic unit. Sharing is the focus. Production on the level of the nuclear family is less important than production on the societal level. And because foraging societies depend on naturally occurring resources, they are aware of the strains that increased population size could place on their subsistence. Recall that many foraging societies, even with infant mortalities, require methods of limiting their births. More adult providers in the nuclear family would gain them nothing—in fact, it would *cost* since adults consume more resources than children do. Anyway, in small societies, polygyny might be difficult since there would hardly be enough "extra" women to go around.

What about polyandry? Why is it so rare? The answer is simple. Although a nuclear family of one woman with several husbands would provide a larger family workforce, there is no greater reproductive potential than in a monogamous family. Polyandry is found where land is scarce and property is inherited through men. So as not to break up land holdings, several brothers may marry the same woman. Property is kept intact and within the family. Several polyandrous societies are found in Tibet, where, obviously, arable land is at a premium.

Nuclear families, of course, are not isolated units. They are strung together horizontally to include persons we refer to as aunts, uncles, and cousins (Figure 9.4). They are also strung together vertically through time to include grandparents and other ancestors. The dimension through time is the **descent line** (Figure 9.5). The female (shaded) is a daughter in one nuclear family. If she marries, she becomes part of two connected nuclear families, the one in which she is a daughter and the one in which she is a wife. The same would hold true for her mother and her daughter, and so on. It is in the descent line that we see some of the most interesting variations in basic social organization.

descent line Nuclear families that are connected through time.

FIGURE 9.5
A simple descent line with nuclear families linked by the female who is a daughter in one family and a wife and mother in the other.

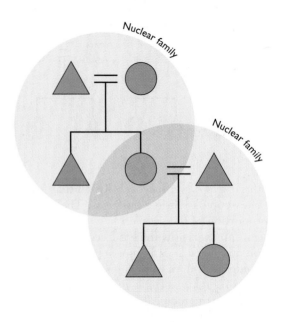

If you were asked to which descent line you belonged, your answer would be both your father's and your mother's. True, you may carry your father's last name, there may be some legal matters that emphasize your ties to one side over the other, and you may feel more personally connected to one side. But in general social and cultural terms, your place in your family is as the product of, and as a member of, both sides. We call this system **bilateral** (literally, two-sided).

A bilateral system makes clear biological sense. But not every society arranges kinship relations around biology. A bilateral system doesn't fill the cultural needs and outlook of every society. Indeed, most societies organize descent lines in very different ways.

Most groups, about 60 percent, are **unilineal** (one line). This means that an individual belongs to only one side of the family. Depending on the society, this is either the father's side, in a **patrilineal** pattern, or the mother's side, in a **matrilineal** arrangement (Figure 9.6). This does not mean that if you live in a patrilineal society you don't know who your mother is, nor that you don't live with her, care about her, and have special emotional and practical relationships with her. But if your whole society is organized according to kinship, for any function in which your place in society is important, you are a member of your father's line, not your mother's. Important functions in this regard might include property ownership and inheritance, military alliances, leadership and other statuses, and potential marriage partners. In North American society, your place in the group is determined by your resi-

bilateral Kinship where an individual is a member of both parents' descent lines.

unilineal Kinship where an individual is a member of only one parent's descent line.

patrilineal Kinship where an individual is a member of the father's descent line.

matrilineal Kinship where an individual is a member of the mother's descent line.

Patrilineal system   Matrilineal system

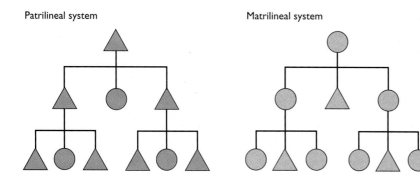

FIGURE 9.6
The members of a patrilineage and of a matrilineage. In a patrilineage, females may be members but cannot pass on their membership to their offspring. In a matrilineage, males may be members but cannot pass on their membership to their offspring. In some patrilineal societies, wives become members of their husband's lineage as well.

dence, occupation, and socioeconomic class. In most societies, though, it's which lineage you belong to.

In unilineal societies, membership in a lineage is inherited through the parent whose sex is the basis for the kinship system. In a patrilineage, you inherit family membership from your father, in a matrilineage, from your mother. You can pass on membership in the lineage only if you are of the corresponding sex. For instance, if I lived in a matrilineal society, I would be a member of my mother's lineage but my children would be members of my wife's lineage. I could not pass on membership in my lineage.

Now, the obvious question: Why? Doesn't unilineality seem to violate logic? In fact, it makes sense in societies that continue to organize themselves using the kinship model but where there are large populations with many family lines. If things like your economic responsibilities, your political and military alliances, and your rights of inheritance are determined by who your relations are, it makes things a lot simpler to cut in half the potential number of your relations. Unilineality makes social organization based on kinship easier and more efficient. Just why each individual system originated and why it has its particular set of rules is another question. Remember, you can't always infer origin from current functional relationships. Nonetheless, some degree of overall social simplicity seems to be an important goal of unilineality, although certain other cultural features that maintain such a system, things like transfer of wealth, can seem even more complicated than in bilateral systems.

Are there any correlations we can make between descent systems and other aspects of culture? Beyond the general function of unilineality, are there reasons why some groups are matrilineal and others patrilineal? And what about bilaterality?

Like monogamy, bilaterality is associated with foraging and complex agricultural and industrial societies—the technologically least and most complex types. For foragers, bilaterality makes obvious sense. It reflects their egalitarian outlook, and the practical implementation of egalitarianism—such as food distribution—is aided by social symmetry. Each person is equally related to both sides of the family. When meat is distributed along kinship lines, this symmetry results in that distribution being simple and equitable. Moreover, bilaterality allows individuals to maximize their kin network. One can find relatives in many if not most other bands within the society.

For complex societies, which are not organized by kinship, no manipulation of the biological categories is required. Kinship is a more personal matter and so the obvious biological relationships hold.

In unilineal societies, the specific type of system seems correlated with economics, in a broad sense. Women perform most of the farming labor in horticultural societies, at least where there is not extensive dependence on crops—that is, where foraging also provides a great deal of subsistence. In such situations, women tend to be the focus of the social structure and these societies tend to be matrilineal. This establishes a stable network of kinship ties and helps provide a high degree of internal political stability.

However, horticulturalists in dense tropical forests often confront a shortage of resources. Farming labor can become more intensive, and competition and even internal warfare are not uncommon within such groups. In these cases, men become a social focus and in such situations we find patrilineal societies.

It should be noted that there are exceptions to these correlations. There are bilateral horticultural societies and unilineal foragers. The above generalizations should not be seen as cause-and-effect relationships, but rather as models for how to think about and analyze the variations in kinship systems among human societies. As we have noted, culture is not a "thing" that responds unvaryingly to certain situations. Culture springs from the minds of people. As anthropologist Roger Keesing, a specialist in kinship, puts it:

> Cultures do not respond to pressures. Rather, individual human beings cope as best they can, formulate rules, follow and break them; and by their statistical patterns of cumulative decisions, they set a course of cultural drift.

It should also be noted that there are other descent systems besides the major ones just described. In some, an individual may choose to belong to either the father's or the mother's side. In others, one is a member of the mother's line for some purposes and the father's for others. These, however, are rare, so we will elaborate on the three major patterns.

Within the major types of descent organization is even more variation. Societies have different specific terminology systems for ordering the exact relationships among individuals. There are about a half a dozen major types. We will look at three to show the kinds of aspects that vary, how we study them, and what they can tell us.

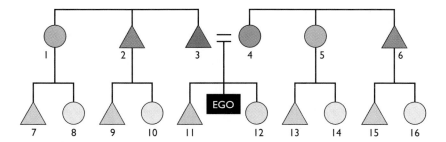

FIGURE 9.7
Eskimo kinship system.

KINSHIP TERMINOLOGY

What do you call the man who is your mother's husband and your immediate male ancestor? That probably appears to be a dumb question. You call him father, of course. And no one else shares that designation. But it's not a dumb question in anthropology because, as you've probably guessed by now, the categories of family relationships differ from society to society as does just about everything else.

Kinship terms are, of course, linguistic, and so it would be unwieldy to describe systems using actual cultural terms. Moreover, each system is used by many societies from all over the world and, thus, uses different languages. We can, however, diagram the systems using symbols. Two individuals who share the same color fall into the same category. In a diagram of a North American family, for example, the color indicating your biological father would be shared by no one else, while the color for your first cousin could be shared by many.

Terms for members of one's family, furthermore, are relative to the point of view of a particular person. You call the man mentioned before "father," but your mother calls him "husband." Your "cousin Tom" is your uncle's "son." So each diagram has one person from whose perspective we're viewing, and we call that person EGO.

Let's begin with the system that should be easiest for us to understand. It's the Eskimo system, so named because it was described in studies of that group (Figure 9.7).

To review, two married individuals, 3 and 4, have three kids, 11, EGO, and 12. Each parent has two siblings, one of each sex, and each of these has two kids. For simplicity, we'll leave out the spouses of the parents' siblings. EGO is of no particular sex, so we can change "its" sex for different examples.

Notice that EGO's biological parents are indicated by colors found nowhere else on the diagram. This means that EGO calls them by terms used for them alone. The parents' siblings fall into two categories, one for males and one for females, but the same categories are used for both sides. In EGO's generation, there are again specific terms for EGO's biological

FIGURE 9.8

Hawaiian kinship system.

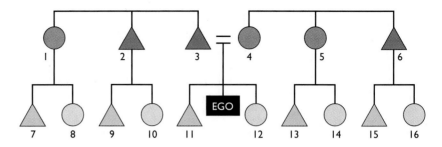

siblings, distinguishing males from females. Finally, all the offspring of EGO's parents' siblings are called by the same term, here with no differentiation for sex (although many cultures using the Eskimo system do make a linguistic distinction).

Look familiar? It should. Just substitute English words for the colors: father, mother, brother, sister, aunt, uncle, and cousin. It would work for other languages as well, including Spanish, French, German, Russian, and many more.

The Eskimo system is found most often at both ends of the continuum of subsistence types. It tends to be used by foragers and by agricultural societies. Why? Look at what is emphasized by the terms: the nuclear family. Within that unit, people are specified. Outside that unit, people fall into a more limited number of categories with no distinction as to side of the family or, in the case of the English "cousin," as to sex. In kinship terminology, specificity indicates emphasis.

The Eskimo system is associated with a bilateral descent line where sides of the family are symmetrical. It reflects an economic emphasis on the nuclear family, as in foraging groups, or a conceptual emphasis on the nuclear family as the only important recognized kinship unit, as in industrial societies. It allows the nuclear family to be set off and persons outside it to be equally important—or equally unimportant. So it works as well among the San as among twenty-first century North Americans.

Probably the simplest system is the Hawaiian (Figure 9.8). In this system persons are distinguished only by sex and generation. This system is found in groups that have bilateral descent or in one of those in which you are a member of either line or different lines for different purposes. Unlike the Eskimo system, also associated with bilaterality, the Hawaiian doesn't focus on the nuclear family but lumps nuclear family members and other close relatives into just a few broad categories. Societies that use this system usually deal with greater numbers of persons than do foragers. There is more emphasis on symmetry of the two sides. EGO's culturally defined relations to a large number of people are thus fairly simple and straightforward.

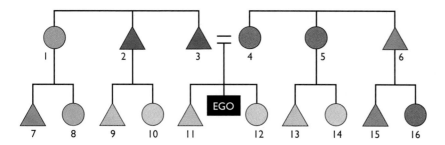

FIGURE 9.9
Omaha kinship system.

There is another aspect of kinship that is linked to terminology—the incest taboo, discussed in Chapter 6. Remember that mating between siblings and between parents and offspring is universally prohibited. Though that taboo may have originated with reference to the biological meaning of those terms, in practice it relates to their cultural meanings as well. In other words, any person to whom you refer using the same term you use for your biological siblings or parents is the *same* as those people. The incest taboo would apply to them as well.

Look back at the Hawaiian system (Figure 9.8). Whom can EGO not marry? Everybody. Everyone on the diagram is the same as the members of EGO's biological nuclear family. EGO must find a mate outside his or her family line.

The terminology systems used by unilineal societies are the most complex. The Omaha system, used by that Native American group as well as many other societies around the world, is a good example (Figure 9.9). It looks very strange at first, but if we take it one step at a time, it makes sense. First, for the moment, ignore persons 9, 10, 13, and 14. They're special and we'll return to them shortly.

Having left those four out, you should notice that on EGO's father's side of the family there are more categories than on the mother's side. In fact, all the members of EGO's mother's family (except 13 and 14— keep ignoring them!) are just male or female, regardless of generation. If we were to add more generations, the situation would still be the same. The color shared by numbers 4, 5, and 16, then, would translate into a word meaning something like "female member of my mother's lineage." Similarly, the color for 6 and 15 means "male member of my mother's lineage."

On the father's side, however, both sex and generation are specified. The color for 2 and 3, for example, means "male member of my father's line *in my father's generation.*" What this tells you is that the Omaha system is associated with patrilineal societies. As EGO, my important culturally defined relationships are with other members of my patrilineage. Thus, it is important for me to specify the categories into which they fall. I am not a member of my mother's patrilineage, though, so those individuals are not as culturally important to me. As a result, they are specified only by their sex.

It is important not to confuse personal recognition with cultural categories here. Certainly, if I were a member of a society using the Omaha system, I would know who those people on my mother's side are, and I would call them all by their personal names. My mother is not a member of my patrilineage but I lived with her when I was growing up and I have close emotional ties with her. She is my mother in every way we understand that term. The categories we're discussing refer to cultural relations—various economic and social rights and responsibilities—that happen to be organized based on kinship.

Now add back those four relations you ignored earlier and look at EGO's generation. The people in this generation fall into many different and asymmetrical categories. Numbers 15 and 16, as we noted, are simply a male and female on the mother's side. Numbers 7 and 8 are individuals with specific terms; we'll get back to them. Numbers 9, 10, 13, and 14, from *both* sides, are the same as EGO's biological siblings.

The Omaha system, as well as some others, makes a distinction between two kinds of children of your parents' siblings. We call them **parallel cousins** and **cross cousins**. Parallel cousins are children of same-sex siblings, your father's brother's kids or your mother's sister's kids. Here they are numbers 9, 10, 13, and 14. Cross cousins are your father's sister's kids and your mother's brother's kids, here numbers 7, 8, 15, and 16.

The origin of this distinction is debatable, but we may show one result—the application of the incest taboo. Numbers 9, 10, 13, and 14, being the same as the biological siblings, clearly fall into the taboo category. In fact, because of the lumping on the mother's side of the family, *everyone* on that side is a prohibited marriage partner. On the father's side, however, 7 and 8 could be acceptable marriage partners. They are neither a member of your mother's lineage nor of yours. They are members of their father's patrilineage, that is, of the lineage of number 1's husband. Such categorization prohibits you (EGO) from marrying into your mother's lineage, which would combine descent lines that the unilineal system has separated. It also prevents you from marrying into your own lineage. But it may allow marriage to persons who are members of what is essentially an unrelated lineage, that of the father of 7 and 8. Indeed, in some cultures with this system, the cross cousins on your father's side are the *preferred* marriage partners.

In actual practice we have to look at each kinship system and see if we can discern the functional relationships involved. As with every other aspect of culture, there are no hard and fast rules. For instance, a few groups that use the Omaha system are matrilineal, so our neat analysis won't work for all unilineal systems.

parallel cousins The children of your father's brothers or mother's sisters.

cross cousins The children of your father's sisters or mother's brothers.

age sets A social unit made up of persons of approximately the same age.

men's associations A social unit made up of a society's men. Common in highland New Guinea.

FIGURE 9.10
Among the Gimi of Papua New Guinea, men and boys sleep in men's houses in the centers of their fenced-in compounds. Women and children are forbidden to enter the men's houses or even to walk on the paths leading to them. They live in smaller houses at the edges of the compounds.

There are more systems of terminology and subsystems within some of these three patterns. They are discussed in the references at the end of the chapter. For the moment, if you're intrigued, consider the Crow system (named after another Native American group). It is the mirror image of the Omaha system and is associated with matrilineal societies. See if you can diagram it.

ORGANIZATION ABOVE THE FAMILY LEVEL

Within societies there are a number of organizing principles in addition to those based on the kinship model. For instance, in many societies there are **age sets**—groups of people born within some limited time range of one another. Age set members remain associated for life and have certain special social and economic rights and responsibilities toward one another.

There are also associations based on gender. **Men's associations,** common in societies in the New Guinea highlands, are as important as any other social category for defining a person's social position and socio-economic relations with others (Figure 9.10). We also find various forms

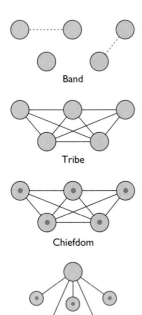

Band

Tribe

Chiefdom

State

FIGURE 9.11
Basic types of political organization. Bands are small autonomous units, without formal leaders, and with informal relationships with one another as the need arises. A tribe is a collection of bands, still without full-time leadership, but with more formalized relations among all the individual units. A chiefdom has formal, full-time leaders of each unit and interactions among the units are conducted through them. States require centralized authority that coordinates and controls the interactions of the individual units, often through the leader of each unit. In reality, for chiefdoms and states, there would be more subunits than depicted here. A chief, for example, might lead a number of villages. A state system can consist of many layers of subunits such as towns, counties, and states, each of which has a leadership structure.

of military associations and associations based on occupation, ethnic affiliation, and region of birth.

As societies get larger and more complex, there is a need for other systems of organization. As anthropologist Elman R. Service puts it:

> Kinship . . . can integrate a society only up to a certain point in its growth. After that, the society must fission into separate societies if growth continues . . . . Only with the achievement of new integrative means can an increase in complexity keep pace with the growth.

The "new integrative means" he refers to is **political organization.** It serves the same functions as organization on the family level, but it involves more people and more-complex interactions. According to Frank Vivelo, political organization

> refers to the means of maintaining order and conformity in a society. It concerns the allocation of power and authority to make decisions beyond the personal level, i.e., decisions which affect the group . . . as a whole. It provides structure through which decisions about social policy, and the implementation of social policy, are effected. In addition . . . [it] also concerns the way a society orders its affairs in relation to other groups.

As you should expect by now, the specific features of political organization vary enormously among different societies. We can, however, categorize the variation into a few general types (Figure 9.11).

Band organization is the simplest and is, in a sense, no political organization at all. It is based on kinship and is characteristic of foraging societies. As you recall, these are made up of small, autonomous, flexible units with no social stratification, although there are individuals who are informally more influential.

Tribal organization is characteristic of horticultural and pastoral groups. Elman Service has referred to these as "collections of bands." The basic organization is still along kinship lines, but now those lines are combined into larger units—often called lineages or clans—and relations exist that unite different kinship units and different residence areas such as villages. Tribes are essentially egalitarian, and there is no central authority, but the problems facing this larger group are generally more complex than those of a band society and so must involve decisions on the part of the tribe as a whole.

Chiefdoms are the next level in terms of integration. There is still no central authority over the whole political unit, but because more people and thus more-complex interactions are involved, there are more individual units making up the whole society. There is a need for some form of formal leadership, at least of the main subunits. These leaders are the chiefs. Such an organization is found in less complex agricultural and large pastoral groups. The basis of organization may still be kinship, since the position of chief is often hereditary. Chiefdoms are socioeconomically somewhere in between egalitarian and class; there are social strata but there is an attempt to smooth out inequalities through redistribution.

States are characterized by having central authority. Complex agricultural and industrial societies are made up of large numbers of people with complex interactions and living in numerous individual units. There is a clear need for all the individual units—even though each may have its own chief—to be integrated. Thus, we find kings, pharaohs, czars, and presidents. The centralized authority itself may be complex and multifaceted, as is the federal government of the United States with its three branches.

Social organization, then, is a broad and complex topic. The general idea, however, is this: The organizing groups may sometimes be based on biological factors like age, sex, and kinship. Nevertheless, the actual categories, the rules for membership, and all the ideals of behavior associated with the categories are cultural inventions geared toward taking care of the needs of the group that uses them. It's in this light that we attempt to understand them.

At least, though, when we're examining the cultural lives of existing peoples, we can actually watch culture in action. We can literally ask the people what they're doing and why. We can go back and check our analyses. Not so with the study of past cultural systems. Some past peoples have left written records that help us reconstruct their cultures, but writing has only been around for 5000 or 6000 years. For all the time before that, our only clues to the lives of people are in the form of the material artifacts they've left behind. Can we hope to understand such abstract things as social organization by looking at ancient garbage? What's the relationship between material culture and whole cultural systems? To explore these questions, we look next at the work of the archaeologist—the anthropological time traveler.

SUMMARY

All groups of living organisms require some mechanism to coordinate the actions of their members. For most living things, this mechanism is genetic. But with large-brained primates—creatures that rely on learned behavior for survival—group organization becomes more complex and variable. In anthropoid primates such as the baboon, chimpanzee, and bonobo, the identity and characteristics of individuals are important in the establishment and maintenance of social organization.

In the human primate, the basis for social organization is, not surprisingly, the nuclear family, the basic reproductive and economic unit. For most human societies throughout most of our evolutionary history, social organization has been based on kinship. But even when populations become large, complex, and composed of many biological kin

political organization The secular, nonkinship means of organizing the interactions within a society and between one society and others.

tribal Political organization with no central leader but where the subunits may make collective decisions about the entire group.

chiefdom Political organization with no central authority but made up of many interacting units, each of which has a leader.

state A political organization with central authority governing all the individual units.

CONTEMPORARY ISSUES

Why Don't Bilateral Societies Have Equality between the Sexes?

It may seem contradictory at first that societies with bilateral descent lines display sexual inequalities. Doesn't the equal relationship of a person to both parents mean that the parents themselves are equal in social and cultural areas? A related question refers to the practice of wives taking their husband's last name and children their father's. Doesn't this actually denote a patrilineal descent system?

In fact, type of descent line and the social and cultural relationships between the sexes are two different issues. North American society is, indeed, bilateral, and yet it has traditionally been dominated by men. Women have only had the vote in the United States since 1920. Until relatively recently far fewer women than men attended college and, if they did, it was often a college solely for women. Those women who worked outside the household did so, to a great extent, in support services. We still picture a woman when we use or hear the terms "nurse" or "secretary." (Notice that the phrase "male nurse" is still common, as if men in that occupation were the overwhelming exception.) When the U.S. Senate and Congress meet in joint session, it is still a sea of male faces (and white male faces at that). Even the two women conspicuous on the current Supreme Court make up only 22 percent of that body. There is still, in some occupations, a disparity in salaries between men and women doing the same work. But *patriarchal* is not *patrilineal*.

Descent systems are a reflection of broad, society-wide, socioeconomic considerations. We can link the different systems (with exceptions, of course) to subsistence patterns. Bilaterality is found in foraging societies that are organized as symmetrical, egalitarian affiliations of fairly small numbers of nuclear families. In these cases,

groups, the organizational structure may still be based on the kinship model. Now, however, kin units are culturally defined and may cross-cut or lump biological categories, and so we see all manner of variation—in one's individual identity as a member of a kin group and in the identity and number of potential marriage partners. These variations may be examined and understood under the assumption that the form of organization works for the people who practice it and is an integral part of their whole cultural system.

When societies become so large and complex that kinship alone can't operate to organize and coordinate them, broader forms of integration must be devised. These are political units. Although many of these still have kin-based aspects, they are largely based on residence and socioeconomic interaction.

In all these aspects of social organization, there are certain correlations with other facets of cultural behavior that we have, and will, examine—things like subsistence pattern and economics.

although there is a sexual division of labor, there is also a basic sexual equality. But bilaterality is also found in complex agricultural and industrial societies where cultural manipulation of biological kinship categories is not necessary, and where the nuclear family has a personal rather than an economic focus. The characteristics of such societies have given rise to at least the potential for inequalities in the relationships between men and women.

In urban and suburban settings especially, a more distinct division of labor evolved. Instead of all members of a household being involved in aspects of the same economic activities, the husband may well leave the house to work. The wife, likely also a mother, would take care of home and children. The sexes were thus isolated from one another for large portions of the day, and women became isolated from public life. They still performed important labor, but it was not labor that generated income. Women thus became economically dependent on men, and, as a result, of-

ten lacked property and power. They became, in a sense, an underclass.

From this male-dominated socioeconomic situation, and from the efforts by men to directly maintain the power and wealth such situations provided them, came the idea that women were "the weaker sex." Women in this country, for example, were seen as unqualified for men's jobs, as incapable and not in need of formal educations, and as needing extra physical protection and care. (Even into the twentieth century, some women were virtually confined to their beds during pregnancy.) Certainly, it was thought, women lacked the mental abilities for commercial or political leadership positions, and a woman doctor or scientist was considered an oddity.

Although the situation is far more equitable today, we are—in both our economics and our world view—still working on an overall equality of men and women in this society. The fact that we organize kinship bilaterally does not require or guarantee that equality.

NOTES, REFERENCES, AND READINGS

The latest information on baboon social organization can be found in Fedigan and Fedigan's *Gender and the Study of Primates*, Barbara Smut's *Sex and Friendship in Baboons*, and Shirley Strum's *Almost Human*. For primate behavior in general, try *Patterns of Primate Behavior* by Claude Bramblett and *The Nonhuman Primates* edited by Phyllis Dolhinow and Agustín Fuentes.

Although it is over twenty years old, I still find Roger Keesing's *Kin Groups and Social Structure* a useful general book on those topics. A good chart on the relationship between kinship and subsistence patterns is on page 134, and the passage I quoted is from page 140.

The survey I mentioned in conjunction with the percentages of cultures exhibiting different descent systems is George Murdock's *World Ethnographic Sample*. Information specifically about the topics of this chapter is in his *Social Structure*.

Descriptions of and discussions about the correlations between marriage, kinship, and subsistence pattern can be found in M. Kay Martin and Barbara Voorhies's *Female of the Species,* sadly now out of print.

Elman R. Service discusses the categories of political organization in *Profiles in Ethnology,* third edition. The passage I quoted is from page 3. The definition of politics I quoted is from Frank Robert Vivelo's *Cultural Anthropology Handbook,* page 135.

10

MATERIAL CULTURE

The Things We Make and
the Things We Leave Behind

How about a multiple-choice question? Which two of the following are in the same category?

a. a beehive

b. a rock used by Egyptian vultures to smash open ostrich eggs

c. a chimpanzee termite stick (see Figure 7.2)

d. a San hut (see Figure 8.5)

They are all some sort of material item, so they all are connected to the topic of this chapter. The vulture, however, doesn't make its tool but simply uses a natural object. That leaves the other three as objects that are manufactured. But the beehive, as with the ant's nests we discussed in Chapter 7, is really a natural object since all the instructions for it, and the "reason" for building it, are programmed in the insects' genes. The termite stick and the San huts, on the other hand, are *artifacts*. They are based on an abstract idea, made according to some general model, and specifically formed to facilitate some need—and all of this is learned extragenetically. In other words, both are cultural as we have defined the term. So the answer is (c) and (d).

One more question. What's the difference between (c) and (d)? Well, the chimp's termite stick, although it fulfills all our criteria for a cultural behavior, is aimed at solving a problem related strictly to the natural environment, namely, how to get a termite snack. The sticks are not part of any larger cultural system. They have no variation that reflects the world view of a society. It is true that chimps show variation in terms of the shape of the sticks and the plants from which they are made, but this seems to be a matter of personal choice, based on who knows what.

The huts of the San, however, besides obviously serving a practical function, are built according to a traditional pattern based on a long history of cultural decisions. The size and number of huts manufactured at any one time is dependent on the number of people who will use them and on the number of persons in the group as a whole. These numbers, in turn, are the results of specific aspects of the San cultural system regarding group size and personal relationships within the group. This last factor also influences the placement of huts within the camp. Who actually builds the huts relates to the society's economic and social organization. And the individual features of the huts are geared to other aspects of San technology, factors like the number and kinds of possessions to be stored in the huts. (Storage is the huts' main function, since they are often too infested with insects to be used as shelters.)

To understand San huts, you have to understand not only what they *do* but also what they *mean*. This is because, as we discussed previously, human artifacts not only help meet basic environmental needs but also implement and reflect cultural ideas about our relation with the environment and with one another—our world view, in other words. Culture adapts to culture as well as to climate and food resources.

All the cultural items we've dealt with in the last few chapters are examples of this concept, as was my necktie story. As another example that concerns a familiar item, consider that paragon of American culture, the automobile.

The purpose of the automobile is to move people and their belongings around quickly and, ideally, with efficiency and safety. The funny thing is, this basic artifact comes in an amazing number of varieties. For 1999, I counted about eighty-seven different models produced by the big three American car manufacturers (General Motors, Ford, and Daimler-Chrysler), and most of those models themselves come in different versions. And then there are all the foreign alternatives. What can we conclude from all this variety about American society? Give that question some thought as we continue.

The idea that artifacts are parts of a cultural system and are reflections of a society's world view is the basis for the work of the anthropologist who tries to reconstruct past cultures from their recovered material remains. This work is archaeology. Of all the subfields of anthropology, archaeology is perhaps the most distinct. Anthropologists specializing in this area tend to identify themselves first as archaeologists. The general public has a good idea what an archaeologist does but has a hard time defining anthropology. This is in part because archaeology is the oldest formal specialty within the field, going back as far as the European Renaissance when "antiquarians" began excavating the remains of the classical civilizations of Greece and Rome.

The most important reason for the distinct status of archaeology, however, is that archaeologists have unique problems with collecting and analyzing their data. Those data, the material remains of past cultures, must usually be dug up—literally. They're most often underground because they're so old and have been buried over the years by things like flooding, windblown dust and sand, volcanic eruptions, and soil buildup. To just find and recover ancient artifacts requires a very specialized set of technical skills. Other techniques and theories are then needed to identify, analyze, and interpret the artifacts.

But don't think this makes archaeology different from anthropology in general. Archaeology is not just finding interesting old stuff in the ground and putting it in museums (although it used to be). The archaeologist uses the recovered artifacts as data to try to answer the same types of questions as any anthropologist—questions about the nature of the human species and its behaviors. Archaeology is the anthropology of the cultural past—no more, no less. Let's see how this works in practice.

ARCHAEOLOGY: RECOVERING AND INTERPRETING THE CULTURAL PAST

Living in New England, I have on hand a very good example of the connection between artifacts and the practical and abstract parts of culture. The artifacts are gravestones carved from the mid-1600s to the mid-1800s.

If you explore old New England cemeteries and look at the stones from that period, you begin to notice that, although there are a number of designs carved into the markers, the majority fall into three broad patterns, called death's heads, cherubs, and urns and willows (Figure. 10.1).

What sorts of things can we tell from these stones? We can certainly tell how old they are. The dates are right on them. And from the epitaphs we can find out about the people buried beneath them: their name, sex, age at death, sometimes the cause of death, and maybe something about their occupation, family, standing in the community, and personality (although, given the context, information on the latter might be biased).

Using historical records, we can sometimes find out who carved the stone (there seem to have been a limited number of gravestone carvers in the area), where the carvers traveled in New England, and even the price paid for the markers. The prices are, in a few cases, carved into the stones themselves.

But the stones can tell us even more. The designs were not carved at random, and they do not exist outside a cultural context. They mean something, and what they mean relates to attitudes toward death and the afterlife—in other words, to religious beliefs as practiced in a given cultural environment. As attitudes changed, so did the statistical frequencies of the designs (Figure 10.2).

The death's head—a grim, grinning skull—symbolized a pessimistic view of life and death. It reminded the living of human mortality, of everyone's inevitable end. The epitaphs on these stones usually read "Here lies buried the body of. . . ." The death's head is associated with the period of orthodox Puritanism from the 1600s to the mid- to late-1700s, depending on the region. The famous witch trials at Salem Village, Massachusetts, in 1692 coincided with the peak in popularity of this design.

As orthodox Puritanism declined beginning in the mid-1700s, attitudes about death changed. The emphasis shifted to resurrection and the rewards to be enjoyed in heaven. This change is reflected in the replacement of the death's head with the cherub—a smiling baby-faced angel with wings—and in epitaphs that stress these more positive aspects of death. "In memory of . . ." began to replace "Here lies the body of. . . ." These new ideas, and the adoption of the new design, seem to have begun in the urban intellectual center of Cambridge, Massachusetts, site of Harvard College (now a university), and spread from there. Moreover, the cherub design in this area was associated with graves of

FIGURE 10.1
An example of each of the three major styles of gravestones in New England from the mid-1600s through mid-1800s: (from top) death's head, cherub, urn and willow. These are from cemeteries in Connecticut.

upper-class, educated individuals. So we see a connection here between artifacts, religious beliefs, and the nature and status of intellectual influence in early New England culture. The gravestone designs themselves, it should be noted, originated in England—a further connection that could be explored.

By the late 1700s, religion had taken on a less emotional nature than it had had under Puritanism. This, in association with a trend toward Greek Revival architecture, gave rise to the classical looking urn–and–willow design. "In memory of . . ." had now completely replaced references to the buried bodies, and some stones simply carried the person's name and dates.

FIGURE 10.2

A graph, called a seriation graph, showing the changes in statistical frequencies of the three gravestone styles in central Connecticut for the years shown. Such a statistical pattern of design replacement is typical for many artifact types analyzed by archaeologists. A seriation graph could also be constructed for more recent artifacts such as automobile or clothing styles.

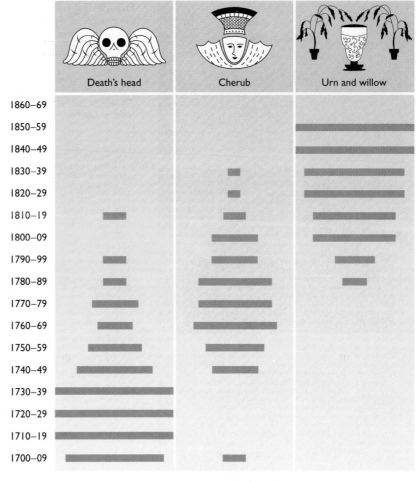

= 10% of the stones in a ten-year period

By the mid-1800s, gravestone designs began to show more variation. This was the result of a combination of factors: greater variety of religious expression, a trend toward more individual freedom, and the immigration of peoples from diverse parts of the world. But in New England during that earlier period, we see clear connections between the gravestones—an artifact—and other facets of culture, even ideological ones.

Now, you're probably thinking that these gravestone are historic, that there's little scientific analysis going on since the basic information is written right on the stones and all the data about the historical and religious context is also written down. Where's the archaeological analysis?

There are several responses to that logical question. First, as surprising as it may seem, there are things we don't know even about cultures with written records, even our own colonial period. People don't write everything down. As we've discussed, people are not always intellectually aware of why they do the things they do. So far as I know, nowhere is there anything in writing that specifically describes the Puritans' motivations for having death's heads carved on many of their gravestones. The connection is something made by scholars later on, looking at the various forms of evidence. So even when we are dealing with historic periods and cultures, archaeological analysis can still tell us some things. Such studies are referred to as **historical archaeology.**

Second, analyses like this, whereby we *can* check out at least some of the connections through written records, form the basis for archaeological analysis in general. In most of the archaeological record we can't see all the facets of culture in operation nor can we read about any of them. We find *only* material remains. So the only things we have on which to base our hypotheses are the actions of living humans and the written records of the recent past.

For example, we can't see an ancient tool being used, so we can't know for sure what it was used for. We can, however, see how similar-looking tools are used in existing or recent societies. By analogy we can hypothesize the same use for the old tool (Figure 10.3). This process is called **ethnographic analogy.** It's a lot like the analysis of fossils. Until we get really complete records of a type of extinct creature, the only way we can categorize a fossil is by deciding which living category it most resembles and tentatively placing it in the appropriate taxonomic group.

So the old gravestones do more than give us some ideas about early New England culture. They also give us some ideas about aspects of culture in general—connections between facets of material culture and abstract belief—that may prove useful to us in other archaeological investigations.

How about something older? There are literally thousands of examples, but one of my favorites concerns a study done by Sir Mortimer Wheeler, one of the most famous of early Old World archaeologists. Using the techniques of archaeological analysis and some basic information from early Roman writings, he reconstructed, in amazing detail, a battle that took place around A.D. 47. In that battle, the Roman commander (and later emperor) Vespasian attacked and conquered a Celtic hill fort, now called Maiden Castle, in southern England (Figure 10.4).

Wheeler was able to tell, for example, that the eastern side of the fort was attacked, what sorts of weapons were used, and that the Romans attacked with arrows first, followed by an infantry charge. He could tell that some huts near the entrance to the fort were burned and that the attackers, possibly because they encountered more resistance than expected, massacred women and children as well as adult male defenders. And when the Romans had won, they proceeded systematically to destroy the fort, tearing down fighting platforms, taking apart gates, and toppling stone walls alongside the entrances.

Soon after the battle (perhaps the next night), the conquered people of Maiden Castle buried their dead in the area of the burned huts. The

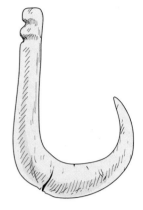

FIGURE 10.3
No archaeologist ever saw this item—from second-century–B.C. Japan and depicted about life size—in use, but it doesn't take much imagination to figure out what it was used *for.*

historical archaeology The archaeology of a society that has written records.

ethnographic analogy Interpreting archaeological data through the observation of activities in existing societies.

FIGURE 10.4

An aerial view of the Celtic hill fort of Maiden Castle, showing the outline of its bank-and-ditch defensive system. The fort was built on a site that had been occupied since about 6000 years ago. At the height of its importance, during the second century B.C., Maiden Castle had timber and stone walls, circular houses, streets, and underground silos for grain storage. These latter features are so extensive it is thought they stored grain for more than just the fort's inhabitants. Maiden Castle was perhaps the capital of a large territory.

burials were hasty (perhaps because the Romans were still around), but the survivors remembered in most cases to include food and drink in the graves for the journey to the next life. Probably the following day, when the Roman soldiers had moved on, the people began cleaning up and putting things back in some order. Eventually they built a new road across the ruins of their old fortifications. They continued to live there under Roman rule for about twenty years, when Maiden Castle was finally abandoned and its remaining walls torn down.

How could Wheeler tell all this? For details I refer you to his fascinating book. But briefly, Wheeler found such evidence as iron Roman arrowheads clustered on the eastern side of the fort. He could tell the order of events by the stratigraphy of the artifacts and other features. For example, the graves were clearly dug *through* the ashes of the burned huts. The skeletons in the graves were not found in any particular position or orientation, and grave goods varied, indicating hurried burials. The bodies showed signs of the wounds that killed them. The brutal nature of the multiple wounds led Wheeler to use the term "massacre."

Finally, it was clear that at least one stone wall was pulled down when the people abandoned the site, sometime in the 60s of the first century A.D., since the remains of that wall are on top of the other features and even block one of the roads built after the battle.

So using knowledge of such things as stratigraphic relationships, weapon types, architecture, technology, **forensic anthropology,** and some details I left out about pottery types and Roman coins, Wheeler was able to paint an amazingly clear and detailed picture not only of the way of life of the people of Maiden Castle but also of a particular event that took place nearly 2000 years ago.

But are those written Roman records bothering you? How about another example from even farther back in time? Something *really* old. In Chapter 5, I noted that the Oldowan tools associated with *Homo habilis* (see Figure 5.10) were not only core tools but also flake tools, and that an important use was the cutting apart of dead animals for meat and marrow. How do we know this? I already mentioned the microscopic analysis of animal bones indicating the presence of stone tool cut marks. Stones themselves may also be studied in this way for wear patterns.

In addition, archaeologist Nick Toth has examined some of the specific sites in East Africa of early stone tool manufacture and has made and used similar tools, a technique known as **experimental archaeology.** Toth has looked at places where stone tools were made by our early ancestors and determined that the stones were often transported from their natural locations for use later on. By making thousands of Oldowan-type tools, Toth has determined what a manufacture site should look like and notes that some of the actual sites show evidence of only partial flaking. This indicates that the tools were worked on over a period of time. Moreover, by comparing his own with actual manufacture sites, he has concluded that some of the variation in core tools was the result of specific flaking methods used to produce different sorts of flake tools (see Figure 10.13). By actually trying out his tools, he has found that flake tools are better for certain important tasks, especially animal butchering.

So using these and other techniques of archaeology, we can reconstruct events from several hundred, to 2000, to 2 million years ago. The three examples above, however, are all about rather specific situations—gravestone design, an ancient battle, and very ancient stone tool manufacture. These are just aspects of larger social and cultural contexts. The ultimate goal of archaeology is to reconstruct past cultural *systems* out of such specific pieces of data and analyses. The three stories were meant to be interesting and memorable ones and to give you examples of the first stage of the science of archaeological investigation.

Now, what are some of the specific techniques the archaeologist uses to locate, recover, and analyze such data? When we talk about archaeological excavations, or "digs," we are reflecting the fact that most archaeological sites are literally underground and must be dug up. An initial question then becomes, How do you find a site in the first place?

forensic anthropology
Subfield of anthropology that applies anthropology to legal matters. Usually used with reference to the identification of skeletal remains and the assessment of time and cause of death.

experimental archaeology
The process of understanding ancient skills and technologies by reproducing them.

FIGURE 10.5

The temples and palaces at the heart of the Maya city of Tikal in Guatemala (left). By 1350 years ago, Tikal had a population of about 40,000 with many thousands more living in the surrounding countryside. Although much of the site was covered by jungle when discovered in the nineteenth century, the tops of the tallest pyramids protrude above the forest canopy. The photograph on the right was taken from the top of an even taller pyramid, rising over 200 feet.

In some cases, of course, the site is obvious. You can't miss the great pyramids of Egypt, for example, or the larger ceremonial cities of ancient Central America (Figure 10.5). Although all the artifacts were within the soil, the outline of Maiden Castle was clearly visible and clearly not natural. In the American Midwest, Native American burial mounds rise out of otherwise flat fields.

In other cases, although the site itself may be hidden, evidence of its presence is uncovered accidentally. A farmer plowing a field in Indiana may turn up a shard of pottery that leads to the discovery of an ancient village. A crew digging a subway tunnel in Boston may come across the remains of an ancient fish weir (a device to trap fish swimming upstream). Wind or water erosion might unearth an artifact long in the ground. Or the vague outline of an old settlement may be noticed from the air even though the slight changes in elevation and vegetation were not readily visible at ground level.

But the vast majority of the time, you simply have to hunt for a site. How you go about this varies greatly depending on the sort of site you're looking for and the time period involved. In the case of Lucy and her contemporaries, for instance, who lived over 3 million years ago in an area noted for its extensive geological changes since then, you pretty much just wander around until you find something, focusing on places where erosion has exposed other fossil beds. For more recent periods, however, there are some specific procedures used to locate sites. As an example, we can look at the situation in Connecticut, where I live.

The basic topography of Connecticut has not changed much since people first lived here. This is because *no one* lived here before the recession of the glaciers about 10,000 years ago (the earliest well-dated site here is 10,100 years old), and the modern form of much of the state is a result of those glaciers. So, if we are looking for habitation sites of Connecticut's ancient peoples, we can begin with an obvious, and answerable

FIGURE 10.6
The floodplain of the Farmington River, Connecticut, as viewed from Talcott Mountain.

question: If we were here several thousand years ago, where would we set up a camp or establish a village? Clearly, we would need to be close to that most vital of resources, water. A flat area, as opposed to, say, the steep side of a mountain, is also an obvious location. In the state of Connecticut there are a number of good-sized rivers with broad, flat, floodplains that have been around for quite a while. That's a good place to begin.

But where on the floodplain of, for example, the Farmington River in central Connecticut would we look? That's a lot of land to cover (Figure 10.6). We might begin by using written records. The state archives contain hundreds of old treaties and deeds, many of which note the locations of Native American villages. Also useful are local informants—farmers who may have plowed up some evidence, or amateur collectors. We may also conduct a surface survey, simply walking around likely spots to see if any artifacts have been brought to the surface by erosion or human activity.

In the end, however, the only way to surely identify a site in an area like this is to dig. Preliminary excavations are called **test pits.** They are around a foot square or so and go as deep as artifacts are found or, more usually, until it is certain that no artifacts will be found (Figure 10.7). Test pits are located so as to provide the best coverage of the area being examined. If a specific place looks promising, the pits may be concentrated there. If it's a very large area, the pits can be placed using techniques of statistical sampling (Figure 10.8). At any rate, it's through test pits that we often determine whether we should conduct more thorough excavations or give up at one spot and move elsewhere.

If test pits reveal the presence of a site, and if it appears that there is more material to be found, the detailed work begins. An excavation is much more than just digging up an area and recovering interesting old objects. When a site is dug, it is literally destroyed. A table full of artifacts in some lab is worthless unless we know precisely where they were found

test pit An exploratory, usually small, excavation made to establish the presence or absence of an archaeological site.

FIGURE 10.7
Test pits are dug with shovels and the soil is screened through hardware cloth with 1/8-inch mesh attached to a wooden frame (foreground). This will reveal even the smallest artifact or piece of an artifact and thus establish the location as a site.

FIGURE 10.8
Excavators digging test pits, here spaced at regular 10-meter intervals along a straight line.

in relation to the site and to each other. Wheeler's conclusions about the battle of Maiden Castle, for example, would have been impossible if all he had to go on were the artifacts themselves. So when excavating a site, detailed and extensive records must be kept of the location of everything. An old cliché says that we should be able to put the whole site back just as we found it.

To record the location of the features of a site, we consider two dimensions. The horizontal dimension is controlled using a grid system (Figure 10.9). The site is marked off, usually with string and small supports, into a set of squares or grids, and each of these is excavated as a separate unit. The size of the grids varies, depending on the nature of the

FIGURE 10.9
A grid system used to control horizontal relationships at a 5000-year-old site in Connecticut. Notice that the excavators are now using trowels rather than shovels. The item in the center background is a larger screening device to separate soil from larger possible artifacts. Note also the surveying equipment (left background) used to maintain precise spatial records.

FIGURE 10.10
The site of Pueblo Bonito in New Mexico, inhabited from A.D. 850 to 1150, includes more than 800 rooms and is three stories high. The rooms and other architectural features form a natural grid system.

site, but an average is a meter square. As artifacts are found, their placement in the grid is noted and drawn or photographed. If the site is something like an old building that is itself already divided into horizontal units (rooms and hallways, for instance), it may not be necessary to impose a grid system (Figure 10.10).

Vertical control, too, may be determined by the site itself—the floors of a building or the rows of stone that make up walls, for example. Or, if the ground is clearly stratified, the natural strata are our units (Figure 10.11).

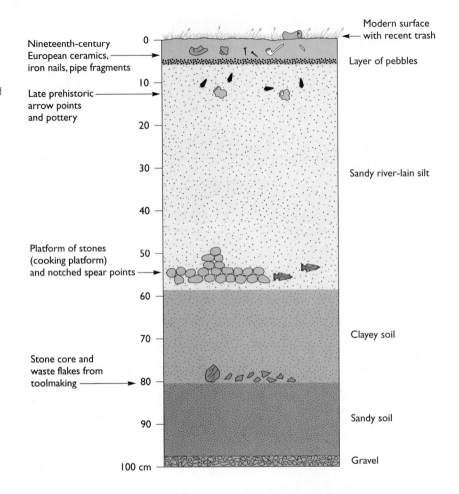

FIGURE 10.11

This stratigraphic section from the Old Farms Brook Site in Avon, Connecticut, shows a sequence of three prehistoric occupations and one historic occupation of the same location.

Nineteenth-century European ceramics, iron nails, pipe fragments

Late prehistoric arrow points and pottery

Platform of stones (cooking platform) and notched spear points

Stone core and waste flakes from toolmaking

Modern surface with recent trash

Layer of pebbles

Sandy river-lain silt

Clayey soil

Sandy soil

Gravel

Often, however, we establish the vertical units ourselves, digging down in layers of a few centimeters at a time so that each artifact may be recorded according to its placement in a certain layer. The vertical dimension is important for determining time and order of events.

The excavation of a site is, of course, only the data collection part of the process. Once a dig is completed, with all the records in order and all the artifacts bagged and labeled, the analysis begins. Artifacts are measured, photographed, compared with those from other sites, and identified. Soil from the site is analyzed for clues to climate and vegetation. Any organic remains are examined to determine the inhabitants' diets. Remains of the people themselves, if found, can be investigated for demographic factors like age and sex distribution and for physical attributes and medical information. Gradually, through these and many other analytical techniques, a picture of the site emerges—a view into the lives of a group of people otherwise unobservable. This view then becomes data itself,

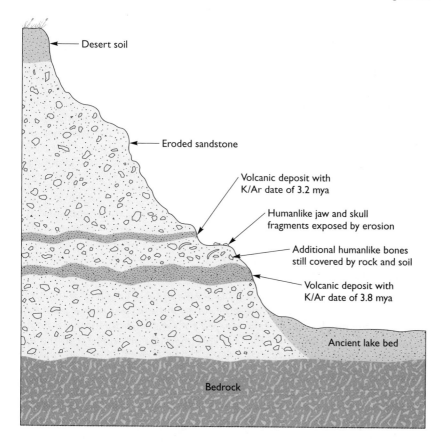

- Desert soil
- Eroded sandstone
- Volcanic deposit with K/Ar date of 3.2 mya
- Humanlike jaw and skull fragments exposed by erosion
- Additional humanlike bones still covered by rock and soil
- Volcanic deposit with K/Ar date of 3.8 mya
- Ancient lake bed
- Bedrock

FIGURE 10.12
Hypothetical geological profile showing human remains between two layers of volcanic rock. The human material must be younger than the volcanic deposit below it (3.8 mya) and older than the volcanic deposit above it (3.2 mya).

and is compared with similar information from other locations in an attempt to derive some generalizations about human behavior.

One aspect of archaeological analysis merits a closer look. All through this book I've been telling how old things are. Lucy is 3.2 million years old. Maiden Castle was conquered in A.D. 47. Life on earth began some 3.6 billion years ago. How do we derive these dates?

There are two major types of dating techniques, **relative dating** and **absolute dating.** Relative dating is when you determine whether something is older or younger than something else or establish the date for one thing based on the date of another. Stratigraphic sequences are the major example of relative dating (Figure 10.12, and see Figure 3.8). Very simply, the deeper something is, the older it is (although there are exceptions in situations where the strata have been disturbed).

We may also obtain relative dates by association. The remains of Lucy, for example, could not be directly dated, since Lucy's bone long ago petrified, that is, turned to stone. However, her petrified skeleton was found between layers of volcanic deposits, which *can* be dated (see below), and in association with some fossils of extinct pigs of known

relative dating Dating that indicates the age of one item in comparison to another.

absolute dating Dating that gives a specific age, year, or range of years for an object or site.

age. Thus, she was dated at 3.2 million years ago, *relative* to other things with established dates.

Absolute dating techniques tell us the actual age of a fossil. Among the best known and most useful are **radiometric** techniques. **Carbon dating** is useful back to about 60,000 years ago and so is relevant to the later period of human evolution. It works as follows: Carbon, in the form of carbon dioxide, is found in all living things, which continuously exchange it with the environment through respiration and metabolism. Most carbon is ^{12}C, indicating that there are twelve particles in the nucleus (six protons and six neutrons). Some carbon, however, is carbon 14 or ^{14}C because it has two extra neutrons. It is formed when cosmic radiation hits nitrogen in the atmosphere. We know the proportion of each form (isotope) of carbon in a living organism. Once the organism dies, however, it is no longer taking in new carbon, and so its ^{14}C—an unstable or radioactive isotope—begins to decay back into nitrogen and does so at a constant rate called a **half-life.** In 5730 years, one-half of the ^{14}C will have decayed. In another 5730 years, half of the remaining half will decay, leaving a quarter of the original, and so on. Now, if we find some organic remains—bone, for example, or even burnt wood—we can test it to see how much ^{14}C is left compared to how much the organism contained when alive. Suppose that our specimen has one-quarter of the living amount. Two half-lives have passed, or 5730 times 2, or 11,460 years. Beyond 60,000 years ago there is not enough ^{14}C left to accurately measure. So how do we date the really old fossils, like Lucy's?

We could use another important method called **potassium/argon** or **K/Ar** dating. Radioactive potassium (^{40}K), found in volcanic rock, decays into stable argon gas at a half-life of 1.31 billion years. Organic matter contains ^{40}K as well, but loses the argon gas that it decays into. Volcanic rocks, formed during eruptions, have a crystalline structure that traps the argon. Using the same reasoning as for carbon dating, we test volcanic deposits for the amount of argon, work backward, and date the rock. With that information, organic remains may be dated relatively. Any fossils found in a layer of volcanic rock are as old as that rock. Fossils found just above are younger; those found just below are older (see again Figure 10.12).

There are many other absolute dating techniques as well. They are based on such factors as changing chemical characteristics of organic compounds in bone; the amount of radiation trapped and released as light in fired clay, pottery, bricks, and burned rock; and the number of electrons produced by natural radiation and trapped in crystalline materials like tooth enamel, mollusk shells, and certain cave deposits. Dendrochronology, the use of tree ring widths, which are unique and nonrepeating, is another dating technique in regions where tree growth responds to yearly climatic fluctuations.

Now, back to the beginning and the basic premise of archaeology—that we can reconstruct cultural systems by using the relationship between

radiometric Referring to the decay rate of a radioactive substance.

carbon dating A radiometric dating technique using the decay rate of a radioactive form of carbon found in organic remains.

half-life The time needed for one-half of a given amount of a radioactive substance to decay.

potassium/argon (K/Ar) dating A radiometric dating technique using the rate at which radioactive potassium, found in volcanic rock, decays into stable argon gas.

those systems and the material artifacts they produce. I asked you to think about the automobile in all its varieties. What would those artifacts tell an archaeologist of the future about modern American culture?

Well, the mere presence of such artifacts—assuming they were found in abundance and accurately interpreted—would indicate that, first, ours was a large population and, second, that it was important for us to move ourselves and our belongings around, sometimes over great distances and with relative speed. The omnipresence of the artifact and the network of roads and other items that facilitate their use would attest to their importance to the entire culture and to the interrelatedness of all geographical and social areas of the society. All this would hint at complex economic transactions and point to a market system.

What about all the different types of vehicles? They indicate that we have labor specialization, for there are obviously different sorts of vehicles for different tasks. But just one type—the basic car—still comes in dozens of different versions, each doing essentially the same thing. That says we are a stratified society, that there are recognized differences in wealth and status that are symbolized in part by the kind of motor vehicle we own and use. Some cost more than others and those, whether or not they actually are mechanically superior, carry more status.

Presumably, this same sort of analysis can be done with other artifacts and for any other society. In the end, archaeology allows us to add now-extinct cultural systems to our database of human cultures, as we attempt to understand our species across space and through time.

SOME PREHISTORIC HIGH POINTS

What have these archaeological theories, skills, and techniques told us about the history of our species? A great deal, of course. There are plenty of books that relate the panorama of human history in great detail, and I'll note a few at the end of the chapter. For our purposes here, however, let's look at three high points of human cultural history that have been illuminated by the anthropological science of archaeology.

Stone Tools

Stone tools are crucial. They were the major type of tool for 99 percent of human cultural history. When they were first invented, around 2.6 million years ago according to the latest evidence, they reflected a jump in our ancestors' conceptual and actual control over their environment. They probably are a major reason why genus *Homo* persisted while the other hominid genera of Africa became extinct. And they are important to the anthropologist because they are often the only remnant of a past culture that is well preserved. Much of what we know about the adaptations and movement of peoples around the world, and of their cultural

FIGURE 10.13
Flint knapping—striking a piece of flint with a harder hammer stone to fracture off a flake of desired size and shape. Notice the flakes on the ground from previous strikes.

systems, is based on our analyses of their stone artifacts. These stone tools come in an incredible array of varieties over space and through time. We can, however, make some generalizations about them.

First, a bit of background about how stone is worked. For the most part, stone tools are made of rock that can be flaked; that is, when struck, shock waves travel through it and produce a fracture that splits off a flake. It looks very much like the chipped lip one sometimes finds on a glass soda bottle. The size and shape of the flakes are determined by how hard, with what, and at what angle the stone is struck. There are no natural planes of cleavage within the rock. Flint, or chert—a type of sedimentary rock rich in silica—flakes well and was used extensively for tools, as was obsidian, a volcanic glass.

To take flakes off a core, you have to hit the core with another hard object, usually another stone. If that sounds simple, it's not. One must understand the nature of the core material and of the tool one is striking it with (Figure 10.13). Manual dexterity is important and practice, as always, is required for anything close to perfection. I've tried flint knapping, as the process of making stone tools is called, usually with disastrous results.

How do we know, especially with these early, relatively simple tools, that they *are* tools? Couldn't they be rocks that were fractured naturally? For one thing, when flint is struck hard enough to detach a flake—something uncommon in nature—the blow leaves a convex surface on the flake called the **bulb of percussion.** Below this there are often concentric rings, like ripples in water, that represent the shock waves. On the

bulb of percussion A convex surface on a flake caused by the force used to split the flake off. Rarely found in a natural break.

FIGURE 10.14
Pressure flaking by pushing a piece of antler against the edge of a core tool. The tool is held in a piece of leather to support it and to protect the toolmaker's hand.

core, there is a corresponding concave surface. Naturally fractured stones rarely exhibit these rings, nor do they show a pattern of flakes. Even in some of the simplest stone tools (as in Figure 5.10), one can see the plan of the manufacturer, the goal of creating a sharp edge or a point.

As technological skills improved, other implements were used to gain more control over the shape of the flakes being removed. A piece of bone, wood, or antler can be used to make a more precise strike or to **pressure flake** the core, which means taking off smaller flakes by pushing the tool against the side of the stone (Figure 10.14). Later still, two tools were sometimes used to acquire even more control—a piece of antler or bone became a chisel when struck by a rock used like a hammer. Finally—a feature associated with early farming societies—stones were ground into the desired shape using a rough rock like sandstone to make a smoother and more durable cutting edge. This practice also allowed people to choose as cores harder rocks, rocks that did not necessarily have the flaking characteristics of flint.

The very first stone tools are from Africa and dated at 2.6 million years ago (see Figure 5.10). As discussed in Chapter 5, they are associated with *Homo habilis*. About 1.4 million years ago, *Homo erectus* elaborated on the earlier toolmaking technique by flaking the entire stone, controlling the shape of the whole core tool. This tool tradition is called **Acheulian**, after the site in France where it was first identified. The core tool produced is the famous hand axe (see Figure 5.15), symmetrical, edged and pointed, and bifacial. In addition to hand axes, *H. erectus* also made tools with straight, sharp edges called cleavers. In making a hand

pressure flake Taking a flake off a core by pushing a wood, bone, or antler tool against the stone.

Acheulian A toolmaking tradition associated with *Homo erectus* in Africa and Europe. Includes hand axes, cleavers, and flake tools.

FIGURE 10.15
The Levallois technique: (a) produce a margin along the edge of the core, (b) shape the surface of the core, (c, d) prepare the surface (the "striking platform") to be struck, (e) remove the flake, and return to step b for additional flake removal.

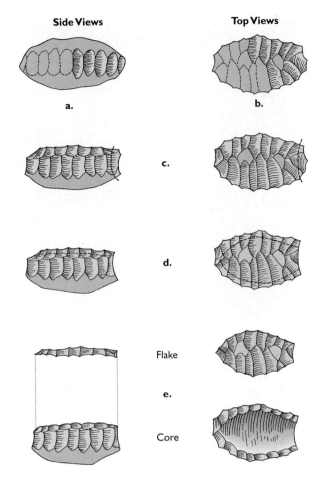

Side Views   Top Views

a.   b.

c.

d.

Flake

e.

Core

axe or a cleaver, a great many flakes are produced—as many as fifty usable ones according to one estimate—and these could be further flaked to produce desired shapes for specific purposes.

Although core tools like the hand axe remained popular for hundreds of thousands of years, flake tools increased in use and diversity. About 200,000 years ago a new and imaginative method of making flake tools appeared, first in Africa and associated with archaic *Homo sapiens*. Called the prepared core, or **Levallois** technique, after the suburb of Paris where it was first recognized, it involves the careful preparation of the rough stone core so that up to four or five flakes of desired shape can be taken off. The flakes can then be used for cutting, scraping, piercing, and so on (Figure 10.15).

Among the well-established accomplishments of the Neandertals, who I defined as a regional population of archaic *Homo sapiens*, was an elaboration on the Levallois technique. Called the **Mousterian** tradition,

Levallois Tool technology involving striking uniform flakes from a prepared core.

Mousterian The culture associated with the European Neandertals.

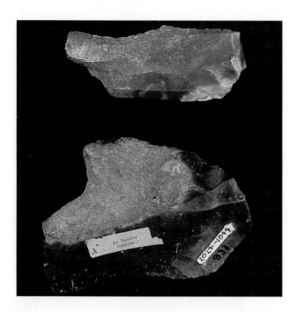

FIGURE 10.16
Retouched Mousterian flakes from the original site of Le Moustier in France.

after the site of Le Moustier in France, it involved careful retouching of the flakes taken off cores. These flakes were sharpened and shaped by precise additional flaking, on one side or both, to make specialized tools (Figure 10.16). One authority has identified no fewer than sixty-three Mousterian tool types.

Several specific uses of Mousterian tools have been inferred from microscopic wear-pattern analysis on specimens from a cave site in Israel. Wear patterns indicate animal butchering, woodworking, bone and antler carving, and working of animal hides. There are also wear patterns like those produced by the friction of a wooden shaft against a stone spear point. The Neandertals may have been the first to haft a stone point.

With anatomically modern *Homo sapiens* came further advances in tool technology. Although much of their tool kit at first resembles that of archaics, artifacts from one of the oldest modern human sites show an important advance. From a site in South Africa, dated to perhaps 120,000 years ago, come long, bifacially worked spear points. These were flaked from cores by the punch technique, where a pointed punch, usually made from antler, is placed on the core and then struck with a stone hammer. This method directs the force of the blow more precisely so that longer, narrower, thinner flakes of predictable shape, called blades, may be taken off. The same technique shows up later in Europe. These blade tools were reworked into detailed and efficient knives, scrapers, and punches, as well as spear and, later, arrow points. In addition, much later, **microliths,** small stones made from pieces of blades, were attached to handles to make sickles, devices for harvesting grasses (see Figure 10.27).

microliths Small stone flakes, usually used as part of a larger tool such as a sickle.

FIGURE 10.17
Bifacially flaked Upper Paleolithic spear points, some of the finest stonework ever seen.

By the time the Neandertals disappeared, about 30,000 years ago, modern *Homo sapiens* had spread all over the Old World, and even as far as Australia, and we enter an important cultural period called the Upper Paleolithic (Late Old Stone Age), known first through finds in Europe. This period is marked by several notable cultural innovations. Blades struck off cores become so precisely and beautifully made as to be virtual works of art (Figure 10.17). In fact, some are so thin and delicate we think they may have been just that. Tools in the Upper Paleolithic were also made from bone, antler, and ivory. Some are practical, such as harpoons, spear points, and shaft straighteners. Some have symbolic significance, and even some of the utilitarian items are decorated (see Figure 5.21). Indeed, art is seen in the Upper Paleolithic in some of its most striking and beautiful forms—a topic we'll take up in the next section.

The final step in stone tool technology, the ground stone tool, is first seen from around 9000 years ago in Europe and Southwest Asia and perhaps even earlier, maybe 20,000 years ago, in Japan and Australia. These earliest artifacts were flaked axes and adzes (like axes but with the head perpendicular to the shaft) with cutting edges made by grinding. Soon, though, grinding was used to give final form to the entire tool.

Grinding is accomplished by rubbing an unformed stone, called a blank, on a gritty stone like sandstone. Using a finer stone with some wet sand on it provides a polish for the finishing touches. The advantage of ground stone is that the smooth surfaces cut better than the rough ones of a flaked tool and that harder stones, less likely to break on impact, can be made into tools.

The use of stone tools persisted even among peoples who learned how to use metal. Some Native American groups, for example, who worked metal for ornaments, still had stone weapons and cutting tools. More recently, small flakes of flint attached to a hammer that struck a metal plate provided the spark in flintlock rifles and pistols, invented in the 1700s. Scalpels for fine surgery (like eye surgery) have been made of obsidian, which is sharper and wears better than steel.

So tools of stone were, and in some places continue to be, major items in the tool kits of humans. And for the prehistoric period of our cultural evolution, they are essential bits of evidence in our reconstruction of past lifeways.

Abstract Thought

Abstract thinking is not completely unique to humans. Chimpanzees think abstractly when they make and use their termite sticks (see Figure 7.2). Dogs think abstractly, in a way, when they make generalizations about behaviors. But what about the level of abstraction that only humans (so far as we know) think at? What about ritual and religion, social responsibilities, and aesthetic appreciation? What evidence have we found for early expressions of these singularly human traits?

Some of the earliest concrete evidence comes from Neandertal times in the form of burials of the dead. Though many previously presumed burials have now been attributed to natural causes, at least thirty-six Neandertal sites, dating from 75,000 to 35,000 years ago, show evidence of intentional interment of the dead, including special positioning of the body, sometimes in a fetal position (Figure 10.18). In about 40 percent of these graves were remains of grave goods—stone tools, animal bones and, possibly, flowers.

There is some debate over the ritual significance of these burials. Did they represent belief in an afterlife or just reverence for the physical remains of the deceased? The pollen found in a Neandertal grave in Iraq may not have been from flowers placed in the grave but may have been brought in by burrowing rodents, carried in by water, or blown in by wind. But whatever the facts—and we will probably never know for sure—it is clear that the Neandertals had some consciousness of and ideas about death and treated the dead in a manner that reflected this.

It has also been suggested that Neandertals were among the first to care for their elderly, ill, and injured; that is, they had ideas about the value of individual lives and some sense of social responsibility. The famous "Old Man" of La Chapelle-aux-Saints in France (the top skull in Figure 5.19) has been interpreted as aged, lacking most of his teeth, and having a debilitating case of arthritis. That he survived for a time with these infirmities, according to traditional assessments, indicates he was cared for by his group. Recent re–examination, however, shows that much of his tooth loss was after death and that his arthritis may not have

FIGURE 10.18
The Neandertal burial from La Ferrassie, France. The body was buried in the flexed position with knees drawn up to the chest, perhaps to mimic sleep. (The basket in the background belonged to the excavators.)

been quite as debilitating as thought. Nor was he really old. He died when he was less than forty, probably rather quickly—as did the majority of people of his time. Care of the elderly was probably not something they had to contend with very often.

On the other hand, there is a skeleton of a Neandertal man from Iraq that shows signs of injuries that resulted in the loss of one arm and possibly blindness. He lived with these conditions for some time and, therefore, was obviously fed and cared for by his comrades.

FIGURE 10.19
A 32,000-year-old engraved bone plaque from Abri Blanchard, France, which Alexander Marshack interprets as a record based on the phases of the moon.

Perhaps the best indication of abstract thought is art—items that are not utilitarian in the sense of directly helping people survive but that may carry symbolic meaning or produce aesthetic pleasure. There are some tantalizing pieces of evidence for very early art—some collections of natural pigments, possibly for body decoration, from a rock shelter in France around 300,000 years ago, and a possible amulet made of a shaped and colored mammoth tooth from 100,000 years ago in Hungary. But we see unequivocal examples of art beginning about 40,000 years ago. These finds are associated with anatomically modern *Homo sapiens*.

From Australia come painted symbols, handprints, and petroglyphs (designs scratched into rock) dated at 43,000 to 36,000 years ago. There is a painting in a cave in Namibia dated at perhaps 29,000 years ago. A carved ivory disk found in a child's grave and a colored pendant in the shape of an animal come from Russia about 28,000 years ago.

The best-known and most evocative early art is that from the Upper Paleolithic in Europe. This does not necessarily mean that Europeans at that time were the best artists in the world. It may simply be that archaeology has been carried out longer and more extensively there than just about anywhere else, so we have found more artifacts and thus know and understand the prehistory of Europe better.

Much of the earliest European art is in the form of carvings. Sometimes tools were decorated (See Figure 5.21). Other carvings had strictly symbolic meaning. From France, dated at 32,000 years ago, is a piece of antler engraved with a curving line of 69 marks (Figure 10.19). Archaeologist Alexander Marshack interprets these as a succession of lunar phases—the correct shape, order, and number for more than two months. This, he thinks, may have been an early lunar calendar.

FIGURE 10.20
The Venus figurine from Dolni Věstonice in the Czech Republic.

FIGURE 10.21
This living ox, at Le Toth museum near the cave of Lascaux in France, has been bred to resemble the aurochs, an ancestor of the modern oxen that was one of the largest mammals of Upper Paleolithic times, weighing more than a ton. The aurochs was hunted for food and was well represented in Upper Paleolithic cave paintings (see Figure 5.22).

FIGURE 10.22

An animal identified as a cow (*vache* in French) and a herd of small horses seem almost to be moving across the cave wall in this painting from Lascaux (see also Figure 5.22) dated to perhaps 17,000 years ago.

Among the most famous of the carvings are the so-called Venus figurines found throughout Europe and dating back to as early as 30,000 years ago (Figure 10.20 , and see Figure 5.21, bottom). These are commonly interpreted as fertility symbols since many depict women with exaggerated secondary sexual characteristics who appear to be pregnant. Others, however, seem to be of women at other stages of life. We may never know just what these figurines meant to those who made them. Clearly, however, they had *some* meaning.

By far the most famous early works of art are the cave paintings, the majority of which come from southern France and northern Spain and are dated at 30,000 to 10,000 years ago. Using natural pigments, the artists rendered accurate depictions of important animals—bison, aurochs (an ancient ox), horses, deer, reindeer, mammoth, ibex (an antelope), and even rhinoceros, lions, and bears, all of which inhabited Europe at the time (Figure 10.21). Some of these paintings are fairly simple and sketchy, but many are beautiful, colorful, and show depth and motion (Figure 10.22, and see Figure 5.22). Sometimes the shape and relief of the rock of the cave wall was incorporated into the painting, giving it even greater realism. Seeing these paintings in person, as I did a few years ago, is a truly moving experience.

As with the figurines, there has been debate over the meaning (or meanings) of these paintings. They most often depict important game animals—and the more important the animals, the more frequently they were painted. Big, dangerous animals, even if rarely a source of meat— mammoths, for instance—were also fairly common. In the recently discovered Chauvet Cave near Avignon, France, rhinoceros, lions, and even a hyena—all nonfood animals—were depicted.

The caves in which these paintings were found were not where people lived. They were sometimes hard to get to, and the painted areas were often far inside them. A source of light was required to travel through the caves and to produce the art. There was clearly something special about these paintings.

Anthropologist Patricia Rice and sociologist Ann Paterson have concluded that the cave art served a combination of purposes: "fertility magic, hunting magic, hunting education, and story-telling about hunting." "Capturing" an animal by painting it may have helped the hunter capture it in reality. Painting a group of animals may have simply helped ensure that they would exist somewhere to *be* hunted. Young men may have been instructed in the hunt with the help of these paintings. And such paintings may also have aided in the recounting of exciting hunting tales (see Figure 8.1). Again, the important fact is that they clearly held meaning of some sort. They stood for and probably helped communicate ideas. It may be no coincidence that these striking cave paintings are found in an area and during a time period that corresponds to a maximum advance of the Pleistocene glaciers—a time and place of social and ecological stress.

Control of Food Resources

In Chapter 8 we discussed the origins of food producing and some of the evidence we use to trace its history. We can now look at some specific locations of early food production, some of the specific crops and animals that were domesticated, and some of the specific evidence used by archaeologists in reconstructing this history (Figures 10.23 and 10.24).

Let's begin with animals. As you might imagine, the first animal to be domesticated was our "best friend," the dog. Evidence of domestic dogs, descended from wolves, has been found at sites in Iraq and Israel dating from 12,000 years ago. (Genetically and reproductively, dogs *are* wolves, although some of the breeds we've created would be incapable of interbreeding with wolves because of their small size.) The Israeli find is the grave of a man whose left hand clutches the skeleton of a puppy—clearly, dogs have held meaning for us for some time. Other early dog remains come from Idaho about 8000 years ago. This domestic animal is known

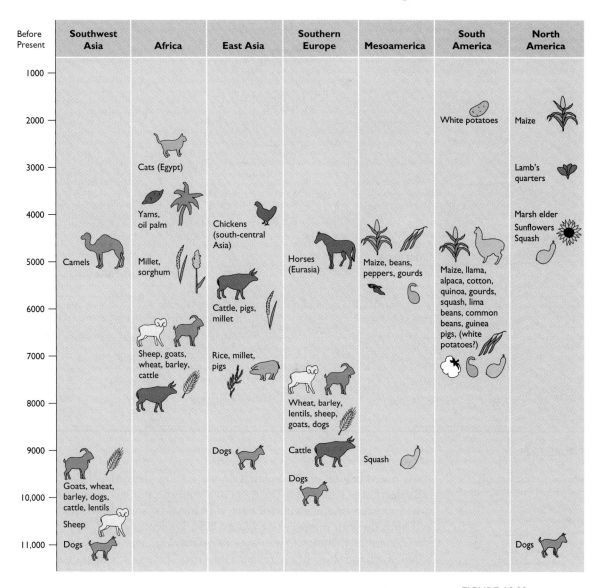

FIGURE 10.23
A chronology of domestication.

worldwide and dogs now come in all sorts of shapes and sizes, but these early ones, little different from their wolf ancestors, display one telling characteristic: Their teeth are crowded together, a result of artificial selection for smaller sizes, or, perhaps, a secondary result of selection for more immature characteristics like docility and subordinate behavior. (Dogs essentially behave like immature wolves.) Although dogs were no doubt used for hunting, another early use was probably as a handy food source. Dogs are still a food source in parts of the world.

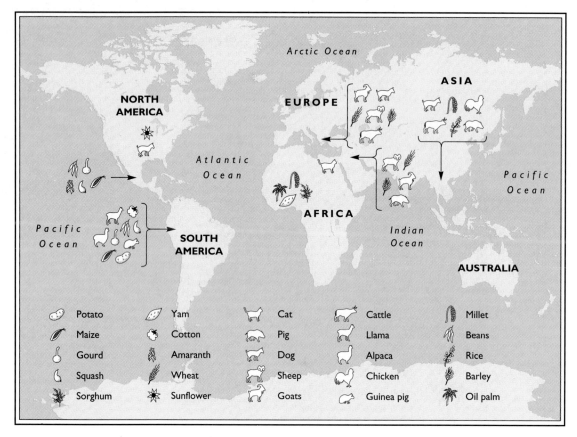

Potato, Maize, Gourd, Squash, Sorghum, Yam, Cotton, Amaranth, Wheat, Sunflower, Cat, Pig, Dog, Sheep, Goats, Cattle, Llama, Alpaca, Chicken, Guinea pig, Millet, Beans, Rice, Barley, Oil palm

FIGURE 10.24

Map of the apparent hearths of domestication of some important plant and animal species.

As noted before, prior to actual domestication (defined as using artificial selection to manipulate the traits of a wild species), people may have learned to exercise some control over wild herds of animals, as modern-day Lapps do with reindeer (see Figure 8.8). Evidence for this in prehistory is, naturally, indirect, but sites in Southwest Asia dating back to 18,000 years ago show heavy reliance on single species of wild animals—wild sheep or goats, specifically. The inference is that herds were followed and exploited on a regular basis and were maybe even controlled as the Lapps do by capturing and castrating a male member of the herd.

Around 10,000 years ago, domestic animals begin showing up all over the Old World. Domestic sheep and goats, differentiated from wild ancestors by such things as horn shape and size, appear in Southwest Asia around that time and in southern Europe and Africa a few thousand years later. Domesticated pigs appear in East Asia over 7000 years ago and cattle about 6000 years ago. Cattle were already found in Southern Europe by 9000 years ago. Domesticated camels appear in Southwest Asia about 5000 years ago and the domestic horse shows up at the same time in Eurasia.

Domestication of both animals and plants generally occurs later in the New World and was never as extensive as in the Old World. There are four reasons for this. First, humans didn't enter the New World until later. Second, wild species with characteristics that lent themselves to domestication were not as numerous. Third, some wild food sources, such as the bison, were already found in great abundance. Fourth, in this region populations became large enough to require manipulation of food sources later than in the Old World. The only New World domesticated animals—which come from Central and South America—are turkeys, alpacas and llamas (Figure 10.25), and guinea pigs (yes, they were food).

Evidence for all these conclusions comes in a number of forms. There are the biological differences already mentioned between wild forms and domestic ones. There is other biological evidence as well, such as finding large numbers of bones of elderly animals at archaeological sites. This indicates that they were kept, for milk or work, beyond the age at which they normally would have been killed if hunted for meat.

There's cultural evidence as well. From Afghanistan 10,000 years ago come small clay tokens, used, it seems, to keep track of trade transactions, that show symbols for sheep and goats. These animals were clearly possessions with specific values attached.

Notice that the animal species first domesticated in each area are species that were native to that area—the same is true of plants. That may seem obvious, but with all the cultural exchanging and borrowing we are used to today, it's good to remind ourselves that you can't, for example, look for domestication of cattle among Native Americans because there were no wild cattle to domesticate. When searching in the archaeological

245

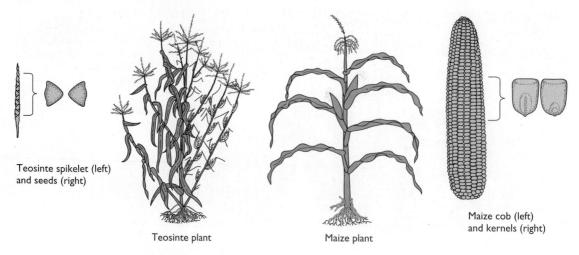

Teosinte spikelet (left) and seeds (right)

Teosinte plant

Maize plant

Maize cob (left) and kernels (right)

FIGURE 10.26

Teosinte, a wild Mexican grass called "God's corn" by the Aztecs, is the most likely candidate for the wild ancestor of maize. Research has indicated that relatively few genetic alterations are required to change the tightly encased seeds and seed spikelet of teosinte into the soft, exposed kernels and cob of maize.

record, we need to understand what wild species were present and the characteristics of those species.

The earliest evidence for plant domestication comes from Southwest Asia from about 11,000 years ago. The plants involved were wheats called emmer and einkorn. There is also evidence of peas and lentils. Other grains like barley, millet, and sorghum appear a little later in Southwest Asia, Africa, and Europe. Rice as a domesticate shows up in East Asia around 7000 years ago. At about the same time we find evidence of maize farming in Mexico.

Evidence of plant domestication, as with animals, comes in part from our knowledge of differences between wild and domestic species. Maize, for instance, is thought to have been domesticated from a wild grass called teosinte, and shows a number of distinctions from its wild relatives in kernel number, overall structure, and the presence of a distinct cob (Figure 10.26, and see also Figure 8.7).

It is no coincidence, by the way, that so many early domesticates—wheat, barley, millet, sorghum, rice, and maize—are grasses. Members of this large family of plants grow rapidly and in great abundance, and they grow from the ground up, meaning that they are not killed off by cutting, grazing, drought, or fire. (That's why we have to mow our lawns *every week*.) In addition, many grasses have a high protein content. Maize does not, but in the New World, beans and squash were also domesticated and they made up the difference; maize, beans, and squash are a very nutritious combination.

Other evidence for early plant domestication is cultural, in the form of tools for planting, harvesting, and storing crops. For example, from several early sites in Southwest Asia and Egypt come remains of sickles (Figure 10.27), presumably used for harvesting plants. These consisted of flint microliths set in a handle of horn, antler, or wood and held in place

FIGURE 10.27
Flint sickle microliths from the fourth century B.C. in Israel. They were originally set in a horn handle with bitumen.

by mastic (a kind of glue) or bitumen (a natural tarlike substance). One of these was found at the bottom of a 6000-year-old coiled basket that also contained some wheat and barley grains. Clinching the assessment that these tools were sickles, microscopic analysis of the flint blades showed a luster on their surface like that caused when flint is brought continually into rapid contact with the silica crystals in the stalks of grassy plants. We also have found stones on which grains were ground to make flour, as well as the stones used for grinding. We know what they are because we've seen present-day peoples using similar items. Storage pits, baskets, and pottery pieces that hold the remains of grains have also been found, all indicating the presence of farming. Later, of course, we find evidence of more–complex farming technology such as plows.

SUMMARY

Material artifacts are the means humans use to implement their solutions to the problems of survival. We make tools geared to dealing with the climate, food sources, and other aspects of the environments in which we live. Material artifacts are also related to our cultural environments. The specific form of an artifact may be more connected to the cultural system than to the natural world. Artifacts have, in other words, styles. And many artifacts, such as the tombstones discussed in the beginning of the chapter, serve the purpose of expressing a society's cultural ideas, ideals, and attitudes.

These connections are used by archaeologists to interpret the remains of past societies and cultural systems in their attempt to reconstruct those societies and systems. These endeavors, of course, aid anthropology as a whole in answering the broad questions we ask about our species and its behavior.

CONTEMPORARY ISSUES

Who Owns Archaeological Sites and Their Contents?

Visit any natural history or art museum in a major western city like New York, London, or Paris, and you will encounter thousands of cultural artifacts and even human biological remains that were originally found in other countries. In some cases, these items were taken from those countries with permission. In many other cases, the justification for taking them was the cultural dominance of the western country or the idea that the scientific nature of the museum somehow gave it the right to have, study, and display the items. Recently, many countries have requested the return of such artifacts and remains, and many institutions have complied. It is now generally felt that paleo-anthropological and archaeological objects are the possessions of the countries in which they are recovered. In many cases, such objects in fact remain in the appropriate country and must be studied there by foreign scientists.

A fairly recent example is the famous "Ice Man" found in an Alpine glacier in 1991—an almost perfectly preserved freeze-dried mummy of a man, along with many of his artifacts, dated to 5300 years ago. He was found close to the Austrian-Italian border but, because the border

was not well marked up in the mountains, it took a while to establish national ownership. The mummy remained for seven years in an Austrian lab since it at first appeared most likely that he was found in that country. In 1997, however, surveyors determined that he had in fact been located inside the Italian border—albeit by a mere 93 meters (305 feet). He now resides in a museum in Bolzano, Italy.

The situation becomes less clear when debates over ownership involve not geopolitical boundaries but biological and cultural descent. For example, for years in North America, otherwise well-meaning scientists enjoyed the freedom to recover, study, and store or display the skeletal remains of the remote and not-so-remote ancestors of living peoples. Many of the thousands of Native American skeletons and related artifacts housed in museums and at universities were literally exhumed from the graves into which they were placed by members of their societies.

Although these remains have provided much information about the original inhabitants of this continent, Native American groups began to object, for obvious reasons. In 1990 Congress

Though our image of archaeology usually centers on the recovery of ancient artifacts, the heart of the data collection phase of this field is record keeping. Without a context for the raw data it would be impossible to see the relationships between artifacts and thus impossible to achieve the real goals of the field. So archaeologists use a precise set of techniques to locate, recover, record, date, and preserve the material remains of ancient lifeways.

The archaeological record of human prehistory is rich and complex. But by looking, even briefly, at some of the high points, we can see that the record tells a story of our species' increasing ability to imagine ways to aid survival and to implement those ideas by mastering technical skills to produce a rich and vast array of material artifacts.

passed the Native American Graves Protection and Repatriation Act (NAGPRA). It said that lineal descendants had a right to the remains of their buried ancestors housed in institutions or discovered on federal or tribal territory. This has led to the removal of large collections of human remains and associated artifacts from museums and labs, and has made new excavations of Native American remains difficult if not impossible. Indeed, before naturally shed remains were excluded from NAGPRA regulations, two local tribes demanded the return of some 10,000-year-old human hair found at a site in Montana, hair that could provide information on the DNA and, thus, on the biological relationships of early Americans.

Is there a compromise between honoring the cultural laws and heritage of peoples and providing science with important data—data that may even shed light on the histories of the peoples in question? In the end, each case must be examined and judged on its own merits. Much evidence of early America is in the form of abandoned and naturally covered-over objects and bones, not intentional burials. Much cannot be reasonably affiliated with any specific living group. Such items should be freely open to scientific investigation. On the other hand, scientists should no longer go into clearly identified burial areas armed with

shovels and trowels. When ancient bones are uncovered by natural processes or accident (say, during a construction project), the group with which those bones are affiliated might allow scientific information to be gathered before the bones are reburied.

This occurred with the well-known African Burial Ground in New York City. In 1991, construction workers unearthed the graves of some 400 African Americans buried between the late 1600s and 1796. (The whole cemetery, most of which is still under the present city, may contain over 10,000 burials.) Because of the wealth of information that could be gathered from the skeletons and the associated artifacts about an otherwise poorly documented group of people, the remains were thoroughly studied by scientists. Then they were reburied with appropriate ceremony.

Whatever the legalities of the individual cases, however, there is one overriding ethical consideration that should guide our actions in these matters: No matter how old (or even from what species) they are, bones were once integral parts of living, breathing, feeling creatures. Artifacts were once important parts of living cultures. Even when we use these things as scientific specimens, they deserve respectful treatment, as do living peoples and cultures associated with them.

NOTES, REFERENCES, AND READINGS

Our discussion of material culture and the area of anthropology that focuses on it took up just one chapter, but the field of archaeology is broad and varied. It covers the whole planet for the whole time our species has been around. It looks at the material culture of premodern humans as well. There are, as a result, many good books and articles about the field. Here are some of my favorites, including those that specifically relate to topics in the chapter.

For a good treatment of the history of archaeology, see Brian Fagan's *The Adventure of Archaeology*. For one example of an archaeological adventure, try Nicholas Clapp's *The Road to Ubar: Finding the Atlantis of the Sands*. It's about the discovery of the location of a fabled ancient Arabian city using a combination of old-fashioned archaeology, high-tech satellite imagery, and, maybe, just a touch of Indiana Jones.

More on New England tombstones can be found in *Gravestones of Early New England and the Men Who Made Them: 1653–1800* by Harriette Merrifield Forbes. Another example of historical archaeology is Ken Feder's *A Village of Outcasts*, about the archaeology of a remote settlement in Connecticut inhabited by Native Americans, African American slaves, and European outcasts from 1740 to 1860. The story of Maiden Castle is in the book of that name by Sir Mortimer Wheeler.

The analysis of toolmaking by *Homo habilis* is from Nick Toth's "The Oldowan Reassessed: A Close Look at Early Stone Artifacts" from *Journal of Archaeological Science* volume 12.

Archaeological theory and method are the topics of Tom Hester et al., *Field Methods in Archaeology*, seventh edition, and Robert Sharer and Wendy Ashmore's *Archaeology: Discovering Our Past*. An excellent collection of thirty-two articles on various aspects of archaeology is Ken Feder's *Lessons from the Past*, and his *Past in Perspective: An Introduction to Human Prehistory* recounts the panorama of human evolution and the evidence used to reconstruct it. The most modern technologies applied to the ancient past are the topic of *Virtual Archaeology: Re-creating Ancient Worlds* edited by Maurizio Forte and Alberto Siliotti. It uses three-dimensional computer reconstructions of ancient sites as well as striking photographs and diagrams that help bring the past to life.

A humorous yet thought-provoking look at what an archaeologist of the future might think of the remains of our culture is David Macauly's *Motel of the Mysteries*.

The analysis of Mousterian tool types, stressing the importance of flake tools, is in François Bordes's *A Tale of Two Caves*, and the analysis of their use based on wear patterns is in John Shea's "A Functional Study of the Lithic Industries Associated with Hominid Fossils in Kebara and Qafzeh Caves, Israel" from *The Human Revolution* edited by P. Mellars and C. Stringer.

A lengthier discussion of Upper Paleolithic art can be found in Ken Feder's and my *Human Antiquity*, third edition, which also includes a detailed discussion of the origins and early history of domestication. Pat Rice and Ann Paterson's conclusions about the meanings of cave art are in their "Cave Art and Bones: Exploring the Interrelationships" from *American Anthropologist* volume 37, pages 94–100. Try also the January 1975 issue of *National Geographic* for an article called "Exploring the Mind of Ice Age Man" by Alexander Marshack.

A discussion of the domestication of plants and animals and their historical ramifications is included in Jared Diamond's Pulitzer Prize–winning *Guns, Germs, and Steel: The Fates of Human Societies*.

11

COMMUNICATION
Sharing What We Need to Know

When a honeybee finds a new source of food—flower pollen and nectar—she flies back to the hive. Within minutes, more bees emerge and, amazingly, fly straight to the food. Their ability to do this is a result of what goes on in the hive after that first bee flies in.

Inside the hive, that bee does a dance, called a waggling dance, to communicate to the other bees the direction, distance, and identity of the food (Figure 11.1). First, because it's usually dark in the hive she emits sound signals that help the other bees determine where she is and how she's moving. She then dances in a figure-eight pattern, waggling only when she is facing the direction of the food source in relation to the sun. The pace of her dancing tells how far away the food is; the faster she dances, the closer the food. At some point, the bees observing the dance emit sounds that vibrate the honeycomb. This causes the dancer to stop, and she gives the watchers small samples of the food so they know its taste, smell, and quality. After receiving the necessary information, the other bees fly out to find the food. They can find food on cloudy days as well as sunny because they can see ultraviolet light.

As amazing as this is, it's just one example of the many ways in which organisms communicate to other members of their species. We sometimes think that humans have the only communication system capable of transmitting such specific information, but, as with other assumed human uniquenesses, that's not the case. The bee dance, as we'll discuss, has the rudiments of some features of human communication.

The important thing here is not to try desperately to come up with a list of traits that distinguish human communication, but to understand what communication is and how it acts as one of a species' survival mechanisms. At the base of this understanding is the simple concept that communication is the way in which information from the nervous system of one organism is transmitted to that of another of the same species. It follows that a species' communication system reflects the species' nervous system and the nature of the information being communicated. A bee, for example, is built to perceive the location and nature of its food source, and it has evolved the ability to share that information with its fellow bees. As you might expect, as simple nervous systems evolved into brains, and as necessary information became more involved, communication systems became more complex.

A look at the specific features of the human communication system will show how this relationship works. Although the term is often used more broadly, I use **language** to refer solely to the human communication system.

language The human communication system.

FIGURE 11.1
A returning bee begins her dance to communicate to the others of her hive the direction, distance, and nature of a food source.

LANGUAGE

Recall from Chapter 7 the abilities of our brains that allow us to have culture. Essentially, our neocortexes can experience not only present events but also events from the past and even hypothetical future events. The human brain can do this because it stores massive amounts of information, derived from experience through the sense organs, and stores that information in such a way that all the individual pieces of data are separately filed but highly cross-referenced. Thus, they can be manipulated—taken apart, modified, and put together in a virtually infinite number of combinations. This ability not only lets us think about experiences, but also enables us to make generalizations about them and derive abstract ideas and concepts from them.

We talk about these mental processes so our communication system must possess features that reflect these processes and make sharing our data and ideas possible. In humans, linguistic abilities are housed in a special area on the left side of the brain (see Figure 4.5), but the functions of that area are basically the same as those of the neocortex in general. Look at the main features of human language.

First, we can talk about things that are not right in front of us, things that are not immediate stimuli. We've been doing that all along in this book, for example. This characteristic is called **displacement.** The subjects of our language can be displaced in time and space.

Second, our language is not made up, as are the communication systems of other species, of a series of individual signals, each with a single and specific meaning. Our ideas are expressed in units of meaning called

displacement The ability to communicate about things and ideas not immediate in space or time.

sentences, which in turn are made up of smaller units called words, which themselves are made up of various combinations of sounds. This feature of language is called **duality.** Language operates on two levels. Individual sounds, **phonemes,** which themselves are meaningless, are strung together in various combinations that have meaning, from the smallest meaningful unit, the **morpheme,** to larger units such as words, sentences, paragraphs, and so on.

Duality makes possible the endless generation of new combinations of these units to express new experiences, new meanings, new ideas, and new concepts. This is called **productivity.** Just as we manipulate the thoughts in our brains, we manipulate the mechanism we use to share those thoughts. If we couldn't do that, we couldn't share those thoughts, and culture, by definition, must be shared.

Finally, since we communicate abstractions, it would be impossible for our language to be made up of sounds that are iconic, that is, that resemble the thing being talked about, or that are specifically linked to one meaning. Rather, our sounds and the units of meaning we combine them into are **arbitrary.** They are culturally agreed-on symbols for facts, ideas, and concepts. That's why every language in the world can have a different linguistic symbol for the same thing. The Tswana, a southern African people, call one species of nut-bearing tree *mongongo* (and the word has been adopted into English). The San call the same tree //"*gxa* (the / is a dental click and the " a glottal flap).

Apply these features to the communication system of the bees. There is a degree of displacement since the flowers are not right in front of the bee who is communicating information about them. She must remember their location for the few minutes it takes her to fly back to the hive and dance. Similarly, the bees receiving the message must remember it long enough to find the flowers. But the bees can't share information about last year's flowers or even yesterday's, and they can't communicate about food sources in the future. Neither is there duality in the bee's communication system. Each aspect of the dance has a meaning of its own, and that's it. Thus, there can be no real productivity. All the bees talk about is the direction, distance, and general type of food. Finally, the bee's communication system is not symbolic. The waggling dance is an analog in that the bee waggles when she's facing in the direction of the food relative to the sun and paces her dance in direct correlation to the distance. That's a lot different from saying, "Fly 300 yards at 10 degrees east of north." Those symbols have meaning only because we have agreed that they do.

What all this amounts to is the same as saying that the features of our languages are cultural, although, of course, the ability to have language is biological. Our languages must be learned. We are no more born knowing how to speak American English than we are born knowing the rules of American culture. Languages use abstract, arbitrary symbols that allow people to speak about abstract concepts. Languages are passed on to future generations not in the genes but by cultural sharing. And language is facilitated through the use of artifacts—written words in

duality Refers to the fact that human language has two levels: units of sound and units of meaning that those units of sound are combined to create.

phoneme The unit of sound in a language.

morpheme The unit of meaning in a language.

productivity Refers to the ability of human languages to generate limitless numbers of meanings.

arbitrary Here, the fact that the features of human languages bear no direct relation to their meanings but are agreed-on symbols.

literate cultures, but also the spoken words themselves; they are artifacts too, because they are created by people.

But the biological basis for our language must not be underemphasized. We have to learn the features of our native language, but that learning itself has a biological component. Before you ever opened a grammar book in elementary school you could already speak your native language with a great deal of fluency. You made mistakes, of course, and we all do even through adulthood. But our linguistic mistakes were, and are, generally exceptions to the basic rules of our language's grammar.

What happens when we are children is that part of our brain is furiously working to take in data about our communication system and to formulate the generalizations about it that will enable us to use it. You don't have to sit down with a child on a regular basis and pound into his or her head all the rules of grammar. The child will learn those rules simply by having heard the language spoken and by trying to speak it.

Consider the grammatical mistakes children make. They are usually matters of not reflecting exceptions to the general rules—exceptions that must usually be specifically and individually learned. A child who says "Yesterday I seed a rabbit" in a language that normally forms the past tense by adding -ed is being perfectly logical and is actually demonstrating an understanding of a basic rule of English grammar.

There's some evidence that language ability decreases with age. It becomes, for most of us, much harder to learn new languages once we're in our teens. Children deprived of human contact and thus of the opportunity to hear and use language have a very difficult time making up for the deficit later on. Language ability is part of our biological makeup and so, it seems, is the ability and process for learning it.

The study of all the arbitrary pieces of human language is called **descriptive linguistics.** To give you an idea as to what is involved and how languages differ from culture to culture, let's just touch on some of the essentials of this field.

The basis for any language is the set of sounds it uses. These are its phonemes, and each language has its own phonemic inventory. Some of these sounds may be used in other languages as well, but some may be unique. For instance, the language of the San contains four phonemes that we refer to as clicks. They are real parts of the language. The difference between one click and another can make the difference between one word and another.

Languages also differ in phonemic distinctions. Two of the most often cited examples involve the presence or absence of certain distinctions in English and Chinese. The *t* phoneme in the words *tack* and *stack* are, to English speakers, the same. To a speaker of Chinese, however, they are different. Say them out loud and notice that the *t* in *tack* has a puff of air after it (called aspiration) but the *t* in *stack* does not. This difference in Chinese could alter the meaning of a word. On the other hand, the first phonemes in *lock* and *rock* are different to an English speaker but are just variations of the same phoneme to Chinese

descriptive linguistics The study of the structure of language in general and of the specific variations among languages.

and Japanese speakers. A supposedly humorous linguistic stereotype in old films and TV shows is based on this.

The arrangement of phonemes also differs among languages. For instance, the *mb* combination is found in final position in English, as in *lamb*, but never in initial position, as in *Mbuti* (say it with two syllables), the name of a Central African people. An initial *nkr*, as in *Nkruma* (also two syllables), the name of the former president of Ghana, is also absent from English.

Phonemes don't have meanings themselves, but they make a difference in meaning within the context of the basic meaningful units of language, called morphemes. A word is a morpheme; it means something. But not all morphemes are words. The word *words,* for instance, is made up of two morphemes: *word,* with its obvious meaning, and *-s*, which means "make the preceding morpheme plural." A morpheme may come in several versions. The English morpheme that, as a prefix, makes the attached word negative, comes in four forms: *im-, in-, ir-,* and *un-,* as in *im*possible, *in*credible, *ir*responsible, and *un*reasonable.

Moreover, pitch and stress can act as morphemes, changing the meaning of a word or set of words. In Chinese, there are four variations in pitch (the rise or fall of the voice) placed on a combination of phonemes basically pronounced *ma*, resulting in four different words. In Russian, the difference between a statement and a question does not have to involve word order, as in English. The changes in pitch as you say the words of the sentence make the difference. Compare the following English and Russian sentences (the Russian is written phonetically, since that language uses a different alphabet):

> I am going to the post office.
> Am I going to the post office?

> Ya idu nah potchtu. (statement)

> Ya idu nah potchtu. (question)

Finally, morphemes are strung together to make up the unit of speech that conveys whole ideas, the sentence. Each language differs in its rules for the order of morphemes in a sentence. This is called **syntax.** For instance, if we want to negate the idea expressed in an English sentence, we usually put a negative morpheme in front of the appropriate word: *I don't love you.* In German, the negative morpheme *nicht* can go at the very end of the sentence: *Ich liebe dich nicht.* (The humorous construction, made famous in the movie *Wayne's World,* of putting *not* at the end of a sentence, as in *I love you . . . not!,* wasn't funny when that movie was translated into German.)

An example of the power of the rules of language—the rules that we generate as children even before we learn them formally—comes from linguist Noam Chomsky. He offers the following sentence:

> Colorless green ideas sleep furiously.

syntax Rules of word order in a language.

Although it has no real meaning, we easily recognize the sentence as grammatical. All the morphemes and the words they make up are in the right places and order. Compare it to this version:

Furiously sleep ideas green colorless.

That one makes no more sense, but neither does it sound like an English sentence. Another famous example comes from *Through the Looking Glass* by Lewis Carroll:

'Twas brillig, and the slithy toves
  Did gyre and gimble in the wabe;
All mimsy were the borogroves,
  And the mome raths outgrabe.

Don't bother consulting a dictionary; you won't find most of those words. But you may have thought they were real because the word structure and order followed the rules of English.

These, then, are the basic pieces of our language systems, pieces that, within certain rules, are broken up, shuffled around, and recombined to facilitate the communication of our thoughts—thoughts that themselves have been through the same kinds of manipulations.

At this point, two questions should come to mind: How did human language evolve? And, just what is it that brings about the differences among human languages?

LANGUAGE AND EVOLUTION

We can generalize and say that the characteristic features of human language make ours an open communication system. Because of its duality and productivity, human language is almost infinitely creative.

The communication systems of nonhumans, on the other hand—even of the nonhuman primates—are closed systems. That is, there are certain calls or other signs that have meanings, but those meanings are specific. For example, chimpanzees have a large repertoire of calls, facial expressions, and gestures, but these normally express emotional or motivational states such as fear, aggression, sexual stimulation, or excitement over something like food or the presence of strangers (Figure 11.2). Thinking back to our discussion of the brain in Chapter 7, we might say that chimps communicate limbic system functions—basic survival-oriented emotions. With few exceptions, the chimps do not *name* things, or, put technically, their communication system is not referential; it doesn't *refer* to something in the physical environment. Nor has anyone ever observed a chimp combining or stringing together calls to convey new meanings.

The exceptions to the nonreferential communication of the chimps are instructive. There is evidence, from studies of chimps and even some African monkeys, that danger calls may differ depending upon the source of the danger, for example, whether it is on the ground (a leopard) or in

FIGURE 11.2
A male chimpanzee showing a "full open grin." This is a sign of excitement, often used by a high-ranking chimp displaying close to a subordinate.

the air (an eagle). Chimps may specify the presence of a snake. If there's anything important enough to "talk" about specifically, it would be potentially lethal predators.

In terms of human evolution, the question now becomes, How did a closed call system, no doubt possessed by our ancestors, turn into an open system? Linguists Charles Hockett and Robert Ascher, in an article called "The Human Revolution," propose a simple model of how this transition may have occurred, which I'm going to simplify even more here. Hockett and Asher suggest that two closed calls were both found, by some human ancestor, to be appropriate for communicating a certain situation. But instead of using both calls, this innovative early hominid combined the calls, perhaps using part of each to make up a brand-new call that conveyed the meaning of both the old calls. Suppose the call for "food" was made up of the sounds ABCD, and the call for "danger" consisted of the sounds EFGH. When a leopard was found standing over a newly killed antelope, both calls would be appropriate. Or, one could be "productive" and use ABEF, meaning "food but danger too." This might make the combination CDGH mean "no food and no danger either," and ABGH "food and no danger." The system is now open, and all the other calls and their parts may become phonemes that can be combined into various morphemes, which can, in turn, be combined into words and sentences. To be sure, it didn't happen this quickly and simply, but the development of language must have entailed a process very much like this.

When did this transition take place? Until people started writing, only around 5000 years ago, language left no physical remains. We must rely on indirect evidence, and this comes in three forms.

First, we know that the brains of living humans are asymmetrical—the right and left hemispheres are differently shaped and perform different functions. Language and the ability to use symbols are in the left hemisphere, and we know with some precision just which linguistic functions are located in which specific areas. By looking back in the fossil record, then, we might try to find at what point modern-looking brain structure appears, especially those features and areas associated with language.

Fortunately, the inside of the skull reflects some of the features of the brain it once held. By making **endocasts,** or using natural endocasts, of the inside surfaces of fossil skulls, we may produce images of the brains of our ancestors (Figure 11.3). What we find, however, doesn't really help answer our question. Asymmetrical brains and language-associated areas are found in all members of genus *Homo* and even in *Australopithecus.* Indeed, we know that chimp brains are also asymmetrical, even in some of the same ways as ours. Until we can discover just what these features were used for by our ancestors, brains can only hint at mental function.

A second type of evidence comes from the use of the base of the skull to reconstruct the vocal apparatus. Even though the vocal apparatus is made up of soft tissue, those parts are connected to bone. The shape of those bones is correlated with the shape of the larynx, pharynx, and other anatomical features (Figure 11.4).

Reconstruction work on australopithecines indicates that their vocal tract was basically like that of apes, with the larynx and pharynx high up in the throat. While this allows them to drink and breathe at the same time (as human infants can do up to about eighteen months of age), it does not allow for the precise manipulation of air that is required for the sounds made by modern human languages. The early hominids could make sounds, but they would have been more like those of chimpanzees.

By the time of *Homo erectus,* however, vocal tracts were more like those of modern humans, positioned lower in the throat and allowing for a greater range and speed of sound production. Thus, *H. erectus* could have produced vocal communication with precise differences among sounds. Whether or not they were doing so, however, can't be inferred from this physical evidence.

endocasts Natural or human-made casts of the inside of a skull. The cast reflects the surface of the brain and allows us to study the brains of even extinct species.

FIGURE 11.3
Natural endocasts from South African australopithecines showing the degree of detail possible. Notice the blood vessels, especially in the upper right cast. Such casts may also be made artificially and allow us to compare the brains of our ancestors with those of modern humans.

The third type of evidence is the least concrete but, to me, the most compelling at this time. We may ask at what point did our ancestors have something to talk *about* that would require the complex features that characterize modern human languages. Here, I come back to *Homo erectus*, who manufactured fairly complex tools, controlled fire, and was able to adapt culturally to a wide range of different and changing environmental circumstances. As impressionistic as this may be, I just can't imagine them using a closed system of communication given the kinds of information necessary to adapt that way. At the same time, I also see language as evolving, not suddenly changing. So I would imagine that, could we hear *Homo erectus* talking, we would not recognize a thing about the communication system. The features of modern languages probably did

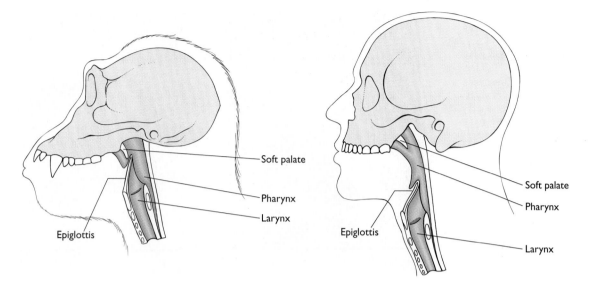

Soft palate
Pharynx
Larynx
Epiglottis

Soft palate
Pharynx
Larynx
Epiglottis

FIGURE 11.4
The vocal tract of a chimp compared to a modern human's. The high placement of the chimp's makes it impossible for it to produce all of the sounds that are part of modern human languages.

not appear at their current level of complexity until much later. According to some, the achievement of that level would have coincided with the increase in cultural complexity evidenced by such things as Upper Paleolithic art (see Chapter 10). So, in general, the question of just when language (as opposed to a closed communication system) evolved remains an open one.

A different sort of linguistic research reminds us of the biocultural nature of human language—and reinforces our acknowledgment of the great apes as our closest relatives. Several chimpanzees, bonobos, gorillas, and orangutans—although all those species lack an open communication system in the wild—have been taught to communicate in a human language, with all the traits that term implies.

A number of attempts were made in the past to teach chimpanzees to actually speak. These attempts were doomed to failure, of course, because of the differences in vocal tracts and facial and tongue muscles between our two species. A chimp named Vicki, for instance, was trained in the 1950s to "speak" a few words—things like *mama, papa,* and *cup.* The vowels in her words, however, were merely puffs of air, and Vicki was forced to hold her lips together with her finger to make the *m* and *n* sounds.

Then, in 1966, a pair of psychologists, Beatrix and Allen Gardner, realized that not all humans are capable of speech and that therefore speech is no indication by itself of linguistic capabilities. Thus they tried a new approach. They acquired a young chimp named Washoe and began to teach her American Sign Language (Ameslan). This is the language used by many hearing-impaired people, and it conveys information with every bit as much detail, efficiency, and nuance as the spoken word. Indeed, because people signing must look at one another, additional information may be included through body language and facial expression (Figure 11.5).

FIGURE 11.5

A sentence in American Sign Language (AMESLAN): "Good morning, have you had coffee yet?" This form of sign language, the most common, does not use signs or fingerspelling for all the words in the sentence and yet clearly conveys the meaning. Facial expressions and body language are important. (a) "Good"—fingers of the hand touch the lips and then move forward. (b) "Morning"—left hand placed in crook of right arm; right arm moves upward (the sun coming up). (c) "Coffee"—the motion of a coffee grinder. (d) "Yet"—palm faces back and hand is moved back and forth several times (being behind). The signer's expression and slightly tilted head make it obvious she's asking a question.

Washoe is now in her thirties and living with four other chimps at the Chimpanzee and Human Communication Institute at Central Washington University. She and her friends know and use hundreds of signs (Figure 11.6). They understand how word order can change the meaning of sentences. They combine words in varying ways to name new objects, for example, Washoe's "water bird" for a swan. They are, thus, using a referential language. One of the chimps, Loulis, is Washoe's adopted son. He learned sign language from Washoe and the other chimps without human input. The chimps sign to each other when humans are not present. They also sign to themselves. They talk about objects and events that are

FIGURE 11.6
A man teaches a chimpanzee to sign the word, "drink." The chimp's signs are easily recognized and interpreted by speakers of American Sign Language.

not present and even about things in the future. Shortly after their special Thanksgiving dinner one year, one of the chimps started signing about a "food tree." He was referring to the fact that Debbi and Roger Fouts, directors of the Institute, would soon put up a Christmas tree, which they decorate with edible goodies. When confronted with a new object, the chimps can categorize it according to attributes it shares with already known objects. In short, they are using—although at the level of a small child—a real human language with all the traits that define that communication system.

Besides the chimps of Washoe's community, there are other chimps, bonobos, gorillas, and orangutans who sign, and yet others who communicate not by signing but by using symbols on keyboards or shaped plastic tokens. Among the most notable are Koko and Michael, signing gorillas, famous for having and naming pet cats (Figure 11.7), and the bonobo Kanzi, who learned a symbolic keyboard language by watching his mother being taught. (Kanzi has also learned how to "knap" stone tools to make flakes with which he cuts string holding closed a box containing food.)

There were—and still are—a few researchers who claim that these apes are just mimicking their trainers and are not really generating language on their own. But most researchers feel that the data from these studies clearly show that apes have the mental capability to learn at least the rudiments of our species' unique communication system. As Koko puts it, "Fine animal, gorilla."

These studies, of course, bring up an obvious question. In the wild, the great apes use closed call systems. Why is it that they have brains capable of learning and using an open communication system, a trait we always thought was ours alone?

Remember that although our language ability is contained in one localized, specialized area of our brain, the basic "wiring" in that area is

FIGURE 11.7
Koko, with Francine Patterson, signs "smoke" in reference to her kitten Smoky.

much the same as that throughout our brain. After all, the nature of the thoughts we transmit is reflected in the nature of the language. Given that the brains of apes have the same sort of wiring as ours, even if not as large and complex, it's not too surprising that they can be taught human linguistic behavior to some extent.

But why have they evolved such brains in the first place—brains that experience events and manipulate data? Simply put, apes lead complex lives. They live in social groups with elaborate personal relationships and interactions. They rely on learning in order to survive in their environments. As we see from the variation in behavior from one group of apes to another, they can alter their behaviors to fit their needs and develop forms of a behavior unique to their group, and then pass on these traditions to future generations. They eat a wide range of foods and need to know where edible foods are, how to get them, when some foods become ripe, when some are bad to eat, and so on. Their brains have evolved to facilitate these adaptations. That they don't have a complex communication system means that they have no need to share some of these specific pieces of information beyond the unintentional sharing accomplished by imitation. Personal knowledge and sharing of emotional states suffices. But, on an individual basis, they need brains with some of the basic abilities that, in one group of apes, would eventually evolve into the human brain. Thus, with proper training, motivation, and a stimulating environment, apes can be taught to use, and even come to intentionally use and generate, a form of our communication system.

LANGUAGE AND CULTURE

Language, of course, is a human cultural universal. But as with other cultural universals, there is an enormous amount of variation from society to society. Can we explain this for language? What is the connection between language and culture?

There are some 3000 languages spoken in the world today. Some of these, like the cultures that use them, are becoming extinct as the modern industrial world spreads over the planet. No doubt a large number of languages we've never heard of have already become extinct.

As with cultures in general, languages are related to one another. They can be arranged taxonomically according to similarities and differences. A common ancestor language can give rise to several new languages. By comparing similarities and differences in certain ways, we can even date the common ancestor of several existing languages and, thus, draw a family tree of language groups (Figure 11.8).

This classification is based on similarities and differences among these languages in such things as rules of grammar, phonemic inventories, and, especially, vocabulary. By examining such elements we can begin to understand the evolutionary histories of languages—which ones gave rise to which other ones. Even extinct languages, like Proto-Indo-European, have been tentatively reconstructed.

This is not an easy task, however, because language is fluid—it changes rapidly and is easily influenced. The French, for example, now commonly use such English derivatives as *le weekend*. In the United States, although we are a Germanic-language-speaking country, we regularly use words whose origins are French, Latin, Greek, Spanish, Hebrew, Italian, and even Sanskrit. Japanese uses many borrowings from English, with the sounds translated to the closest Japanese sounds. Thus, they enjoy the American national pastime, *basu-boru*. Japanese workers often finish the day at *happii awaa*. My Japanese counterpart would now be sitting at his *konpyutaa*.

As a result, when trying to classify and reconstruct languages, we use words that are less likely to change with contact between cultures or the introduction of new technologies. These include words for body parts, numbers, and family relations. We call words that are related by descent **cognates** (Figure 11.9).

English speakers, of course, are familiar with the degree of linguistic variation in other Indo-European languages. Most of us have taken courses in one or more of these, and many of us actually speak another Indo-European language. But many of us lack an appreciation of the

cognates Words that are similar in two or more languages as a result of common descent.

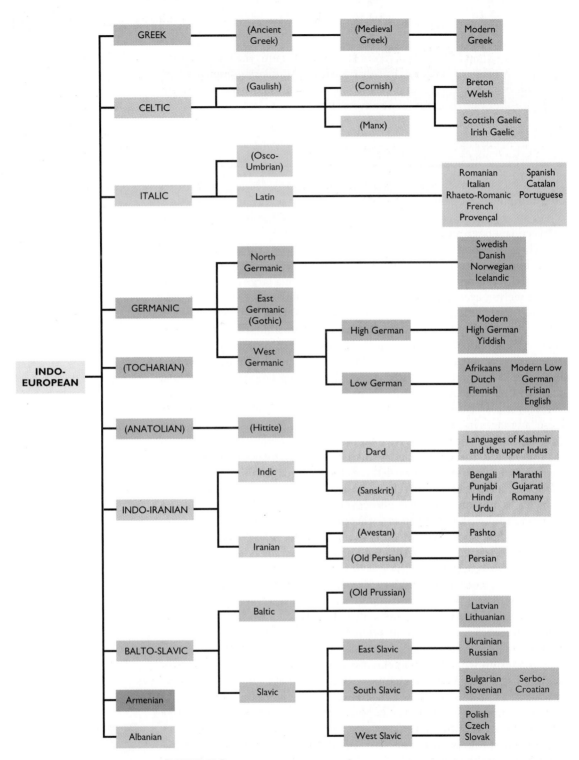

FIGURE 11.8

A family tree of Indo-European languages. The languages in parentheses are no longer spoken, although some may survive in written form.

Indo-European Languages						
English	one	two	three	mother	brother	sister
German	ein	zwei	drei	Mutter	Bruder	Schwester
French	un	deux	trois	mère	frère	soeur
Latin	unus	duo	tres	mater	frater	soror
Russian	odin	dva	tri	mat'	brat	sestra
Old Irish	oen	do	tri	mathir	brathir	siur
Lithuanian	vienas	du	trys	motina	brolis	seser
Sanskrit	eka	duva	trayas	matar	bhratar	svasar
Non-Indo-European Languages						
Finnish	yksi	kaksi	kolme	äiti	veli	sisar
Fore	ka	tara	kakaga	nano	naganto	nanona

FIGURE 11.9

Some words in Indo-European and non-Indo-European languages. (The words are rendered phonetically where the alphabet is different, as in Russian, or the language is not written, as in Fore.) Notice the similarities among the Indo-European words. These are cognate words. (From Diamond 1992:250)

enormous variation found around the world. I've heard someone describe other people as being able to "speak African." It would probably amaze the person who said that to find out there are some 800 languages spoken in Africa. On the island of New Guinea, which is smaller than Alaska, there may be (or at least have been in the recent past) as many as 1000 distinct languages spoken.

Our surprise at these facts shows the importance of language to a culture and its people. Those of us who grew up speaking English think of it as normal. It's difficult for us to really speak, much less think in, another tongue. Language is central to the success of a culture. It is the most important way we learn our culture in the first place—and how we will pass that culture on. To truly understand another language is to truly understand the culture it represents. And that's a monumental task.

An ongoing project since the beginnings of anthropology has been to discover the relationships between a cultural system and the language its people speak. Can everything about a language—its phonemes, morphemes, rules of grammar—be related to the culture that it expresses?

There have been many attempts to describe such relationships, and they have nearly all met with failure. There seems to be no practical reason why French has gutteral *r*'s and Spanish speakers roll theirs; why German can tack *nicht* to the end of a sentence but English, a closely related language, can't; and why clicks as phonemes are found mainly in southern Africa. Like genes, the specific features of languages seem to undergo flow, drift, and mutation—random changes not related directly to cultural adaptation.

What *is* connected to cultural systems directly, however, are the words themselves. What people call things tells us what sorts of categories they recognize. How they express ideas tells us how they view their world. We have already discussed one example of this—kinship terminology (Chapter 9). Although we used graphic symbols instead of actual words, our symbols (for example, see Figure 9.7) represented word usage, and the study of which relatives were called by what terms told us something about the cultures that practiced each system we described.

This phenomenon of grouping things according to a society's world view is called folk taxonomy. The study of folk taxonomies is known as **ethnosemantics,** or "cultural meanings." As a classic, but often misunderstood example, we can look at words for the white, crystalline matter that falls from the sky in winter. In English, we call it "snow." We modify that word by adding an adjective, depending on our situation. Thus, when I look out on my snow-covered driveway, I wonder if it's a deep snow or a shallow snow, or heavy or light snow. When I was a kid, I cared whether it was wet snow or dry snow, the former being better for snowballs and snowforts. Skiers listen for reports of powder or granular snow.

The Shuar (formerly called the Jivaro), an indigenous group in the forests of Ecuador, perhaps best known for their shrinking of human heads, are said to incorporate the phenomenon of snow into a single concept represented by a single term. It refers to the Andes Mountains, with which they are familiar but which play no direct role in their lives. The term includes the mountains, the snow, the idea of high altitude, and so on. In short, it means something like "the way it is up there."

At the other extreme are the peoples of the American Arctic. An old interpretation from the early days of anthropology (and repeated through the years by many anthropologists, including me), held that the Eskimo had many separate words for different kinds of and conditions of snow, with no single root word for snow at all. That sounded good, but linguistic anthropologist Laura Martin has shown that the Eskimo do indeed have a root word for snow. However, their way of modifying words is so different from English that their snow words looked completely different to English-speaking anthropologists. This doesn't, however, change the point. Because snow is important to the Eskimo, they recognize and name many different types and conditions of snow. In other words, their categories—their folk taxonomy—for snow reflects the role snow plays in their lives. Travel, tracking game, the very presence of game, the temperature and wind—all these depend on, and can be in part predicted by, the nature and condition of snow. Thus, they modify the root word, in the case of Eskimo languages by adding suffixes. For example, they have a word for falling snow and another for snow on the ground; one word for drifting snow and another for a snow drift; a word for snow that can cause avalanches; even a word for the bowl-shaped hollow in the snow around the base of trees (something many of us may never even have noticed). The words and categories of words that a language uses are intimately related to the environment, world view, and cultural system of the society that uses the language.

Other folk categories have also been studied. Color terms, for example, vary greatly from society to society. Some groups, like the Dani of New Guinea, have only two color terms, roughly corresponding to *light* and *dark*. In Western societies, we have dozens of recognized, agreed-on color terms. It's not that the perceptual abilities—the eyes and

ethnosemantics The study of the meanings of words, especially as they relate to folk taxonomies.

brains—of the Dani are different. All normally sighted humans see the same color spectrum. What's different is the cultural importance each group gives to distinguishing and naming the different sections of the visible spectrum. Explanations for this diversity are still being sought. It may have something to do with the nature of the group's environment. People living in areas with fewer natural colors—the Arctic or a desert— may have a simpler color taxonomy than rain forest peoples. It may also have to do with art styles. Where a society has art that attempts to be realistic, it becomes important to re-create and name the great diversity of colors in nature.

Number systems, too, vary. The number system we recognize goes on counting forever. The Dani, on the other hand, recognize "one," "two," "three," and "many." Again, there is no perceptual or intellec- tual difference between us and them. It's just that, within their cultural system, it is not necessary for them to tally or keep track of the specific number of anything beyond three. Don't assume, however, that one can easily account for all such differences by relating them to environments or overall levels of cultural complexity. Another highland New Guinea group, the Kapauku, count into the thousands. As with all cultural phe- nomena, the interrelationships can be obscure and complex, and with language they seem especially so.

Languages also have histories, and a language is related to the cultural history of a society. The Hutterites, for example, are trilingual. They speak English to outsiders like me. They use German for religious ritual, and it is the language in which all their literature, both sacred and secular, is written. To one another they speak "Huttrish," their unique language.

The Hutterites originated in a German-speaking region and their conservative outlook and lifestyle would predict that they would keep the language that was first used to communicate their thoughts and cultural ideas. Moreover, the German they use is "High" German, an old form. English is utilitarian. The Hutterites now live in English-speaking coun- tries in North America. Their own language, with which they communi- cate information about everyday matters, has a practical history. It includes words derived from the languages common to the areas in which the Hutterites have lived during their nearly 500 years. Even with my meager linguistic abilities, I was able to pick out some German and Russ- ian, along with the English in their speech. For example, they called me *der fingerprint mensch,* a German-English mix. In fact, their language uses words and phrases not just from those major languages but from specific dialects of those languages.

So language is an intimate part of any cultural system. It is the mech- anism whereby each of us, as a youngster, learns the basics of our cultural system, and it is the means we use to communicate to others, in the present and the future, the facts, ideas, and norms of our culture. One feature of a language—the words, their meanings, and their categories— are a reflection of the very basis of a cultural system, its world view.

CONTEMPORARY ISSUES

Are Written Languages More Advanced Than Unwritten Ones?

The modern world would be inconceivable without written language. It is now absolutely essential to record massive amounts of information accurately and efficiently and to share it accurately and quickly. All the world's major languages, and many less common ones, are now written. We usually refer to those that are not written as *preliterate*, as if literacy were the natural outcome of all language evolution, and thus, as if preliterate languages were somehow less than fully evolved—less complex, less accurate, less efficient. Is this the case?

Jared Diamond discusses these issues at length in *The Third Chimpanzee* and *Guns, Germs, and Steel*. We can summarize his conclusions. First, we need to understand that, as Diamond says in the first of those books, there is no correlation between the complexity of a society and the complexity of its language. To be sure, complex modern industrial societies have larger vocabularies than small, isolated foraging groups. My *New Shorter Oxford English Dictionary* (abridged from the longer version by including only words in use after 1700 or that appear in the works of Shakespeare) still contains over half a million words. But that's because societies that use English have more things to name and more involved relationships to precisely describe.

That does not mean, however, that English is more complex than San or one of the thousand or so languages from the New Guinea highlands. Diamond mentions, as just one example, that the language of the Iyau people of New Guinea uses pitch, changes in which may give a single vowel as many as eight different meanings. Other so-called primitive languages have grammatical rules that are far more complex than those of English and related languages, and thus far more convoluted to nonnative speakers (such as the linguistic anthropologist trying to describe them).

Diamond does note that pidgin languages are much simpler than established languages. Pidgins arise when groups from two cultures come into intimate contact with one another—for example, colonists and native workers—and the two groups need to

One of the things we talk about is especially important, for it is a direct statement about our world view. It is the way we pass on and maintain that view. It is our means for understanding our relationship with our environment and with each other, and for translating that understanding into articulate rules of behavior. It is religion and the secular systems derived from religion.

SUMMARY

A communication system functions to transfer information from the nervous system of one organism to that of others of its species. It is therefore a reflection of the structure and function of that nervous system. Human communication—language—has features that enable us to share information and ideas that are cultural. The traits of human language reflect the features of our brains that make culture possible. Thus, human language is very different from the communication systems of even our closest relatives.

communicate. They concoct a crude and variable language that uses combinations of sounds and words from both standard languages. If, however, the next generations of the groups involved begin using the pidgin as their native language in more social situations than those in which the pidgin arose, they may find its simplicity inadequate. They will spontaneously expand the pidgin into a creole—a formal language with larger vocabulary, more-complex grammar, and more consistency. Still less complex than established languages, creoles nonetheless have many of the attributes of those languages and may take on even more over time.

Now, what about writing? In the second of the books mentioned, Diamond notes that writing is invented under very special circumstances. In fact, it appears to have been independently invented in only four locations, the Fertile Crescent of Southwest Asia, Mexico, China, and Egypt (and the last two are disputed by some authorities who say these cultures either borrowed writing from neighboring cultures or were inspired to invent it by example). What do these societies have in common? It was in these locations that food production first started. Thus, it was in these areas where we find the first large, sedentary, stratified societies with cities and state political systems. It was these societies that first required writing for economic, political, and military record keeping and for disseminating important information. From these powerful societies, writing or the idea of writing spread to other populations.

But what about some large food-producing societies with complex political systems that did not have writing? These include the Inca of South America, the Hawaiians, large societies and states of sub-Saharan Africa, and the large North American societies of the Mississippi Valley. Were the four states that independently invented writing more evolved? Only in the sense that—because of accidents of geography, climate, availability of domesticable species, and need—those four populations developed food producing earlier than the others and so early on required and developed that sociocultural ramification of food producing, the city-state. Writing, like so many other cultural innovations we've discussed, is the result of a need, not of some inevitable stage of progress toward which all cultures naturally move.

We have only indirect evidence for when language evolved in hominids, but we can get a glimpse into how it evolved by comparing our communication system to that of the great apes and trying to determine under what circumstances a closed call system would have evolved into an open symbolic language. The fact that under certain conditions apes can be taught to use a human language shows us again just how similar our species are in terms of mental abilities. At the same time, since the apes don't use such a system in the wild, these studies also show us how intimately connected are language and culture.

The specific connections between a particular language and the culture that uses it are not, as previously believed, on the level of sounds and grammatical structure. There are, however, direct connections between the world view of a society, the words people use to talk about that world, and the categories into which those words are organized. On a broader scale, features of a language can reflect something about a society's cultural history.

NOTES, REFERENCES, AND READINGS

A recent article on the communication of bees is "The Sensory Basis of the Honeybee's Dance Language" by Wolfgang Kirchner and William Towne in the June 1994 *Scientific American*. Notice that these authors, as do many, use language and communication interchangeably.

For overviews of linguistics try A. R. Akmajian et al., *Linguistics*, and for anthropological linguistics, see Zdenek Salzman, *Language, Culture, and Society.*

See Jane Lancaster's *Primate Behavior and the Emergence of Human Culture* for a detailed discussion of the differences between human language and the communciation systems of other primates. For other evolutionary perspectives see Richard Passingham's *The Human Primate* and Jared Diamond's *The Third Chimpanzee*. The famous article by Charles Hockett and Robert Ascher, "The Human Revolution," is in *Current Anthropology*, volume 5.

A good summary of the status of the ape-language studies, focusing on Washoe and her community, is "Chimpanzee Sign Language Research" by Roger and Debbi Fouts in Phyllis Dolhinow and Agustín Fuentes, *The Nonhuman Primates*. A more detailed treatment is Roger Fouts's *Next of Kin*. The linguistic achievements of Koko and Michael are discussed, with lots of pictures (including one Koko took of herself) in "Conversations with a Gorilla" by Francine Patterson in the October 1978 *National Geographic*. An article about Kanzi and his linguistic and toolmaking abilities called "Ape at the Brink" by Sue Savage-Rumbaugh and Roger Lewin is in the September 1994 issue of *Discover*.

An interesting discussion of language families and their relationships to cultural and genetic groups is "Genes, Peoples and Languages" by L. L. Cavalli-Sforza in the November 1991 *Scientific American*.

For the origins of English words, look in any dictionary or try a dictionary of foreign words and phrases such as that published by Oxford University Press. An interesting article about recent English borrowings into Japanese was in the *New York Times* April 4, 1999, titled "Help! There's a Mausu in My Konpyutaa!" by N. Kristof.

More on folk taxonomies can be found in Ronald Casson's *Language, Culture, and Cognition*. The technical article on Eskimo snow words is by Laura Martin in *American Anthropologist* volume 88, number 2, and, for a delightful description of those words and the conditions they describe, see *The Secret Language of Snow* by Terry Tempest Williams and Ted Major.

The various connections between languages and history are discussed in Jared Diamond's *The Third Chimpanzee* and *Guns, Germs, and Steel*. The former includes a description of the reconstruction of Proto-Indo-European.

12

MAINTENANCE OF ORDER

Making the World View Real

Network television is not known for its profundity, but on occasion it does provide a memorable line. One of my favorites is from the comedy series *Taxi,* which ran in the '70s and '80s. In one episode, the other employees of the Sunshine Cab Company ask Latka, a generic foreigner played by the late Andy Kaufman, why his upcoming wedding ceremony is so bizarre and complex. Latka answers that in his country there is a saying that what separates man from the animals is "mindless superstition and pointless ritual."

And don't we in fact often think of the beliefs and rituals of other peoples as mindless and pointless? We even have that view of some beliefs and rituals found in our own culture—the ones that we don't happen to practice. It's a natural reaction, and there's a good reason for it.

We see the beliefs of others, and the ways in which they express those beliefs, as mindless and pointless because ours are so basic to us. Other people may dress differently from us, and we may see other modes of fashion as a little strange, but those things are not really so important. Beliefs *are* important, however, because beliefs—as we discussed in Chapter 7—are a direct reflection of our world view, our set of assumptions, attitudes, and responses that give rise to and hold together the cultural fabric of our lives. Except for personal survival, nothing is more important or more central to our existence.

Specific cultural expressions that reflect world view can generally be termed **religion,** although in complex and multicultural societies, secular **legal systems** take the place of religious concepts as rules for human behavior. Still, as we'll see, such legal systems are themselves often secular restatements of religious principles.

For a formal definition of religion, I don't think we can do better than that offered by anthropologist Edward Norbeck. Religion, he says, is a

> distinctive symbolic expression of human life that interprets man himself and his universe, providing motives for human action, and also a group of associated acts which have survival value for the human species.

Moreover, he sees the roles of religion

> as explanatory, and in many ways psychologically reassuring, and as socially supportive by providing validations for existence, motives for human action, and as a sanction for orderly human relations.

Religions, or legal systems that derive from them, are our way of making our world view real. They provide us with a means for communicating

religion A system of ideas and rules for behavior based on supernatural explanations.

legal systems A set of secular rules governing the behavior of individuals and institutions within a society.

our assumptions about the world. They give us a medium for formulating values of behavior that correspond to the world view. They provide a framework for putting those values into action in our everyday dealings with one another and with the world around us. Furthermore, they are the way in which we impart our world view to future generations. Little wonder, then, that *our* religion seems so natural and *theirs* so strange.

As with any facet of culture, however, our overriding assumption is that a religious system makes sense to the people who practice it. We already saw this when we examined some features of Eskimo religion and compared it with those of Southwest Asia. Let's now look more closely at religion and related cultural phenomena and see in what ways cultures are similar and different in their expressions of this important behavior.

RELIGION AND RELIGIOUS SYSTEMS

Edward Norbeck's definition indicates what religion does, but just what *is* it? Religions vary greatly from society to society but the one trait they all have in common is the supernatural. Religion is a set of beliefs and behaviors pertaining to the supernatural.

By "supernatural" we mean something—a force or power or being—that is outside the known laws of nature. Thus, one difference among societies is in which phenomena are dealt with by religion—a belief system —and which are dealt with using scientific knowledge (see Chapter 2). Most North Americans, for instance, deal with disease in a scientific fashion. But for the Fore of New Guinea (see Chapter 13), disease is explained as the work of sorcery—a supernatural explanation.

Not only is a belief in the supernatural universal among religions (indeed, it defines religion), but religion itself is a cultural universal. As with the other cultural universals we discussed in Chapter 6, the universality of religion requires an explanation. Might religion have some biological basis?

There would not seem to be any behavior among nonhumans that could have been translated into this particular cultural behavior—nothing like pair bonding and sexual consciousness (marriage, in cultural terms) or avoidance of mating with siblings (the cultural incest taboo). But a biological basis of religion can be found in our big brain. Such a brain, with its complex functions and abilities, evolved as our species adapted through understanding its environment and by using that understanding to manipulate the environment for survival. The potential to understand, however, does not guarantee that everything will be understood. Some natural phenomena are within the intellectual grasp of a group of humans, but others are not. These, however, also need to be explained—which is where forces outside of nature come in.

For example, our species has had a science of making stone tools for millions of years. The abilities of the human brain were brought to bear on the problem of selecting and modifying natural objects into artifacts, and the efforts that resulted were quite successful. But what about a phenomenon like the weather? Or the movement of stars? Or death? Relatively speaking, we have only recently begun to understand these things scientifically because such understanding requires groundwork in the form of data, experimentation, the generation of theory, and the technology to acquire the data and conduct the experiments. Some aspects of phenomena like death, of course, are beyond the reach of science.

But all these phenomena are important to all people—including our remote ancestors—who seek to explain them. People need to feel some control over the facets of their worlds, even if only in the form of understanding those facets. So, when some natural phenomenon was beyond the reach of a people's scientific know-how, the supernatural was invoked. If the phenomenon seemed to be beyond the laws of nature, so then was the explanation. Thus, all aspects of their world were put into concrete terms that could be communicated. The world view, in other words, was made real.

Recall, for example, the Eskimo, who saw what must have seemed like random changes in their challenging environment. They explained these as the work of individual spirits with individual control over their physical embodiments. What seals did, for example, was determined by the spirit of the seal. If the seals were to behave as the Eskimo needed them to in order to hunt them, certain behaviors geared toward appeasing the seal spirit were required. These gave the people a sense of control, even if indirectly, over their world.

Death, one of the greatest of natural mysteries, is commonly dealt with by a belief in some sort of afterlife in which the body or some essence of the deceased goes back to some region from which it came, enters a whole new dimension, or simply hangs around the present world as a ghost. In all cultures, care is taken through ritual to make sure the person gets where he is supposed to go, and, as with the ancient Egyptians, quite elaborate procedures often were involved (Figure 12.1, and see Figure 10.18). And in many societies, in order to get to the proper place after death, one must behave in a certain fashion while living. Thus, the explanation for this most fearful of natural phenomena not only interprets something about humans and their world, but also supplies a reassuring story, provides motivation for human actions, and acts as a sanction for orderly human relations—all functions appearing on Norbeck's list.

The universality of religion, then, is a result of the blessing of our big, complex brains with their ability (and desire) to understand the world around us and the curse that those big brains can't understand everything and are acutely aware of that fact. We are also cursed with knowledge of our own mortality—a focus of much religious belief and ritual.

As we have done throughout this book, we should ask again if there are any antecedents to human religion to be found among nonhumans.

FIGURE 12.1
Rituals performed around death and burial are not just recent cultural phenomena. In this grave from the nearly 7000-year-old site of Vedbaek in Denmark, a mother and newborn child were buried together. The mother's head was placed on a cushion of material decorated with snail shells and deer teeth. Similar materials were found around her waist, evidence of some sort of dress. Her child was buried with a flint knife, as were all males in this cemetery, and was laid to rest on the wing of a swan. Although we can't know the exact meaning of these features, they clearly meant something.

Are there any clues that some other creatures might even dimly ask some form of the questions that religions answer? There is one. Granted, it's open to interpretation, but it's also rather tantalizing since it comes from our close relatives, the chimpanzees.

During a violent thunderstorm at the Gombe Stream Reserve in Tanzania, Jane Goodall observed what she called a "rain display" or "rain dance." At the height of the storm, several male chimps took turns running to the top of a hill and then hurtling down it screaming, jumping into trees along the route, tearing branches from the trees, and waving them around (Figure 12.2). When one male reached the bottom, he returned to the top to start over, during which time other males performed. All this was observed by a gallery of females and youngsters

FIGURE 12.2
Artist's depiction of a chimp "rain dance." As lightning flashes in the background, several males hurtle down the hill, swinging around trees and tearing off branches while females and young watch safely off to the side.

lining the sides of the route. This was an uncommon event; Goodall saw it only a few times during her more than thirty years at Gombe.

Just what the rain dance means to the chimps is probably an unanswerable question. One is tempted, however, to imagine the dance as a reaction to the anxiety that the chimps feel toward what must, even for wild creatures, be a frightening phenomenon. Perhaps the chimps are trying to scare away the storm that is scaring them. As Goodall says "With a display of strength and vigor such as this, primitive man himself might have challenged the elements." If that's the case, their dance may be seen as having the rudiments of a religious ritual. Maybe, of course, they are just performing what animal behaviorists call a displacement activity, like our whistling in the dark. Or, as Goodall also proposes, perhaps all that running around just helps them keep warm.

Could human religion have started in a similar way—by some behavior aimed at influencing a natural, but otherwise frightening or unexplained, phenomenon? Neandertal burials (see Chapters 5 and 10) probably had the objective of somehow influencing the event of death—either for the benefit of the deceased, if the burials demonstrated a belief in an afterlife, or for the benefit of the emotions of the living, if the burials simply show a reverence for the physical remains of a member of the family and group. In either case, something beyond concrete, observable nature is being invoked.

The same can probably be said of the Upper Paleolithic cave art (Chapters 5 and 10). One hypothesis as to the meaning of this art is that it influenced natural phenomena such as fertility or hunting success. The recognition of some agent beyond nature (that is, a supernatural agent) would seem to be a necessary component of such a perceived connection between art and nature.

Let's look at the ways in which religious expression differs among cultures. Like any cultural expression, religion varies in how it is geared to individual culture systems and in how it changes to keep pace with them. There are, of course, as many specific religious systems as there are cultures, but we can get an overview by noting the variation in some general aspects of religion.

We've already discussed, in Chapter 7, the distinction between monotheistic and polytheistic religions and the connection between these and some general types of world view. Polytheism tends to be found in societies, like the foraging San or Eskimo, that interact with their environments on a more personal level, where the people see themselves as one of many natural phenomena. Groups practicing polytheism tend not to have political systems with formal leadership. The supernatural reflects the natural in terms of social organization as well.

Monotheistic systems or hierarchical polytheistic systems (such as in ancient Egypt) are found in groups that have gained distinct control over their habitats—groups like the early agriculturalists of Southwest Asia. Such groups tend to have a hierarchical political system with formal leadership and full-time labor specialists.

As usual, such a dichotomy doesn't always work out exactly. It has been said, for instance, that true monotheism is rare. For example, while Christianity has a single, all-powerful deity, that deity comes in three forms indicated by three distinct terms. This is the Holy Trinity of Father, Son, and Holy Ghost or Holy Spirit. Moreover, the Virgin Mary has been virtually deified by some Christian churches, and all sorts of angels and saints are included among Christianity's beings with supernatural powers, as is the devil.

Judaism, on the other hand, from which Christianity branched, is more truly monotheistic (although it also recognizes angels and the devil). The difference in the recognized number of supernatural beings between Judaism and Christianity probably can be traced to the wide spread of the latter and the diversity of the cultural systems that adopted it (voluntarily or otherwise), each system giving the basic religion a slightly different spin. Remember, world view is generated by a combination of environment plus history.

The nature of the supernatural beings also differs among humankind's religions, and we can categorize three basic kinds of beings or forces. The first is sometimes called by a Polynesian word, *mana*. It refers to a force possessed by a person, a place, or a nonliving thing (Figure 12.3). Charms, like lucky rabbits' feet or New Age crystals, have mana. So do the sacred black and green stones venerated by the Dani of New Guinea. People have mana as well—for example, the San who possess healing

FIGURE 12.3
The town of Sedona, Arizona, and the surrounding area are said to contain numerous vortexes, places with supernatural properties, specifically where energy is concentrated in such a way as to enhance one's psychic powers. At this vortex area in Boynton Canyon, believers have left offerings atop a tree stump at the supposed heart of the vortex. This vortex is said to help one recall past lives. (It didn't work for me.)

power (see Figure 8.6). And many cultures have taboos against contact with certain objects, like the "unclean" foods listed in the Bible (see Chapter 13). They have negative mana.

Other supernatural beings are of human origin—ancestors and ghosts. Recall the importance of ghosts of the deceased for the San (Chapter 8). The lives of the Dani are very much ruled by the ghosts of their ancestors. Such supernatural beings are important among peoples for whom the kin group is the major social, political, and decision-making unit. Thus, not only are living humans important, so too are the spirits of deceased humans. Again, the real and the supernatural reflect one another.

Finally, there are supernatural beings of nonhuman origin. These are beings who created themselves and then made the world with all its creatures, including people. These beings may take the form of a single, all-powerful god or a number of individual spirits, like those that control the natural features of the Eskimo's world.

A culture, of course, can have a combination of types of supernatural beings. The San, for instance, have both human ghosts as well as spirits of natural phenomena to deal with. They also recognize two powerful gods who created everything in the first place and who generally keep things going. What anthropologists must do is look at the specific nature of the beings and forces recognized by a culture and the ways in which the people deal with those beings and forces. In this way, we may see how these beings and forces act, for that culture, to fulfill all the roles that religious beliefs play in human cultural and psychological life.

Supernatural beings also differ in personality. Some are benevolent, some malevolent, some mischievous. This may be connected to how a group of people perceives their environment: Is it harsh, as for the Eskimo? Or is life fairly easy and predictable, as for the Dani? Indeed, for the horticultural Dani, basic subsistence seems so easy that their main supernatural beings, the ghosts of their ancestors, are known mostly for their mischievous deeds, their specifically good or evil acts associated with special circumstances. The supernatural forces recognized by another New Guinea group, the Fore, are mostly malevolent, as we will discuss in Chapter 13.

It has also been suggested that the personality of the supernatural may correspond to a society's childrearing habits. If they treat their children gently, their gods are gentle gods. If they are strict disciplinarians, the gods are to be feared. Notice how the Christian deity is referred to as "God the Father," and the followers as "His children" or "His flock." Gods are often linguistically classified as parents.

Also showing variation is the degree to which the supernatural intervenes in the daily affairs of people. Generally, the more important scientific knowledge is to a people, the less direct is the influence of the gods. Natural phenomena, including human actions, are attributed to natural forces. The degree and kind of intervention may also be related to the complexity of the social order. Especially where there are inequalities in wealth and power, rules for human behavior that are said to come directly from the supernatural may help to maintain the existing order (and, thus, the wealth and power of those who have it).

The kind of person who specializes in taking care of the religious knowledge and welfare of a people varies as well. Here, we may define two basic categories. The first are part-time specialists, usually called on only in times of crises like illnesses. They are often referred to as **shamans** (after a Siberian word). Shamans receive their powers directly from the supernatural; they are "chosen" for this position. This type of religious specialist is found in egalitarian or less complex horticultural societies where there are no full-time specialists in anything and where religious knowledge, so vital to survival, is known and practiced by everyone. Only special situations, like curing, require the extra help of shamans. The San healers would be an example.

More-complex cultures have **priests.** In anthropological terminology, priests are full-time specialists who train for their profession, learning what is passed down by their predecessors. They are the repository of religious knowledge and thus are the persons who know best what the gods say, how best to interpret their words, and how best to get in touch with the gods. Where shamans have real supernatural power, priests have knowledge of the supernatural. Put another way, priests tell us what to do on behalf of the supernatural and shamans (often for a fee from a

shaman A part-time, supernaturally chosen religious specialist who can manipulate the supernatural.

priest A full-time, trained religious specialist who can interpret the supernatural and petition the supernatural on behalf of humans.

FIGURE 12.4
A Catholic priest conducting a mass. He is a priest in the anthropological sense in that he has chosen his profession and has trained for it. Priests possess knowledge rather than supernatural powers, as shamans do.

client) tell the supernatural what to do on behalf of us. Priests in the Catholic Church would be an example of priests in the anthropological sense (Figure 12.4).

With priests' knowledge often comes power of a more down-to-earth nature—political power. In some cultures it can be difficult to separate the political system from the religious system and political leaders from the religious ones. This was true among the ancient Aztecs of Mexico, for instance, and to a great extent in medieval and Renaissance Europe.

Finally, the ways in which people get in touch with the supernatural show variation. People may pray, in a congregation or alone. The prayer itself may be individual or may involve group recitation of prescribed words. Some form of eating may be involved—everything from a feast to the taking of communion, the symbolic ingestion of the body and blood of Christ.

Sacrifice is a common way of pleasing the supernatural. It may take the actual killing of an animal or a human to do this (the latter also found among the Aztecs), or it might involve some sort of abstinence, as some Christians practice during Lent and some Jews on the Sabbath.

Music, noise, and dance are also ways of attracting the attention of the gods or spirits, as is art—drawings or some symbol representing the supernatural. And in some cases, people feel closer to the supernatural during a transcendent experience, sometimes brought about by taking drugs. The Shuar of Ecuador and the Yąnomamö of Brazil do this (Figure 12.5). Such psychological states may also be brought on by fasting, exhaustion, or by physical abuses like self-mutilation. The Dani, for instance,

FIGURE 12.5
Yãnomamö men take hallu-cinogenic drugs nearly daily. A powder is made from the leaves of a plant and is then blown up one's nose by a friend through a long, hollow tube. This is said to bring a man closer to important beings in the spirit world.

cut off the finger joints of female relatives of a person who has died. In James Michener's famous novel *Hawaii* there is a graphic description of a man from that culture mutilating himself following a relative's death. Walking on fire, self-flagellation with whips and chains, and piercing the cheeks with long skewers all fall into this category.

Two other terms should be noted in this consideration of variation in religious expression: **magic** and **sorcery**. Magic refers to situations where people feel they have control over the supernatural rather than the other way around. Instead of pleasing the supernatural through acts, or asking for favors through prayer, magic seeks to manipulate it. This manipulation can be for either good or evil. If for evil, it is usually called sorcery.

Such practices are found in less scientific societies, where natural phenomena are explained through the action of the supernatural. What magic and sorcery do is give people a feeling of some degree of control over important events. The Fore, for example, see disease as a result of sorcery, that is, as the result of humans acting with the help of supernatural agencies or powers. A result of this kind of explanation, of course, is that since the diseases are caused by humans, other humans can take actions against them. A sense of control is achieved. We will see this in action among the Fore in the following chapter.

magic Ritual acts where people control the supernatural.

sorcery Rituals that control the supernatural for evil purposes.

A belief in sorcery, of course, doesn't disappear with cultural complexity and science. There were several periods in Europe between the thirteenth and seventeenth centuries when witches were accused and burned by the thousands, and I noted in an earlier chapter the famous Salem witch trials in Massachusetts in 1692. Even lately, ideas about witches, magical powers, and psychic abilities have risen in popularity once again (see the Contemporary Issue feature for this chapter).

This, then, is what religion is and some of the general ways in which it varies from culture to culture. The richness of this variation, and the explanations for individual expressions within particular cultures, is a broad and complex field. We may, however, take a closer look at one religion and see how some of its major features relate to the overall cultural systems of its followers and how these features have changed over time and space. We can then look at some of its variations.

It's easier, in a way, to examine the religion of some "exotic" group of people. We can analyze such a religion from afar, dissociated from any cultural or emotional connection to it. But that's too easy. Let's instead discuss a religious tradition that many of us either practice or are at least familiar with—one that, in a broad historical context, helps make up the moral and ethical outlook of North American society. It's also a religion about which we have extensive written records. Let's look at Christianity.

RELIGION AND CULTURE

From an anthropological perspective, Christianity must be viewed as a branch of Judaism, because that's how it originated. Judaism, a monotheistic religion, dates back, at least as a tradition if not a formal religion, to the time of Moses, probably the thirteenth century B.C. The first Jewish kingdom was founded by David (of David and Goliath fame) in Palestine in the early 900s B.C. David was considered a *messiah*, which originally meant one who had great holiness and power. Shortly after David's death his kingdom was divided, and a few hundred years later it was conquered. There followed hundreds of years of oppression of the Jews by several other nations. The last of these, the Roman Empire, virtually brought an end to the Jewish homeland in A.D. 135.

A result of this long period of colonialism and economic oppression was the development of the idea that someday, if the Jews kept their covenant with God, a messiah would come. This messiah would lead the Jews in military conquest over their oppressors. The idea peaked during Roman rule, which began in 40 B.C. During that time, a number of "messiahs" appeared and led groups of Jews in what anthropologist Marvin Harris calls guerrilla warfare against the Romans. At first little more than a nuisance, these uprisings soon became a threat to Roman power, and the Jews involved were typically executed if captured—which they nearly always were.

It was into this political environment that Jesus was born. He is seen today, of course, as a peaceful messiah, but there is good evidence that he was, in his time, part of the military messiah tradition. There is no reason to think that the Jews of Jesus' time would have followed anyone claiming to be the messiah who advocated peace with the Romans. The goal was military overthrow.

Jesus, of course, was captured and crucified—the standard form of execution for such rebels because it was slow and painful and provided a powerful warning to others. Death had ended the brief tenures of Jesus' predecessors, but a number of his ardent disciples claimed that, rather than proving Jesus *wasn't* the promised messiah, his death was a test of his followers' faith. If they kept that faith, he would one day return. So, while most Jews still awaited a military savior, a small cult of Jewish Christians formed and began to spread, preaching this new variation of Jewish doctrine but still maintaining ties with the religion at large. Over the next thirty years (Jesus was killed in A.D. 33), the cult had spread as far as Rome itself and had begun to be taken up by some non-Jews.

This last fact began a split between the Jews of Palestine, where the new Jewish Christians still considered themselves Jews, and those outside the homeland, where the differences were emphasized. The separation became complete when, after the Jewish uprisings had become a serious problem for the Romans, a major military campaign was launched, under the leadership of Vespasian and his son, culminating in the destruction of the temple in Jerusalem in A.D. 70 and the fall of the famous fortress of Masada in A.D. 73 (Figure 12.6). (You should remember Vespasian from the story of Maiden Castle in England.)

Incredibly, the military messianic tradition persisted quietly for the next sixty years and arose again in earnest in A.D. 132. This resulted in the founding of an independent Jewish state which lasted until A.D. 135. In that year, the Romans mounted a fierce and bloody campaign that ended in the destruction of Jewish settlements, the deaths of hundreds of thousands, and the taking of more thousands into slavery. But the earlier Roman victory—in Jerusalem in A.D. 70—showed the might of the Roman Empire and brought about the cultural changes we're concerned with.

With the temple—the heart of Judaism—destroyed, connections between Jews and the Jewish Christians were severed. The Palestinian Jews had to cease, or at least not actively pursue, their messianic beliefs—for a time anyway. The Jewish Christians, though, responded differently. Especially in other parts of the Roman Empire, including Rome itself, it was simply not wise to continue following the cult of Jesus as it then existed, particularly since the belief was that he would one day return. The nature of this messiah, then, gradually changed. He became a peaceful savior, bringing salvation not in this world but in the next—hardly a threat to the Romans. It was about this time that the first of the Gospels, the book of Mark, was written. (The Gospels do not appear in the Bible

FIGURE 12.6
The Romans laid siege to the fortress of Masada (left center) for several months in A.D. 73, living in camps like the one near the cliff in the foreground. Finally, when it was clear they could hold out no longer, the 960 defenders of Masada chose suicide rather than surrender.

in the order in which they were written.) The Gospels tell the story of Jesus and outline his teachings, confirming his emphasis on heavenly rather than earthly reward (although they retain some of his more militant statements). Differences between the new Christianity and Jewish tradition were formalized. The food laws from the Old Testament, for example, were ignored and circumcision was no longer prescribed. Christianity, as we recognize it today, had begun.

Numbers of communities banded together to await the Second Coming of Jesus and to preach the teachings of this new religion. Some of this early history is recounted in Acts of the Apostles in such passages as 2:44: "All that believed were together, and had all things common." Sound familiar? It's the passage on which the Hutterites base their communal lifestyle. We can now see this lifestyle as a direct descendant of that of some of the first Christian communities.

The origin of Christianity, then, can be understood as a branching off from the long-standing traditions of Judaism, stimulated by a particular set of historical circumstances and the reactions of a group of people to them. The basic tenets of the religion are a reflection and an affirmation of a particular world view—a view generated by all the aspects of the founding group's environment and history.

Over nearly 2000 years, the history of Christianity became complex, as the basic idea spread throughout the world, was adopted by many different societies, developed all sorts of variations, and underwent historical changes. Suffice it to say that there are now three recognized major branches: Roman Catholic, Eastern Orthodox, and Protestant, each, especially the latter, with a number of subbranches. Let's look at two subbranches of Protestantism as further examples of the anthropology of religion.

The first—the Hutterites—we've already covered at some length. You recall that the Hutterites were founded as part of the Anabaptist movement of the early 1500s that involved many groups that repudiated infant baptism (hence the name), believed in a literal interpretation of the Bible (especially the New Testament), and disliked state-controlled religion.

At the time of the Anabaptist movement, a major change was taking place in Europe in terms of people's ability to acquire information. Specifically, new innovations in printing had put the Bible in the hands of the common citizen. Now, for literate persons (mostly townsfolk and artisans), or persons who knew someone who could read, there was no need to rely on the church for knowledge about the content and interpretation of the Bible. Some people began to think for themselves about religious issues, and the Anabaptist ideas noted above were three important and common conclusions.

Such conclusions, however, were not viewed kindly by the mainstream Catholic and Protestant churches, which were, at the time, inextricably linked to the state. Repudiating infant baptism had been considered

FIGURE 12.7
Torture and public burnings of witches and heretics, such as the Anabaptists, were not uncommon in Europe from the 1400s through the 1600s.

heresy for some time, and this was used to punish the Anabaptists and similar groups. Their "real" crime, of course, was their threat to the church's and state's hold over the religious lives—and, thus, the economic lives—of its subjects. Many of the religious rebels were tortured and burned at the stake (Figure 12.7). Among them was Jacob Hutter, whose followers took his name in tribute.

Living communally, apart from society at large, was not an original part of the Anabaptist belief system, but it became necessary in the face of continual persecution to live separately and to develop a social system that was self-sufficient and had internal strength and cohesion. The self-sufficiency was possible since many of the people, as noted, were literate urban artisans and craftspersons. So the early Hutterite communities began to produce their own food and to manufacture their own houses, clothing, and other artifacts (Figure 12.8). The agricultural life, of course, has lasted to the present. So too has the craftsmanship. One still finds shoemakers, carpenters, and even bookbinders in a Hutterite colony.

Again, the ideological basis for such economic and social communism was found, not surprisingly, in the Bible. The social system of the Hutterites—having "all things common"—is modeled after the communities of early Christians, who gathered together, separate from the larger society, to follow the teachings of Christ while awaiting his return—as the Hutterites do.

FIGURE 12.8
Eighteenth-century illustration of Hutterite straw roof construction. The Hutterites became well known for their self-sufficiency, the quality of their products, and their farming techniques.

Now, compare the Hutterites' version of Christianity with that of another North American group. This branch is generally less well defined than the Hutterites and is quite variable, but we can focus on its most extreme form. It's called by a number of names depending on the region, but a common one is the Holiness Church, and its followers the Holy Ghost People. Sometimes, for reasons that will become clear, they are referred to in a derogatory fashion by outsiders as the "Holy Rollers."

Holiness churches started in the first decade of the twentieth century in Tennessee and are now found mostly in Appalachia and the Southeast—Georgia, the Carolinas, Florida, Virginia, West Virginia, Kentucky, Tennessee, and Ohio. The basis for their form of Christianity comes from the Gospel of Mark, 16:17–18. Speaking to his disciples, Jesus says,

> And these signs shall follow them that believe; In my name shall they cast out devils; they shall speak with new tongues; They shall take up serpents; and if they drink any deadly thing, it shall not hurt them; they shall lay hands on the sick, and they shall recover.

The Holy Ghost People feel that if they believe strongly enough, the Holy Ghost enters their bodies. The manifestations of this are, as predicted in Mark, "speaking in tongues" (a babbling, rolling sort of speech whose meaning is only intelligible to others with the Holy Ghost), convulsive dancing and trancelike states, the ability to "lay hands on" the sick and cure them, and a "call" to handle venomous snakes or drink poison (Figure 12.9).

FIGURE 12.9
This man, at a Holiness service, has been called by the Holy Ghost to show his faith by handling poisonous snakes.

The snakes are local rattlesnakes and copperheads. The poison is a dilute strychnine solution. The meaning of these acts, always performed at the height of the service, when the music is loud and many persons are manifesting the Holy Ghost, has to do with professing one's faith. "God," they are saying, "will protect me from this dangerous act, so strong is my belief. But if I die from it, that's God's will, and I will accept it." Persons bitten by the snakes or who become very ill from the poison will not accept medical aid. At least twenty people associated with this religion are known to have died in the last eighty years from snakebite. As a result, the practice is outlawed in most of the states listed. It goes on, however.

Besides these biblically sanctioned features, there are some others that characterize and distinguish Holiness church services. There is often, for example, no formal minister, no one who is trained or ordained to conduct the services. The leader is chosen much like the San choose the man to ask about where to hunt. It is based on outgoingness, charisma, speaking ability, or, perhaps, just whoever gets up and starts. Sometimes, it's the person who has been bitten by snakes most often.

What goes on during a service, moreover, is often individual rather than group-oriented. People pray in their own words, kneeling if they want, or standing, dancing, or lying down. This makes sense, of course, since possession of the Holy Ghost is an individual matter. It doesn't happen to everyone, and for those to whom it does happen, how they manifest the experience is up to the Holy Ghost. A Holiness service appears rather chaotic once it gets going. There are quiet periods when the collection plate is passed or when individuals "testify," telling personal stories about their experiences with the Holy Ghost. But the main event finds some participants playing music, some praying, others dancing or laying hands on the sick, and still others handling snakes or drinking poison.

The attitude of the Holy Ghost People toward their relationship with God is unique in Christianity. Most Christians' prayer is in the form of a request to God. But as one man puts it in a film of a Holiness service, these Christians feel that "if you believe, God is obligated to answer your prayer." God is still supreme and can do with his followers as he chooses. But a strong enough faith on the part of the people "obligates" God to them.

How may we interpret this somewhat unusual version of Christianity? The fact that they are Christians lies in the history of the culture of which they are a part, but their particular practices would seem to be explained in economic and social terms. The Holiness Church is largely a phenomenon of poor, rural Appalachia (although it has moved into urban areas with the migration of people). People in parts of Appalachia are among the least economically well off in the United States. They are small-scale farmers, local merchants, or employees of coal-mining or other large companies. They don't, in other words, have the kind of control over their economic welfare that many Americans have—or think they have.

Not many of us do, of course. But the image of American affluence that comes across in books, magazines, and television is quite different from the lives led by the folks in poor, rural America. Having little more than this image with which to compare themselves, they feel out of step with mainstream American life. The religious expression of the Holiness Church provides a sense of control. The practitioners of this religion have a oneness with God in the possibility that they might be possessed by the Holy Ghost, which then can choose to act through their bodies. In fact, simply by believing strongly enough, they can even obligate God to them.

Moreover, in an environment economically near the bottom of America's social stratification, the Holiness service is an opportunity for a little egalitarianism. There is no formal hierarchy. Everyone is important. Everyone expresses him or herself as an individual. The only difference between people—the possession of the Holy Ghost—is a difference that can be eliminated by strong belief. Possession of the Holy Ghost is open to all.

Finally, anthropologist Westen LaBarre has suggested that the Holiness service may provide a mechanism for sexual expression. No sex is taking place at the services, of course, but *social* intercourse between the sexes is taking place. And such public interaction is something not done regularly in conservative societies like the ones in which we tend to find the Holiness Church.

Open sexuality is not part of these peoples' lives, yet it is characteristic of American society as a whole. Just watch television for a couple hours—programs and commercials. As with economics, there may be a feeling of being out of step with an important aspect of American culture—and perhaps with some basic human tendencies (see Chapter 6). At any rate, a look at a Holiness service, such as that depicted in the film *Holy Ghost People,* reveals a good deal of touching between members of the opposite sex, and not always between members of a recognized couple. (I've seen that film at least fifty times, and I've come to know the people well enough to make this observation.) The idea is to pass on and share the presence of the Holy Ghost. There is no overt sexuality involved, but the touching and dancing may function to provide an outlet for sexual identity and expression that are normally repressed.

As with most other cultural (and biological) behaviors, however, these practices developed gradually—in other words, they evolved—and their current functions don't necessarily account for their origins. Nor are people always consciously aware of those functions. In the case of the Holiness Church, though, the facts that it is of recent origin and is still found in its place of origin lend support to the idea that, here, current functions are original functions.

From this brief examination of Christianity in general, and of two expressions in particular, you should have an idea of how anthropology looks at religion. There are some general principles regarding what types of religions one tends to find in what types of cultures. Then, specific religious traditions are examined by delving into the cultural histories of the societies involved and into the peoples' reactions to social, political, and economic situations that make up the tapestry of this history. Religion is part of a cultural system, intimately connected to all other parts.

This scientific approach, it must be noted, does not make a religion any less real for those who practice it. So basic are religious beliefs to peoples' lives—as members of cultures and as individuals—that they cannot entirely be reduced to or explained by the objectivity of scientific investigation. The reality of religious beliefs operates at many levels.

If religion acts to provide motivations and sanctions for human actions, what about societies that are so populous, complex, and technologically and scientifically elaborate that religion has ceased to be at the center of human life? What maintains order in such societies?

LAW

We may lump other order-maintaining systems into a single category and call them legal systems. Legal systems are secular—that is, not religious—but they perform many of the same functions religious systems do. They define the premise on which human interactions in the society are based. They outline specific behaviors that correspond to this premise, and they provide rules for handling disputes about and transgressions of these behaviors. Though secular, they are often based on the religious principles that express the world view of the culture in question.

Take the United States as an example. If the foregoing is the case, the basis of our legal system should be found in Judeo-Christian religious tradition. What is at the center of that tradition with regard to how humans ought to act toward one another? If you boil it down, it is expressed by such ideas as "Thou shalt love thy neighbor as thyself" (Leviticus 19:18); "all things whatsoever ye would that men should do to you, do ye even so to them" (Matthew 7:12); and "Judge not, and ye shall not be judged" (Luke 6:37).

What is the essential premise of our legal system? Nowhere is it better stated than in the Declaration of Independence:

> We hold these truths to be self-evident, that all men are created equal, that they are endowed by their Creator with certain unalienable Rights, that among these are Life, Liberty, and the pursuit of Happiness.

The Constitution lays out the foundation of a government formed to

> establish justice, insure domestic tranquility, provide for the common defense, promote the general welfare, and secure the blessings of liberty.

In the first ten amendments, or Bill of Rights, the Constitution includes some specific ideas aimed at protecting the rights named in the Declaration and at fairly punishing those who are accused of trespassing on the rights of others. Viewed in this way, our legal system is a translation of some basic Judeo-Christian religious principles into secular terms, and the formulation of specific laws to implement those principles in the real world.

All this seems rather obvious and, for us, there seems no other system that could protect and ensure those rights. But there are. Although it would be accurate to say that all people seek to be alive, free, and happy, just how cultures define those ideals in practical terms differs greatly.

For the Dani of New Guinea, for example, the taking of human lives is a regular, formalized occurrence that makes up a central focus of their existence. The Dani have a system of ritualized warfare (which we will examine more fully in the next chapter) that involves the killing of an enemy to placate the ghost of a slain member of one's own group. Then the enemy must slay a member of the other your group to placate the ghost of its member, and so on. These groups, it is important to understand, are groups *within* Dani society. They are not outsiders. And so important is this revenge cycle that a woman or child may be killed in place of a male warrior if too much time has passed.

Although we have our own share of murders and wars, a system like the Dani's seems at least exotic if not barbaric to us. It's difficult to maintain one's cultural relativity when looking at their system because it seems to violate principles central to our system. We must remember, however, that there is a reason for their behaviors within their larger cultural system, and that through it they are pursuing happiness as they define it— just based on a very different premise from ours. One might say (and I don't mean this as sarcastically as it may sound) that their premise is something like "do unto others what others did unto you." And yet their culture has persisted successfully for thousands of years.

The chapters in Part Three have discussed the major categories of human adaptive behavior. We have covered the possible origins of our behaviors as well as the variations we observe in them from society to society. And we have talked about how we as anthropologists go about trying to understand these behaviors.

If that were all there was to anthropology, my job would be a lot easier. But there's more. We don't look at cultures as groups of people who are eating and communicating and maintaining order and making tools. A culture is a whole—an integrated system with all its individual features and all the people involved interacting in a complex web of relationships. Although most anthropologists would, I think, agree in principle with my filter diagram (see Figure 7.4), we don't all agree on exactly how all those aspects interact in terms of the human motivations behind them and the immediate functions they fulfill. Have we so successfully taken care of practical needs that all our actions have only symbolic value? Or do we still do things for down-to-earth practical reasons? Or both?

Furthermore, has our successful cultural adaptation left biology behind? Or are we still, and will we be forever, biological organisms? And just how much can we say about the biological bases for certain cultural behaviors?

It's time now to put all this together and discuss some general ideas about human behavior.

SUMMARY

World view is an abstract set of conditions and assumptions about those conditions that are at the integrative center of any cultural system. But world view requires a mechanism to give it reality, to allow it to be transmitted among a people and to future generations, to provide answers to questions about the world, to translate its assumptions into values that regulate human behavior, and to formulate rules of behavior that put those values into action. These are the functions of religion and of secular legal systems.

Religion, distinguished from secular systems by its focus on the supernatural, is, like any facet of culture, highly variable from society to society. It is, however, a cultural universal, that universality explained by the need for a way to help people understand the complex world around them and to coordinate their actions accordingly. Many features of the natural world can be explained scientifically, but many cannot. They require explanations that are beyond science. There is also the need to regulate the various levels of human interaction—to tell us how to behave.

As one of several aspects of cultural behavior, we can find correspondences between variables of a religious system and other features of the culture of which it is a part. Since history also affects world view, we find that we must look at the historical dimension of a religious system in order to understand its origins, basic characteristics, and meaning.

In many if not most societies, some of the rules of life have evolved away from the strictly religious and have become phrased in secular terms. In societies like our own, where the answers to world view questions are largely scientific and rational, the vast majority of our basic rules are secular laws. Laws perform the same functions as religious systems, at least with regard to defining the premises for human action and outlining the specific actions that correspond to these premises. Laws also take care of disputes about those regulated actions and provide for punishment of those who transgress them. Even where a society is regulated almost exclusively by a secular legal system, there is often at the basis of that system a religious tradition. The religious rules have been translated into secular ones.

NOTES, REFERENCES, AND READINGS

My favorite work on the anthropology of religion is still Edward Norbeck's *Religion in Human Life: Anthropological Views*. It defines religion and its roles and gives numerous ethnographic examples. The passages I quoted are from pages 6 and 23.

A good collection of readings is Arthur Lehmann and James Myers's *Magic, Witchcraft, and Religion: An Anthropological Study of the Supernatural.*

The chimpanzee "rain dance" is described in Jane Goodall's *In the Shadow of Man*. The quote is from page 67.

My discussion of the origins of Christianity is largely from Marvin Harris's *Cows, Pigs, Wars, and Witches: The Riddles of Culture*. Harris's treatment includes some of the specific evidence for the original identity

CONTEMPORARY ISSUES

How Can We Account for the Recent Interest in Witchcraft?

Witches have been showing up with increasing frequency in the popular media lately. There are television shows like *Buffy the Vampire Slayer* (where one main character and several minor ones are witches); *Charmed;* and *Sabrina, the Teenage Witch* and movies like *Practical Magic* and *The Craft.* Since popular media are a reflection of general cultural trends, these examples hint that some larger cultural phenomenon is taking place. And, indeed, there are those who claim to be witches and to practice witchcraft. Many of these people belong to a movement called Wicca (from the Old English for "sorcerer" and the origin of the word "witch").

Wicca (which can trace its modern form to the 1950s) is a somewhat loosely defined religious movement with no central authority, with several subgroups, and with accepted diversity among its individual units, called "covens." There are, however, some general features. Wicca's followers claim to be "white" witches, that is, witches that do good rather than evil. Indeed, one of their basic tenets is to "harm none." The powers of these witches seem based mostly on a learned ability to connect with and channel natural forces (herbal medicines, for example), although one gets the sense that some feel a more innate source. A reverence for nature and fertility is common, as are elaborate and colorful rituals, and, according to Jeffrey Burton Russell, a sense of "restrained hedonism" and "release from guilt" regarding sexual pleasures, so long as such behavior harms no one. In the words of a Wicca website (www.wicca.com), Wicca is a "peaceful, harmonious and balanced way of thinking and life which promotes oneness with the divine and all which exists."

Wicca celebrations seem to be a mix of astronomical events like the solstices and equinoxes and largely Celtic celebrations such as *Samhain,* the precursor of Halloween. At the same time, there is, in the basic tenet that one should do no harm to others, a Judeo-Christian ethical overtone. A close examination of Wicca shows, in fact, that it draws its features from a number of religious traditions. Finally, Wicca should not be confused with Satanism or with the heretical witchcraft of medieval and early modern Europe. Wiccans reject the existence of the Devil, since that is a specifically Judeo-Christian idea.

Now, in this age of both the growth and ubiquity of scientific knowledge and the existence of a number of larger, better-defined, better-accepted, and more established religions, why would people be attracted to the idea of witchcraft, with all its negative connotations and

of Jesus as belonging to the military messianic tradition. Among this evidence are some passages from the Bible such as "Think not that I am come to send peace on earth: I came not to send peace, but a sword" (Matthew 10:34) and "he that hath no sword, let him sell his garment, and buy one" (Luke 22:36).

For more on the Hutterites, see the references cited in Chapter 1.

The Holy Ghost People are described and analyzed in detail in Westen its scientifically unsupported ideas of the supernatural?

The answer probably varies with each individual, but we can propose some explanations in keeping with our theme of the integrated nature of cultural systems. First, one purpose of any religion is to give its followers some sense of control over their lives, or at least some sense of predictability. There have always been those for whom the orthodox religions of the time proved unsatisfactory in fulfilling these roles, but the modern world seems, to say the least, a particularly unpredictable one and one over which many people feel a decreasing sense of control—the power of science notwithstanding. At the same time, according to Barry Singer and Victor Benassi, traditional religions have lately recognized a "more abstract, less personal deity" and have focused their activities more on secular concerns (human rights and so on) and less on "individual parishioner's needs." People, however, still require the personal benefits of religious beliefs, so some have converted to less orthodox religions—like Wicca—that provide a more personal sense of knowledge, control, and even power, and a degree of individual freedom from specific doctrine. Few of us are not at least entertained by the possibility of possessing the kinds of knowledge and powers exhibited by television and movie witches.

Second, some authorities (such as Singer and Benassi) also connect the current interest in witchcraft to deficiencies in modern science education. Not understanding how science works and how it can examine and evaluate natural phenomena may lead people to uncritically accept the kinds of powers sometimes claimed by or attributed to witches. Certainly, this problem contributes to the proliferation of pseudoscientific nonsense that shows up in supermarket tabloids and on television—alien abductions, Atlantis, and psychic powers, to name a few.

But regarding modern witchcraft, I think an assessment by Marcello Truzzi rings truer. He sees some of the current interest in witchcraft as well as other aspects of the occult as actually "a kind of victory over the supernatural" and "a demystification-process of what were once fearful and threatening cultural elements." In other words, people may not always fully understand science but most people do understand that it accurately tells us how the world works and how we may utilize the natural processes of that world. They also know that most claimed supernatural phenomena, occult occurrences, and the like, don't really exist. So, dabbling in the occult, as Truzzi notes, is often a leisure activity and those involved often have an attitude of "playfulness" toward their involvement. It's fun, and it gives one at least a sense of what it must be like to possess the kinds of knowledge and powers claimed.

LaBarre's *They Shall Take Up Serpents*. It gets a little heavy on the symbolic, psychoanalytic side, but it's worth reading.

The references I used for the Contemporary Issue on Wicca are from three articles in the Lehmann and Myers's reader noted above. They are: "Witchcraft" by Jeffrey Burton Russell, "Occult Beliefs" by Barry Singer and Victor A. Benassi, and "The Occult Revival as Popular Culture: Some Observations on the Old and the Noveau Witch" by Marcello Truzzi.

THE EVOLUTION OF OUR BEHAVIOR

Pigs, Wars, Killer Proteins, and Sorcerers

Anthropologists agree that all the facets of a cultural system are integrated—they are connected to one another by a complex web of interactions, both at any given time and over the course of time. I have tried to show this integration in the last five chapters by pointing out some of the interrelations involved within the individual aspects of cultural adaptations and some examples of connections among cultural features.

Anthropologists agree, as well, that culture has two interacting roles: as the means by which our species and its societies respond adaptively to their natural environments, and as the means by which we respond to our cultural environments—that is, the ways in which we maintain the integrity and meaning of our cultural systems (see Chapter 7 and Figure 7.4). A cultural behavior, then, can have practical value, or it can have meaning. Usually, it has both.

Now we must try to put all these ideas together and see how they work when we look not just at individual aspects of a cultural system but at cultural systems as wholes. When we do this, we begin to find some disagreement among anthropologists. These disagreements can be complex, but most of them focus on which role of culture is most important—that is, which role is being fulfilled by the features of a cultural system within the minds of the people practicing those features and within the actual living, working culture?

Some anthropologists emphasize the practical adaptive role of culture, maintaining that the ultimate explanation for cultural phenomena lies in the fulfillment of basic needs such as providing food, water, and shelter. Others focus on culture itself, stressing that cultural phenomena need be explained only by their meaning within a given cultural system. Put another way (in the words of anthropologist Marvin Harris), the debate asks in which direction is the relationship between ideas and behavior. Does behavior guide ideas (the practical adaptive explanation), or do ideas guide behavior (culture as meaning)?

I believe that cultural phenomena fulfill many roles in a complex feedback system, far more complex than this dualistic, either-or debate indicates. I will apply this idea to two cultural examples in the second section of this chapter. First, however, I think I can best demonstrate the integrated roles of culture by looking at two existing and diverse explanations for a particular cultural expression. The proponents of these explanations are British anthropologist Mary Douglas and American anthropologist Marvin Harris, and the topic of their debate—going back to that most basic of human concerns—is food, specifically the lists of clean and unclean foods from the Bible.

OF THEIR FLESH YE SHALL NOT EAT

Jews are forbidden to eat the flesh of swine. So, too, are Muslims. For these religions, pigs are considered unclean creatures: "Of their flesh shall ye not eat, and their carcasses shall ye not touch." But you may not be aware that this taboo is part of a long list of foods considered unclean by the ancient Hebrews. (Pork is the only specific meat prohibited in Islam, although anything already dead or any animal sacrificed to another religion is also inedible.) You'll find this more interesting if you begin by reading the list yourself. You can find it in both Leviticus 11:1–47 and Deuteronomy 14:1–21. Read them both, as each has some specific information not included in the other. It takes a little patience to sort out all the generalizations, and wording varies depending on the version of the Bible you have, so here's a summary.

Among the important animals that are acceptable to eat are those that have parted or cloven hooves and chew their cud (some ungulates regurgitate partially digested food and chew it again to extract more nutrition). Creatures in this category include oxen, sheep, goats, and various wild deer and antelope.

However, any creature that has *only one* of these attributes is unclean and cannot be eaten. The camel chews its cud but does not have a cloven hoof. The coney (or hyrax, a rabbitlike animal) and the hare don't actually chew cud but look like they do, and neither has anything like a hoof, so they cannot be eaten. And the pig, which has cloven hooves but does not chew cud, is prohibited by the same criteria (Figure 13.1).

Water creatures are easily defined in this system. If they have fins and scales, you can eat them. If they have neither or only one, you can't. Thus, trout can be eaten, but eels and sharks (which have no scales) or clams and lobsters (which have neither fins nor scales) are unclean.

The longest specific list of prohibited food sources is for birds. Most of those considered unclean are birds of prey—those that clearly eat large creatures such as mammals, other birds, or fish—and scavengers. (Notice that bats, which are, of course, mammals, are listed as prohibited birds, an interesting taxonomic error.) Also prohibited are waterbirds like the swan and cormorant and "all fowls that creep, going on all four," presumably a reference to flightless birds. (Of course, no bird goes on "all four," so, unless the ancient Hebrews couldn't count, I attribute this to poor translation. It must simply refer to creatures whose primary locomotion is walking.) Leviticus says nothing about which birds may be eaten, and Deuteronomy says only "of all clean fowls ye may eat." But how do we know, then, which are clean? What are the criteria? For the moment, let's go on.

All insects (the Bible says "every creeping thing that flieth") are unclean except those that "have legs above their feet, to leap withal upon the earth." These may be eaten, and locusts, grasshoppers, and beetles are specifically listed as edible.

FIGURE 13.1
Domestic pigs showing the cloven or split hoof that became one characteristic that placed these animals in the category of prohibited foods among the ancient Hebrews.

There is an unspecified mention of things with "paws." This would probably include mammals like dogs and cats, certainly wild and possibly domesticated. Finally, there is a list of prohibited "creeping things that creep upon the earth," specifically weasels, mice, tortoises, ferrets, chameleons and other lizards, snails, and moles. In addition, there is a general prohibition against eating anything that has already died, even if it is one of the clean creatures.

Now, how do we explain these clean and unclean animal food sources? We can, with reference to the pig as an example, discount the conventional wisdom that pigs are literally unclean because they are dirty and carry disease. They are, in fact, no dirtier than any other domestic animal, nor are they the only animal that can be a source of disease. The parasite usually associated with pigs, the trichina worm, is rare in hot climates, can be controlled simply with proper cooking, and its existence only became known in the nineteenth century—long after the lists of clean and unclean food were created. Moreover, many of the other creatures labeled as unclean are perfectly fine, safe sources of food. There's obviously some other explanation.

FIGURE 13.2
A Kosher deli with separate sinks and utensils for meat and dairy products. The Hebrew food laws include rules about consistency, uniformity, and lack of confused categories. Thus, "Thou shalt not seethe [cook] a kid in his mother's milk" (Deuteronomy 14:21).

Mary Douglas emphasizes the symbolic functions of cultural practices. Once beyond the obviously practical (things like tools to acquire food and so on), the functions of most acts, she feels, are aimed at conforming to and thus reinforcing our basic assumptions about our world, our world view. The food taboos, she feels, reflect some broad idea, serving an abstract cultural need rather than a practical one. Ideas, in other words, guide behavior.

Douglas's argument is detailed in her book, *Purity and Danger.* Most of the taboos, she feels, are aimed at preserving peoples' "holiness" (Leviticus 11:43–47), which she takes to mean wholeness, completeness, and consistency (Figure 13.2). Things of this world should not be confused and must be uniform, integrated, conforming: "Holiness requires that individuals shall conform to the class to which they belong. And holiness requires that different classes of things shall not be confused."

It follows from this general principle that one of the most vital aspects of the world, food, should be categorized in such a way that the categories ("classes") are clear and that creatures conform to the characteristics that define their class. If they don't, they are not holy—and are thus unclean.

So, Douglas says, water creatures that lack fins and scales fail to conform to the criteria defining this class of organisms. Creatures that "go on all four" but that fly are also unclean because they fail to behave appropriately for legged land creatures, which should be jumping or walking. This is why locusts, beetles, and grasshoppers, even though they fly, are edible. Animals with "paws," she says, are unclean because they have "hands instead of front feet" and so "perversely use their hands for walking." And all those "creeping" creatures are taboo because of their "indeterminate form of movement."

The list of unclean birds doesn't seem to work well with Douglas's interpretation. A raven is not fundamentally different from, say, some perching bird like a robin, which, I assume, would be acceptable to eat. Douglas addresses this by suggesting that the list may be poorly translated, the translators using modern names of species for old Hebrew and Greek names of quite unrelated species. If the list could be retranslated, she offers, we might find the unclean birds to be birds that can't fly or that swim and dive as well as fly, and that, therefore, are "not fully birdlike."

Now, before we get to her discussion of the cloven-hoofed, cud-chewing animals, let's examine her idea so far. To be sure, the lists of creatures that can and cannot be eaten or even touched serve an important symbolic purpose. They maintain the "holiness" of those who adhere to their principles. It reminds them constantly of their relationship with God, from whom the rules came. "By rules of avoidance holiness was given a physical expression in every encounter with the animal kingdom and at every meal, " says Douglas.

Though categorization itself may serve this function, Douglas's interpretation doesn't explain why the animals are categorized as they are in the first place. Who says creatures with fins and scales are the "proper" kind of water animal? Indeed, there are more kinds of marine animals without these two traits than there are with them. Who decided that a huge number of insects don't conform to their category because they have feet but also fly? What's wrong with creeping? And paws?

And notice what's missing from the list: plants. Surely there are plants that are bad to eat or fail to conform to some taxonomic norm. Clearly, there's more to the story, and a clue can be found in Douglas's discussion of livestock.

Here, the criteria for cleanliness are clearly based on practical matters. Douglas says, "Cloven-hoofed, cud-chewing ungulates are the model of the proper kind of food for a pastoralist." Why? Not because of the presence of a particular set of "proper" traits, as with the other categories, but because the rules are an "*a posteriori* [after the fact] generalization of their habits." In other words, the rules reflect what the people were already doing with regard to eating animals. Behavior, in this case, was guiding ideas. And we must assume that with something as vital as food, what they were already doing had practical reasons behind it.

This is where another view of cultural analysis, expressed by Marvin Harris, comes in. Harris is a cultural materialist, someone who sees cultural patterns not as "random or capricious" but as based on "practical circumstances" and "ordinary, banal, one might say 'vulgar' conditions, needs, and activities." People may do things for reasons that are symbolic on the surface, but beneath it all, their cultural practices originate in down-to-earth, "mundane," usually economic matters. Says Harris,

> Practical life wears many disguises. Each lifestyle comes wrapped in myths and legends that draw attention to impractical or supernatural conditions. These wrappings give people a social identity and a sense of social purpose, but they conceal the naked truths of social life.

Harris's ideas on cultural materialism are detailed in a technical book by that name and in two popular books, *Cows, Pigs, Wars, and Witches* (the inspiration for the subtitle of this chapter), and *Cannibals and Kings: The Origins of Cultures*. Here is what he says about the dietary laws.

Harris would agree with what Douglas said about the livestock—that the dietary laws are after-the-fact generalizations of already existing habits. And the habits in question revolve around the fact that the people among whom these laws originated emphasized farming as a source of food. Recall that Southwest Asia was one of the areas where agriculture first appeared. Part of the reason for its emphasis in that area is that, given the ecological conditions there, farming is a much more efficient source of nutrition than is herding. You get, says Harris, about ten times the number of calories back per calorie expended in farming as you do in raising livestock. Moreover, as the emphasis on farming increased in the area, it brought about ecological changes itself, turning forests into grasslands, which themselves sometimes converted to deserts (Figure 13.3). These environmental changes also made most hunting a costly proposition in terms of nutrition returned for energy expended.

This emphasis on farming explains why plants are not given clean and unclean labels. So central was the raising of plants that there was no need for any formal reinforcement of the habits, or for reminders about which plants to grow and which to avoid. Plant foods weren't special. That information was a given.

Thus, the practical concern of cost versus benefit for various sources of food was, according to Harris, at the heart of the matter. People gradually stopped hunting for wild creatures, especially those that provided little meat and were hard to catch. They were also careful about the animals they herded; such animals had to be useful alive (for work, milk, and fertilizer) as well as on someone's dinner plate. Otherwise, the cost in energy was too high.

This explains the prohibition of eating pig. Pigs are useful only when dead, and then just for meat and leather. They are hard to herd—indeed, they are not creatures that herd naturally. They cannot digest cellulose and thus are not grazing animals suited to the natural flora of Southwest Asia. In fact, their digestive system is much like our own (part of the reason fetal pigs are often dissected in biology labs), so they actually compete with humans for the same food sources. Finally, they are hard to raise in hot, dry climates because they don't sweat. They need an external source

FIGURE 13.3
View of the Gaza Strip along the Mediterranean Sea, taken from a space shuttle. Years of grazing and climatic changes have removed much of the vegetation and turned the area into desert. Note particularly the very light strip along the shore. North of the clearly defined border between the Egyptian Sinai and southern Israel, irrigation has allowed farming, as seen by the dark fields. Assessing the costs versus benefits of raising different foods in such ecological conditions helps explain the biblical dietary laws.

of moisture to cool their bodies and roll in mud or even their own excrement if no other source is available—the origin of the notion that they are especially dirty. It was, in short, not a good idea for the peoples of Southwest Asia to raise pigs. Although they did at one time (archaeologists have found bones of domestic swine), they gradually stopped doing so as the area's ecology changed. These compelling reasons for eliminating pig raising, and thus pork eating, must also explain the Muslim prohibition.

What about animals that *were* herded—sheep, goats, and cattle? All these animals can thrive under the ecological conditions of Southwest Asia and can, because they are naturally herding animals, be easily controlled. They serve functions other than as sources of food. They all provide milk. Sheep have wool. Cattle can be used for agricultural work and, when dead, as a source of meat and leather. The benefits of herding such species outweigh the costs.

Some wild animals are also listed in the cloven-hoofed, cud-chewing category. Harris feels that whether they are clean or not depends on the same basic criterion: cost effectiveness. Wild deer and antelope have long been successfully hunted (see Figures 5.22 and 10.22) and provide a good deal of meat. Hares and hyraxes, on the other hand, are harder to find and kill and are not worth the effort.

To round out this part of the list, we have the camel, an animal so useful for transportation and other work that to eat it would have been detrimental in terms of energy efficiency. The same could be said for the horse and donkey. The latter was widely used in the area, but neither is included in the lists, although Harris says that rabbinical scholars have normally added them. Again, their use alive was so important that eating them was out of the question—so much so that it may simply have not been necessary to list them.

In support of this part of Harris's materialist interpretation is the fact that the Koran (the sacred book of Islam) specifically releases Muslims from the prohibition against eating camel flesh. Many Islamic pastoralists used the camel for long trips through desert areas and, in an emergency, eating camel might have been the only means of survival. A prohibition would have been decidedly counterproductive.

The hunting idea seems also to apply to birds. Such birds as eagles and vultures (both unclean) were hard to catch and would not provide much nutrition for the effort. (I'll bet they're not very tasty either.) And there might be another factor, not mentioned by Harris, that relates to practical concerns of cleanliness and health. Recall that many of the prohibited birds are birds of prey or scavengers. They eat other animals, including ones that are already dead. The eating of carrion is prohibited by both the Bible and the Koran, probably because of the recognition of the potential ill effects of eating decaying flesh. (It is true that our earlier ancestors were scavengers. They certainly could have eaten already dead animals with impunity, but I also imagine some of them suffered for it.)

Harris also applies the inefficiency of most hunting to explain the taboo against finless, scaleless aquatic animals like clams, eels, and shrimp—which were not common in the interior of Southwest Asia. Nor would animals with "paws" and those "creeping" things have been very energy efficient sources of food.

Neither would most insects. But those that were edible—locusts and grasshoppers, especially—were big, meaty bugs that are most abundant and easily captured when they are swarming and eating people's crops. There is surely some practical sense in eating these insects, and folks did (Figure 13.4).

Now, we seem to have two quite diverse points of view here: Douglas, who feels the explanation for the laws lies in their symbolic and organizing value, and Harris, who thinks they all stem from practical considerations. I think they are both right and that each emphasizes a different aspect of the same story. When you read them carefully, you see that they realize this as well.

Harris explains the origin of the laws as religious expressions of preexisting practical habits. Douglas as much as acknowledges that in the passage I quoted about the cloven-hoofed, cud-chewing ungulates.

FIGURE 13.4
A farmer in Burkina Faso in West Africa raises a horde of locusts from a tree whose vegetation might have fed livestock. A locust swarm in Somalia in 1958 is said to have measured 400 square miles and numbered 40 billion insects capable of eating 80,000 tons of food plants a day.

But the fact that the laws are expressed in terms of loose zoological categories labeled "clean" and "unclean" may be explained by the need for people to order their world and to do so in a way that makes sense culturally and symbolizes basic cultural ideas. The categories are folk taxonomies. And Harris admits that some of the prohibited creatures, especially some of those in that rather diverse "creeping" list, may have been prohibited

> not for ecological reasons but to satisfy random prejudices or to conform to some obscure principle of taxonomic symmetry intelligible only to the priests and prophets of ancient Israel.

Now, once the laws are in place, serving to codify and maintain certain practical habits, they may also function—since they are in religious terms—to remind people of their identity and relationship with the supernatural, even after their practical functions are no longer important. Harris again:

> Food taboos and culinary specialties can be perpetuated as boundary markers between ethnic and national minorities and as symbols of group identity independently of any active ecological selection for or

against their existence. But I don't think such beliefs and practices would long endure if they resulted in the sharp elevation of subsistence costs.

In short, Harris and Douglas do not really hold completely opposite views on the analysis of cultural phenomena. Rather, they each emphasize a different process in what amounts to a complex feedback loop. For another example, consider that although both religions arose from the same general geographical area and share much history and many beliefs, Islamic dietary laws are much less restrictive than Jewish ones. Muslims can, for instance, eat shellfish; Jews who keep kosher cannot. Many Jews have held on to this prohibition even if they live in areas where shellfish are nutritious, easily obtained food sources. For cultural reasons, the symbolism of the prohibition is more important than material concerns. The Muslims did not carry over this restriction (although, recall that they did with the pork taboo) for reasons that may involve practicality (the presence and abundance of shellfish in coastal areas) or symbolism (to differentiate their beliefs from Jewish tradition) or some combination of both. Specific cultural systems are explained by the specific and complex histories and environments of the societies in question.

To summarize:

It makes sense that many if not most cultural behaviors originate for practical reasons. If a society can't satisfy its basic biological needs, symbolism and meaning become irrelevant. Once a basic set of behaviors is in place, they become part of an integrated, meaningful, complex cultural system. In Harris's words, behaviors have guided ideas. Then, however, the ideas that those practical behaviors generated become integral parts of the cultural system and of the lives of the people who practice it. Those ideas, then, act as guides for behaviors. And, of course, both these processes are always in operation within any cultural system at any given time and through time. Both these directions of influence must be looked for and considered when we attempt to understand a system of culture, be it someone else's or our own.

Now, how does this work when we look at more than just a society's dietary laws? As examples, let's examine more closely two fascinating stories from New Guinea.

PEACEFUL WARRIORS AND CANNIBAL FARMERS

That both my examples come from New Guinea does not mean that the analytical process I've described is applicable only to peoples from that large island in the western Pacific. It can be applied to any culture. It's just that these two examples are among my favorites and are two you are not likely to forget.

The Dani

The Dani, whom I've mentioned several times, live in the western half of New Guinea called West Irian or Irian Jaya, now a part of Indonesia. The lives of the Dani have, of course, changed over the last several decades as industrial societies and technologies have increasingly invaded their once isolated mountain valley. The Dani I'll describe are the Dani of the late 1950s and early 1960s, when anthropologists first extensively studied them and before much outside contact had changed forever a way of life they had led for perhaps thousands of years. I'll speak in the present tense, what we call the "ethnographic present." My information comes largely from ethnographic studies by anthropologist Karl Heider.

There are about 100,000 people who speak the Dani language, but the group we're concerned with, about 50,000 individuals, lives in the Grand Valley of the Balim River, an area of about 250 square miles. The Dani are horticulturalists, using only digging sticks and human labor to break ground and plant, care for, and harvest their crops. They use an extensive system of ditches that have four functions: to bring water to crops, drain excess water away from crops, protect crops from pigs, and make compost.

Their major crop, making up perhaps 90 percent of their diet, is the sweet potato. Almost their only source of meat comes from domestic pigs. In contrast to Southwest Asia, highland New Guinea is an ideal place for pigs—not too hot, plenty of moisture, and, because of the successful sweet potato farming, plenty of food for both pigs and people. There was little natural game to begin with, and much of that has been hunted out.

In general, the Grand Valley is a nice place to live. The average year-round temperature is about 70° Fahrenheit and there is plenty of rain. Although there are seasonal fluctuations in rainfall and temperature, there is essentially a year-round growing season. The elevation is high enough so that common tropical diseases are uncommon. One might think that people in such a place would live happy, peaceful lives. Happy, perhaps; indeed, Heider describes the people themselves as "gentle" and "nonaggressive." But peaceful, hardly. For the Dani are continually at war, and not with outsiders, but with one another.

The Grand Valley Dani are divided into about twelve alliances, which are subdivided into a total of about fifty confederations. There has existed, for how long no one knows, a state of ritual war between various alliances. The motivation is the placation of ghosts. The ghost of a person slain in warfare demands revenge. This requires that the life of an enemy be taken in return. That death, of course, requires revenge as well, making the cycle self-perpetuating.

The opportunity to take lives is provided by large battles. These take place, by mutual agreement, on a no-man's-land between alliance territories, usually only on days when the weather is nice. The weapons used

FIGURE 13.5
A Dani war dance.

are 13-foot-long spears and bows and arrows. These weapons are not particularly well made, and an alert warrior can usually see them in flight and avoid being hit. When a man is killed or badly wounded, however, the battle ceases, for there is concern that no more than one life be taken in revenge. In the case of multiple deaths—on either side—the rules still require only one death to be taken in revenge. It all has the appearance of a huge game, though one with very high stakes.

If several of these battles fail to result in the death required, the group needing the kill may resort to ambush. Here, an unwary woman or child can be the victim and serve the purpose of revenge as well as a warrior in battle. When a person has been killed, all other activities cease and both sides celebrate: One has a dance of joy that their ghost has been avenged while the other stages a funeral with all the display of emotion one would expect, especially if the deceased is a child (Figure 13.5).

On reading about the Dani, or on seeing Robert Gardner's marvelous film, *Dead Birds* (so called because the Dani see themselves as birds, which are mortal, as opposed to snakes, which shed their skins and so are immortal), many people see such a cycle of death as incongruous given the relatively "temperate" (as Heider says) conditions of their environment and personalities. Why do people who seem to have no real economic hardships and who feel normal emotions of grief and

311

FIGURE 13.6
Holistic summary of Dani warfare.

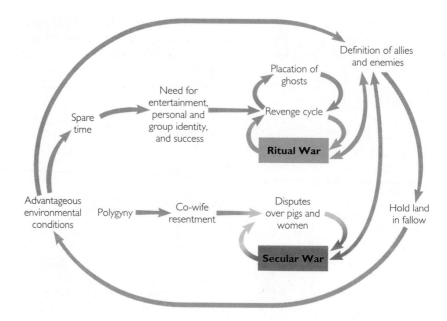

sorrow have a cultural practice that ensures that a violent death takes place on a regular basis? Moreover, the men seem obsessed by war and death, as most of their daily activities are centered on watching for the enemy, making weapons, and weaving bands decorated with shells that are traded only at funerals. How can we explain such a cultural system?

Some cautions: Just because we will have to cover the features and relationships of this cultural system in some order doesn't mean that that is the order in which they developed or that what is discussed first is the cause and subsequent features the results. We're talking about an evolving holistic system that developed through time (Figure 13.6). As a result, what might have been a functional relationship in the past may not hold true in the present. Without written records, the best we can do is point out the functional relationships that were observed by anthropologists over about a ten-year period and then hypothesize about the nature of those relationships in the past.

You should know that the ritual war is not the only kind the Dani fight. They also have periodic secular wars. These are fairly rare, occurring maybe every ten years or so—so rare, in fact, that Heider didn't know of their existence when he first studied the Dani. These secular wars take place for secular reasons, usually arguments over wives or pigs (both are commodities and signs of status to the polygynous Dani) or some other matter that gets out of hand and cannot be resolved peacefully. Conflict resolution is something the Dani don't seem to be very good at.

Secular wars are usually fought between confederations within an alliance because it is between such groups that the economic and social relations occur about which conflicts arise. Secular wars are not played by rules. The idea is to kill members of the enemy confederation and to take their goods and land. The last such war took place in 1966, when some 125 people, of both sexes and all ages, were massacred. It was this war that prompted the Indonesians, who had taken over Irian Jaya from the Dutch in 1963, to step up their attempts to pacify the Dani.

War, as most of us normally think of it, is thus possible within the Dani cultural system and has obviously been part of it. These secular wars, however, are few and far between. The ritual war is continuous. It almost appears as if the ritual war fills in the time between "real" wars— and, to an extent, I think that's the case.

The ecological conditions of the Grand Valley make basic subsistence a fairly easy task, given the technology the Dani possess. With relatively little labor, sweet potatoes can be grown in sufficient quantities to feed everyone, and this vegetable seems to be nutritious enough to make up the bulk of the Dani diet. Similarly, the pigs, raised and cared for with little labor, provide the additional sustenance available from meat. The majority of the food-related labor, in fact, is done by women and children. The men usually break ground for a new garden, the hardest work involved, but after that women do the farming—children are largely responsible for the pigs. The men, as a consequence, have lots of spare time.

Now, don't get the idea that the men dreamed up this elaborate game to relieve their boredom. It's not that simple. It's more accurate to say that an important *current function* of the ritual war, and part of the reason it persisted, is that it gives the men something to do. It provides a focus for their daily lives. It gives them a social and personal identity. It's exciting. But this is not why it *originated*.

It would be more reasonable to assume that the ritual war derived from some already existing behavior—namely, the secular wars—and that the secular war came about for some down-to-earth practical reasons. Secular wars came about, and were made possible, because there are a large number of people living isolated in a bounded area (the Grand Valley), who are spread out over that area in individual units. Thus, there is a sense of "mine" and "thine." Moreover, the subsistence pattern is successful enough that the beginnings of social stratification are seen. Differences exist in number of pigs owned, in amount of land farmed, and in numbers of wives. Conflicts could easily arise over these factors as well as over matters of relative power, influence, and social status. Polygyny itself carries the seeds of tensions, because the common phenomenon of **co-wife resentment** can sometimes send one wife back to her parental village, which in turn causes ill will toward her kinsmen on the part of her husband.

co-wife resentment Tension among the wives of one man in polygynous societies often caused by the differing statuses of those wives.

In other words, these conditions, and the Dani's reactions to them, set the stage for a world view where tension and potential conflict are normal (or at least not abnormal) states of affair. There were territories established, statuses acknowledged, and wealth unequally distributed—all things we don't see among egalitarian foragers, who may experience violent behaviors toward one another, but not on the scale of warfare.

So the ritual war has derived from—is an extension of, a symbol of, a metaphor for—the secular conflicts and the conditions that brought them about. The exact relationship and history we'll probably never know. But the ritual war caught on, in part because of its identity as a derivative of the other tensions and conflicts and in part because it filled the time and provided a major theme for Dani life.

The importance of the ritual war is evidenced by its justification within the Dani religious system. It is not just a frivolous game but a vital part of their world view and most deeply held beliefs. A behavior (the tensions and secular wars), in other words, gave rise to ideas (the revenge cycle for ghosts of the slain), which then guided behavior (the ritual war and its central place in Dani culture).

Are any other relationships in operation here? During the ritual war, a no-man's-land exists between rival factions. This land is not planted, although when alliances shift (confederation and alliance membership is not stable) it may be farmed once again. After a secular war, there is usually much shifting of people, alliance membership, and land. This shifting allows areas of land to lie fallow for a time, which lets the nutrients build back up, which in turn may add to the overall success of Dani farming. Whether the Dani are aware of this is unclear, nor do we know whether it really makes a difference. But it's one route of possible investigation.

Another economic relationship exists as well. Tension and war are justifications for ceremonies—not only funerals but also feasts that help strengthen alliance relationships. Ceremonies are not only important symbolically but are also events during which food is consumed and goods exchanged. Pigs, for example, are normally eaten only in some ceremonial context. Ceremonies, then, keep Dani wealth in circulation, acting as a means of redistribution of wealth—both symbolic shell bands and pig flesh.

One would think that when the Dutch and then the Indonesians pacified the Dani and put an end to the warfare cycle, the whole of Dani society would unravel, lacking such an integral part of their culture. Something with so many interrelationships and to which the Dani devote so much time and concern must be something they can't do without. But that's not what happened. The Dani took the imposed change quite calmly. The men continued to sit in watchtowers guarding against an enemy attack that would never come. They found occasions to eat pigs. They carried their weapons and wore their finest battle garb for fights that would never happen. Taking away the actual war made little difference to them.

What we see here, then, is a complex interaction of ideas and behaviors that evolved over many years and resulted in the manifestation of Dani culture in the early 1960s. (And what I've outlined is only part of the story; see Karl Heider's book for more detail.) Although we have been able to see how all the aspects of Dani culture *can* interact, we can't know for certain how they really do and did interact. Obviously, the calm with which the Dani accepted pacification tells us there's something else involved. The above analysis is only a hypothesis that requires testing. Because of the changes to Dani life, such testing may be impossible. At any rate, it is by observing, describing, and proposing relationships between ideas and behaviors that we may begin to approach the understanding of individual cultural systems and of culture in general.

The Fore

For a second example, let's move to the eastern half of New Guinea, now the independent nation of Papua New Guinea, and another society I've mentioned elsewhere in this book, the Fore.

There are about 14,000 people who consider themselves Fore. The example in question, however, refers to a subgroup, the South Fore, who number about 8000. Like the Dani, the Fore are horticulturalists and pig keepers. Also, like the Dani, their major crop is the sweet potato, although they grow a greater variety of minor crops. The Fore also do more hunting than the Dani.

As with any culture, the Fore exhibit a set of cultural features that make them unique. But when first extensively studied, they exhibited another distinction as well—a disease, found occasionally in surrounding groups but heavily concentrated among the South Fore. They call the disease *kuru,* and we have adopted that name. It is a degenerative disease of the central nervous system. Its symptoms follow an almost unvarying pattern, starting with loss of balance, followed by loss of motor coordination, slurred speech, abnormal mental behavior (such as uncontrollable laughter), and finally complete motor incapacity and death. It takes on average a year for this sequence to progress (Figure 13.7).

When first discovered among the Fore, the cause of kuru was a mystery, and it displayed a strange distribution. Between 1957 and 1968 there were 11,000 deaths from kuru, accounting for about 80 percent of Fore deaths. The most common victims by far were adult women, in whom it was nearly eight times as frequent as in adult men. Following the women, children of both sexes were the next most common victims, followed by elderly men. There was clearly a lot to explain.

Shirley Lindenbaum's *Kuru Sorcery* has more details. Here, though, are the major features of the story, which suffice to demonstrate the importance of the interaction of ideas and behaviors as we've discussed. And more recently, we have come to know much more about the disease itself.

FIGURE 13.7
A Fore woman in the terminal phase of kuru, supported by her husband. She can no longer sit up unaided and, although she appears to be smiling, has in fact lost control of her facial muscles.

The first problem to solve was the cause of the disease. At first, because of its isolated nature, kuru was thought to be genetic. But there is no genetic mechanism that would account for the distribution of the disease among the Fore, with adult women, children of both sexes, and elderly men being the most common victims. Anyway, it was too frequent to be genetic. A disease that is 100 percent lethal would have been selected out of existence, except for isolated new cases, long ago.

A clue came from veterinary medicine. It was reported that a similar disease called *scrapie* was known among sheep and goats. Kuru was then considered a "slow infection"—one with a long incubation period —and thought to be caused by a virus. Some symptoms were similar, and autopsies of kuru victims showed similar features of deteriorated brain tissue.

We now know that kuru is caused by a still-mysterious and frightening protein called a prion protein. Not living organisms, prions are normal proteins in the nervous tissue (of no known function) that (for no known reason) sometimes fold up in an abnormal configuration. In this form they trigger the same folding up of the normal proteins, which then build up in brain tissue, which they eventually destroy. The condition is

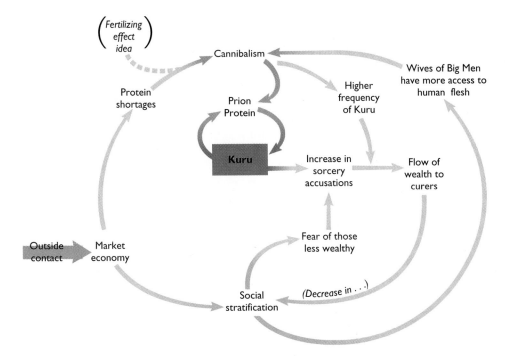

FIGURE 13.8
Holistic summary of kuru phenomenon among the Fore.

called *spongiform encephalopathy*. Mad cow disease in cattle, scrapie in sheep and goats, Creutzfeld-Jakob disease and kuru in humans, are all examples. Although the trigger for the abnormal shape of the protein may come, not surprisingly, from a genetic mutation (since, as you recall, genes code for the synthesis of proteins), the frightening thing about prions is that they can be transmitted across species. Moreover, they are very hard to destroy. Mad cow disease may have been spread because cattle in England were fed meal that contained the remains of other domestic animals. Even though these remains were rendered (cooked and processed into meal), the prions survived and were passed to other cows through ingestion. Several human cases of Creutzfeld-Jakob in England can be traced to human consumption of infected beef. In other words, these are all essentially the same disease.

Since people the world over may get the disease—albeit rarely—why was it so concentrated among the Fore? How was it being passed from one person to another, and why in such an odd pattern? The answer, first proposed by anthropologists Shirley Lindenbaum and Robert Glasse, was cannibalism, which was largely practiced by women who shared the human flesh with their children and, sometimes, with elderly men. Consuming the flesh of someone who died from kuru, even though the flesh is cooked, passed the prion proteins on to others. Because they practiced **endocannibalism,** the disease was concentrated and found almost exclusively among the South Fore (Figure 13.8).

endocannibalism The eating of human flesh from members of one's own society.

Why were they practicing cannibalism, and why was it mostly the women who practiced it? Fore cannibalism seems to be practiced for reasons somewhere between ritual and nutrition. Rather than feeling they are gaining some power from the deceased, they seek to acquire a "fertilizing" effect. As Lindenbaum states, "Dead bodies buried in gardens encourage the growth of crops. In a similar manner human flesh, like pig meat, helps some humans regenerate. The flesh of the deceased was thought particularly suitable for invalids."

But when we step back and look at broader relationships, we may see this practice as having a more material origin. It appears to have been taken up by women—in the relatively recent past, an idea borrowed from some surrounding societies—to supplement their diet in what was fast becoming a protein-poor society where men, who dominate Fore society, had first access to the small supply of wild game and pigs that were available. So indeed, cannibalism here does seem to have a nutritional function at its origin.

Why was the society becoming protein-poor? Complex economic changes brought about by the Australian government (which then controlled Papua New Guinea) had turned these former foragers and horticulturalists into settled farmers, with an emphasis on the sweet potato and the pig, as well as on cash crops (such as coffee). This way of life, and the larger, more sedentary populations it produced, had gradually depleted the forests and the game they contained, making protein increasingly scarce. Moreover, now that they were part of a larger, money-oriented economic system, these fairly egalitarian people began to exhibit stratification in both wealth and status. Large-scale historical changes had affected the specific environment of the Fore, initiating (or at least promoting) the practice of cannibalism, which seems quickly to have become part of the Fore cultural system, endowed with symbolic meaning. Again, we see the mutual influences of behaviors and ideas. In a tragic coincidence, then, the practice of cannibalism transmitted and increased the frequency of a devastating disease, which otherwise would have only affected the few individuals in whom the still-mysterious protein anomaly occurred.

But this cycle caused even more changes. The Fore explain serious diseases as the work of sorcerers, people who for one reason or another bear a person ill will and act to cause that person harm. As kuru increased, the Fore began to fear that their women would all die and that they as a society would perish, and they naturally explained this in terms of the acts of many powerful sorcerers. Who were these sorcerers? People who were not faring well in the new economic stratification. So the increase in kuru coincided with the coming of economic differences and rivalries. In addition, it seems as if the wives of the "Big Men"—those with the most power and wealth—had more access to human flesh than the wives of the less powerful, with the result that kuru was more frequent among families of the Big Men, who, then, naturally saw themselves as being victimized by those of lesser status and wealth. The invocation of sorcery to explain the disease thus made perfect sense within the Fore cultural system.

Finally, to whom did the Big Men turn to try to counteract this sorcery? To their own sorcerers, of course, who did not come cheaply. Thus, the wealth of the Big Men began to pass from them to others in the form of fees to the counter-sorcerers or bribes to the accused sorcerers themselves. Lindenbaum calls this an example of redistribution, which acted to even out some of the differences in wealth and status.

These two examples from New Guinea and the brief analysis of the biblical food laws show the intimate connection not only among different aspects of cultural systems but also between culture and biology. We had to understand the biology of pigs, for example, and the nature of a bizarre anomalous protein in order to explain cultural phenomena and the cultural systems of which they are a part. But are there any more-direct connections between biology and culture? Is our behavior totally generated by culture, or does it have a biological component? If so, just how much influence does biology have over our actions?

BIOLOGY AND CULTURE IN INTERACTION

On the cold, stormy evening of January 13, 1982, during the Washington, D.C., rush hour, Air Florida flight 90 out of National Airport apparently iced up during takeoff and moments later crashed into the Potomac River, killing 78 people. Only a handful of the plane's passengers survived, and one of them probably owes her life to a young man named M. L. Skutnik.

Skutnik, a government worker, was stopped in the traffic jam resulting from the crash. He was watching the rescue operations when he noticed a woman survivor in the water unable to grab onto a lifeline. Removing his coat and shoes, he dived into the icy Potomac and saved her life.

In June of the following year, Kansas City Chiefs running back Joe Delaney saw three young boys in trouble out in the water of a Louisiana lake. Delaney jumped in to try to help them. Others came to their aid but, unfortunately, one of the boys drowned. So did Delaney, who couldn't swim.

These heroic deeds fall into a category of behavior called **altruism**—acts performed for the benefit of others with no regard to the performer's welfare. The question that comes immediately to mind is why anyone would perform such an act. Why did these two men do what they did?

Perhaps they were responding to learned cultural ideals. There would, however, have been no retribution—legal or moral—if they hadn't acted.

altruism Acts that benefit others without regard to the welfare of the organism performing those acts.

Under the circumstances, their deeds were extremely dangerous. No one and nothing was forcing them to act. No one would have blamed them if they hadn't. Perhaps, on the other hand, what they did was an automatic response to some biological instinct, coded somehow in their genes. But one of the strongest instincts is surely that of personal survival, and both these men put their lives at risk (and Delaney lost his) for people they didn't even know. Perhaps, then, their deeds involved some complex interaction between culture and biology.

Such questions are part of a larger issue that has long been debated in many scholarly areas. As you might imagine, we can describe two extreme points of view on the subject, which we can call **biological determinism** and **cultural determinism** or, more simply, "nature versus nurture." The first position holds that much human behavior is biologically determined, though, of course, mediated by culture. The second feels that humans are born pretty much as behavioral "blank slates" and that culture then "writes in" everything that needs to go on those slates. These extremes are rarely held today, although there are those who lean in one direction or the other. As so often occurs in such cases, evidence points to an interaction of biology and culture, a middle ground between the nature and nurture extremes. But, let's first examine the extremes.

The nurture, or cultural determinism, school of thought is clearly untenable. It posits, to use a computer metaphor, that we arrive in this world like computers with internal hardware but nothing programmed. One can't load data into a computer without the appropriate application software. If the human brain were not already "programmed," for example, to learn language, no amount of exposure to language would result in a person's being able to speak.

This point of view also implies that at some point in our evolution we left behind our biological heritage and became something qualitatively different. But obviously, we carry the anatomical and physiological imprints of our evolutionary past. Why not the behavioral ones as well, even if only in terms of general behavioral themes?

A strict nature, or biological deterministic, point of view is also untenable, but for more complex reasons, and a real or perceived support of this position is what has generated the controversy around this question.

It's obvious, and uncontroversial, that the behavior of non-culture-bearing species is programmed in their genes in a complex series of stimulus-response reactions. The nest-building behavior of the weaver ants I described in Chapter 7 is an example. It has even been shown that social behaviors can be biologically based and, thus, explained by the operation of natural selection—even behaviors that may benefit the group rather than the individual.

Take altruism, for example, which—in its broad definition—seems to exist in nonhuman species. In some mammalian species like ground squirrels and prairie dogs, certain individuals act as guards or sentinels,

biological determinism
The idea that human behaviors have a biological basis, with minimal influence from culture.

cultural determinism The idea that human behaviors are almost totally the result of learned cultural information, with little or no instinctive responses.

FIGURE 13.9
A prairie dog who has acted as a sentinel, giving what animal behaviorists call a "jump-yip," a signal meaning "all clear."

watching for predators while the others forage (Figure 13.9). If a predator is sighted, the sentinel gives an alarm call and the others literally "hit the dirt." In some species there is evidence that the sentinel is at more risk than the others. How, then, could such behavior have been selected for if it might lead to *less* chance of passing on one's genes?

The proposed answer is a phenomenon called **kin selection.** If the members of such a mammal group are closely related, they share many of their genes. As a result, the fitness of a set of genes (and, thus, the adaptiveness of the phenotype) is not only measured by the reproductive success of the individual but also by the reproductive success of all those possessing the gene. Thus, any behavior that aids the passing on of the gene in question is selected for. This would include any behavior that

kin selection Promoting the passing on of one's genes by aiding the survival or reproduction of one's close kin.

benefits the related group as a whole, even if it might not necessarily benefit particular individuals. Over time, a set of genes for sentinel behavior would increase in frequency because, at any given time, some individuals possessing those genes will perform guard duty and, even if they are eaten and lose their opportunity to pass on any more genes, they have helped save the lives of many related individuals who share the genes.

So, complex behaviors—even seemingly maladaptive behaviors—in other species can be accounted for in Darwinian terms, that is, in terms of natural selection and the other processes of biological evolution. The problem arises when such reasoning is applied to humans. Could there be a similar biological basis for our behaviors? Some areas of study, variously known as **sociobiology, evolutionary psychology,** or **behavioral ecology,** have suggested that this is possible—that certain typical human behaviors arose and became part of our behavioral repertoire because they conferred a reproductive advantage on those possessing them. In other words, because they had a genetic basis, they developed through the mechanism of natural selection.

One reaction to this model came from those who interpreted "biologically based" to mean "biologically determined," that is, that this idea implied severe limits on human free will and thus on the power of culture. Other objections were more political. They claimed that the idea was racist and sexist, or at least potentially promoted racism and sexism. The reasoning behind such accusations was that if human behaviors are genetically determined, then the *differences* in human behaviors lie in genetic differences, and so the two sexes and people from different populations, being genetically different, could thus be seen as unequal on a very basic biological level.

But there are scientific, as well as political, objections to an extreme nature viewpoint. Essentially, this model implies that our behaviors are all aimed at maximizing our reproductive success. It could even be seen as implying that cultural variations on these behaviors have evolved for that reason. Some of the more popular versions of this idea assume that people, in performing some behavior, are at some level still aware of the biological advantage that may have selected for the behavior in the first place. But, as Marvin Harris points out, not all cultural behaviors and ideas are aimed at reproductive success. Polyandry, for example (see Chapter 10), is hardly the best method of passing on a maximum number of one's genes. Rather, there are important and complex *cultural* reasons for this variation on the nuclear family model.

To give another example, journalist Robert Wright, in his book *The Moral Animal,* posits that infanticide may be the result of a "mental organ that implicitly calculates when killing a newborn will maximize genetic fitness." In noncultural creatures, this may be the case. Lions kill offspring of lionesses so they can mate with them and produce cubs that will inherit their genes. But in humans, I don't think infanticide is always

sociobiology The scientific study that examines evolutionary explanations for social behaviors within species.

evolutionary psychology A synonym for sociobiology.

behavioral ecology A synonym for sociobiology.

done with *this* calculus anywhere in mind. People kill infants to maximize *something*, and so clearly the potential to kill one's offspring is there, but what's maximized is not always, and maybe never, just one's genetic fitness. For example, the Yąnomamö of Brazil regularly killed female infants. The reason was their emphasis on male warriors—because of tension and competition among Yąnomamö villages, the very survival of each village depended on the ability to defend and conduct offensive war, which was a vehicle for procuring land for farming and hunting. So women must give to their husbands and their villages new potential warriors and a first-born daughter or the second of two daughters born in a row was commonly killed. The benefit is symbolic. In fact, it's actually counter-productive genetically, since Yąnomamö villages often have, as a result, a shortage of marriageable females, and so another reason to go to war is to steal women to provide wives. The behavior is important and it was *culturally* selected for, but there's no logic in thinking it evolved in any biological Darwinian sense.

Can these two extreme views be reconciled (as I tried to do for the two extreme explanations for the food laws)? In fact, I've already discussed two related examples at length (Chapter 6): marriage and the incest taboo. We may come "preprogrammed" with some general behavioral themes or potentials—such as the attraction and bonding between males and females and the avoidance of mating with immediate family members. These may, in our evolutionary past, have been so important adaptively (in maximizing reproductive potential) that they channeled and placed strict limitations on our behavior. That's why our cultural translations of those behavioral themes—marriage and incest taboos—are cultural universals. The web of relationships that make up a cultural system provides the motivating factor for how specific versions of those themes are expressed and explains the specific function of those expressions. Culture, as in the case of inbred ancient Egyptian royalty, can reverse the behavioral norm. But these cultural expressions may still be seen—in all their rich diversity—as variations on behavioral themes that were selected for before we became the cultural primate. In this way, biology and some general aspects of cultural systems interact.

Now, what about Skutnik and Delaney? Is this model applicable to their deeds of heroism? Perhaps the *fact* that they were able to spontaneously place their own lives at risk to help fellow species members is based on some ancient biological program similar to the noncultural one that programs individuals in other species to act as sentinels for their group or to defend their young. But those behaviors can be seen as having evolved to promote the passing on of one's genes, even if they are in the body of a related individual. Skutnik and Delaney didn't even know the people they went to rescue.

Maybe, as with the case in the kibbutzim (see Chapter 6), culture has fooled Mother Nature. Those two men may have been among those who

CONTEMPORARY ISSUES

Are Humans Naturally Violent?

Perhaps the most common question regarding the issue of a biological basis for our species' behavior involves human violence. A brief glance at human history—or simply a look at today's newspaper—could easily convince you that the answer to the question posed in this feature's title must be yes. Although most people probably go through their entire lives without committing a truly violent act, the frequency of human violence and the intensity of some violent acts—from individual murders to the genocide of millions—certainly can make it seem reasonable that aggression is part of our species' behavioral repertoire and that, although most of us can suppress or rechannel our aggressive tendencies, those tendencies can, under sometimes inexplicable circumstances, be expressed. This has been the premise of a number of popular and even scientific works, perhaps the most famous (or infamous) of which were *African Genesis* (1961) and *The Territorial Imperative* (1966), both written by playwright-turned-amateur anthropologist Robert Ardrey. They are better written than most examples of the genre, but their arguments are typical.

Based on the accepted fact that humans are the products of an evolutionary history, Ardrey claimed that the violent acts humans commit toward one another can be traced to our descent from apes that were "armed killers"—that is, our australopithecine ancestors whom he characterized as roaming the savannas of Africa with weapons, killing other animals for food and, on occasion, killing one another in defense of their territories. An instinct for violence is thus, he said, in our genes, and it is expressed by war and other aggressive acts that seem at times to have become

a hallmark of our species. Indeed, Ardrey claims war, territoriality, and competition have led to the great accomplishments of civilization but that, at the same time, "civilization is a compensatory consequence of our killing imperative; the one could not exist without the other." This is because civilization is also a natural result of evolution that acts to sublimate and inhibit our "inherent talent for disorder."

As further evidence of the instinctive nature of human aggressiveness, Ardrey offers the observation that we *also* possess instinctive behaviors that seek to limit aggression, much like the submissive behavior of dogs and wolves or the threat gestures of some nonhuman primates—behaviors that make the point of showing who's boss without bloodshed. A good example is "that innate aggressor, the athlete . . . [who] accepts and absorbs the rules and regulations of his sport without, in many cases, benefit of a registerable IQ." Aggression, competition, and violence are so much a part of our biology, says Ardrey, that we can't do without them, so we also have evolved ways of inhibiting them to keep "within the bounds of danger." Oftentimes, however—whether in athletic competition or the waging of war—we go well beyond those bounds. So, by such arguments, violence is a natural behavior because it makes Darwinian sense—having been selected for because it conferred such a powerful reproductive advantage for early hominids that it became part of our species' behavioral repertoire.

Are we biologically capable of violence? Of course; humans commit violent acts. Might violence have a specific biological component? There have been some demonstrated correlations between tendencies toward violence in some individuals and imbalances in important brain chemicals. But is violence necessarily Darwinian —that is, something we have inherited from our evolutionary past because it was naturally selected for and still makes sense in terms of enhancing one's reproductive success? We have already discussed this issue with regard to other human behavioral themes, but let's look specifically at this one. It is an important issue, and such arguments can be quite persuasive.

The first problem with Ardrey's idea is that he lumps diverse acts together under one category. Killing something for food—which he claimed our remote savanna ancestors did, and which is an aggressive act—is *not* necessarily the same as the planned genocide of other members of one's species because they have ethnic, religious, or political differences. A hunting instinct has very different origins, immediate motives, and functions from conscious and planned murder.

Even if we could consider all examples of human aggression as the same, there is no evidence that the australopithecies were "armed killers" (and the evidence was slim when Ardrey was writing). They did not make stone tools, there is no evidence of other tools (much less weapons as Ardrey claims), and, if they ate any meat, they scavenged it. Nor is there evidence of any territorial homicide.

Second, such ideas assume that even if a connection existed between a behavior and reproductive success, that connection has existed through the millions of years the behavior was passed along in our evolution and still exists now. As we discussed with the issue of infanticide or the more benign practice of polyandry, there are presumably *reasons* for these behaviors but the reasons may have nothing to do with repro-

ductive success. They can be explained as parts of cultural systems, and both their functions and the motives underlying them may have nothing to do with reproduction. In fact, they can be counterproductive in this regard. Certainly murder seldom serves to promote the passing on of one's genes.

Biology and culture are in complex interaction throughout our evolutionary history and at any point in that history. But seeking to explain specific cultural phenomena as the result of naturally selected behaviors that maximize reproductive success both oversimplifies the complex nature of natural selection and minimizes the nature of cultural systems and the power of cultural motivations.

Acts of aggression expressed by human beings need to be examined and dealt with as cultural phenomena. We may have the biological potential to commit violent acts against members of our species, and the basis for that potential may lie within some basic instincts— unsurprising and uncontroversial things like self-preservation or protection of family members. But these acts (except for those clearly the result of neurological or neurochemical defects) are triggered by cultural ideas and ideals. They are responses of human beings as members of cultural systems—as individuals or groups of individuals interpreting and responding to their world and world view. As a result, we can deal with the problem of violence neither with simplistic measures (since the reasons for violence are embedded deep within cultural systems) nor with some fatalistic, pessimistic idea that all violent acts are expressions of some ancient genetic program that we're stuck with.

take seriously the cultural idea that all men are brothers or that we should treat others as we would be treated. Naturally, neither man felt the same about all people, but their belief in a moral abstraction was enough to trigger an altruistic response and lead to what, by adaptive criteria, were irrational acts—but acts full of positive cultural meaning.

SUMMARY

Culture consists of both ideas and behaviors. One area of debate within anthropology focuses on the direction of the influence between the two. Some feel that behaviors give rise to and guide ideas; others say that ideas give rise to and guide behaviors. An examination of cultural phenomena shows that the influence is in both directions. Practical behaviors become translated into ideas that become part of integrated, holistic cultural systems. Ideas then influence behaviors, since behaviors must meet practical needs as well as remain consistent with and help maintain the cultural system itself. This mutual influence can be demonstrated more persuasively when entire cultural systems (or at least large portions of them) are examined.

A long-standing question in anthropology and other human-oriented disciplines relates to the relative influences of biology and culture on human behavior patterns. As with the issue above, there have been two extreme views. One claims that culture creates minor modifications in some biologically based and naturally selected-for behaviors. The opposite view says that biology has little or no real influence and that human behaviors are entirely cultural. Again, examining behaviors seems to show a complex interaction between biology and culture. While the immediate motivation for and function of our behavior patterns relate to their place within our cultural systems, those general patterns themselves may have been selected for in our precultural stage because they conferred an adaptive—that is, a reproductive—advantage. Variations in behavior patterns such as marriage, incest taboo, and language are explained by variations in cultural systems. That there *is* marriage, incest avoidance, and the ability to produce symbolic language have, at their base, a biological explanation.

NOTES, REFERENCES, AND READINGS

The debate over the direction of influence between ideas and behaviors in culture is discussed in Marvin Harris's latest book *Theories of Culture in Postmodern Times,* in which, among other things, he evaluates an extreme nature position on the influence of biology.

Mary Douglas's model of cultural analysis can be found in her *Purity and Danger: An Analysis of Concepts of Pollution and Taboo.* The discussion here is from her chapter "The Abominations of Leviticus." Marvin Harris's ideas on cultural materialism are detailed in his technical *Cultural Materialism: The Struggle for a Science of Culture* and more entertainingly in *Cows, Pigs, Wars, and Witches: The Riddles of Culture* and *Cannibals and Kings: The Origins of Cultures*. The quotes I used are from page 5 of *Cows, Pigs, Wars, and Witches* and pages 202 and 206 of *Cannibals and Kings*.

For more information about the Dani see Karl Heider's *Grand Valley Dani: Peaceful Warriors*. Be sure to see Robert Gardner's movie *Dead Birds,* which can be rented through a number of academic film rental organizations. The story of the Fore and kuru is detailed in one of the best examples of holistic anthropology available, Shirley Lindenbaum's *Kuru Sorcery: Disease and Danger in the New Guinea Highlands*. A more recent piece, which also talks interestingly about some aspects of scientific research, is "Fieldwork in the South Fore: The Process of Ethnographic Inquiry" by Robert Glasse and Shirley Lindenbaum. A more up-to-date discussion of kuru, related diseases, and prion proteins (with a graphic description of Fore cannibalism) is *Deadly Feasts,* by Pulitzer Prize–winning author Richard Rhodes.

Still a good book on the Darwinian basis on animal behavior, and the book that started the modern nature-nurture controversy through its application of sociobiological ideas to human behavior is Edward O. Wilson's *Sociobiology: The New Synthesis*. A collection of works on all sides of the debate, and on the debate itself, is Arthur Caplan's *The Sociobiology Debate,* which is now out of print but worth looking for. A new collection on all aspects of human behavioral evolution is *The Biological Basis of Human Behavior: A Critical Review* by Robert Sussman. Robert Wright's recent argument for a biological basis for specific human behaviors is *The Moral Animal: Evolutionary Psychology and Everyday Life.*

For a different interpretation of some altruistic-looking behavior among animals, see "Selfish Sentinels" by Daniel Blumstein in the June 4, 1999 issue of *Science,* page 1633.

For an extreme nature, or biological determinist, point of view on human violence, see *African Genesis* and *The Territorial Imperative* by Robert Ardrey. The quotes used in the Contemporary Issue feature are from pages 355 and 359 of the former and page 317 of the latter.

PART FOUR

The Species Today, the Species Tomorrow

14

HUMAN VARIATION
Different Looks, Different Behaviors

The 6 billion human beings on earth today come in an amazing variety of shapes, sizes, colors, appearances, beliefs, and behaviors. We speak, idealistically, of celebrating this rich diversity. This seems especially applicable in the United States—a nation and a culture synthesized from the cultural systems of both indigenous peoples and immigrants from every corner of the world. The fact is, however, that while many nations (the United States included) do a relatively good job of integrating and appreciating the diversity of their peoples, there is still a great deal of misunderstanding about just what our species' diversity means. There are now, and always have been, conflicts—from the ideological to the bloody—based on different interpretations of the origin and meaning of biological and cultural differences.

We have spent much of this book looking at the nature of cultural differences. What about biological differences? Where do those come from? What do they mean? How are they connected to differences in behavior? The search for answers to these questions is, I believe, one of anthropology's most important contributions.

Let's begin with one of my favorite photographs (Figure 14.1). It shows *National Geographic* photographer George Steinmetz and some Yali men from the highlands of New Guinea. I need not point out who is who. You can guess from what I've said who's who. In fact, if I hadn't said anything about them, you might still have guessed from what part of the world they come, even without the cultural cues of clothing. Steinmetz looks European. The Yali men look like people from the interior of New Guinea. (Compare their features with those of the people in Figures 8.9, 13.5, and 13.7).

This photo beautifully represents the wide range of phenotypic variation within the human species. Imagine some extraterrestrial scientist seeing these men as the first specimens of our species. He or she (it?) might initially think they represented two profoundly different and distinct biological groups. This, in fact, was what the first Europeans thought when they encountered peoples from highland New Guinea.

We know now, of course, that the men in the photo are members of the same biological species, *Homo sapiens*. We can provide detailed evidence of their genetic similarities, and the ultimate test of species identity—the ability to produce fertile offspring—has been demonstrated many times.

So, the people in this photograph belong to the same species. But look at them! They are distinct in a number of striking physical features,

subspecies Physically distinguishable populations within a species; the concept is falling from use.

races In biology, the same as subspecies. In culture, cultural categories to classify and account for human diversity.

FIGURE 14.1
A European American photographer who is 6 feet 2 inches tall with a group of Yali people from the highlands of Irian Jaya (the western half of New Guinea). There is little doubt as to who is who, nor that members of our species can display a striking degree of phenotypic variation. The major question then becomes: Does this degree of variation mean that there are distinguishable human races?

and you could accurately place them geographically. Surely, they must represent definable, nameable groups *within* the human species. And so, by implication, there are surely other definable, nameable human groups. In other words, surely the human species is divisible into a number of biological **subspecies** or, to use a more common term, **races.**

I'll answer that right away. It is now a well-established fact that, biologically, humans races do *not* exist. There is no scientifically valid way to divide us up into any number of biologically meaningful groups below the species level. But this area of human biological diversity is rife with all sorts of social, ethical, political, historical, philosophical, and personal implications. And it's a subject in which wishful thinking is sometimes allowed to stand in for rigorous science.

So it pays to articulate *why* there are no biological races. It's not enough to be sure it's the case or to assume it is because it makes us feel good. We need to be able to explain it, to present the *evidence* for it.

WHY ARE THERE NO BIOLOGICAL RACES WITHIN THE HUMAN SPECIES?

There are four intersecting, interrelated types of evidence that we can examine to address this question. As we discuss them, we need to be as objective as possible, to try not to argue to a predetermined conclusion. In the end, this will make our conclusion all the more meaningful.

The Concept of Race within Biology

Since we humans are a biological species, major theoretical conclusions that apply to other species should apply to us. We may ask, then, what evolutionary biologists in general say about categories below the species level, that is, subspecies or races.

Subspecies names—that is, a third taxonomic name after the genus and species name, indicating a distinct group—have been in common use

FIGURE 14.2
North American populations of caribou are considered by some to represent subspecies or races.

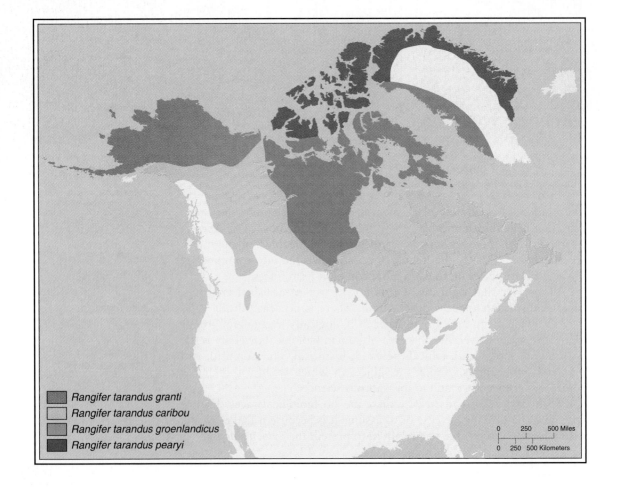

- Rangifer tarandus granti
- Rangifer tarandus caribou
- Rangifer tarandus groenlandicus
- Rangifer tarandus pearyi

0   250   500 Miles
0   250   500 Kilometers

FIGURE 14.3

The caribou, *Rangifer tarandus*. This woodland caribou of Alaska and Canada is sometimes classified as subspecies *Rangifer tarandus caribou*. Well adapted to a wide range of environments, the caribou has such traits as hollow outer guard hairs that give it extra buoyancy for swimming and extra insulation for warmth. This feature makes caribou hides a favorite material among the Inuit for making parkas.

for years. Figure 14.2, for example, shows the ranges of four named subspecies of caribou, a large North American member of the deer family (Figure 14.3). The problem here is obvious: Since all populations of caribou compose a single species and maintain that species identity through the flow of genes among their populations, then these subspecies distinctions are rather artificial. In reality, the dividing lines shown on this map don't exist. The caribou at the extremes of the range may look quite different (in size, color, and branching pattern of antlers) but one doesn't step over one of these geographical lines and find the caribou suddenly looking completely different. Rather, their variable traits will grade into one another over geographical space. This is called a **cline,** or *clinal distribution.*

Figure 14.4 shows the size variation (based on sixteen skeletal measurements) of the common house sparrow. There are certainly some interesting facts revealed here. For example, northern sparrows tend to

cline A geographic continuum in the variation of a trait.

FIGURE 14.4

Distribution of size variation in male house sparrows, determined by sixteen skeletal measurements. The larger the number, the larger the sparrow. The classes, however, are arbitrary. If a line is drawn from Atlanta to St. Paul or from St. Paul to San Francisco, the size variation in the sparrows is distributed as a cline, a continuum of change from one area to another.

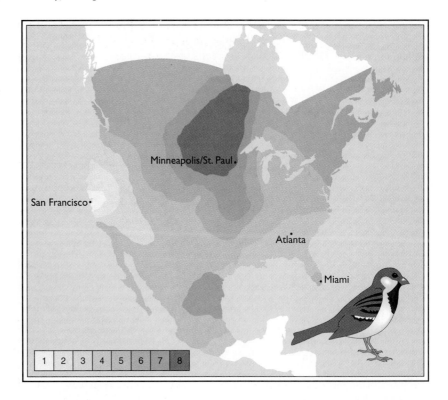

semispecies Populations of a species that are completely isolated from one another but have not yet become truly different species.

be larger, an adaptation to cold. But, again, the categories are artificial. We could divide the size variation of this species up into more categories, or into fewer. In no case would those categories deserve formal names. Notice that, rather than coming in distinct subspecific groups, sparrow size variation is distributed as a cline. Draw an imaginary line from Atlanta to St. Paul or from St. Paul to San Francisco and you can see the continuum of change.

I conducted a limited but representative sampling of recent texts in evolutionary biology and found that the concept of subspecies or race is formally recognized less and less. In one major text, for example (*Evolution* by biologist Mark Ridley), neither term appears in the index or glossary, nor is either formally used in the discussions of species variation or species formation.

The terms *are* used in another book (*Population Genetics and Evolution* by Mettler et al.), but race is said to be "a subjective convenience" and, in place of subspecies, the authors suggest **semispecies** to indicate groups within a species that have become isolated and distinct enough to be at an intermediate stage toward becoming actual separate species. An example would be the caribou of North America and the reindeer of Eurasia. Members of these two groups—although they do have some biological differences—can interbreed under artificial conditions (such as zoos), so they are technically the same species; but they don't interbreed in nature because they've been isolated in separate hemispheres for about 10,000 years (since the last glaciers receded and a rising sea level inundated the Bering Land Bridge).

So evolutionary biology is tending to formally recognize biological groups within species only on those relatively rare occasions when we've caught speciation in the act. Otherwise, variation within species is distributed clinally, making the naming of meaningful subspecies or racial groups impossible.

Human Biological Variation

How then does the human species compare with other species as regards races or subspecies? Could we—like caribou and reindeer—come in distinct enough groups to be considered semispecies, thus deserving formal third names after *Homo sapiens*? Or—like the populations of house sparrows or the North American caribou—are we a large, widely dispersed, physically variable single species in which variable traits are distributed as clines such that no truly distinct biological populations exist? Let's look at some of our variable biological traits, called **polymorphisms,** and their distributions.

One obvious and important human polymorphism is skin pigmentation—a criterion, by the way, used for racial classification not just in the West. Skin color is the result of several pigments, the most important of which is **melanin,** produced by specialized skin cells called **melanocytes.** A function of melanin is to absorb ultraviolet (UV) radiation, which can damage tissues, from the sun. Under the influence of increased UV radiation, melanocytes increase their melanin production and darken the skin. This, of course, is known as tanning, and even dark-skinned individuals can exhibit this response.

Ultraviolet radiation varies with latitude. Sunlight strikes the earth more directly at the equator and at more of an angle the farther one gets from the equator. Hitting at an angle, the solar radiation also travels through more atmosphere and thus more UV is absorbed by ozone. Not only do humans have the ability to tan in response to increased UV levels, but, as is obvious to us all, populations are genetically programmed for differences in skin color and these differences also vary by latitude. In general, peoples that live closer to the equator have darker skin. Skin color gradually gets lighter in populations farther away from the equator (Figure 14.5), although, for complex astronomical and meteorological reasons, UV radiation is greater south of the equator than north, so people in the Southern Hemisphere have darker skins than those in the Northern Hemisphere even at equivalent latitudes. Notice that the average skin color of Tasmania (about 40° south) is darker than that of Japan (about 40° north). (These generalizations refer to indigenous populations, those with a long history in an area. The average skin color of people in a cosmopolitan city—say, New York—would obviously be meaningless.)

polymorphisms Variations in phenotypic traits that are the results of genetic variation.

melanin The pigment largely responsible for human skin color.

melanocytes Specialized skin cells that produce the pigment melanin.

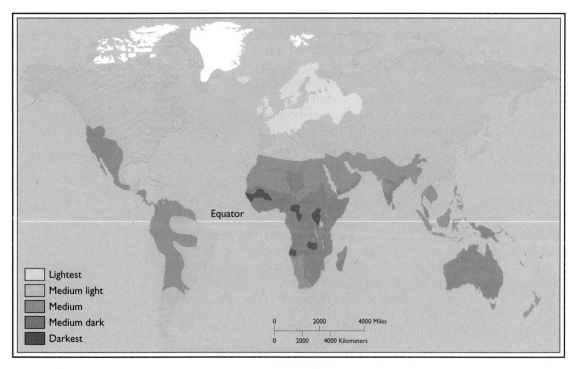

Lightest
Medium light
Medium
Medium dark
Darkest

Equator

0   2000   4000 Miles
0   2000   4000 Kilometers

FIGURE 14.5
Skin color distribution.
Darker skin is concentrated
in equatorial regions.

It is generally agreed that the relationship between dark skin and high levels of UV radiation is an example of an adaptive response. Because of the damaging effects of UV, peoples in or near the equator have undergone selection for permanently higher levels of melanin production. Darker-skinned people do not have more melanocytes than lighter-skinned ones, just more melanin. By implication, of course, dark skin was the original human skin color, since—at least according to the latest evidence—our species first evolved in equatorial Africa.

Why, then, did populations that moved away from the equator evolve lower melanin production and therefore lighter skin? It is easiest to say that since dark skin was no longer needed, it became light. Evolution, however, does not always work this way. More likely, there was an adaptive reason why lighter skin was actively selected *for*.

A common answer has to do with vitamin D production. Vitamin D can be synthesized in lower layers of skin when a precursor of the vitamin is activated by UV radiation. This vitamin is important in regulating the absorption of calcium and its inclusion in the manufacture of bone. Deficiency in vitamin D can lead to a skeletal deformity known in children as rickets. (There is an adult version of the abnormality as well.) Bones with rickets are also more prone to breakage, and deformity of the pelvis can make childbirth difficult.

It has been thought that, as populations moved away from the equator, those with darker skin could not manufacture sufficient vitamin D for normal bone growth and maintenance. Those with lighter skin, therefore, were at an adaptive and, thus, a reproductive advantage. Over time, lighter skin became the normal, inherited condition in these groups. Skin color was thus seen as a balancing act—dark enough to protect from the damaging effects of UV and light enough to allow the beneficial effects.

This explanation has, however, recently been questioned. Rickets is associated with recent urban populations and is seldom found in rural areas. Indeed, there is little evidence for rickets in the fossil record. Moreover, although dark skin does slow down the production of vitamin D, it can still allow for sufficient synthesis to maintain healthy levels. Vitamin D synthesis may not have been a selective factor for our ancestors.

Now, of course, we can also obtain vitamin D through vitamin supplements and by adding it to milk. It is also found in fish liver oils and egg yolks. A correlation between dark-skinned urban populations and rickets—once proposed as evidence for the adaptive connection—may be based more on socioeconomic factors resulting in poor diet than on skin color differences.

Another possible factor for the adaptation of light skin concerns injury to the skin from cold. Data from the military show that darker skin is more prone to damage from frostbite than is lighter skin. Selection for light skin may not be related to ultraviolet radiation but to temperature, while selection for darker skin remains related to UV.

Now, look back at the map (Figure 14.5). Although skin color varies by latitude, and ranges from the very dark to the very light, in no way does this variation assort into distinct geographical groups. My categories (lightest, medium light, and so on) are arbitrary, as are my geographical dividing lines. I could have demonstrated the relation between skin color and latitude with any number of different schemes. I could even have used numbers, by actually measuring the color variation in skin, but, even then, the groups I divided the range of numbers into and the lines I drew on the map would have been arbitrary. Skin color, like sparrow size, is distributed as a cline, gradually getting lighter or darker across geographic space. So, dark skin, often associated with Africa, is, in fact, an equatorial expression and is also found—as you have seen—halfway around the world in New Guinea. It does not correspond to one particular population.

Skin color is, however, a trait of continuous variation, that is, the trait itself does not come in nice, neat categories but, rather, ranges from light to dark with all shades in between. What about traits that come in discrete, either-or categories? Maybe these could be used to divide our species into subspecific or racial populations. The well-known ABO blood types are a good example. Everyone on earth is either type A, type O, type B, or type AB—there are no other categories and no intermediates. The variation is the result of four alleles of the single gene that codes for a chemical on the red blood cells. How is this polymorphism distributed?

Figure 14.6 shows the distributions for type A and type B blood. There appears to be no correlation with any obvious environmental factor such as latitude or climate. Type A is totally absent in some native South American groups, but is found in over 50 percent of some populations in parts of Europe and native Australia. Type B, found in very low frequency among Native Americans, comes in high frequencies in Asia—where Native Americans originated. Type O, the most common for the whole species, ranges from 40 percent in parts of Asia to 100 percent among some native South Americans.

It has been suggested that this trait is adaptively neutral, that is, that blood type is not related to health or reproductive success, but is just a matter of the random processes of evolution, gene flow, and genetic drift (see Chapter 3). The great apes also have these blood types, so the variation could go well back into our evolutionary history. Others have proposed an association between blood type and susceptibility or resistance to various diseases. There is some statistical evidence for this, but no well-established cause-and-effect relationships.

The point here is that, as with skin color, the distribution of blood types is of no help in defining human races. The categories on the maps are arbitrary. I could have divided the range of frequencies into more groups or into fewer. The maps then would have looked quite different. But, again, notice that the distribution of the frequencies is actually clinal. If I had more categories this would be even clearer.

In fact, no matter what traits one uses, the human species simply cannot be divided into distinct subgroups based on biological differences. Nor will such division work when using combinations of traits, because the distributions of traits are discordant—that is, a particular expression of one trait does not necessarily predict a particular expression of another (Figure 14.7). The nature and distribution of human polymorphisms, then, is like that of other species. Because we are a single species with extensive gene flow, our variable traits are distributed as clines, with no clear-cut boundaries. The distribution of one trait does not match the distribution of others. Clearly defined biological groups below the species level are not scientifically supported for *Homo sapiens* by these data.

Evolutionary Theory and the Nature of the Human Species

Let's look at the question from a more general perspective. We could ask whether—given the nature of our species and what we know of the workings of evolution—groups distinct enough to be semispecies (the only group below the species level that is scientifically supported) *could* exist within *Homo sapiens*. After all, semispecies have developed in 10,000 years in *Rangifer tarandus* (reindeer and caribou) and, even by the most conservative estimates, our species is ten times as old.

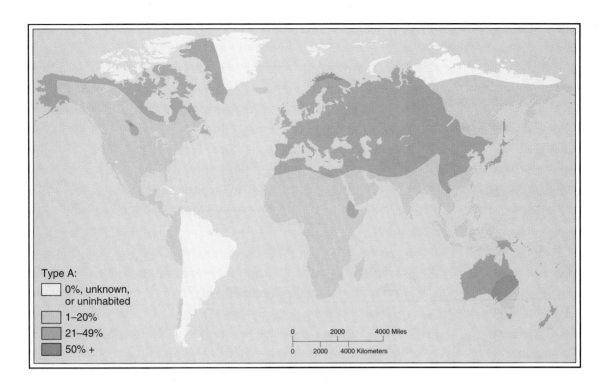

Type A:
- ☐ 0%, unknown, or uninhabited
- ☐ 1–20%
- ☐ 21–49%
- ■ 50% +

0   2000   4000 Miles
0 2000 4000 Kilometers

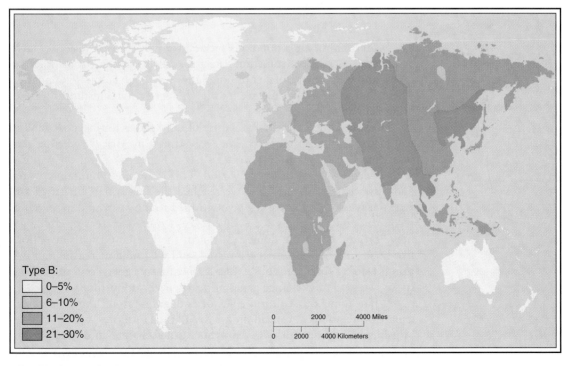

Type B:
- ☐ 0–5%
- ☐ 6–10%
- ☐ 11–20%
- ■ 21–30%

0   2000   4000 Miles
0 2000 4000 Kilometers

FIGURE 14.6

Approximate frequency distributions of type A and type B blood, demonstrating the lack of a pattern in the distribution of this polymorphism.

FIGURE 14.7
Diagram of discordant variation. Each layer represents the geographic variation in one polymorphism. Each "core," or cylinder, represents a sample of individuals from a particular area. Notice that each core is different and that any other four cores are very likely to be different as well. The expression of one trait does not predict a particular expression of another. There are no natural racial divisions based on specific combinations of traits.

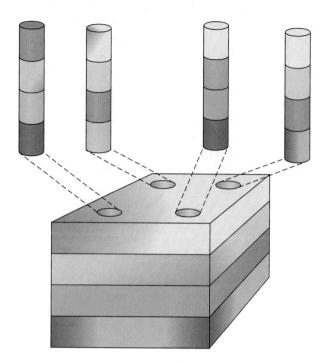

Moreover, we are a populous species; we live in a vast variety of environmental conditions, sometimes in areas fairly isolated from other regions; and we further isolate our populations through cultural boundaries. These characteristics would seem to be the perfect circumstances for creating definable groups.

However, one noteworthy feature of our species for its entire biological history has been mobility. We evolved first in Africa—whether that was 2 million or 200,000 years ago (see Chapter 5)—and then spread with amazing speed all over the Old World, despite mountains, water, and other barriers. And when we reached the far corners of Africa and Eurasia, we did not stay put. We continued to move around in search of resources and space. As we evolved, we acquired increasing ability to move around (with the domestication of the horse and with inventions like boats and navigation instruments), and we found increasing motivation for doing so. Such mobility leads to extensive gene flow, and it's fair to say we tend to exchange genes at nearly every opportunity.

What about our cultural rules of endogamy; don't they genetically isolate populations at certain times? Recall the Hutterites, who have been largely endogamous for 470 years. Such rules change, and the political, ethnic, and religious populations they define change through time. The Hutterites' nearly half a millennium history is not all that long in evolutionary terms; not much genetic variation can arise in that period, especially in a species with a long generation time. Moreover, rules of endogamy are not always fully upheld. Biological isolation through the cultural institution of endogamy is a temporary condition.

Gene flow, then, is the norm for our species, and, as widespread as we are, we still manage to exchange enough genes—through intermediary populations—to prevent any group of humans from being isolated long enough to evolve the differences sufficient for semispecies status.

Finally, what about all the different environments our species inhabits? Couldn't natural selection have led to differentiation of some populations? Certainly, the variation and distribution of some of our polymorphisms— skin color, for example—can be attributed to natural selection. But our major adaptive mechanism is culture, with its values, social systems, and, especially, its technologies that, to a great extent, have increasingly buffered us against the constant editing of natural selection. Adaptively, we change less biologically than we do culturally. Culture and the big brains that make culture possible are species characteristics, shared by all humans. They are the basis of our modern identity. Culture, in a sense, *is* our environment, and we may say that, for some time, our species has experienced little of the kind of environmental variation that would lead to the development of distinct, isolated subpopulations. As anthropologist C. Loring Brace puts it, we all have undergone the "same selective pressures" leading to essentially the "same lifeway."

Genetics

The last decade has seen amazing advances in our ability to look into the very code of life, genes. This is a complex topic but suffice it to say that we can analyze small differences in the very letters of the genetic code (called, technically, the base pair sequence). Especially important are noncoding genes—that is, the 90 percent or so of the 100,000 human genes that do not code for the building of proteins and so, apparently, vary randomly. When we look at such base pair sequences we see, for one thing, minute but distinct differences among individuals. These are the so-called genetic fingerprints one hears about in criminal cases.

We can also see differences among populations at this most basic genetic level—enough to allow researchers to construct family trees for human populations (Figure 14.8). C. Loring Brace calls this "kinship writ large." Such data, especially when compared with linguistic and archaeological information, have also allowed us to hypothesize migration times and routes for human groups (Figure 14.9). Human populations, in other words, have genetic and biological histories just as they have cultural ones.

These small differences are interesting and can be useful, but when we step back and use modern techniques to look at the human genome as a whole, what we find is remarkable homogeneity. An estimated 75 percent of our genes are functionally identical for all humans (that is, they

FIGURE 14.8
A genetic family tree for 42 populations based on a comparison of 42 genetic systems with a total of 120 alleles (variations of genes).

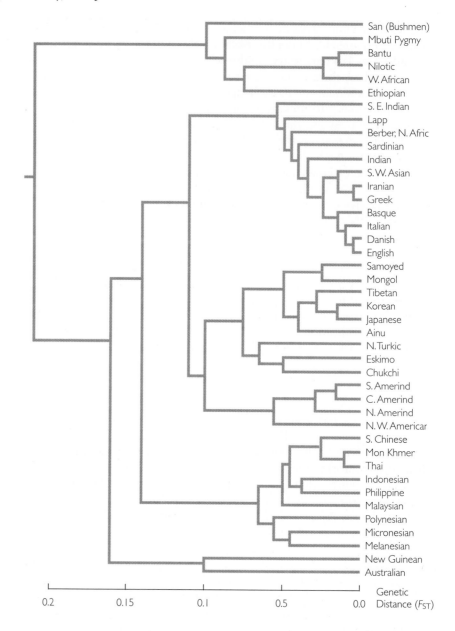

may not have exactly the same code letters but they *do* the same thing). This is less variation than is found in chimpanzees, who inhabit just the center of one continent and number only about a quarter million. And many genes that do vary are involved with differences between the sexes. In other words, all our polymorphic features are accounted for by a relative handful of genes.

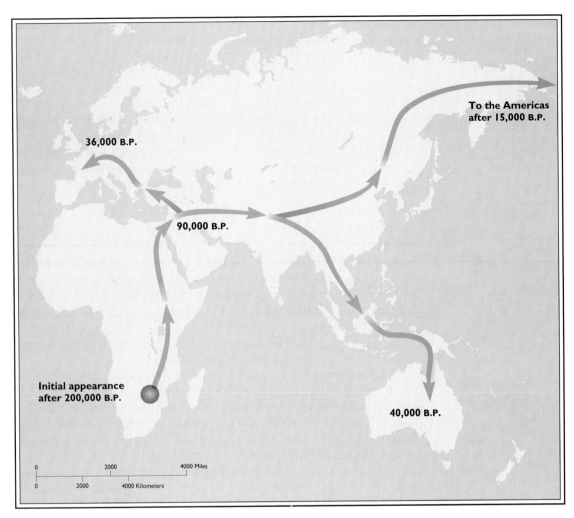

36,000 B.P.

90,000 B.P.

To the Americas after 15,000 B.P.

Initial appearance after 200,000 B.P.

40,000 B.P.

0 · 2000 · 4000 Miles

0 · 2000 · 4000 Kilometers

FIGURE 14.9
Hypothesized migration routes and times of modern *Homo sapiens,* based on detailed genetic comparisons of living populations. (This model assumes the species *Homo sapiens* is 200,000 years old. As discussed in Chapter 5, there are other estimates for the age of our species.)

Moreover, those variable genes are more evenly distributed than one might imagine. Population geneticist Richard Lewontin has calculated that if some great cataclysm left only Africans alive out of all humans, that remnant of our species would still retain 93 percent of the variable genes of the former species (although, of course, some of the variations would be found in higher frequency than the previous average, for example, those for greater melanin production).

Now, this is not to say that—either physically or genetically—every population is the same. Obviously they're not. Try this analogy: Our species is *not* like a can of paint where the paint is a complex color made up of many individual tints but so evenly mixed that we can't discern the individual components. Rather, we are like a pot of stew cooking on the stove. Some of the components (like the water) are evenly distributed.

But at any point in time one can pick out some of the other individual ingredients—chunks of potato, slices of carrot, pieces of meat (for you carnivores). There might even be a clump of some spice down in one corner of the pot where we haven't stirred well. But, as the stew cooks and we continue to stir, the ingredients are always changing position—the potatoes get broken up, the spices better distributed, and so on. There's no way you could divide the stew into any distinct and meaningful subdivisions. In other words, there is variation, and it is unevenly distributed, but there are no dividing lines. In the same way—whether we are examining phenotypic features or genetic variations—there is biological variation in humans but there are no biological races.

WHAT, THEN, *ARE* HUMAN RACES?

Having said all the above, we are still left with the question stated in the heading—because races *are* real. We talk about them. We casually identify ourselves as belonging to one race or another. We identify one another as belonging to a particular race. We are asked on various forms to identify our race. Decisions about our lives are made according to our race. And, certainly, one can't open the newspaper without reading some story related to race. So, if not a biological category, what *is* race?

The answer is that race is a folk taxonomy, a cultural classification (see Chapters 6 and 11). You recall that societies interpret and translate biological differences in sex into cultural categories called gender that include attitudes about men and women as well as norms of identity and behavior. In other words, sex is a biological category; gender is a folk taxonomy. Biological variation and race are similar.

All cultures have folk taxonomies for the human variation they are aware of. Isolated societies may have a very simple racial classification: us and them. And often their word for "us" also means something like "human" or "the people," while "them" may imply, well, something other than "the people." Societies having more contact with other groups will, obviously, have more complex folk taxonomies for race and more complex attitudes reflected by the implications of their names and categories. (Of course, even complex cultures may still talk about "us" and "them" with reference to political or ideological differences between certain groups—for example, "us" the free world countries as opposed to "them" the Iron Curtain countries during the Cold War. But for isolated societies, "us" and "them" may be the *only* categories, racial or political.)

The racial categories we are familiar with in the United States are no less a folk taxonomy than anyone else's. Our basic scheme of categories is something we all are aware of. I once gave a class a weekend assignment: They were to find ten people—preferably of different ages, both sexes, and different ethnic backgrounds—and ask them two questions: How many races are there? What are they? Some of my students got some odd responses, such as "three races: black, white, and

Polish." Jewish was a race according to some informants. Some listed Native Americans. But the majority gave some form of racial classification that corresponded to our familiar categories—Caucasian, black, Asian; or African American, white, Oriental. They used different terms depending on their own age and background, but the similarity of responses indicated that some basic taxonomy is shared among members of our society.

Now, since these are cultural categories, we should be able to trace their origins historically. At the risk of oversimplifying European and American history, I can surmise that our racial categories can be traced back to European knowledge and attitudes first acquired during the Age of Exploration. European explorers used mostly water transportation, and so were limited in the range and distribution of human variation they could observe. They sampled points along the continuum of human biodiversity. Because these points could differ greatly from one another, it appeared that human variation fell into a number of relatively discrete categories (Figure 14.10).

In addition, peoples contacted were not seen as merely different human beings. Instead they were compared to and ranked against European peoples and cultures, usually unfavorably. After all, they looked different, spoke differently, had different cultures, often were less technologically complex, and were not Christians or Jews. In addition, the motivation for exploration was often less to acquire knowledge than to acquire spices, precious metals, territory, and labor. An attitude of profound difference and dominance was built into European relationships with the people contacted. (Notice, in Figure 14.10, the men erecting a cross to claim the land for Spain.) A racial folk taxonomy naturally developed to organize this variation and these attitudes.

These folk taxonomic categories were formalized in 1758 by Linnaeus. His species *Homo sapiens* was divided into five varieties: *Homo sapiens ferus* (wild men, possibly to accommodate tales of retarded and abandoned children supposedly raised by animals), then *H.s. americanus*, *H.s. europaeus*, *H.s. asiaticus*, and *H.s. afer*. (Interestingly, despite his obvious biases, he doesn't place Europeans either at the beginning or end of the list, as one would expect.) His descriptions of these races—and this is typical of racial folk taxonomies all over—are blends of biological generalizations, perceived cultural traits, and what anthropologist Stephen Molnar calls "personality profiles." For example, here's his description of *Homo sapiens afer*:

> Black, phlegmatic [sluggish], relaxed. Hair black, frizzled; skin silky, nose flat; lips tumic [swollen]; crafty, indolent, negligent. Anoints himself with grease. Governed by caprice [impulse].

Europeans, by comparison, were "covered with cloth vestments" and "governed by laws."

Because the history of the United States has been so influenced by European cultures, it makes sense that these basic categories would be

FIGURE 14.10
Columbus's first contact with natives of the New World. To the Europeans, the Indians were so strikingly different in physical and cultural features that it was natural to consider them as a distinct category of human. Notice the men planting the cross to claim the land as theirs. (From a seventeenth-century Spanish version of a 1594 engraving by de Bry. The Granger Collection.)

carried over to this country and altered by its subsequent history. For example, the reason we distinguish Hispanics from other European-Americans is, in part, because of the conflicts between Spain and other European countries over territory in the New World and later between Mexico, a former Spanish colony, and the United States. Notice, too, that in some lists of race Puerto Rican has been separated from Hispanic. It's not that some new group of people has arisen, but, rather, that for certain purposes, we choose to distinguish people from that U.S. territory—people who, previously and still in other lists, are categorized as Hispanic.

Race is a folk taxonomy—a cultural translation of human diversity, variable across space and through time. But I should offer a caution: Having dismissed the idea of biological race, and having identified race as a folk taxonomy, let's not relegate the race concept to *just* a folk taxonomy, and by doing so imply that the problems inherent in, derived from, and justified by our racial categories are not real. They are. Folk taxonomies are powerful things, not just isolated phenomena of exotic cultures—Eskimo snow words, Crow kinship terminology, or the Dani counting system. All cultures categorize their worlds with folk taxonomies. Even us. And even when we are aware of our taxonomies, we still respond to and perceive our world according to them.

RACE, RACISM, AND SOCIAL ISSUES

The issue of race is not just a matter of whether or not to apply the biological concept of the subspecies to divisions among humans. Would that it were. Rather, the idea of race can be, and is, used to make prejudgments about people and to determine a person's place in society, often without regard to that person's individual traits, skills, and talents. This is **racism**. The moral dimension of this problem, although it should be important to everyone, is beyond the scope of this brief book. We can, however, show how the approach of anthropology has examined two claimed connections between racial categories and biological traits and, in the process, remind ourselves just what race is—and what it is not.

One issue is the claim that certain human societies, because they live at a less complex cultural level than most, are somehow less evolved and, thus, less intelligent. There are, sadly, many examples of such ideas and their applications in human history. One striking example involves the natives of Tasmania, an island about 130 miles south of Australia (Figure 14.11).

When first contacted by Europeans in the seventeenth century, there were about 5000 indigenous Tasmanians, living with one of the least complex technologies of any modern peoples. Their tools were simple stone and wood artifacts. They lacked metal, domesticated plants and animals, pottery, and bows and arrows. All these were lacking in Australia, too. But the Tasmanians also lacked things found commonly in Australia, such as boomerangs, dogs, nets, hafted stone tools, barbed spears, fishing, sewing, and even the ability to make a fire.

The European settlers—observing this lack of artifact complexity, not appreciating the richness of the more abstract aspects of the Tasmanian's cultural system (such as language), and, no doubt, with preconceived notions of racial superiority—saw the natives of Tasmania as less than human—perhaps, some scientists suggested, as missing links between humans and apes. They were enslaved, killed, and relocated to isolated areas. A cash bounty was offered for natives captured alive. Some were hunted for sport. By 1869 there were only three native Tasmanians left, two of whom were further denigrated even in death as their bodies were

racism Judging an individual solely on his or her racial affiliation.

FIGURE 14.11
Eight of the last native Tasmanians.

dissected, some of the pieces used as souvenirs, and their bones put on public display. (Not surprisingly, however, there are still some descendants of Tasmanian women and white settlers.)

Such behavior is, of course, unconscionable, and its morality needs no discussion. But we can still try to account for the great disparity in technological complexity that the Europeans used to support and justify their ideas about and treatment of native Tasmanians. Was there something profoundly different about Tasmanians themselves that prevented them from inventing some very basic tools and technologies?

The answer is that such differences in cultures are explained not by evolutionary level but by very practical considerations of geography, environment, and mobility. A group of people is adapted, in the most

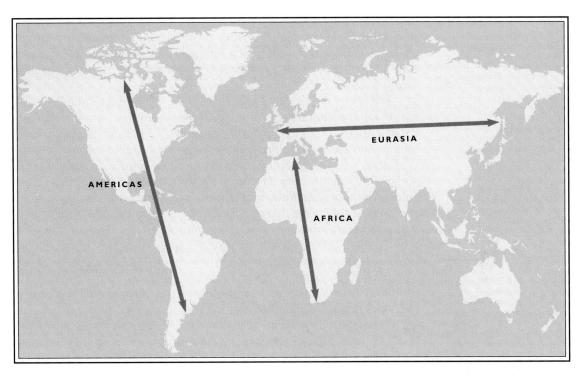

AMERICAS

EURASIA

AFRICA

FIGURE 14.12
The major axes of the continents. The long east-west axis of Eurasia allows rapid and extensive movement of people and domestic species on that continent because it involves less latitude change and thus less climatic change. The major axis of Africa is north-south, making movement more limited, and in the Americas, movement is severely limited because of the major axis. (From a discussion by Jared Diamond in *Guns, Germs, and Steel: The Fates of Human Societies.*)

basic sense, to the environment in which it lives. They can only use what resources their habitat provides. They must contend with the climatic conditions of their area.

Although people have lived successfully in just about every set of environmental circumstances on earth, these variables—resources and climate—can make a big difference. As we pointed out in Chapter 8, the first farming occurred where there were wild plants with characteristics that lent themselves to domestication. It is not surprising that areas rich in wild grasses were among the first to see farming; grasses are hardy, nutritious, and easily selectively bred. Similarly, domesticable wild animals must be present for that cultural change to take place. The relative lack of domestic animals in the New World is thus accounted for. Where wild horses were available, on the other hand, their domestication gave people a source of labor and mobility that brought about major historical changes. The cultures and languages of peoples with horses often had an immense influence on and power over other groups.

Another broad geographical feature is also important. As physiologist and science writer Jared Diamond points out, the major geographical axis of Eurasia runs mostly east and west, while those of Africa and the New World run north and south (Figure 14.12). People and their plants and animals, and, thus, their technologies can move over great distances in Eurasia without major changes in latitude, thus not encountering temperature and seasonal changes. Ideas and inventions can spread farther and faster there. In Africa, such cultural ideas are more limited in their movement, and in the Americas most movement involves latitude changes and is thus slow. It took a very long time, for example, for maize, first domesticated from a wild plant in Mexico, to move to northern North America.

And the movement of peoples with their ideas and technologies is a factor of vital importance to our question about level of cultural complexity. Societies rely on contact with other societies for the majority of their cultural items, often referred to as their cultural inventory. By some estimates, only 10 percent of a given society's cultural inventory originated within that society. The other 90 percent was borrowed from other cultures in a process known as **diffusion** (a topic we'll discuss in more detail in the following chapter). Thus, populations isolated from contact with others are left very much to their own devices. They are, as Diamond puts it, "confined to their private universe." Societies that inhabit isolated regions change slowly. On the other hand, societies that live along major migration routes have contact with various peoples and cultures and have ample opportunity to observe, borrow, and adopt new ideas and items. They change rapidly.

During the Pleistocene glacial advances, Tasmania was connected many different times to Australia, and Australia itself, while never connected directly to Southeast Asia, was more accessible to that region via a string of islands exposed when sea levels dropped. This is how people got to Tasmania in the first place. But with the last glacial recession 10,000 years ago, Tasmania and Australia were separated from one another by a broad strait that the Tasmanians' simple watercraft were incapable of navigating. The hunter-gatherer population of the island was thus virtually completely isolated until Europeans arrived in 1642. They changed, to be sure, but slowly, and there is even archaeological evidence that their culture actually lost some items—fishing, sewing, bone tools—that they once had.

Major differences in level of cultural complexity can be striking, and we can be tempted to explain them through differences in biology—evolutionary level or mental facility. But there is no evidence for such biological differences, and there are perfectly sound explanations based on the nature of culture as an adaptive mechanism.

A second claimed connection between race and biology is the idea, related to the cultural complexity issue, that among the biological differences of human populations is a difference in intelligence. If one's goal is to limit the social position and power of a particular group, one of the strongest arguments you can propose is that the population in question possesses some unalterable biological difference that inherently limits their abilities and therefore justifies their lower social position. Slavery in the United States was often justified by the claim that the black slaves were less intelligent than the whites and therefore could never hope to attain the dominant race's social, political, and intellectual level.

Such broad statements are so clearly motivated by social and eco-

diffusion The movement of cultural ideas and artifacts among societies. Cultural borrowing.

nomic situations as to be at least questionable, if not obviously false. Perhaps more dangerous, however, are the more subtle correlations whose propositions are based on scientific investigation. Ideas that sound scientific are often treated more seriously, especially because, even today, many people feel that science is something so complex and obscure that only a handful can really understand it: Many people take the position that if something sounds scientific and they don't get it, it must be valid.

Such is the case for the claimed connection between the American black and white races and IQ (intelligence quotient). The most infamous example is educational psychologist Arthur Jensen's 1969 article in the *Harvard Educational Review* titled "How Much Can We Boost IQ and Scholastic Achievement?" A more recent work on the same topic is *The Bell Curve* by R. J. Herrnstein and C. Murray (1994). It is far more complex than Jensen's article but expresses the same basic argument, so we can focus on the older work.

Jensen attempted to explain the documented fact that American black children score, on average, 15 points lower on IQ tests than American white children. He wondered why programs aimed at the obvious solution of culturally enriching children's lives had pretty much failed. Some studies showed that the 15-point IQ difference remained. Hence, the title of his article (this time with emphasis for the right intonation): "How much *can* we boost IQ and scholastic achievement?"

Jensen's first conclusion is that IQ tests measure general intelligence—a biological, inherited entity. He also accepts that 80 percent of the variation in intelligence within a population is explained by genetic differences and that only 20 percent is the result of members of that group having been brought up in different cultural environments.

The obvious conclusion, then, is that the difference in intelligence between the two racial groups must be largely the result of some genetic difference, and, thus, all the cultural enrichment programs in the world can only have a limited effect. Jensen's answer to the question in his title is, "Not much." He states: "No one has yet produced any evidence based on a properly controlled study to show that representative samples of Negro and white children can be equalized in intellectual ability through statistical control of environment and education."

But Jensen went further. He compared scores from different parts of IQ tests and concluded that the different IQs of blacks and whites result from their having different kinds of intellectual abilities. Whites are better at problem solving and abstract reasoning, while the abilities of blacks are focused on memorization, rote learning, and trial-and-error experience.

His ultimate conclusion was that education should be as individualized as possible, taking into account not only individual differences in ability and skill, but these racially based ones as well.

As you can imagine, Jensen's article caused a great deal of controversy. He was labeled a racist, and, certainly, those with racist leanings embraced his work enthusiastically. Let's examine his argument more scientifically, however.

The idea that IQ tests measure some innate mental ability is fraught with problems. It has been said that IQ tests measure the ability to take IQ tests. This is not, as it sounds, just a sarcasm. IQ tests, in fact, measure particular knowledge and abilities that are largely learned through one's culture. They are valuable. Relatively low scores may, sometimes, point out a learning disability that has a biological basis. Because they measure the kinds of skills required by education in our culture as well as by many occupations, they do have predictive value as to one's success within the culture.

We do not, however, even know what intelligence is. How can we—through a test given in a cultural language, in a cultural setting, with cultural problems—apply a single number to such a complex and multifaceted concept? When we do this, we are practicing what is called **reification**. With IQ scores we have reified intelligence—translated a complex idea into a single number, which we then use to classify people into various groups, for example, different learning tracks in schools.

As anthropologist Jonathan Marks suggests, there is a difference between *ability* and *performance*. One's score on an IQ test is a score of one's performance. Certainly some internal factor—innate intellectual ability, whatever that *is*—plays a part in your IQ performance. But that performance is also affected by all sorts of external factors. In test taking, for example, your cultural background, quality of education, personality, home life, even your mood on the day of the test can all affect your performance. We cannot, therefore, infer innate abilities from a test score, any more than we can infer a person's athletic abilities from their performance in just one game.

The inherited nature of IQ is a complicated issue but we can point out a major problem here. Heritability studies—that estimate the genetic and environmental components of the phenotypic variation in a population—are done regularly, but they are carried out using organisms like fruit flies, where the genetic mechanisms for phenotypic traits are well known (and can even be manipulated) and where the environmental variables can be controlled in detail. Numbers may be placed on these genetic and environmental variables, which may then be plugged into a heritability formula. To apply the heritability formula to humans, however, is virtually impossible. What numbers can we place on the environmental variables that affect us? How, in other words, can we reify culture? What number is applied to having a culturally enriched childhood, being a member of a minority group, or having a poor early education?

To further claim that two races have different kinds of intellectual abilities is to ignore the very nature of the modern human species. This claim denies to a large number of people the very abilities—to solve problems, to formulate abstractions and generalizations—that are a hallmark of our species' evolution. Certainly, we express individual variation in some of these abilities, and some of this variation may well be based on some biological difference. I have no doubt that Beethoven and Einstein had some

reification Translating a complex set of phenomena into a single entity such as a number.

fundamental innate processes going on in their brains that I don't. But to think that natural selection would promote profoundly different expressions in the major adaptive mechanism of a species makes little sense in light of what we know about the workings of adaptive evolution.

Finally, if you are looking to make biological comparisons between two groups, the groups need to be biologically defined. American whites and American blacks are decidedly not biological races. We have already established that race is not a biological concept for the human species in the first place. What variation does exist is distributed in such a way as to make distinct, discrete groups of *Homo sapiens* nonexistent. We perceive differences in these two racial groups—skin color, major geographic area of origin, even relative frequency of some genes—but the groups themselves are cultural. There's simply not much genetic difference, certainly not on the level of genes for different intellectual abilities. Indeed, it has been estimated that about 15 percent of all genes in African Americans have come from European Americans because of the extent of gene flow between the two populations over the last several hundred years.

Our folk taxonomies are powerful and influential. We respond to them often without realizing that they are *our* culture's way of ordering *our* world and are not necessarily scientific universals. The influence of the American folk taxonomy for race can easily be seen in Jensen's work. By understanding what race is and what it's not, and by applying what we know about the workings of genetics and evolution, we may see the fallacies of this particular piece of research, and we have a perspective from which to evaluate other such claims.

SUMMARY

The issue of race is one of the most contentious that face us today. The contribution of anthropology is the objective examination of the facets of human variation and the drawing of conclusions about what that variation entails, how it came about, and what it does and does not mean. Armed with such information, we are at least a little better able to confront the social, ethical, political, and personal aspects of race.

Scientific data from evolutionary biology, biological anthropology, and genetics show us clearly that while human biological variation exists across geographical space and can be examined and explained, the human species simply cannot be divided up into any number of meaningful biological units. In other words, biological races do not exist for our species.

Race, of course, does exist, but it is a cultural classification—based on a society's knowledge of human diversity, its history, and its attitudes about various human groups. Just as societies culturally translate sexual differences into gender categories, they also translate human biological and cultural diversity into racial categories.

CONTEMPORARY ISSUES

Are There Racial Differences in Athletic Ability?

Having established that race has no biological meaning for the human species, we can translate the question to ask whether there are average differences in athletic ability among populations from different regions of the world. Of course there are. Look again at Figure 14.1 as one example. How many heavyweight boxers or 400-meter sprinters could hail from the highlands of New Guinea where people, on average, are much smaller than most Europeans or Africans? There are phenotypic differences within the human species, and some of these would certainly have an effect on performance in particular athletic contests.

The question, however, commonly refers to American sports, where, for example, even a casual look at a National Basketball Association game would give one the clear impression that African Americans are better basketball players than European Americans. The biggest recent stars of the game, with the notable exception of Larry Bird, are African Americans like Michael

Jordan, Shaquille O'Neal, and Charles Barkley. The stereotype has become part of our folk culture—we say as a joke that "white men can't jump." But don't we really believe it? How reasonable is our inference about race and sports?

For one thing, we cannot infer a generalization about a whole group of people from a small sample. All professional basketball players are people who, due in large measure to some innate abilities and physical features (like, simply, above-average stature), excel at the skills required for the game. But in no way does it follow that all blacks have those skills or that only blacks have them, any more than it follows that all white European males or only white European males have the ability to write the Ninth Symphony (Beethoven's or Mahler's). It does not even follow that blacks are *more likely* to possess those skills than whites.

Why, then, the prevalence of blacks in the sport? As Jonathan Marks has pointed out, and as we noted in the chapter, sports involve innate

Political, ideological, and economic motivations have led societies to propose connections between racial categories and biological traits. Differences in cultural level have been interpreted to reflect differences in intelligence or evolutionary level. IQ test scores have been said to show differences in intellectual abilities between races. There is no sound evidence for such profound biological differences. Rather, there are logical reasons for differences in test scores and level of technology that are grounded in what anthropological data and theory have shown us about the nature of culture as an adaptive mechanism and as the complex environments in which we, as individuals and members of our societies, live.

NOTES, REFERENCES, AND READINGS

The two books in evolutionary biology to which I referred are *Evolution* by Mark Ridley and *Population Genetics and Evolution* by Lawrence Mettler et al.

skills, but, like IQ tests, they are also performances and, as such, are influenced by complex external factors. The difference in socioeconomic status of those identified as white and black has created differences in the opportunities people have to play certain sports. In fact, just a few generations ago, most professional basketball players were white, because, except for boxing, blacks had little or no opportunity to participate in professional sports.

Even now that sports are open to all groups, the effects of those socioeconomic differences have an influence. To practice the skills of basketball, one needs only a hoop of some sort, an area to play, and a ball. These prerequisites can be found in every neighborhood. Swimming pools, golf gear and courses, tennis courts, even baseball equipment are not as inexpensive or as readily available. Moreover, with career choices traditionally more limited for black youths than for whites, an easily practiced sport becomes an increasingly popular focus. There may well be many white youths who have the innate abilities of a Jordan, O'Neal, or Barkley, and people from all groups

enjoy the game at an avocational or scholastic level, but more athletically inclined black youths are interested in a *career* in basketball and so pursue it. Thus, more men who become professional basketball players are black, and this is a major reason for the skewed racial distribution within that sport.

Does this cultural explanation necessarily rule out the existence of some physical or physiological feature related to basketball prowess that shows an average difference between Americans of African descent and those of European descent? Certainly not. There are other features—most notably skin color—that show an average difference. To my knowledge, no one has found any such basketball trait, but if they did, so what? We each possess features that both enable and limit us in terms of what we can do. Some of these features may relate to our geographic heritage. Better to understand the facts behind such features and their effects than to concoct myths about them and to prejudge an individual's abilities based simply on the group to which he or she belongs.

There are many good books on the nature of human biodiversity. I recommend *Human Variation: Races, Types, and Ethnic Groups* by Stephen Molnar; *Human Diversity* by Richard Lewontin; and *Human Biodiversity: Genes, Race, and History* by Jonathan Marks. The figure about the remnant Africans possessing 93 percent of human variable genes is from page 123 of the Lewontin book. The estimate of 15 percent European genes among African Americans is from page 114. The Marks book includes an expanded discussion of race and athleticism and the distinction between performance and ability. For some of the latest information on the distribution of skin color differences, see "Hemispheric Difference in Human Skin Color" by John H. Relethford in the December 1997 issue of the *American Journal of Physical Anthropology*.

For a collection of articles on the nonexistence of biological races, see *The Concept of Race*, edited by M. F. Ashley Montagu. For a nice treatment of the history of race studies, including a discussion of Linnaeus's taxonomy, try Kenneth Kennedy's *Human Variation in Space and Time*.

The story of the Tasmanians can be found in Jared Diamond's *The Third Chimpanzee* and in his *Guns, Germs, and Steel.* Both these books also discuss the origins of differences in cultural level and the idea of the different axes of the continents.

Arthur Jensen's article, "How Much Can We Boost IQ and Scholastic Achievement?" is in the Winter 1969 issue of the *Harvard Educational Review.* The quoted passage is on pages 82–83. For a more detailed version of the same argument see *The Bell Curve* by Richard Herrnstein and Charles Murray.

Perhaps the best book on racism, emphasizing an examination of scientific attempts to find correlations between race (and sex) and intelligence is Stephen Jay Gould's *The Mismeasure of Man* (revised and expanded). It includes a detailed critique of *The Bell Curve.*

15

CULTURE CHANGE

Processes, Problems, and the Contributions of Anthropology

It should be obvious by now that cultures are anything but static and unchanging. Although we can try to describe the interrelationships among the features of a cultural system at any given point in time (as we did in Chapter 13), many of those features are changing as we're studying and analyzing them. Culture change is the norm, not the exception. Some cultures change slowly, as did, for example, the Tasmanians we discussed in the previous chapter. Many change rapidly. But they all change. Think of the changes you've witnessed in your culture.

We have already noted some major changes and their effects—things like the beginning of domestication and the origin of cities. But culture change involves smaller changes as well. And any change acts to alter the cultural system of which it is a part, because culture works *as* a system, with all its facets operating together and interacting with one another. All those facets, in turn, are related to the society's world view, which is the collective interpretation and response of the people to their natural and cultural environment.

How do cultures change? Are there any specific processes that account for changes in cultural systems? The answers to these questions can help us explain changes in the past, understand changes that are going on now, and give us some guidelines for thinking about changes in the future as the rate of culture change accelerates in the modern world.

THE PROCESSES OF CULTURE CHANGE

Every cultural alteration—every new idea or new artifact—must start somewhere. Thus, at the base of all culture change are the related processes of **discovery** and **invention**. Discovery is the realization and understanding of some set of relationships—anything from the nature of fire to the reaction of the people of a society to some aspect of their environment. Invention refers to the creation of artifacts, whether concrete (tools) or abstract (institutions), that put the discovery to use. Discovery is knowledge; invention is application.

For example, discovery of the nature of fire was necessary before fire could be used for cooking, light, heat, and scaring away animals. The fact that flint struck with another rock would produce a spark or that wood rubbed against wood would produce heat had to be discovered before fire could be purposely made. Discoveries, of course, may be intentionally sought after (since, as the saying goes, "necessity is the mother of invention"), or they may be accidental. I'm confident that the

discovery The realization and understanding of a set of relationships. An addition to knowledge.

invention The creation of new artifacts. The application of discovered knowledge.

spark-producing qualities of flint were discovered as a by-product of knapping stone tools (see Figure 10.13).

Nor need discoveries—additions to knowledge—be concrete. One may, for example, "discover"—in the sense of proposing an idea—that societies should be based on the premise that each person possesses the right to life, liberty, and the pursuit of happiness. Then one can invent a social system that implements that idea, that puts it into action in the complex, everyday, real world.

A discovery may not always lead to all the inventions that outsiders would think of as its obvious applications. The applications of a discovery must fit within the existing cultural system. As a classic example, consider the wheel in Mesoamerica. The properties of the wheel—contrary to the common misconception—*were* discovered in the New World. The idea was just never put to use as it had been in the Old World, where it was used for wheeled vehicles and for making pottery. The only known use of the wheel in the New World prior to European contact was for children's toys—clay animals with axles and wheels (Figure 15.1). Without domestic draft animals, there was no need to invent wheeled vehicles, and perfectly usable pottery was already being produced without potter's wheels.

A current example involves electric automobiles. They exist, some have been sold, and they work well and don't pollute the atmosphere, but don't expect one to be owned by every family in the near future. The current limits on their speed and range don't fit the fast-paced needs of our society, and their fuel source is a major concern to the petroleum industry, which wields a great deal of political and economic power. So a perfectly good idea has not been, and, in the foreseeable future, will not be adopted.

Sometimes a discovery is not accepted if it appears inconsistent with some aspect of a cultural system. The discovery by Copernicus, later verified by Galileo, that the earth was not the center of the universe violated mainstream religious interpretations of the Bible, which were said to indicate that the earth did not move. The telescope, however, the instrument Galileo used to gather supporting data for this idea, was readily adopted for acceptable uses such as keeping track of the comings and goings of merchant vessels in the port of Venice. In a similar vein, when the Fore (see Chapter 13) were first told the scientific explanation of the outbreak of the disease kuru, it made no sense to them. The idea of disease as the result of sorcery was too central to their world view and cultural system.

Finally, it is important to understand that, once adopted, a new discovery and its initial applications become part of a cultural system, where their presence brings about changes in the system. We saw the profound changes that resulted from the inventions of farming techniques (see Chapters 8 and 10). Or think about such things as the domestication of the horse, the invention of wheeled vehicles, and more recent innovations such as the production and harnessing of electricity; the understanding of the energy within the atom; and the inventions of the transistor (a small device for controlling the flow of electricity without the presence of a vacuum), the laser, and the microchip (a tiny integrated circuit with multiple transistors). As an exercise, count the number of items in your household that include microchips and think about how they have changed life in modern times. Then realize that when I started college thirty-five years ago, those things didn't exist or at least were not so commonplace.

As we discussed in the previous chapter, however, each society can only discover and invent so much. Thus, the second basic process of culture change is the diffusion of discoveries and artifacts, the giving and taking of culture among different societies. This is thought to be responsible, on average, for 90 percent of a society's cultural inventory. Though we are, by our very nature, an inventive, creative species, we nonetheless rely heavily on borrowed items for stimulating and bringing about change. Societies isolated from outside contact change slowly. Those with greater opportunity for contact—and thus for borrowing—change more rapidly.

This emphasis on diffusion is sometimes hard to grasp because once an item is borrowed it is modified and adapted to the borrowing culture and becomes a part of its cultural system. It becomes so firmly a part of that system that we don't think about the fact that it may not have originated within that culture. The classic and often-quoted attempt to make this point comes from anthropologist Ralph Linton's article "One Hundred Percent American." It was written in 1937 so some of the references are a bit outdated, but the point is still clear. It follows a typical American man through the first part of his day. Here are excerpts:

> Our solid American citizen awakens in a bed built on a pattern which originated in the Near East but which was modified in Northern Europe before it was transmitted to America. He throws back covers made from cotton, domesticated in India, or linen, domesticated in the Near East, or wool from sheep, also domesticated in the Near East, or silk, the use of which was discovered in China. . . . He takes off his pajamas, a garment invented in India, and washes with soap invented by the ancient Gauls. He then shaves, a masochistic rite which seems to have been derived from either Sumer or Egypt. . . . On his way to breakfast he stops to buy a paper, paying for it with coins, an ancient Lydian invention. . . . As he absorbs the accounts of foreign troubles he will, if he is a good conservative citizen, thank a Hebrew deity in an Indo-European language that he is 100 percent American.

Cultural ideas and technologies are not, of course, always borrowed intact, nor is everything borrowed that *could* be borrowed. If, to take a hypothetical example, a Native American people from before European contact had seen wheeled vehicles, they may well have rejected the idea of incorporating them since they lacked domesticable large animals to pull them. Other items may be rejected because they conflict with religious or ethical beliefs. Anthropologists Carol and Melvin Ember point out that, although the Japanese borrowed much from the Chinese, they never adopted the idea of binding the feet of women because Japanese culture traditionally abhors any type of body mutilation. Clothing styles seem particularly open to diffusion (American jeans are sought after all over the world), but differences in standards of modesty cause many styles to be rejected. As immodest as the clothing styles in the United States are considered by some societies, I doubt whether we would ever adopt the male attire of many societies of the New Guinea highlands (see Figure 14.1).

Items that *are* borrowed are usually modified to fit the receiving society's cultural system. So central is wine in French culture that when fast-food restaurants like McDonald's diffused there, wine was added to the menu. English missionaries introduced the game of cricket to the Trobriand Islands (now part of Papua New Guinea) in the early twentieth century. The game was enthusiastically adopted, but the Trobrianders quickly made it their own, changing the rules, redesigning the equipment, and using the game as a substitute for intervillage warfare and for the establishing of alliances. And their team names, often sexual references, seemed quite contradictory to the English intent of using the game to "civilize" the natives.

Adaptation of borrowed items is often strikingly seen in religion. Because of the cultural and psychological importance of religion, people are obviously reluctant to give up their religious beliefs, even under pressure. Thus, new beliefs are often incorporated into existing ones to produce a synthesis. This is called **syncretism.** Voodoo (or voudou), for example, a religion of Haiti, derives from several West African cultural traditions and is heavily influenced by Catholicism. Part of the explanation for the great variety of specific beliefs and rituals within Christianity is the wide spread of that religion and the synthesis of basic Christian ideas with existing religious traditions of the cultures adopting, or forced to adopt, it. Many non-European expressions of Catholicism still include, at the specific urging of the Vatican, traditional local elements.

There are two other basic recognized processes of culture change that are, in a sense, extreme forms of invention and diffusion. One is **acculturation,** defined as rapid diffusion under the influence of a dominant society. This may occur voluntarily or by force and with violence.

Examples of the latter are all too common. Native Americans, for instance, were quickly acculturated into the European-based society of the colonial powers and later the United States. As just one example, many Indians in the American Southwest still practice Catholicism and have Spanish surnames, a remnant of several hundred years of Spanish presence in the region (Figure 15.2). Slaves are acculturated into the societies of their owners. Countries conquered during war are forced to take on at least some of the cultural aspects of their conquerors, although the conquerors can also be influenced by the cultures they defeat. For example, when the European Christians conquered and ruled Islamic Spain, from the eleventh through the fifteenth centuries, they found a wealth of written knowledge in science, mathematics, and philosophy, some of it passed down from classical Greece. This knowledge then entered and had a profound effect on Western Europe's history.

An example of more voluntary acculturation is the phenomenon of the cargo cults. Peoples of a number of South Pacific island societies, from New Guinea to Fiji, came into brief contact with industrialized technologies during World War II. Liking what they saw, they wanted the benefits of some of that technology, which came to be generally called—borrowing the English word—"cargo." Once the war was over, the islands were left pretty much as they had been. To get the cargo back, peoples of some of these societies took on many of the trappings of Western culture as they remembered them. They began to use English words. They started to dress and mimic the military personnel they had observed, sometimes marching and carrying rifles carved from wood (Figure 15.3). They worshipped sacred objects—old helmets, dog tags, and other military and personal items the western military had left behind. They created gods to whom they prayed for the return of the cargo. One of these gods, on the island of Tanna in the Republic of Vanuatu, was named John Frum, another English borrowing.

Another process of culture change is **revolution.** Usually thought of in the context of violent overthrow of an existing government—as in the American, French, and Russian revolutions—a revolution can also refer

syncretism The synthesis of existing religious beliefs and practices with new ones introduced from the outside.

acculturation Rapid diffusion of cultural items either by choice of the receiving society or by force from a more dominant society.

revolution Rapid and extensive culture change generated from within a society.

FIGURE 15.2
The cemetery at Taos Pueblo, New Mexico, a Tiwa-speaking community. The symbols are Christian and the surnames on the graves are Spanish, results of Native American acculturation to Spanish culture during the colonial period.

to a radical change in other aspects of society. There are scientific revolutions. The discoveries of Copernicus, Darwin, and Einstein come to mind—discoveries that radically and fairly rapidly changed the very way we think. We have already noted some technological revolutions such as the invention of the microchip. A revolution in the sense of a process of culture change can, I believe, be thought of as rapid invention—new

FIGURE 15.3
Some men from the island of Tanna in Vanuatu march with bamboo rifles and "U.S.A." painted on their chests in the hope that by mimicking the behavior of Western soldiers they can attract a messiah named John Frum, who will bring material goods.

stimulus diffusion When knowledge of a cultural trait in another society stimulates the invention of a similar trait.

ideas and applications from within a society (or borrowed and radically adapted from outside) that thoroughly alter that society.

In this sense, then, a revolution can also involve a strong cultural statement on the part of a portion of a society that quickly affects and alters the society as a whole. The Protestant Reformation may be thought of in this way. Even the social changes we saw in this country in the 1960s—trends toward greater individual freedom of expression and behavior and more tolerance of varying lifestyles—were a result in part of a strong statement by America's youth in conjunction with elements of its artistic and academic culture. The statement caught on and has affected our entire social and cultural system to the present.

All these processes should not be thought of as independent and separate, of course. As with other processes we've discussed (such as the processes of biological evolution), they can work together in interaction. For example, the stimulus for an invention can diffuse from another culture, even if the invention itself does not. This, in fact, is known as **stimulus diffusion**. The French Revolution, for instance, was influenced in part by the success of the American Revolution. And, in the early nineteenth century, a Cherokee named Sequoyah invented an alphabetic system for writing his language, stimulated by his knowledge that whites had a means for inscribing their language.

These are the processes that bring about changes in cultures. But we are still left with some major questions that bring us back to the topic of evolution, with which we began. In terms of the history of culture, can we perceive any overall trends? Are there any general rules of culture change? Any particular direction that culture change takes? The search for answers to such questions characterized much of the early history of anthropology.

THEORIES OF CULTURAL EVOLUTION

By the last third of the nineteenth century, largely as a result of the work of Charles Darwin, the idea was reasonably well accepted that humans had evolved from other creatures and that our evolution had taken place over millions of years. Furthermore, because of extensive exploration over the previous 350 years, Western knowledge included a great deal of information about the vast diversity of cultural systems that existed among the world's peoples. It became only natural then to attempt to explain this cultural diversity in terms of the new evolutionary framework. In other words, if we had evolved biologically, we had certainly evolved culturally. As we discussed in Chapter 14, there were attempts to account for racial variation in an evolutionary context. Why not account for cultural variation in general in a similar fashion, searching for the same sorts of trends and directions that were being proposed for biological change through time?

One of the first schools of thought on this subject is associated with the English anthropologist Edward B. Tylor (1832–1917) and the American Lewis Henry Morgan (1818–1881). It is called **classical** or **unilineal evolutionism.** The idea was that all societies pass through the same series of major evolutionary cultural stages which Morgan termed "savagery," "barbarism," and "civilization." The savage stage is characterized by foraging and the use of fire and the bow and arrow; barbarism by domestication of plants and animals, pottery, and the beginnings of metallurgy; and civilization by writing and the invention of phonetic alphabets. Each stage could be represented by existing societies and, thus, the obvious explanation for the diversity of culture was simply that some societies had progressed farther along the series, while others had changed more slowly and were still in earlier stages.

The problems with this model should be obvious. First, it required that all societies, as they evolved, independently invent the same innovations and artifacts and undergo parallel development through the stages. Influence among societies—that is, diffusion—was not part of the model.

classical evolutionism
The same as unilineal evolutionism.

unilineal evolutionism
Now-outdated concept of cultural evolution where all societies pass through the same series of stages from savagery to civilization.

Second, it set up a predetermined and fairly simple scheme into which data were forced. In other words, every culture was pigeonholed into one of the three stages according to a limited set of criteria. In this, the model failed to do justice to the wealth of cultural diversity and to the complexity of cultural evolution. Third, it assumed that the goal of cultural evolution—civilization—was the stage reached by the society to which the theorists belonged. It was, in short, quite ethnocentric, and in this regard it mirrored many of the studies of racial classification being conducted at the same time.

As if to answer the problem of too much focus on independent invention, the **diffusionist** school arose. We have discussed the importance of diffusion in culture change. But this school of thought, popular in the first decades of the twentieth century, oversimplified the process by claiming that cultural innovation arose in only a few centers of culture (or even just one) and then spread to the rest of the world. One group, enamored of ancient Egypt, supposed that Egypt had been the source of almost all cultural innovations except for the simplest of hunting tools. Everything we think of as complex culture—from artifacts to social institutions—had been invented in ancient Egypt and diffused from there.

There were, however, less extreme forms of diffusionism. One, originating in Germany, proposed a number of early cultural centers from which cultural traditions spread in ever-widening circles. This is the *Kulturkreise* ("cultural circle") model. It explains the modern presence of "less advanced" societies by supposing that they failed to acquire the cultural innovations of the expanding circle as a result of being pushed into out-of-the-way geographical regions by more advanced populations.

Diffusionism also suffers from the problem of being a predetermined scheme into which data are fit rather than allowing the data to generate the models to be tested. Moreover, it's clear that culture is far too complex and variable to be accounted for by having spread from a small number of centers. Finally—just the opposite of unilineal evolutionism—diffusionism doesn't give *enough* credit to independent invention. It assumes most peoples are not capable of coming up with new ideas and technologies, which apparently require an intellect found only among a few populations.

The American school that has come to be called **historical particularism**, associated with the famous Franz Boas (1858–1942), attempted to overcome some of the objections to these other models. It rejected the idea of parallel development driven by some universal law of cultural evolution. For one thing, there was insufficient information about various cultures to propose any generalizations. Boas, as a result, is responsible for anthropology's focus on fieldwork, on the accumulation of firsthand data about societies and their cultures (Figure 15.4). Moreover, Boas said this fieldwork should be holistic, looking at all aspects of a culture

diffusionism Now-outdated concept of cultural evolution where major cultural advances were made by one or a few societies and spread from there to all other societies.

Kulturkreise ("culture circle") School of cultural evolution originating in Germany that proposed a small number of early cultural centers from which cultural traditions spread in ever-widening circles to encompass and influence other societies.

historical particularism American school of cultural evolution that rejected any general theory of culture change but believed that each society could only be understood with reference to its particular history.

FIGURE 15.4
Margaret Mead (left) doing fieldwork in Samoa in the 1920s. Mead is famous for her fieldwork as well as for being one of the first well-known women anthropologists. As her clothing suggests, she also advocated the idea of "participant-observation" in fieldwork—that the anthropologist could better understand a society and its culture by trying as much as possible to be a part of it.

and their interrelationships, and should be relativistic, understanding a culture within the context of its cultural system. It was Boas who was the first to formalize these concepts—of data collection, holism, and relativism—and make them important parts of anthropology.

With this approach, however, Boas implicitly rejected the possibility of *any* generalizations about culture and cultural evolution. Each culture, he said, could only be understood and explained by intensive study of its particular history (hence the name of the model). If there were similarities among cultures it was because of diffusion, often through trade, or because of similar cultural responses to similar environmental circumstances. In fact, the Boasians thought there was so much diffusion that it was difficult if not impossible to classify individual cultures. Instead, they developed lists of specific cultural traits that defined broad culture areas, rather than looking at boundaries between individual societies.

Still, Boas advanced the study of cultural evolution by finding some middle ground between the simplistic and extreme focuses of the independent invention and diffusionist schools—realizing both processes were important. He also proposed a relationship between culture and environment, getting away from both ideas—a unilineal evolution of all cultures regardless of environment and the diffusion of cultural items without any sort of adaptive selection and modification by the receiving society. And, once again, it was Boas and his followers who made scientific data collection through field research, holism, and relativism parts of the very identity of the discipline.

As we detailed in Chapter 13, there are still individual theoretical approaches to the analysis and explanation of individual cultural systems and of the diversity among them. Mary Douglas's symbolic approach and Marvin Harris's cultural materialism are only two. Which school of thought one supports will, of course, also influence how one sees the processes of culture change as they affect societies and their cultural systems. An examination of these approaches is beyond the scope of this book. There are some references listed at the end of the chapter that can guide you to further study.

It is safe to say, however, that—no matter how one sees them specifically affecting cultural systems—invention and diffusion are the driving forces behind culture change. *With caution,* we may propose an analogy to the processes of biological evolution. Invention is like mutation—the source of new variation. As a mutation spreads through heredity and gene flow, a new cultural innovation spreads through diffusion, either when the idea itself moves among societies or when the people migrate and carry the idea with them. But the success of a mutation is dependent on its adaptive value. If it is useful, it's selected for by natural processes of differential reproduction. If not, it is selected against. The same holds true for cultural innovations. They are not just blindly accepted. Rather, they undergo cultural selection with regard to their value to and fit within the new cultural system. The difference in the two sets of processes—*and this is extremely important*—lies in the fact that cultural innovations arise through conscious, purposeful thought (although discoveries may originally be accidental), while biological mutations are random, unconscious, and undirected. Natural selection is an unconscious process; cultural selection is a conscious one. That added dimension—of human motivation, consciousness, and will—makes all the difference.

CHANGE IN THE MODERN WORLD

Although culture change may be the norm, it can present problems, especially during the process of acculturation or when a society is trying to realign and maintain its system in the face of change. Such situations are, of course, becoming increasingly frequent as the world in which we live becomes effectively smaller. Let's look at recent changes in some of the societies we've discussed as just a few representative examples.

In the summer of 1983, ten years after my first visit, I went back to some Hutterite colonies to collect more data and to get some photographs and video footage. This time I visited two American *Bruderhofs,* and the differences I perceived between the Canadian and United States Hutterites, and the difference of a decade, were striking.

It had been said, and it was my impression (although based on a small sample) that the American Hutterites tended to be a little less open and a little more suspicious of outsiders than those in Canada. This may be in part because during World War I many U.S. Hutterites who resisted the military draft because of their pacifist beliefs were jailed as draft resisters. In fact, two Hutterites died in prison as a result of maltreatment. In addition, the Hutterites felt that how their colonies were taxed in the United States was unfair. As a result, most Hutterites moved to Canada, where they were not drafted and where some tax arrangements were made. (Since then, the United States has made similar accommodations, and about 29 percent of Hutterite colonies are in this country.)

In addition, I sensed, although I can't document it, more jealousy on the part of non-Hutterites in the United States over the large and prosperous tracts of land that the Hutterites own and the large-scale farming operations they maintain. This may be because land is somewhat more plentiful in Canada (although there have been legal restrictions on the establishment of new colonies in Canada). At any rate, one of the two colonies I visited in 1983 was unwilling to let me do anything more than talk to one young man and take still photographs. This was in contrast to the Canadian colonies in 1973, who had gladly and cooperatively allowed me to take fingerprints and collect family and individual histories. Obviously, however, a more extensive study with a far larger sample would be necessary to support my impressionistic conclusions.

The modern world has brought changes to the Hutterite way of life. The colonies depend on the income acquired from the sale of produce and, to a lesser extent, of handmade goods and of services such as the repair of farm equipment. Hutterites must be, and are, well versed in the ins and outs of the market system. That system, however, is becoming increasingly complex, as is farming and the technologies needed to support it. As a result, more information is required, enough to warrant the Hutterites changing their educational practices.

FIGURE 15.5
My informant and his first child, one of the next generation of Hutterites.

Until recently, Hutterite youths received standard schooling on the colony from an outside licensed teacher just until they were old enough to legally drop out. With the need for more education, Hutterites now go to school through grade twelve, and in 1994 the first of them received high school diplomas. This need, in turn, has led to the desire to have their own licensed teachers, and in 1996 the first Hutterites received teaching degrees. There are also plans for some young people to acquire vocational degrees as well as degrees in some of the technological skills required to maintain the colonies' self-sufficiency.

At the same time, the Hutterites must try even harder to keep the outside world from influencing their young people too much and threatening the very continuation of their culture. This is a problem. The young man that became my informant had, in fact, left the colony for a time to attend college. He had had no plans to return, but found himself unable to adapt to the kind of individualized existence found on the outside and missed the security of colony life. After a few years he returned. His sister, however, had left and married a non-Hutterite. One of his brothers had also left, and a second brother I met—with styled hair, jeans instead of homemade pants, and Nike running shoes—struck me as at least a potential candidate for leaving. Even the young man himself, although he had returned, married, and had a son, was different from other Hutterites (Figure 15.5). He had an extensive library that reflected his continued interest in worldly matters outside the concerns of most colony members. A Bible and a few works by Hutterites were the usual extent of a member's reading material.

FIGURE 15.6
A Dani man in traditional dress tries to warm himself in the evening chill amidst the shops and traffic of modern Wamena, Irian Jaya.

Because keeping young people on the colony means the survival of the culture, the Hutterites were reluctant to talk about how many people have left. Though I could get no hard data, I had the distinct impression that the case of this one family was not unusual. After over 400 years of successfully maintaining their separation *from* the world while still being *in* it, they are now confronting a situation where that kind of separation seems impossible. On their solution to this problem rests their very future.

One approach—and, in a way, one they have always used—is to let in just enough of the outside world to maintain the financial success that sustains their independence and to keep their young people from feeling too out of touch and different from mainstream culture. Sending some young people to college is part of this. And, recently, a group of Hutterite high schoolers in Manitoba have created a web site with extensive data about the lives, history, and beliefs of the society. There is a saying in anthropology that cultures change just enough so they don't have to change profoundly. That seems true of the Hutterites and is, I think, along with their devout religious beliefs, a key to their longevity.

The Dani have not had the luxury of exercising so much control over changes. When Karl Heider last visited the area in 1970, the Indonesian government had stopped the warfare, and there were a government army and police post (inside which the Dani were not permitted to carry their weapons), a first aid station, a landing field, a Catholic mission, a school, and even tourists. Today, a major road, the Trans-Irian Highway, connects the north and south coasts of the country, running through the Grand Valley town of Wamena. That town, not even mentioned on the earliest maps of the region, now has a population of 17,000 (Figure 15.6). Although the Dani try to cling to old ways—many still dress in the traditional style—they are now involved in growing rice for sale, leading tourists on treks, and worshipping at Christian churches. A Dani Baptist deacon is quoted as telling his congregation, "There is no fighting. You don't have to hunt or garden. Everything good comes to you."

The San have experienced what anthropologist Richard Lee calls "directed social change." In 1960 the San of Namibia, then a country under the control of South Africa, were settled in an area set aside for them as part of South Africa's apartheid (racial separation) policy. Some of the men worked on road gangs or in workshops, but many were unemployed—a concept that would have made no sense to them just a few years before. Women spent their time with household chores and the children were supposed to go to school, but absenteeism was high. Everyone was fed by the government. The results were no surprise. Boredom, alcoholism (alcohol was an important item the government made available in their stores), and violence increased.

Starting in 1966, some native peoples of Namibia began fighting for independence from South Africa under the South-West African People's Organization (SWAPO). To combat SWAPO, the South African government not only sent in its own troops but also recruited locals, including the San (Figure 15.7). Induced by good wages (up to $500 a month), the San joined up in large numbers, for a war that few really understood and that involved the killing of an "enemy" made up of some of their fellow Namibians. Raids were even made over the border into neighboring Angola. Besides the obvious dangers of warfare and the further divisions among the indigenous peoples, the pouring of large sums of money into the lives of the San led to social stratification of a once-egalitarian people, with the consequent resentments and conflicts. Alcoholism and violence further increased. In one two-year period (1978–1980), Lee recorded seven homicides—a huge number for a people who had been relatively peaceful for years.

Namibia became independent in 1990, initially a mixed blessing for the San, according to Lee. Many former soldiers were back home with nothing to do. Once-protected San land was being eyed enviously by cattle herders, many of whom moved onto the land before legal restrictions

FIGURE 15.7
A San woman nurses her baby while listening to a tape deck at a military camp in Namibia in the early 1980s, before independence. She touches her husband's foot with her own to maintain physical contact, an important concept to the San. The man wears military clothing from the South African army, indicating he probably volunteered to fight for wages against SWAPO.

were enacted (those restrictions were the result of work by a foundation set up by anthropologists and an indigenous farmer's cooperative and union). Additional problems, however, came from within, as this traditionally egalitarian society had to elect leaders, own and divide land, and speak as a whole people rather than as small family groups. Simply being independent after thirty years of colonialism can also be a problem. Lee, however, says the San's new empowerment is "a modest basis for optimism."

What of the San in neighboring Botswana? Private ranching syndicates have encroached on much of their land, the grazing turning once-rich areas into dustbowls. Government-controlled stores, schools, feeding programs, and local officials have transformed the San, as Lee puts it, "in a generation from a society of foragers . . . to a society of small-holders who eked out a living by herding, farming, and craft production, along with some hunting and gathering." Some San from Botswana had crossed the border into Namibia to fight against SWAPO. Changes in health and nutrition have been documented, with an increase in hypertension and heart disease, a result of changes in diet, more alcohol, and more smoking. A craft production organization brought a good deal of money into the area, but much of that money is spent on alcohol and prepared foods, there being still too few opportunities to purchase farming equipment and other necessities. However, under the influence of the Namibians and their indigenous political organizations, the Botswanans are beginning to mobilize, and some changes may be forthcoming. The results, of course, remain to be seen.

There are many other examples of both progress and problems as the rich diversity of the world's peoples and their cultures encounter the global village, global economy, and global ecosystem our planet is fast becoming. What role can anthropology take in the modern world?

APPLYING ANTHROPOLOGY

There is nothing wrong, of course, with knowledge for its own sake, and anthropology has inarguably added to our understanding of our species through its holistic scientific studies. Some of this understanding might be merely interesting, but much of it can be applied to helping societies—including ours—cope in today's complex, fast-changing world.

Anthropology has shown how science—often stereotyped as being concerned only with chemicals, heavenly bodies, and atoms—can be applied to an understanding of the evolution and nature of human behavior. As we confront differences in behaviors among societies as well as disturbing increases in anomalous behaviors—violence, to name an obvious example—such potential understanding is of great importance.

The nature of relations between the sexes and the multitude of ideas and attitudes regarding gender are a clear focus of anthropology's contribution. We now have an understanding of the difference between sex and gender, the relationship between those two categories, and the cultural variations that exist. We can shed some light on what have traditionally been considered deviations from normal sexual and gender behavior and place them in cultural (and, perhaps, biological) contexts.

Anthropology has shed light on issues of health, including the nature and causes of variation in disease frequency among societies and the different ways societies categorize and think about diseases. The application of this understanding to AIDS—its origin, spread, and attitudes about its victims in different societies—is obvious. By comparing the health of modern industrial peoples with that of foragers, we may even be able to suggest some ways we could alter our lifestyles for better health.

Forensic anthropology is a growing specialty. Its techniques have been applied to solving crimes, identifying accident victims, and disclosing war crimes such as those committed in Kosovo in 1999.

In a broad perspective, anthropology has provided insight into historical trends, giving us the potential to make general predictions about what circumstances might tend to lead to what results. The archaeological record, for example, has shown why farming originated and what benefits and problems resulted from that change in subsistence. The more we understand the past, the better is our ability to understand the present and guide the future.

With the world's societies in increasing interaction with one another, anthropology offers a perspective with both ethical and practical applications. Knowing what culture is, how it operates, and why it varies helps us understand—on a profound level—cultures other than our own. Indeed, when we better understand our *own* culture from an anthropological perspective, we better understand others. This has obvious humanistic relevance, and, on a practical level, is necessary for doing international business. Businesspersons from other societies may be involved in a global economy, but they are still members of their own cultures, and how one conducts business with them can be important. Multinational corporations frequently hire anthropologists as consultants in such matters.

One of anthropology's most important contributions has been in its investigation of the nature of biological diversity and the cultural phenomenon of race. Understanding what race is—and what it is not—can go a long way toward eventually addressing the social problems that a lack of understanding has burdened us with.

As the world population increases and puts further pressure on resources and our ability to govern and serve our peoples, anthropology can aid in the dissemination of family planning information and technologies. For many cultures, the idea of limiting one's family is unnatural, even if it might make sense. Understanding another society's traditional views on this matter can be vital to introducing its people to relevant information and techniques.

In a world where conflict and war are so commonplace that we are almost inured to it, understanding the cultural reasons for violent conflict is essential. Wars are fought for a multitude of reasons. To be able to discern the reasons for a specific conflict goes a long way toward dealing with and, hopefully, ending that conflict with negotiation rather than with more violence.

Finally, though change is inevitable and no society is immune to change, most people feel that a society undergoing change should have some say in the speed, direction, and nature of the changes affecting it. This, of course, is not always the case. Some dominant cultures have no desire to give subservient ones any voice in what happens to them. In other cases, imposed change may be well meaning but misguided due to a lack of knowledge about another culture and, thus, about the potential results of change. Anthropology can make a tremendous contribution by using its understanding of other peoples to help give them a voice and to help predict and guide changes as they take place. To finish bringing the story of the San up to date, let's use them as an example.

As changes to the San's way of life were imposed from the outside and were taking place within, the simple accumulation of basic anthropological knowledge was important. No help and no understanding on the part of outsiders is possible without the documentation and dissemination of basic data about the people in question. Among the data documented, of course, were data on changes that had already taken place and their effects on the San.

Some anthropologists became advocates for the rights of these (and other) indigenous peoples. Two formed the Nyae Nyae Development Foundation of Namibia to lobby nationally and internationally to preserve land rights for the San and raise funds for that purpose. Much of their work involved communicating information about the San to relevant agencies.

Other anthropological researchers focused on helping the San themselves to apply their traditional ideas to the new situations that were confronting them. Having, in a way, a dual perspective—as members of a multicultural, international, industrial society and as scientists with a holistic knowledge of their subjects—anthropologists are uniquely able to do this. Among specific services they may provide is translation to and from indigenous languages, their dual cultural perspective enabling them to be, perhaps, more accurate than other translators.

Anthropologist and filmmaker John Marshall, who has documented the lives of the San since the 1950s, notes that the anthropologist also plays the role of listener or "cultural therapist" as the people themselves discuss and try to work out their situation in the face of change. Much like some psychological analysts, the anthropologist can, without interfering or coercing, suggest different perspectives and give the people in question what is perhaps their most powerful weapon—knowledge.

The application of anthropology in these ways is not without its controversies. We'll take these up in the Contemporary Issues feature of this chapter. But the application of anthropological knowledge in today's world attracts many people to the discipline and has become a growing specialty within the field.

SUMMARY

Cultures change at different rates and times, but change is inevitable for any society. Two basic processes bring about culture change. The first of these is the interacting processes of discovery and invention—the addition of new knowledge about the world and the application of that knowledge through the creation of concrete or abstract artifacts. Innovations are selected and modified to fit a society's existing cultural system.

Possibilities for innovation within any given society are limited. The second process of culture change—diffusion—is responsible for the majority of any society's cultural inventory and explains the diversity in level of complexity among societies. Diffusion is the process of cultural borrowing. Isolated societies, with limited opportunities to come into contact with the innovations of other groups, change slowly. Societies that live in areas with greater intercultural contact change more rapidly. As with innovations, potentially borrowed items are selected for their fit within the receiving society's system. When borrowed, they are modified to fit the system.

Acculturation is rapid diffusion under the influence of a more dominant culture. This may take place by force, as in military conquest, or voluntarily, as with the cargo cults of Melanesia.

Revolution is rapid invention—change from within a society that alters the whole social fabric. Revolutions may involve violent overthrows of existing governments, or more peaceful cultural statements, such as religious revolutions or some of the changes seen in United States society that began in the 1960s.

Early theories of cultural evolution were often oversimplified models stressing one process of change—either independent invention or diffusion. Thanks in part to the Boasian school of thought, we now see that all the processes of change work together in complex ways that vary with each society's particular history.

As change in the modern world accelerates, it brings both benefits and problems, especially to societies with little or no say in how and in what direction they change. Some important roles of modern anthropology are to understand and disseminate knowledge about cultural systems, to document the effects of changes on societies, to advise agencies on the possible outcomes of alterations to certain societies, and to help monitor the progress of those changes.

NOTES, REFERENCES, AND READINGS

Ralph Linton's famous article appeared in the *The American Mercury* (1937) and is reprinted in numerous collections of anthropological literature.

A good article on the much-misunderstood religion of voodoo, with information about its syncretic nature, is "Voodoo" by Karen McCarthy Brown. It can be found in the Lehmann and Myers reader, *Magic, Witchcraft, and Religion,* cited in Chapter 12.

A well-illustrated piece on the cargo cults is in the May 1974 *National Geographic* titled "Tanna Awaits the Coming of John Frum" by Kal Muller.

For a comprehensive collection of pieces on anthropological theory, with commentary through introductions and extensive footnotes, see *Anthropological Theory: An Introductory History* by R. Jon McGee and Richard Warms.

Have a look at the Hutterites's web site, www.hutterianbrethren.com.

For an idea, with pictures, about how the Dani and their country have changed over the last decades, see three articles in *National Geographic:* "Netherlands New Guinea" (May 1962) by John Scofield; "Two Worlds, Time Apart: Indonesia" (January 1989) by Arthur Zich; and

CONTEMPORARY ISSUES

Can Anthropology Be Both Scientific and Humanistic in Today's World?

Let's begin with the answer: Anthropology *can* be both scientific and humanistic, and, in today's world, it *must* be.

In Chapter 2, I indicated that one of the appeals of anthropology to many people, and one of its major contributions, is its humanism—its understanding of and concern for other peoples and their cultures and for humanity in general. That aspect should now be clearer as we've examined all the methods, topics, and conclusions of the discipline. Obviously, in the process of studying a society's culture, one comes to know its people in a profound way, and one recognizes—beyond all the striking differences—the essential similarities among all humans. I had chosen the Hutterites as subjects to help me answer a biological question. But during my brief fieldwork, I came to know many of them quite well, and I became deeply interested in their way of life, their attitudes, and their problems. I never thought for a second about living that life; it was foreign to many of my beliefs, habits, and likes. Nor did I get along with every Hutterite I met; some I was friendly with, some I never warmed up to, and I'm sure the feeling was mutual. But I went away with a better understanding of their culture, and still have a deep respect and concern for the culture and the people who practice it.

This phenomenon is true for most anthropologists, I believe. Certainly, it occurs among cultural anthropologists who study living peoples and cultures. But even archaeologists, who study cultures and peoples no longer living, can develop an intimacy with and respect for those societies. And many ancient societies still have identifiable living descendants with whom archaeologists can form professional and personal relationships. Indeed, even paleoanthropologists studying long-extinct species of hominids may still acquire a feel for their subjects, so detailed and personal is the nature of anthropological data. We can't, for example, help but speculate how Lucy died 3.2 million years ago, because we feel some connection even across so many millennia. Her well-preserved bones conjure up a picture of her death on the shore of a body of water, with her corpse sinking into the thick silt at the bottom to slowly decay.

This intimacy with and concern for other peoples has led to an increase in the desire of anthropologists to apply their knowledge (from their privileged positions as members of affluent societies) to address the concerns and problems of their subjects. Many peoples—especially those in isolated, poor, minority, or subservient societies—are at best ignored and at worst denigrated, exploited, and violently persecuted. No thinking person can ignore this, and anthropologists—immersed as they are in the lives of others—must confront it head-on. As a result, many anthropolo-

"Irian Jaya" (February 1996) by Thomas O'Neill. The quote from the Dani deacon is from page 24 of the latter.

Richard Lee's *The Dobe Ju/'hoansi*, second edition, has several chapters on the recent changes to beset the San and includes additional information about how anthropologists are offering help. Part of the topic of the Contemporary Issues feature is discussed in Chapter 12.

gists have lately focused on advocacy—speaking, lobbying, and collecting money for people in the societies they have studied and come to know. As indicated by the example of the Ju/'hoansi, such activities can be profoundly helpful.

But the anthropology-as-advocacy approach has led to criticism. Anthropologists involved in these sorts of activities have been accused of abandoning anthropology as science. They are not, it has been said, advancing our knowledge of peoples, cultures, and humanity in general, but have become politically oriented and, as such, let beliefs and opinions rather than facts influence how they describe and analyze a group of people and their culture.

For their part, some anthropologists whose focus is on advocacy for a particular group have expressed a suspicion of science as cold, detached, and dehumanizing and even a tool of the politically powerful to justify some social-economic-political status quo. A result has been something of a split within the discipline (sometimes actually reflected in the division of university departments) between science-oriented and advocacy-oriented anthropology, and the debate has taken on varied (and complex) philosophical dimensions.

Does this mean the demise of anthropology as we have known it, a field that has been called "not only scientifically important but intellectually bold and morally brave"? I certainly hope not, nor do I think this will be the outcome. But a solution rests with the realization that science and humanism can and should work together in this field, that they are not mutually exclusive, and that the free discussion of differences in philosophy and theory drives progress in knowledge and its applications.

The subject matter and methodology of anthropology make it uniquely qualified to speak with and for peoples of other cultures or subcultures in the face of the extensive and accelerating change that is part of the modern world. Indeed, anthropologists would be remiss if they did not apply their knowledge and skills in this way. At the same time, offering opinions on real, concrete matters without factual information to support them ranges from ineffectual to dangerous. If we are to provide a forum and voice for the people of other societies, we must do so with the best information at hand—and some of the best information about societies and their cultural systems comes from anthropology in its role as a scientific discipline. All the best intentions for another people will do them no good unless reality is taken into account, and, as anthropologist Robin Fox says, "Science, with its objectivity . . . remains the one international language capable of providing objective knowledge about the world. And it is a language we can all use and share and learn. . . . " To not apply science—especially when that application can assist people in achieving the basic human right of exercising control over their lives—is arguably immoral. Thus, the reconciliation of the scientific and humanistic roles of anthropology is a bold, brave, and important goal.

A good collection of articles about applications of anthropology is *Applying Anthropology: An Introductory Reader,* fifth edition, edited by Aaron Podolefsky and Peter Brown.

For introductions to applied anthropology as a new subfield within the discipline see *Applied Anthropology: A Practical Guide* by Erve Chambers and *Applied Anthropology: An Introduction* by John van Willigen.

The Contemporary Issues feature just scratches the surface of a continuing and very complex debate within anthropology. For an introduction to the subject, I recommend the last section of the McGee and Warms book (page 480ff.). The quotation about the important, bold, and brave nature of traditional anthropology comes from Paul Gross and Norman Levitt, the authors of a staunchly pro-science—and sometimes overstated—book called *Higher Superstition: The Academic Left and Its Quarrels with Science,* page 213. Robin Fox's quote is on page 82 of that book. A work about the possibility and, indeed, the need for unifying areas of knowledge is Edward O. Wilson's *Consilience: The Unity of Knowledge.*

16

STATE OF THE SPECIES

The Edge of the Future

Since anthropology is the holistic study of the human species, it is only fitting that we end by standing back and seeing if we can assess the state of our species today and, perhaps, make some guesses as to where—based on our present state—we might be headed in the future. Of course, even using the best scientific methodology and techniques at hand, analyzing a situation we're right in the middle of and which seems to change by the minute, not to mention making predictions about the future, is risky. Still, the anthropological perspective and some of the data and conclusions we've discussed in this book might be useful starting points for thinking about these matters.

THE HUMAN SPECIES TODAY

There are two general criteria for evaluating the success of a biological species. One, obviously, is reproductive success. Reproductive success is, after all, the measure of species adaptation and the factor that drives natural selection. The second criterion is longevity—how long the species has maintained an adaptive fitness that allows it the chance to perpetuate itself.

In strict numerical terms, we are clearly reproductively successful. Our population is at 6 billion and counting. We're projected to reach 8.5 billion by 2050. But there's another variable in reproductive success besides sheer numbers. A species can be *too* reproductively successful and then risks both running out of space and resources and putting pressure on those behaviors that have evolved to maintain social order among its members. Successful species have mechanisms for limiting their total population relative to existing environmental conditions. Sometimes this is simply a matter of an increased death rate when some environmental variable is abnormal—lack of food or water, a climate that is too hot or too cold, and so on. Sometimes it's more subtle, as when environmental disruptions lead to interruptions in mating behavior or reproductive physiology.

But our species manipulates environmental variables through culture. We can protect ourselves from the elements, find alternative sources of food, migrate to new areas, and deal with some injuries, illnesses, and handicaps in a way that makes them no longer impediments to reproduction. These steps all sound good on the surface—but they have consequences that, even today, we sometimes do not fully appreciate. First, of course, we run the risk of producing too many people for the resources at hand. It can be convincingly argued that we have already done this. True, there are many people in the world today for whom the necessities of life are readily and easily available. Indeed, many resources go to waste in affluent societies. But there are even more people on this planet who do not receive adequate food, water, and shelter. In some cases, of course, this is because of the political situations in their countries, not because of availability. After all, there are homeless and underfed people in the wealthiest of nations. But, in broad perspective, if large numbers of the species do *not* have access to adequate resources, those resources are effectively *not* available. If there's not enough to go around, for whatever reason, we've run out. In ecological terms, we've reached our **carrying capacity.**

The second consequence of our species' ability to keep on reproducing by manipulating the environment is that each time we manipulate the environment in the face of depleted resources and increased population, we have to intensify that manipulation—hunt more animals, farm more land, use more water, divert sources of water to new locations, use more wood and other raw materials to construct more shelters, and so on. Each time, the environment is affected, with the result that alternative resources and space are increasingly less available for the next time. And with less availability, we have greater need to further and more frequently intensify. Eventually, something has to give.

This consideration brings up the matter of species longevity. The relationship between a species' evolutionary health and how long it has been around is, of course, relative to the nature of the species. For some species of bacteria, with a generation turnover time of one hour, a short tenure on earth can indicate success. For a large species with a long generation time, a longer time in existence is required to say the species has been successful. By the most liberal of definitions (see Chapter 5) our species is 2 million years old—not a long period for a large mammal with a generation time in double digits—so we would be premature to say humans are successful based on the time we've been around.

But even time itself is not a good measure. To be considered adapted, a species must be in some equilibrium with its environment—extracting enough to survive, but not extracting so much that it depletes the resources it needs and, thus, in the end, adversely affects itself. Since we began farming, we have increasingly taken more out of the environment than we have put back. That is, we are sort of "out of the loop" in the food chain. We don't trap solar energy like green plants. We don't provide a food source for other creatures except decomposers like bacteria and fungi, and some of our funerary practices like embalming and cremation even deprive those organisms. Rather, we have altered the natural ecology of much of the planet, including, through our waste products, changing the very chemical makeup of the land, water, and atmosphere. We have brought about the extinction of many species. Indeed, the rate of extinction in the past few hundred years appears to be more rapid than

carrying capacity The maximum population of a species allowed by existing environmental conditions and resources.

during any of the five previous mass extinctions (for example, the one 65 million years ago that included the dinosaurs). This has led some to refer to the last century or so as the "sixth extinction." While the causes of some previous extinctions are still being debated, that of the current one is clear—it's us.

So, one could conclude that—although many of us live relatively healthy, safe lives with adequate nutrition, water, and shelter—the species as a whole is not in the best state of health. What can we say about the prognosis?

THE HUMAN SPECIES IN THE FUTURE

If we are to extrapolate into the future, we must (as we noted in Chapters 14 and 15) understand the nature of change, and we must appreciate the inevitability of change. To think about change in a broad perspective, we must understand the concepts of **contingency** and constraint.

In the early 1980s, I wrote the following:

> Considering our current situation, we can see ourselves standing on the edge of a lush Eden of scientific, technological, medical, and social advances that make all our lives longer and happier. Or we might be poised on the edge of a cliff, below us a deadly cauldron —a polluted, violent, nuclear nightmare.

At the time, the Soviet Union still existed and tensions between the United States and that nation were, at times, high. There was serious talk of the possibility that a small conflict somewhere in the world would escalate into nuclear war—and the stockpiles of nuclear weapons in some half-dozen countries at the time were the equivalent of 20 billion tons of TNT, about 1.6 million times the power of the bomb that destroyed Hiroshima in 1945. At my university, there was a faculty-student group whose focus was to educate about the threat of and results from nuclear war. Our "bible" was Jonathan Schell's *The Fate of the Earth,* a book that painted a grim picture of the world after a nuclear conflict as "a republic of insects and grass," two groups of organisms that seem to be little affected by nuclear radiation. Other problems, of course, existed, but, for a time in the 1980s, they seemed to pale before the vision of a world devastated by nuclear war. We dreamt, as did Schell in his book, of how different the world would be if that threat, which we had lived with for nearly forty years, could be lifted. At the time, it seemed like no more than a dream.

contingency The idea that events are dependent upon all preceding events and that a change in one event will affect all that follow from it.

Now, less than two decades, later, I know what that world is like. In the early 1990s the Soviet Union collapsed and with it the sense of the imminence of a worldwide nuclear holocaust—what we used to term the "unthinkable," because, truly, it was impossible to conceive of, there being no prior experience with anything of that magnitude. We have now, of course replaced it with the "thinkable"—that is, the possibility that any of a number of current violent conflicts could result in the localized use of nuclear arms. For that, because of Hiroshima and Nagasaki, we have a reference point.

Even if nuclear weapons are not part of the picture, we are still beset with local but sometimes terribly bloody wars. As I write in the summer of 1999, there are ongoing conflicts, recent conflicts, or potentially violent tensions in the Balkans, Mexico, Colombia, along the Indian-Pakistani border, central Africa, Northern Ireland, South Africa, China, the Middle East, Timor, and others. By the time you read this, the list will no doubt have changed.

Our image of nuclear war—an act of humans—as the event that will bring about the end of the world as we know it has been replaced by, metaphorically speaking, an act of god. There have been two recent theatrical movies and one made-for-television movie about the devastation of the earth from an impact by a giant asteroid. This idea has been fed by the increasingly good evidence for an asteroid impact as the initial cause of the mass extinction 65 million years ago. Evidence for other impacts in the past has also come to light. Instead of the so-called Star Wars technology, which was supposed to protect the country from missile attack with laser-armed satellites, we now hear arguments for the development of new technologies that will protect us from killer asteroids and comets.

Although environmental problems—pollution, extinction, destruction of the rainforests—are still very much with us and have, in fact, gotten worse, they seem to have been overshadowed by a newly realized problem, one that has direct effects on us and so seems of more immediate concern. As our population expands and as we move into new areas—especially in the tropics—we are coming into greater contact with other species that carry diseases to which they are immune but that prove deadly to us. HIV, the virus that causes AIDS, came from a species of African monkey that had evolved the ability to carry the virus without being adversely affected. A new strain of HIV, the virus that causes AIDS, seems to have come from a West African population of chimpanzees that had evolved the ability to carry the virus without being adversely affected. Another strain of HIV came to humans from a species of African monkey. AIDS is now the leading cause of death in Africa, where it accounted for 1.8 million deaths in 1998, and the fourth leading cause of death in the world, accounting for 91 percent of AIDS deaths worldwide. In Zimbabwe, over one-quarter of the population is HIV positive or has AIDS, and the disease is spreading rapidly, especially in populous countries like India, China, and Brazil. Hanta virus from rodents; ebola virus from an as-yet-unknown source; and *campylobactor,* a bacterium from chickens, are other examples of pathogens that have recently jumped from other species to ours with serious consequences. We discussed in Chapter 13 still another example of an **emerging disease,** the prion protein disorders, which are also transmitted between species.

emerging disease Any of a group of diseases of various causes that have newly appeared or are rapidly expanding their range in the human species.

The point is that, even in the mid-1980s, these specific changes were largely unforeseen. We might have assumed, based on twentieth-century history and facts about the possession of nuclear weapons, that *if* the Soviet Union collapsed the imminent threat of all-out nuclear war would be ended. But who could have guessed with any certainty that the Soviet Union would collapse, and that conflict would flare up among the former Soviet-controlled countries and the former Soviet republics? Could we have predicted that within a few years, a number of deadly diseases would emerge, one of which is now changing the demographics of a whole continent? Who would have thought that with the threat of nuclear war between the superpowers virtually eliminated, we would need some other apocalyptic scenario and pick an extraterrestrial impact to worry about?

The reason these things, so familiar and explicable to us now, were unpredicted just a decade and a half ago is because history is contingent. That is, each event is dependent on the series of events that preceded it. Historians and evolutionary scientists engage in reconstructing contingent series of events to explain why the world is as it is. But, as Stephen Jay Gould puts it, we explain "in retrospect what could not have been predicted beforehand." A change in any preceding event will change the events that follow, but, because so many interacting events are involved, we have little predictive ability to foresee *how* a particular change will alter subsequent events. Thus, each specific sequence of events in history is unique and unrepeatable, although, in hindsight, each makes sense.

Try it with your own life. Here's an example from mine: If I had taken the job that was offered me when I was a freshman in college, photographing fossil plants for one of my professors, would my life be different now? Sure. How? No way to know. I might just be an anthropologist who knows something about fossil plants. Or I might now be a paleobotanist. I could, of course, be an accountant. Or maybe I'd be married to someone I met while doing that job. My life has turned out the way it has because of the particular sequence of events that I've experienced. But it could have turned out a million other specific ways if any preceding events were different from what they actually were.

So, can we say *anything* with confidence about our species' future? Or is history an "anything goes" situation? Are all conceivable paths and outcomes possible?

Despite the contingent nature of history, there are constraints and limitations that lead to general trends. Let's take examples from biological evolution. Some specific results of life's history would seem highly improbable and, thus, based on a unique and contingent sequence of events. In other words, if something had been different in the past, that result might not have occurred. So far as we know, among the countless millions of species that evolved on this planet, only one small group possesses the consciousness required for complex abstract conceptualizing and a language capable of sharing such concepts. If some past events had been different, a species like ours might well have not evolved.

On the other hand, once the basic vertebrate body design appeared, a certain limited set of features evolved independently in three lineages of vertebrates that adapted to an aquatic life—fishes, cetaceans (whales and porpoises), and ichthyosaurs (extinct marine reptiles)—because that basic shape is obviously a very good way to propel a creature through the water. We see here a basic general trend in evolution, although we might still say that trend—the vertebrate body plan—was a unique event.

How may we apply this to the future of the human species? In trying to predict our future, we are clearly limited in making specific forecasts. Look, for example, at how difficult it is for economists to predict exactly what will happen with global monetary trends. Dealing with human beings, their psychologies, and their cultural systems—in all their rich variety— it seems as if almost anything is possible. And yet the past has shown us trends that do provide us with predictive ability. We know, for example, that despite our intellect and our ability to understand and manipulate our environments and their resources, we are constrained by our biology and by certain biological and ecological laws. The natural resources of the planet are limited. Just as medieval alchemists could not turn lead into gold, we cannot make more basic resources, at least not without using up others. Eventually something will run out. The planet has a carrying capacity for each species, even ours. And we have data, at relatively small scales, for what happens when things do run out. History provides us with many examples of famine and the resultant starvation and war. We might reasonably expect, given our increasing global population and the limitations of the earth's resources, to see these events at increasingly larger magnitudes.

But the purpose and value of prediction—even if it is limited to general trends with specific events being so contingent as to be unpredictable—is not to be able to foretell doom and destruction. The value is that, from those general trends we have come to understand, we can, as the cliché says, learn from the past—if only we pay heed to its lessons and try to apply them.

Knowledge, in the modern world, is accumulating at a frustrating rate. It becomes more and more difficult to stay current in one's own field, much less to be minimally conversant even in related fields. We are seeing an increasing specialization in scientific and other scholarly disciplines. But, at the same, we must maintain an appreciation for the holistic perspective and encourage holistic and multidisciplinary approaches—because the real world doesn't divide itself into nice, neat categories. In this regard, anthropology—with us as its subject and holism as its central principle—can be in the forefront as we face the challenges at the edge of the future.

NOTES, REFERENCES, AND READINGS

On the idea of the "sixth extinction," see Richard Leakey and Roger Lewin's book of that name. The story of humankind's changing relationship with the environment is covered in *Dominion: Can Nature and Culture Co-exist?* by Niles Eldredge.

Although the threat of our extinction from global nuclear war seems remote at the moment, Jonathan Schell's *The Fate of the Earth* is still relevant and thought-provoking.

On emerging diseases, see *Virus X* by Frank Ryan, and *Viral Sex: The Nature of AIDS* by Jaap Goudsmit.

I related my view as to the relative importance and interaction of contingency and constraints in evolution and history. This topic, however, is still a matter of intense debate, with the major opponents being Stephen Jay Gould for contingency and Simon Conway Morris for constraints. Gould's description of contingency in evolutionary history is nicely covered in an article called "Eight Little Piggies" in his book by the same name. The quote is from page 77. Detailed arguments in the debate are in Gould's *Wonderful Life* and Conway Morris's *The Crucible of Creation,* and nice summaries of their points of view are in the December 1998–January 1999 issue of *Natural History,* "Showdown on the Burgess Shale."

An up-to-date and timely discussion of the nature, importance, and application of anthropology and its holistic approach is in Marvin Harris's *Theories of Culture in Postmodern Times.*

Glossary

absolute dating Dating that gives a specific age, year, or range of years for an object or site.

acculturation Rapid diffusion of cultural items either by choice of the receiving society or by force from a more dominant society.

Acheulian A toolmaking tradition associated with *Homo erectus* in Africa and Europe. Includes **hand axes**, cleavers, and flake tools.

adapted When an organism has physical traits and behaviors that allow it to survive in a particular environment.

age sets A social unit made up of persons of approximately the same age.

agriculture Farming using animal or mechanical labor and complex technologies.

alleles Variants of a gene that code for different expressions of a trait.

altruism Acts that benefit others without regard to the welfare of the performer.

amino acids The chief components of proteins.

apocrine glands Specialized sweat glands that secrete a substance that gives off an odor thought to be related to sexual stimulation.

arbitrary Here, the fact that the features of human languages bear no direct relation to their meanings but are agreed-on symbols.

arboreal Adapted to life in the trees.

archaeologist Specialist in a subfield of anthropology that recovers evidence of the human cultural past and reconstructs past cultural systems.

artifact Any object that has been consciously manufactured. Usually refers to human-made objects, but now includes some items made by other primates.

artificial selection Selection for reproductive success in plants and animals that is directed by humans. Also called selective breeding.

asexually Reproducing without sex, by fissioning or budding as in many single-celled organisms.

balanced reciprocity Giving with expectation of equivalent return. See **general reciprocity.**

bands Small autonomous groups, usually associated with **foraging societies.**

behavioral ecology See **sociobiology.**

belief systems Ideas that are taken on faith and cannot be scientifically tested.

bifacial A stone tool that has been worked on both sides.

bilateral Kinship where an individual is a member of both parents' descent lines. See **unilineal.**

biological anthropologist Specialist in a subfield of anthropology that studies humans as a biological species.

biological determinism The idea that human behaviors have a biological basis with minimal influence from culture.

bipedal Walking on two legs.

brachiating Moving using arm-over-arm swinging.

bulb of percussion A convex surface on a flake caused by the force used to split the flake off. Rarely found in a natural break.

carbon dating A **radiometric** dating technique using the decay rate of a radioactive form of carbon found in organic remains.

carrying capacity The maximum population of a **species** allowed by existing environmental conditions and resources.

caste A system of socioeconomic stratification where **strata** are closed and a person's membership is determined at birth.

chiefdom A **political organization** with no central authority but made up of many interacting units, each of which has a leader.

chromosome Strands of DNA in the nucleus of a cell.

civilization Cultures with an agricultural surplus, social stratification, labor specialization, a formal government, rule by power, monumental construction projects, and a system of recordkeeping.

cladistic A classification system based on order of evolutionary branching rather than on present similarities and differences.

class A system of socioeconomic stratification where the **strata** are open and a person may move to a different stratum.

classical evolutionism The same as **unilineal evolutionism.**

cline A geographic continuum in the variation of a trait.

co-wife resentment Tension among the wives of one man in **polygynous** societies, often caused by differential statuses of those wives.

codify To arrange systematically. To put into words.

codominant When both **alleles** of a pair are expressed in the **phenotype.**

cognates Words that are similar in two or more languages as a result of common descent.

contingency In history, the idea that events are dependent on all preceding events and that a change in one event will affect all that follow from it.

cross cousins The children of your father's sisters or mother's brothers.

cultural anthropologist Specialist in a subfield of anthropology that focuses on human cultural behavior and cultural systems and the variation in cultural expression among human groups.

cultural determinism The idea that human behaviors are almost totally the result of learned cultural information, with few or no instinctive responses.

culture Ideas and behaviors that are learned and transmitted. Nongenetic means of adaptation.

deduction Suggesting specific data that would be found if a hypothesis were true. Works from the general to the specific. See **induction.**

deoxyribonucleic acid (DNA) The molecule that carries genetic code.

dependency Here, the period after birth during which offspring require the care of adults to survive.

descent line Nuclear families that are connected through time.

descent with modification An old term for what we now call biological **evolution.**

descriptive linguistics The study of the structure of language in general and of the specific variations among languages.

diffusion The movement of cultural ideas and artifacts among societies. Cultural borrowing.

diffusionism Now outdated concept of cultural evolution where major cultural advances were made by a few, or by a single society and spread from there to all other societies.

directional selection Natural selection for new adaptations in response to changing environmental conditions.

discovery The realization and understanding of a set of relationships. An addition to knowledge. See **invention.**

displacement The ability to communicate about things and ideas not immediate in space or time.

diurnal Active during the day.

division of labor When certain individuals within a society perform certain jobs. Usually refers to the different jobs of men and women.

dominance hierarchy Individual differences in power, influence, and access to resources and mating.

dominant The **allele** that is expressed if in a pair of unlike alleles. See **heterozygous.**

duality Refers to the fact that human language has two levels: units of sound and units of meaning that those sounds are combined to create.

ecofact A natural object used as a tool but not modified.

ecology The science that studies the network of relationships within environmental systems.

ecosystem A specific set of environmental relationships. The unit of study within ecology.

egalitarianism The practice of not recognizing, and even eliminating, differences in social status and wealth.

emerging disease Any of a group of diseases, of various cause, that have newly appeared or are rapidly expanding their range in the human species.

endocannibalism The eating of human flesh from members of one's own society.

endocasts Natural or human-made casts of the inside of a skull. The cast reflects the surface of the brain and allows us to study the brains of even extinct species.

estrus In mammals, including nonhuman primates, the period of female fertility or the signals indicating this condition.

ethnocentrism Making value judgments about another culture from the perspective of one's own cultural system.

ethnographic analogy Interpreting archaeological data through the observation of activities in existing societies.

ethnosemantics The study of the meanings of words, especially as they relate to **folk taxonomies.**

evolution In biology, the idea that **species** change through time and that existing species give rise to new species.

evolutionary psychology See **sociobiology.**

experimental archaeology The process of understanding ancient skills and technologies by reproducing them.

fission Here, the splitting up of a population to form new populations.

folk taxonomies Cultural categories for important items and ideas.

foraging society Another name for a **hunter-gatherer** society.

forensic anthropology Subfield of anthropology that applies anthropology to legal matters. Usually used to identify skeletal remains and assess the of time and cause of death.

fossils Remains of life-forms of the past.

founder effect Genetic differences between populations produced by the fact that genetically different individuals founded (established) the populations.

gamete sampling The genetic change caused when genes are passed to new generations in frequencies different from those of the parental generation.

gametes The cells of reproduction, which only contain half the **chromosomes** of a normal cell.

gender The cultural categories and characteristics of men and women.

gene flow The exchange of genes among populations through interbreeding.

gene pool All the alleles in the population.

general reciprocity Giving with no expectation of equivalent return. See **balanced reciprocity.**

genes Technically, those portions of the **DNA** molecule that code for the production of specific **proteins.**

genetic drift Genetic change based on random changes within a species' **gene pool;** includes **fission** and the **founder effect,** and **gamete sampling.**

genotypes The **alleles** possessed by an organism.

glaciers Massive sheets of ice that expand and move.

grooming Cleaning the fur of another animal; an activity that, in primates, also promotes social cohesion.

haft To attach a handle to a shaft.

half-life The time needed for one-half of a given amount of radioactive substance to decay.

hand axe A **bifacial,** all-purpose stone tool, shaped somewhat like an axe head.

heterozygous Having two different **alleles** in a gene pair.

historical archaeology The **archaeology** of a society that has written records.

historical particularism American school of cultural evolution that rejected any general theory of culture change but rather saw each society as understood only with reference to its particular history.

holistic Assuming an interrelationship among the parts of a subject.

hominids Modern human beings and our ancestors, defined as the primates who walk erect.

homozygous Having two of the same **allele**.

horticulture Farming using human labor and simple tools such as digging-sticks and hoes.

hunting and gathering A society that relies on naturally occurring sources of food.

hypotheses Educated guesses to explain natural phenomena.

incest taboo A cultural rule that prohibits **marriage** with persons defined as being too closely related.

indigenous Native; refers to a group of people with a long history in a particular area.

induction Developing a general explanation from specific observations. See **deduction**.

industrialism Sometimes recognized as a subsistence pattern characterized by a focus on mechanical sources of energy and food production by a small percentage of the population.

infanticide The killing of infants.

inheritance of acquired characteristics The incorrect idea that adaptive traits can be acquired during an organism's lifetime and be passed on to its offspring.

intensive foraging Hunting and gathering in an environment that provides a very wide range of food resources.

invention The creation of new artifacts. The application of discovered knowledge. See **discovery.**

kin selection Promoting the passing on of one's genes by aiding the survival or reproduction of one's close kin.

kinship Your membership in a family and your relationship to other members of that family. May refer to biological ties or cultural ties modeled on biological ones.

Kulturkreise ("culture circles") German school of cultural evolution that proposed a small number of early cultural centers from which cultural traditions spread in ever-widening circles to encompass and influence other societies.

labor specialization When certain jobs are performed by particular individuals.

language The human communication system.

legal systems A set of secular rules governing the behavior of individuals and institutions within a society.

Levallois Tool technology involving striking uniform flakes from a prepared core.

limbic system A portion of the brain involved in emotions such as fear, rage, and caring for young.

linguistic anthropologist Specialist in a subfield of anthropology that studies language as a human characteristic and attempts to explain the differences among human languages and the relationships between a language and the society that uses it.

macromutations Mutations with extensive and important **phenotypic** results.

magic Ritual acts where people attempt to control the supernatural. See **sorcery.**

market system Where **money** is used for exchange in place of the actual exchange of goods and services.

marriage A set of cultural rules for bringing men and women together to create a family unit and for defining their behavior toward one another, their children, and society.

matrilineal Unilineal kinship where an individual is a member of the mother's **descent line.**

melanin The pigment largely responsible for human skin color.

melanocytes Specialized skin cells that produce the pigment **melanin.**

men's associations A social unit made up of a society's men. Common in highland New Guinea.

microliths Small stone flakes, usually used as part of a larger tool such as a sickle.

money Symbolic representation of wealth. Used for exchange in place of the exchange of actual products or services.

monogamy The marriage unit made up of only one husband and one wife.

monotheistic Refers to a religious system that recognizes a single supernatural being.

morpheme The unit of meaning in a language.

Mousterian The culture associated with the European Neandertals.

mutagens Environmental factors that cause genetic **mutations.**

mutation Any spontaneous change in the genetic code.

natural selection Evolutionary change based on the differential reproductive success of individuals within a species.

neocortex A portion of the brain involved in conscious thought, spatial reasoning, and sensory perception.

niche The environment of an organism and its adaptive response to that environment.

nocturnal Active at night.

nomadic Referring to societies that move from place to place in search of resources or in response to seasonal fluctuations.

nuclear family The family unit made of parents and their children.

olfactory Referring to the sense of smell.

opposability The ability to touch the thumb to the tips of the other fingers.

ovulation The period when an egg cell matures and is capable of being fertilized.

paleontology The study of life-forms from the past using fossil remains and their geological contexts.

parallel cousins The children of your father's brothers or your mother's sisters.

pastoralism The subsistence pattern characterized by an emphasis on herding animals.

patrilineal Unilineal kinship where an individual is a member of the father's **descent line.**

phenome The unit of a sound in a language.

phenotype The chemical or physical results of the genetic code.

pheromones Chemical substances secreted by an animal that convey information and stimulate behavior responses.

physical anthropologist The traditional name for biological anthropologist.

Pleistocene The geological time period, from 1.6 million to 10,000 years ago, characterized by a series of advances and retreats of polar and mountain **glaciers.**

political organization The secular, nonkinship means of organizing the interactions within a society and between one society and others.

polyandry A marriage system that allows multiple husbands for one woman.

polygamy Any marriage system that allows multiple spouses. See **polygynous** and **polyandry.**

polygynous Refers to a society where a man may have multiple wives.

polymorphisms Variations in **phenotypic** traits that are the results of genetic variation.

polytheistic Refers to a religious system that recognizes multiple supernatural beings.

postpartum sex taboo The practice of prohibiting sex for a certain period of time after a woman gives birth for purposes of limiting the birth rate.

potassium/argon (K/Ar) dating A **radiometric** dating technique using the rate at which radioactive potassium, found in volcanic rock, decays into stable argon gas.

prehensile Having the ability to grasp.

pressure flake Taking a flake off a core by pushing a wood, bone, or antler tool against the stone.

priest A full-time, trained religious specialist who can interpret the supernatural and petition the supernatural on behalf of humans.

productivity Here refers to the ability of human languages to generate limitless numbers of meanings.

prognathism The jutting forward of the lower face and jaw area.

proteins Molecules that make cells and carry out cellular functions.

protocultural A behavior having most but not all of the characteristics of a cultural behavior.

pseudoscience Scientifically testable ideas that are taken on faith, even if tested and shown to be false.

quadrupedal   Walking on all fours.

R-complex (Reptilian complex)   A primitive portion of the brain involved in self-preservation behaviors such as mating, aggressiveness, and territoriality.

races   In biology, the same as **subspecies.** In culture, cultural categories that classify and account for human diversity.

racism   Judging an individual solely on his or her racial affiliation.

radiometric   Referring to the decay rate of a radioactive substance.

rank   Refers to a society that strives for equal distribution of goods and services but that achieves this through the use of recognized status differences. See **redistribution.**

recessive   An **allele** that is only expressed if present in a matched pair. See **homozygous.**

redistribution   Where surplus goods are collected centrally and then given out to those persons in need of them.

reification   Translating a complex set of phenomena into a single entity such as a number. IQ test scores are an example.

relative dating   Dating that indicates the age of one item in comparison to another.

religion   A system of ideas and rules for behavior based on supernatural explanations.

revolution   Rapid and extensive culture change generated from within a society.

ribonucleic acid (RNA)   The molecule that, in two forms, translates and transcribes the genetic code into **proteins.**

savannas   The open grasslands of the tropics, usually with reference to the plains of Africa.

science   The method of inquiry that requires the generation, testing, and acceptance or rejection of hypotheses.

scientific method   The process of conducting scientific inquiry.

sedentary   A human settlement pattern in which people largely stay in one place year-round, although some members of the population may still be mobile in the search for food and raw materials.

semispecies   Populations of a **species** that are completely isolated from one another but have not yet become truly different species.

sexual dimorphism   Physical differences between the sexes of a species not related to reproductive features.

shaman   A part-time, supernaturally chosen religious specialist who can manipulate the supernatural.

social stratification   The presence of acknowledged differences in social status, political influence, and wealth among the people within a society.

sociobiology   The scientific study that examines evolutionary explanations for social behaviors within **species.**

sorcery   Rituals that attempt to control the supernatural for evil purposes. See **magic.**

speciation   The evolution of a new **species.**

species   A group of organisms that can produce fertile offspring among themselves but not with members of other groups.

stabilizing selection   Natural selection that maintains a species' adaptation to a particular set of environmental circumstances.

state   A **political organization** with central authority governing all the individual units.

stereoscopic   Three-dimensional vision; depth perception.

stimulus diffusion   When knowledge of a cultural trait in another society stimulates the invention of a similar trait.

strata   Layers; here, the layers of rock and soil under the surface of the earth, or the socio-economic levels within a society.

stratigraphy   The study of the earth's **strata.**

subsistence pattern   How a society acquires its food resources.

subspecies   Physically distinguishable populations within a **species.** The concept, as a formal **taxonomic** unit, is falling from use.

syncretism   The synthesis of existing religious beliefs and practices with new ones introduced from the outside.

syntax   Rules of word order in a language.

taxonomy A classification based on similarities and differences. Includes a nested set of categories of increasing specificity.

test pit An exploratory, usually small, excavation made to establish the presence or absence of an archaeological site.

theory A **hypothesis** that has been well supported by evidence and testing. A general idea that accounts for a set of phenomena.

tribal A **political organization** with no central leader but where the subunits may make collective decisions about the entire group.

unilineal evolutionism Now outdated concept of cultural evolution where all societies pass through the same series of stages from savagery to civilization.

unilineal Kinship where an individual is a member of only one parent's descent line. See **bilateral.**

world view The collective interpretation of and response to the natural and cultural worlds in which a group of people live. Their assumptions about those worlds and the values derived from those assumptions.

Bibliography

Akmajian, A., R. Demers, A. Farmer, and R. Harnish. 1991. *Linguistics*, 3rd ed. Cambridge, Mass.: MIT Press.

Ardrey, R. 1961. *African Genesis: A Personal Investigation into the Animal Origins and Nature of Man.* New York: Dell.

Ardrey, R. 1966. *The Territorial Imperative.* New York: Dell.

Attenborough, D. 1979. *Life on Earth.* Boston: Little, Brown.

Attenborough, D. 1984. *The Living Planet.* Boston: Little, Brown.

Attenborough, D. 1990. *The Trials of Life: A Natural History of Animal Behavior.* Boston: Little, Brown.

Baird, R. M., and S. E. Rosenbaum. 1991. *Animal Experimentation: The Moral Issues.* Buffalo: Prometheus Books.

Balikci, A. 1970. *The Netsilik Eskimo.* Garden City, N.Y.: Natural History Press.

Benedict, R. 1934. *Patterns of Culture.* New York: Mentor.

Blumstein, D. T. 1999. Selfish sentinels. *Science* 284 (4 June): 1633–34.

Bordes, F. 1972. *A Tale of Two Caves.* New York: Harper and Row.

Bowen, E. S. (L. Bohannon). 1964. *Return to Laughter.* Garden City, N.Y.: Anchor Books.

Bowlby, J. 1990. *Charles Darwin: A New Life.* New York: Norton.

Brown, K. M. 1987. Voodoo. In *Magic, Witchcraft, and Religion: An Anthropological Study of the Supernatural,* ed. A. C. Lehmann and J. E. Myers. Mountain View, Calif.: Mayfield.

Calvin, W. H. 1996. *How Brains Think: Evolving Intelligence, Then and Now.* New York: Basic Books.

Caplan, A. L. 1978. *The Sociobiology Debate.* New York: HarperCollins.

Cavalieri, P., and P. Singer, eds. 1993. *The Great Ape Project: Equality Beyond Humanity.* New York: St. Martin's Griffin.

Cavalli-Sforza, L. L. 1991. Genes, peoples and languages. *Scientific American* (November): 104–10.

Chagnon, N. A. 1974. *Studying the Yąnomamö.* New York: Holt, Rinehart and Winston.

Chagnon, N. A. 1993. *Yąnomamö,* 4th ed. Fort Worth, Tex.: Harcourt Brace.

Chambers, E. 1989. *Applied Anthropology: A Practical Guide.* Prospect Heights, Ill.: Waveland.

Clapp, N. 1998. *The Road to Ubar: Finding the Atlantis of the Sands.* Boston: Houghton Mifflin.

Cohen, J. E. 1996. Ten myths of population. *Discover* (April): 42–47.

Conway Morris, S. 1998. *The Crucible of Creations: The Burgess Shale and the Rise of Animals.* Oxford: Oxford University Press.

Conway Morris, S., and S. J. Gould. 1998/1999. Showdown on the Burgess Shale. *Natural History* 107 (10): 48–55.

de Waal, F. B. M., and F. Lanting (photographer). 1997. *Bonobo: The Forgotten Ape.* Berkeley: University of California Press.

Dettwyler, K. A. 1994. *Dancing Skeletons: Life and Death in West Africa.* Prospect Heights, Ill: Waveland Press.

Diamond, J. 1991. Curse and blessing of the ghetto. *Discover* (March): 60–65.

Diamond, J. 1992. *The Third Chimpanzee: The Evolution and Future of the Human Animal.* New York: HarperCollins.

399

Diamond, J. 1997. *Guns, Germs, and Steel: The Fates of Human Societies.* New York: Norton.

Dolhinow, P., and A. Fuentes, eds. 1999. *The Nonhuman Primates.* Mountain View, Calif.: Mayfield.

Eldredge, N. 1995. *Dominion: Can Nature and Culture Co-exist?* New York: Henry Holt.

Fagan, B. M. 1989. *The Adventure of Archaeology.* Washington, D.C.: National Geographic Society.

Feder, K. L. 1994. *A Village of Outcasts: Historical Archaeology and Documentary Research at the Lighthouse Site.* Mountain View, Calif.: Mayfield.

Feder, K. L. 1999a. *Frauds, Myths, and Mysteries: Science and Pseudoscience in Archaeology,* 3rd ed. Mountain View, Calif.: Mayfield.

Feder, K. L. 1999b. *Lessons from the Past: An Introductory Reader in Archaeology.* Mountain View, Calif.: Mayfield.

Feder, K. L. 2000. *The Past in Perspective: An Introduction to Human Prehistory,* 2nd ed. Mountain View, Calif.: Mayfield.

Feder, K. L., and M. A. Park. 1997. *Human Antiquity: An Introduction to Physical Anthropology and Archaeology,* 3rd ed. Mountain View, Calif.: Mayfield.

Fedigan, L. M., and L. Fedigan. 1988. *Gender and the Study of Primates: Curricular Module for the Project on Gender and Curriculum.* Washington, D.C.: American Anthropological Association.

Forbes, H. M. 1927. *Gravestones of Early New England and the Men Who Made Them: 1653–1800.* Princeton, N.J.: The Pyne Press.

Forte, M. and A. Siliotti, eds. 1996. *Virtual Archaeology: Re-creating Ancient Worlds.* New York: Harry N. Abrams.

Fortey, R. 1998. *Life: A Natural History of the First Four Billion Years of Life on Earth.* New York: Knopf.

Fossey, D. 1983. *Gorillas in the Mist.* Boston: Houghton Mifflin.

Fouts, R. (with S. T. Mills). 1997. *Next of Kin: What Chimpanzees Have Taught Me About Who We Are.* New York: William Morrow.

Fouts, R. S., and D. H. Fouts. 1999. Chimpanzee sign language research. In *The Nonhuman Primates,* ed. P. Dolhinow and A. Fuentes. Mountain View, Calif.: Mayfield.

Gaffney, E. S., L. Dingus, and M. K. Smith. 1995. Why cladistics? *Natural History* 104 (6): 33–35.

Galdikas, B. 1995. *Reflections of Eden: My Years with the Orangutans of Borneo.* Boston: Little, Brown.

Glasse, R. and S. Lindenbaum. 1992. Fieldwork in the South Fore: the process of ethnographic inquiry. In *Prion Diseases of Humans and Animals,* ed. S. B. Prusiner, J. Collinge, J. Powell, and B. Anderson eds. West Sussex, England: Ellis Horwood Limited.

Goodall, J. 1971. *In the Shadow of Man.* Boston: Houghton Mifflin.

Goodall, J. 1990. *Through a Window: My Thirty Years with the Chimpanzees of Gombe.* Boston: Houghton Mifflin.

Goudsmit, J. 1997. *Viral Sex: The Nature of AIDS.* New York: Oxford University Press.

Gould, S. J. 1980. *The Panda's Thumb.* New York: Norton.

Gould, S. J. 1983. *Hen's Teeth and Horse's Toes.* New York: Norton.

Gould, S. J. 1989. *Wonderful Life: The Burgess Shale and the Nature of History.* New York: Norton.

Gould, S. J. 1993a. *The Book of Life: An Illustrated History of the Evolution of Life on Earth.* New York: Norton.

Gould, S. J. 1993b. *Eight Little Piggies.* New York: Norton.

Gould, S. J. 1996. *The Mismeasure of Man,* 2nd ed. New York: Norton.

Greene, J. C. 1959. *The Death of Adam.* New York: Mentor Books.

Gross, P. R., and N. Levitt. 1994. *Higher Superstition: The Academic Left and Its Quarrels with Science.* Baltimore: Johns Hopkins University Press.

Harris, C. L. 1981. *Evolution: Genesis and Revelations.* Albany: State University of New York Press.

Harris, M. 1974. *Cows, Pigs, Wars and Witches: The Riddles of Culture.* New York: Vintage Books.

Harris, M. 1977. *Cannibals and Kings: The Origins of Cultures.* New York: Random House.

Harris, M. 1979. *Cultural Materialism: The Struggle for a Science of Culture.* New York: Random House.

Harris, M. 1999. *Theories of Culture in Postmodern Times.* Walnut Creek, Calif.: Altamira Press.

Heider, K. 1979. *Grand Valley Dani: Peaceful Warriors.* Fort Worth, Tex.: Harcourt Brace.

Herrnstein, R. J., and C. Murray. 1994. *The Bell Curve: The Reshaping of American Life by Difference in Intelligence.* New York: Free Press.

Hester, T. R., H. J. Shafer, and K. L. Feder. 1997. *Field Methods in Archaeology,* 7th ed. Mountain View, Calif.: Mayfield.

Hockett, C. F., and R. Ascher. 1964. The human revolution. *Current Anthropology* 5: 135–68.

Hostetler, J. A. 1974. *Hutterite Society*. Baltimore: Johns Hopkins University Press.

Hostetler, J. A., and G. E. Huntington. 1996. *The Hutterites in North America*. Fort Worth, Tex.: Harcourt Brace.

Jensen, A. R. 1969. How much can we boost IQ and scholastic achievement? *Harvard Educational Review* 39 (Winter): 1–123.

Johanson, D. C., and M. A. Edey. 1981. *Lucy: The Beginnings of Humankind*. New York: Simon and Schuster.

Johanson, D., and J. Shreeve. 1989. *Lucy's Child: The Discovery of a Human Ancestor*. New York: William Morrow.

Keesing, R. M. 1975. *Kin Groups and Social Structure*. New York: Holt, Rinehart and Winston.

Kennedy, K. A. R. 1976. *Human Variation in Space and Time*. Dubuque, Iowa: W. C. Brown.

Kirchner, W. H., and W. F. Towne. 1994. The sensory basis of the honeybee's dance language. *Scientific American* (June): 74–80.

Kottak, C. P., J. J. White, R. H. Furlow, and P. C. Rice. 1997. *The Teaching of Anthropology: Problems, Issues, and Decisions*. Mountain View, Calif.: Mayfield.

Kristof, N. 1999. Help! There's a mausu in my konpyutaa! *New York Times* (Sunday, April 4): WK4.

LaBarre, W. 1962. *They Shall Take Up Serpents*. Minneapolis: University of Minnesota Press.

Lancaster, J. 1975. *Primate Behavior and the Emergence of Human Culture*. New York: Holt, Rinehart and Winston.

Leakey, R., and R. Lewin. 1992. *Origins Reconsidered: In Search of What Makes Us Human*. New York: Doubleday.

Leakey, R., and R. Lewin. 1995. *The Sixth Extinction: Patterns of Life and the Future of Humankind*. New York: Doubleday.

Lee, R. 1993. *The Dobe Ju/'hoansi*, 2nd ed. Fort Worth, Tex.: Harcourt Brace.

Lehmann, A. C., and J. E. Myers. 1993. *Magic, Witchcraft, and Religion: An Anthropological Study of the Supernatural*. Mountain View, Calif.: Mayfield.

Lewontin, R. 1982. *Human Diversity*. New York: Scientific American Books.

Lindenbaum, S. 1979. *Kuru Sorcery: Disease and Danger in the New Guinea Highlands*. Mountain View, Calif.: Mayfield.

Linton, R. 1937. One hundred per cent American. *The American Mercury*, 40.

Lopez, B. 1986. *Arctic Dreams: Imagination and Desire in a Northern Landscape*. New York: Bantam Books.

Macauly, D. 1979. *Motel of the Mysteries*. Boston: Houghton Mifflin.

Marks, J. 1995. *Human Biodiversity: Genes, Races, and History*. New York: Aldine de Gruyter.

Marshack, A. 1975. Exploring the mind of ice age man. *National Geographic* 147 (1): 64–89.

Martin, L. 1986. Eskimo words for snow: A case study in the genesis and decay of an anthropological example. *American Anthropologist* 88 (2): 418–19.

Martin, M. K., and B. Voorhies. 1975. *Female of the Species*. New York: Columbia University Press.

McGee, R. J., and R. L. Warms, eds. 1996. *Anthropological Theory: An Introductory Reader*. Mountain View, Calif.: Mayfield.

McGraw, W. C. 1998. Culture in nonhuman primates? *Annual Review of Anthropology* 27: 301–28.

Mettler, L. E., T. G. Gregg, and H. E. Schaffer. 1988. *Population Genetics and Evolution*. Englewood Cliffs, N.J.: Prentice Hall.

Mithen, S. 1996. *The Prehistory of the Mind: The Cognitive Origins of Art, Religion and Science*. London: Thames and Hudson.

Molnar, S. 1992. *Human Variation: Races, Types, and Ethnic Groups*, 3rd ed. Englewood Cliffs, N.J.: Prentice Hall.

Montagu, M. F. A., ed. 1964. *The Concept of Race*. New York: Collier Books.

Muller, K. 1974. Tanna awaits the coming of John Frum. *National Geographic* 145 (5): 706–15.

Murdock, G. P. 1949. *Social Structure*. New York: Macmillan.

Napier, J. R., and P. H. Napier. 1985. *The Natural History of the Primates*. Cambridge, Mass.: MIT Press.

Norbeck, E. 1974. *Religion in Human Life: Anthropological Views*. New York: Holt, Rinehart and Winston.

O'Neill, T. 1996. Irian Jaya. *National Geographic* 189 (2): 2–33.

Park, M. A. 1999. *Biological Anthropology*, 2nd ed. Mountain View, Calif.: Mayfield.

Passingham, R. 1982. *The Human Primate*. New York: Freeman.

Patterson, F. 1978. Conversations with a gorilla. *National Geographic* (October): 438–65.

Pfeiffer, J. E. 1982. *The Emergence of Humankind*. 3rd ed. New York: Harper and Row.

Podolefsky, A., and P. J. Brown, eds. 1999. *Applying Anthropology: An Introductory Reader.* Mountain View, Calif.: Mayfield.

Rachels, J. 1990. *Created from Animals: The Moral Implications of Darwinism.* Oxford: Oxford University Press.

Relethford, J. H. 1997. Hemispheric difference in human skin color. *American Journal of Physical Anthropology* 104: 449–57.

Rhodes, R. 1997. *Deadly Feasts.* New York: Simon and Schuster.

Rice, P., and A. Paterson. 1985. Cave art and bones: Exploring the interrelationships. *American Anthropologist* 87: 94–100.

Ridley, M. 1996. *Evolution,* 2nd ed. Cambridge, Mass.: Blackwell Science.

Robey, B., S. O. Rutstein, and L. Morris. 1993. The fertility decline in developing countries. *Scientific American* (December): 60–67.

Rollin, B. 1992. *Animal Rights and Human Morality,* rev. ed. Buffalo: Prometheus Books.

Rowe, N. 1996. *The Pictorial Guide to the Living Primates.* East Hampton, N.Y.: Pogonius Press.

Russell, J. B. 1993. Witchcraft. In *Magic, Witchcraft, and Religion: An Anthropological Study of the Supernatural,* ed. A. C. Lehmann and J. E. Myers. Mountain View, Calif.: Mayfield.

Ryan, F. 1997. *Virus X: Tracking the New Killer Plagues out of the Present and into the Future.* Boston: Little, Brown.

Sagan, C. 1977. *The Dragons of Eden: Speculations on the Evolution of Human Intelligence.* New York: Ballantine Books.

Sagan, C. 1996. *The Demon-Haunted World: Science as a Candle in the Dark.* New York: Random House.

Salzmann, Z. 1993. *Language, Culture, and Society: An Introduction to Linguistic Anthropology.* Boulder, Col.: Westview.

Savage-Rumbaugh, S., and R. Lewin. 1994. Ape at the brink. *Discover* (September): 91–98.

Schell, J. 1982. *The Fate of the Earth.* New York: Knopf.

Scofield, J. 1962. Netherlands New Guinea. *National Geographic* 121 (5): 584–603.

Service, E. R. 1978. *Profiles in Ethnology.* New York: HarperCollins.

Sharer, R. J., and W. Ashmore. 1993. *Archaeology: Discovering Our Past,* 2nd ed. Mountain View, Calif.: Mayfield.

Shea, J. 1989. A functional study of the lithic industries associated with hominid fossils in Kebara and Qafzeh Caves, Israel. In *The Human Revolution: Behavioural and Biological Perspectives in the Origins of Modern Humans,* ed. P. Mellars and C. Stringer. Princeton, N.J.: Princeton University Press.

Shepher, J. 1983. *Incest: A Biosocial View.* New York: Academic Press.

Shreeve, J. 1994. *Erectus* rising. *Discover* (September): 80–89.

Singer, B. and V. A. Benassi. 1993. Occult beliefs. In *Magic, Witchcraft, and Religion: An Anthropological Study of the Supernatural,* ed. A. C. Lehmann and J. E. Myers. Mountain View, Calif.: Mayfield.

Sisson, R. F. 1980. Deception: Formula for survival. *National Geographic* 157 (3): 395–415.

Smith, J. M. 1984. Science and myth. *Natural History* 93 (11): 10–24.

Smuts, B. 1985. *Sex and Friendship in Baboons.* Hawthorne, N.Y.: Aldine de Gruyter.

Stringer, C. B., and R. McKie. 1996. *African Exodus: The Origins of Modern Humanity.* New York: Henry Holt.

Strum, S. 1987. *Almost Human.* New York: Random House.

Sussman, R. W. 1999. *The Biological Basis of Human Behavior: A Critical Review.* Upper Saddle River, N.J.: Prentice Hall.

Tattersall, I. 1993. *The Human Odyssey: Four Million Years of Evolution.* New York: Prentice Hall.

Teitelbaum, M., ed. 1976. *Sex Differences: Social and Biological Perspectives.* Garden City, N.Y.: Anchor Books.

Toth, N. 1985. The Oldowan reassessed: A close look at early stone artifacts. *Journal of Archaeological Science* 12: 101–20.

Trefil, J., and R. M. Hazen. 1995. *The Sciences: An Integrated Approach.* New York: Wiley.

Truzzi, M. 1993. The occult revival as popular culture: Some observations on the old and the nouveau witch. In *Magic, Witchcraft, and Religion: An Anthropological Study of the Supernatural,* ed. A. C. Lehmann and J. E. Myers. Mountain View, Calif.: Mayfield.

van Willigen, J. 1986. *Applied Anthropology: An Introduction.* South Hadley, Mass.: Bergin and Garvey.

Vivelo, F. R. 1978. *Cultural Anthropology Handbook: A Basic Introduction.* New York: McGraw-Hill.

Wheeler, M. 1943. *Maiden Castle.* London: Society of Antiquaries of London.

Williams, T. T., and T. Major. 1984. *The Secret Language of Snow.* San Francisco: Sierra Club/Pantheon.

Wilson, E. O. 1975. *Sociobiology: The New Synthesis.* Cambridge, Mass.: Harvard University Press.

Wilson, E. O. 1992. *The Diversity of Life.* Cambridge, Mass.: Harvard University Press.

Wilson, E. O. 1998. *Consilience: The Unity of Knowledge.* New York: Knopf.

Wolpoff, M., and R. Caspari. 1997. *Race and Human Evolution.* New York: Simon and Schuster.

Wright, R. 1994. *The Moral Animal: Evolutionary Psychology and Everyday Life.* New York: Vintage.

Zich, A. 1989. Two worlds, time apart: Indonesia. *National Geographic* 175 (1): 96–127.

Credits

Index

409